Developments in Forecast Combination and Portfolio Choice

SERIES IN FINANCIAL ECONOMICS
AND QUANTITATIVE ANALYSIS

Developments in Forecast Combination and Portfolio Choice

Edited by

Christian Dunis

Allan Timmermann and

John Moody

JOHN WILEY & SONS, LTD

Chichester • New York • Weinheim • Brisbane • Singapore • Toronto

Other Wiley Editorial Offices

John Wiley & Sons, Inc., 605 Third Avenue,
New York, NY 10158-0012, USA

Wiley-VCH GmbH, Pappelallee 3,
D-69469 Weinheim, Germany

John Wiley & Sons Australia Ltd, 33 Park Road, Milton,
Queensland 4064, Australia

John Wiley & Sons (Asia) Pte Ltd, 2 Clementi Loop #02-01,
Jin Xing Distripark, Singapore 129809

John Wiley & Sons (Canada) Ltd, 22 Worcester Road,
Rexdale, Ontario M9W 1L1, Canada

Library of Congress Cataloging-in-Publication Data

Developments in forecast combination and portfolio choice/edited by Christian Dunis,
Allan Timmermann and John Moody.
     p. cm.—(Wiley finance series)
     Selected proceedings from a conference held in London in June 2000.
     Includes bibliographical references and index.
     ISBN 0-471-52165-5
     1. Investment analysis—Congresses. 2. Portfolio management—Congresses. I. Dunis,
Christian. II. Timmermann, Allan. III. Moody, John. IV. Series.

HG4529 .D48 2001
332.6—dc21   2001024348

British Library Cataloguing in Publication Data

A catalogue record for this book is available from the British Library

ISBN 0 471 52165 5

Typeset in 10/12pt Times by Laser Words Private Limited, Chennai, India
Printed and bound by CPI Antony Rowe, Eastbourne

Contents

Contributors

GEORGE T. ALBANIS
Enron Europe Ltd, London, UK

GUSTAVO M. DE ATHAYDE
Banco Itaú, São Paulo, Brazil

ROY BATCHELOR
City University Business School, London, UK

MICHEL BEINE
University of Lille, France

AURÉLIE BOUBEL
University of Evry, France

FRÉDÉRICK BOURGOIN
Barclays Global Investors, London, UK

RICCARDO BRAMANTE
Milan Catholic University and Pavia University, Italy

NEIL BURGESS
Morgan Stanley Dean Witter, London, UK

BARBARA CAZZANIGA
Price Waterhouse Coopers, Milan, Italy

STÉPHANE CHAUVIN
Technological Knowledge Institute, Universidad Complutense, Madrid, Spain

CHRISTIAN L. DUNIS
Liverpool Business School, John Moores University, Liverpool, UK

LAURENT FERRARA
Centre d'Observation Economique (COE), Paris, France

DOMINIQUE GUÉGAN
Department of Mathematics, University of Reims, France

EMMANUEL JURCZENKO
University of Panthéon-Sorbonne and ESCP-EAP Business School, Paris, France

SÉBASTIEN LAURENT
University of Liège, Belgium

JASON LAWS
Liverpool Business School, John Moores University Liverpool, UK

BERTRAND MAILLET
University of Panthéon-Sorbonne and ESCP-EAP Business School, Paris, France

JOHN MOODY
Oregon Graduate Institute of Technology, Oregon, USA

MATTIAS PERSSON
Department of Economics, Lund University, Sweden

ALLAN TIMMERMANN
University of California, San Diego, USA

NEVILLE TOWERS
London Business School, London, UK

About the Contributors

GEORGE T. ALBANIS

George T. Albanis has worked as a Quantitative Analyst at Enron Europe Ltd. He has submitted his Ph.D. thesis at City University Business School, London. He holds a B.Sc. (Economics) from the University of Piraeus, Greece and Master's degrees in Business Finance and in Decision Modelling and Information Systems from Brunel University, London. An experienced programmer, his interests are applications of advanced data-mining techniques for prediction and trader support in equity and bond markets. E-mail: g.albanis@soi.city.ac.uk.

GUSTAVO M. DE ATHAYDE

Gustavo M. de Athayde is a Senior Quantitative Manager at Banco Itaú and a Ph.D. student at the Escola de Pós Graduação em Economia, Fundação Getúlio Vargas, Rio de Janeiro. He has a practical knowledge of the Brazilian financial markets and his present research interests include portfolio design, in static and dynamic settings, and the econometrics of risk management models. E-mail: gustavo.athayde@itau.com.br

ROY BATCHELOR

Roy Batchelor is HSBC Professor of Banking and International Finance at City University Business School in London. He teaches, researches and consults in the areas of financial and economic forecasting, and financial derivatives. He is an Associate Editor of the *International Journal of Forecasting*. Current projects include evaluating the performance of technical analysts, and developing nonlinear classification models for real-time stock market forecasting. E-mail: r.a.batchelor@city.ac.uk

MICHEL BEINE

Michel Beine is Lecturer in Economics and Applied Econometrics at the University of Lille 2 in France. He has published several papers in the fields of International Macroeconomics, International Finance and Financial Econometrics, particularly focusing on the foreign exchange market. E-mail: beine@hpsc.univ-lille2.fr

AURÉLIE BOUBEL

Aurélie Boubel is currently a Ph.D. student at the University of Evry (France). The focus of her thesis is the study of the relationship between exchange rate volatility and economic fundamentals. Her research interests include the analysis of high frequency financial data, volatility modelling, market microstructure and exchange rate dynamics. E-mail: boubel@eco.univ-evry.fr

FRÉDÉRICK BOURGOIN

Frédérick Bourgoin is an Associate in the Active Fixed Income Portfolio Management Team at Barclays Global Investors in London. Prior to joining BGI, he was a risk manager at UBK Asset Management in London. He holds an M.Sc. in Finance from ESSEC Graduate Business School and a postgraduate degree in Econometrics from Paris II University. E-mail: frederick.bourgoin@barclaysglobal.com

RICCARDO BRAMANTE

Riccardo Bramante is Professor of Economic Statistics at Milan Catholic and Pavia University. He also works as a consultant to Finanza e Gestione and CSC (Computer Sciences Corporation). He is a member of the Laboratory of Applied Statistics within Milan Catholic University. E-mail: iststat@mi.unicatt.it

NEIL BURGESS

Neil Burgess has published over 30 papers in the field of Computational Finance and has acted as a programme committee member for the international conferences: Forecasting Financial Markets, Computational Finance, and Intelligent Data Engineering and Learning. His research is focused on developing and exploiting emerging computational techniques as a means of avoiding the restrictive assumptions required by more established modelling tools. He obtained his Ph.D. from London University and is currently working for Morgan Stanley Dean Witter in the area of quantitative programme trading. E-mail: neil.burgess@msdw.com

BARBARA CAZZANIGA

Barbara Cazzaniga works as a consultant to PriceWaterhouseCoopers. She is also Lecturer at Milan Catholic University. E-mail: barbara.cazzaniga@it.pwcglobal.com

STÉPHANE CHAUVIN

Stéphane Chauvin received his Ph.D. in Applied Mathematics from ENST in Paris. He currently works at the Technological Knowledge Institute of Spain (University of Madrid) and as a consultant in the field of data mining. He teaches, researches and consults in the areas of knowledge discovery and knowledge management. He is a specialist in

Bayesian Networks for symbolic data fusion applied to Customer Relationship Management. Current projects include evaluating the application of technical analysts and knowledge representation by the combination of classification models, decision tree models and neural network models. E-mail: itc@sis.ucm.es

CHRISTIAN L. DUNIS

Christian L. Dunis is Girobank Professor of Banking and Finance at Liverpool Business School, and Director of its Centre for International Banking, Economics and Finance (CIBEF). He is also a consultant to asset management firms and an Official Reviewer attached to the European Commission for the evaluation of applications to finance of emerging software technologies. He is an Editor of the *European Journal of Finance* and has published widely in the field of financial markets analysis and forecasting. He has organised the Forecasting Financial Markets Conference since 1994. E-mail: cdunis@totalise.co.uk

LAURENT FERRARA

Laurent Ferrara is a statistician and researcher at the Centre d'Observation Economique (COE). He holds a Ph.D. in Statistics from the University of Paris 13, on generalised long memory processes. His research interests focus on time series modelling, parameter estimation, forecasting and applications. He has published in the *Journal of Forecasting*, the *Revue de Statistiques Appliquées* and the book *Advances in Quantitative Asset Management* (edited by C.L. Dunis). He also gives lectures on time series analysis and statistical packages. E-mail: lferrara@ccip.fr

DOMINIQUE GUÉGAN

Dominique Guégan is Professor in Statistics in the Department of Mathematics at the University of Reims (France). Her research concerns time series modelling (heteroskedastic and long memory models), and dynamical systems (chaotic processes). Most of her publications are on identification theory, estimation, tests and prediction and also the probabilistic aspects of dynamical chaotic systems. Currently, she supervises Ph.D. students on these various subjects. She is regularly invited to international congresses and workshops on these topics. She has published in many international journals in the areas of Probability, Statistics and Physics. E-mail: dominique.guegan@univ-reims.fr

EMMANUEL JURCZENKO

Emmanuel Jurczenko is reading Finance at the University of Panthéon-Sorbonne and at ESCP-EAP Business School, Paris. He is also a Visiting Professor at University Saint-Joseph, Beirut. His research is concerned with higher moment asset pricing models. E-mail: ejurczenko@aol.com

SÉBASTIEN LAURENT

Sébastien Laurent is a Ph.D. candidate in Econometrics at the University of Liège in Belgium. His research interests are in the field of Financial Econometrics, particularly in time series modelling and forecasting of high-frequency data. E-mail: s.laurent@ulg.ac.be

JASON LAWS

Jason Laws is a Lecturer in International Banking and Finance at Liverpool Business School (Liverpool John Moores University, UK). He has taught extensively in the area of financial markets at all levels, with particular specialisms in option pricing and international finance. His research interests are focused on volatility modelling and the implementation of trading strategies. He is also the Course Director for the M.Sc. in International Banking, Economics and Finance at Liverpool Business School. E-mail: j.laws@livjm.ac.uk

BERTRAND MAILLET

Bertrand Maillet is a Lecturer in Economics at the University of Panthéon-Sorbonne and an Associate Professor of Finance at ESCP-EAP Business School (Paris). His research interests concern technical analysis trading rules, asset pricing models, performance and risk measures. E-mail: bmaillet@univ-paris1.fr

JOHN MOODY

John Moody is the Director of the Computational Finance programme and a Professor in Computer Science at the Oregon Graduate Institute. His research interests include computational finance, time series analysis and machine learning. He has served as Programme Co-Chair for the Forecasting Financial Markets and Programme Chair for the Neural Information Processing Systems Conferences. Professor Moody has held positions at Yale University and the Institute for Theoretical Physics. He received his B.A. from the University of Chicago and his Ph.D. from Princeton University. E-mail: moody@cse.ogi.edu

MATTIAS PERSSON

Mattias Persson has a B.A. in Philosophy, he is a Ph.D. candidate and Lecturer at the Department of Economics at Lund University. His research is concerned with issues in portfolio selection such as downside risk, long term investment and risk estimation. E-mail: mattias.persson@nek.lu.se

ALLAN TIMMERMANN

Allan Timmermann is an Associate Professor of Economics at the University of California, San Diego. He is a Departmental Editor of the *Journal of Forecasting* and an Associate Editor of the *Journal of Business and Economic Statistics*. His research is concerned with modelling the dynamics and predictability of returns in financial markets. Professor Timmermann has held positions at Birkbeck College and the London School of Economics and obtained his Ph.D. from Cambridge University. E-mail: atimmerm@ucsd.edu

NEVILLE TOWERS

Neville Towers is pursuing a Ph.D. degree at London Business School on the development of decision modelling techniques for exploiting predictability in financial markets. His research interests include reinforcement learning, neural networks, trading rules, heuristic optimisation techniques and value-at-risk. He is currently working as a Senior Risk Analyst at London Electricity. E-mail: neville_towers@londonelec.co.uk

Series Preface

This series aims to publish books which give authoritative accounts of major new topics in financial economics and general quantitative analysis. The coverage of the series includes both macro and micro economics and its aim is to be of interest to practitioners and policy-makers as well as the wider academic community.

The development of new techniques and ideas in econometrics has been rapid in recent years and these developments are now being applied to a wide range of areas and markets. Our hope is that this series will provide a rapid and effective means of communicating these ideas to a wide international audience and that in turn this will contribute to the growth of knowledge, the exchange of scientific information and techniques and the development of cooperation in the field of economics.

Stephen Hall
Imperial College Management School, UK

Preface

"Developments in Forecast Combination and Portfolio Choice" is a book of selected proceedings from the FFM2000/CF2000 Conference focusing on the themes of risk, forecasting and asset management.

For the Millennium, the organisers of the Forecasting Financial Markets Conference and the organisers of the Computational Finance Conference decided to hold a joint venue of both Conferences in London in June 2000. During the three days of the event, over 90 high-quality papers were presented, and the task of selecting only a handful has been extremely difficult.

Rather than mixing a set of papers whose only common factor would be quantitative finance, we have chosen to focus this book on three themes that address current frontier research in quantitative finance. The first theme deals with the combination of forecasts used in asset allocation decisions. Many researchers in finance are coming to the conclusion that all individual forecasting models are misspecified in some dimensions and that the identity of the "best" model changes over time. In this situation it is likely that a combination of forecasts will perform better over time than forecasts generated by any individual model that is kept constant.

Although the identity of the best model can change over time, it is still important to use models that represent the data-generating process as closely as possible. One of the stylised facts of many financial return series is that the autocorrelation of absolute or squared returns dies out very slowly, giving rise to what is known as "long memory". However, it is still not known whether such long memory behaviour should be modelled as a fractionally integrated process or by allowing for "rare" structural breaks in the mean or, possibly, volatility of the return series. Nor is it known how to best estimate the parameters of processes with long memory. The second part of the book addresses this important issue.

Finally, there has recently been considerable interest in extending much of the classic work in portfolio analysis that assumes a quadratic, or mean–variance, utility function. If investors' preferences are more general, it becomes an issue to model properties of the return distribution other than the mean and variance, e.g. skewness and kurtosis. It is also not clear how the conclusions from the CAPM regarding the equilibrium properties of asset returns change. These are questions addressed by the third part of the book.

In the following we provide further details on the individual papers included in the book.

I   MODEL AND FORECAST COMBINATIONS

This was one of the major themes emanating from the Conference; indeed, model combination is attracting increasing interest among practitioners and academics alike. The vast majority of work in finance uses a two-step procedure, which in the first step generates an econometric model to produce a sequence of forecasts of asset returns and their correlations. In the second step the forecasts are used for portfolio selection, taking the first step forecasts as given and treating them as if they came from the "true" model. This procedure is now widely acknowledged to be sub-optimal and recent work has concentrated on integrating the two steps as well as devising strategies for combining forecasts from different models, each of which captures different characteristics of the return-generating process.

To cover this area, we have selected the following five articles.

- *"What Exactly Should We Be Optimising? Criterion Risk in Multicomponent and Multimodel Forecasting"* by A.N. Burgess: this article investigates the risks and inefficiencies resulting from the use of different optimisation criteria at different stages of the modelling process, and from the use of model combination techniques. It presents a population-based algorithm whose purpose is to optimise the joint performance of a combination of different models rather than the performance of each individual model. The algorithm is first applied to synthetic data with known properties, and then to two portfolios of statistical arbitrage stock market models, one using daily data, the other intraday hourly data. Both empirical applications of the algorithm demonstrate the consistency and robustness of the resulting trading performance.
- *"A Meta-parameter Approach to the Construction of Forecasting Models for Trading Systems"* by N. Towers and A.N. Burgess further analyses the issue of joint optimisation of the forecasting model and trading strategy used in a trading system. It presents a combination of the forecasting procedure with the optimisation of the rest of the decision-making process. It is shown that, on a set of 50 "statistical mispricings" within the UK equity market, when compared to a naïve approach, joint optimisation improves trading performance by more effectively compensating for the presence of market frictions such as transaction costs.
- *"The Use of Market Data and Model Combination to Improve Forecast Accuracy"* by C.L. Dunis, J. Laws and S. Chauvin addresses three issues pertinent to modelling the volatility of exchange rates. The first issue is whether a single parametric model, chosen from a set of popular specifications including GARCH, stochastic volatility and autoregressive or moving average representations of squared returns, dominates other alternatives. It is found that this is generally not the case. The second question, following from the finding that no single model dominates, is whether combined forecast models lead to improvements in volatility forecasting. Here it is found that it is possible to improve various measures of forecasting performance by model combination. Finally the paper investigates the extent to which inclusion of an implied volatility variable improves the forecasting performance of statistical volatility models that only use information from past returns. It is found that this is the case, even though the implied volatility tends to be well above 21- and 63-day moving average estimates of volatility and hence provides a biased out-of-sample forecast.

- *"21 Nonlinear Ways to Beat the Market"* by G.T. Albanis and R.A. Batchelor applies five statistical classification methods to identify high and low performing shares among about 700 stocks traded on the London Stock Exchange in the period 1993–1997, and proceeds to combine their forecasts using a majority and a unanimity voting principle. It is shown that all classification methods produce excess returns, but that greater gains can be achieved through the combination procedures. In particular, the unanimity voting principle where a share is not classified as "high performing" unless all five classifiers agree produces superior trading results and also lower trading costs as it implies trading an overall lower number of shares.
- *"Predicting High Performance Stocks Using Dimensionality Reduction Techniques Based on Neural Networks"* by G.T. Albanis and R.A. Batchelor: using the same dataset as in the previous paper, this article looks more specifically at ways to combine optimally the information available in a dataset consisting of a large number of inter-related variables. This is achieved through alternative dimensionality reduction techniques, transforming the original dataset into a substantially smaller set of uncorrelated variables, which nonetheless contain a substantial proportion of the information available in the original dataset.

II STRUCTURAL CHANGE AND LONG MEMORY

This is again a very active research area. Asset allocation models traditionally assume a stationary return process, but recent developments have questioned this assumption either by allowing for structural breaks or by letting the effects of shocks on returns die out very slowly, which gives rise to long memory in returns. Recent research also suggests that structural breaks, either of the deterministic type or of a type that is generated by an underlying stochastic process such as a mixture model, can give rise to high persistence in the return-generating process when such breaks are not controlled for in the econometric modelling or forecasting exercise. There are many unresolved issues remaining in this area. Key is perhaps the above question of observational equivalence between long memory and structural break or regime switching processes with persistent states. Although these processes may be similar in some respects, they differ in others. It is therefore important both for asset allocation and forecasting exercises to be able to identify the underlying data-generating process for a given return series. The papers by Beine and Laurent and Boubel and Laurent make good progress on this issue and shed light on the complex interaction between long memory and regime switching.

Long memory makes estimation of the parameters of the data-generating process notoriously difficult since key parameters depend on what happens in the long run. The relatively short samples typically available to researchers do not provide much information on the long run. Therefore it is important to explore the performance and robustness across competing estimators, a question addressed by Ferrara and Guégan. In this area, we have selected the following three papers.

- *"Structural Change and Long Memory in Volatility"* by M. Beine and S. Laurent introduces a Markov regime-switching model with fractional integration (MS-FIGARCH) that allows the persistence in the conditional volatility to decay at a hyperbolic rate. By jointly estimating the switching and long memory parameters, the authors can address issues related to spurious shifts in the mean or spurious second-moment persistence that could arise in the context of the separate, nested models. It is found that the fractional integration coefficient estimate drops significantly after introducing two regimes compared to a single state model. However, the results also suggest that both regime switching and fractional integration characterise the daily Deutsche Mark–US Dollar exchange rate.

- *"Long-run Volatility Dependencies in Intraday Data and Mixture of Normal Distributions"* by A. Boubel and S. Laurent studies long memory in the Deutsche Mark–US Dollar exchange rate through a fractional integration model that allows for volatility clustering. Two basic specifications are investigated: one assumes that the residual is drawn from a normal distribution, while the other also includes a jump component that follows a Bernoulli process without memory. The purpose of the second component is to pick up isolated outliers and thus reduce the kurtosis in the residuals. In an analysis of a high-frequency data sample it is found that accounting for such outliers also brings down the fractional integration coefficient and hence reduces the extent of long memory in the series. This is an interesting finding with consequences for interpretation of the sources that give rise to long memory.

- *"Comparison of Parameter Estimation Methods in Cyclical Long-memory Time Series"* by L. Ferrara and D. Guégan compares semiparametric and pseudo-maximum likelihood estimation methods applied to generalised long memory processes which comprise both autoregressive fractionally integrated (ARFIMA) and seasonal long memory processes. A variety of techniques, including tapering and smoothing, are explored. It is found that a two-step procedure which first uses the log-periodogram to estimate points at which the spectral density peaks (Gegenbauer frequencies) followed by pseudo-maximum likelihood estimation of the long memory parameter works quite well. Model performance is measured in terms of penalised likelihood or information criteria. In an empirical application to an error correction term from the Nikkei 225 spot and futures indexes, it is found that the generalised long memory specification outperforms a standard autoregressive fractionally integrated model.

III   CONTROLLING DOWNSIDE RISK AND INVESTMENT STRATEGIES

Building on the classic work on portfolio analysis by Nobel laureate Harry Markowitz, the most widely used methods have assumed that investors have a quadratic loss function and hence minimise portfolio variance subject to achieving a certain expected return. However, most players in the financial markets have far more sophisticated loss functions that treat losses differently from gains of similar size. Markowitz understood this, and was the first to propose semivariance as a measure of risk.[1] However, extensive investigation of risk-averse utilities, skewed or heavy-tailed returns and downside risk was hampered for decades by analytical difficulties and computational limitations. In the past several years, the emergence of risk management as a discipline, a wide appreciation of the importance of loss aversion and dramatic increases in computing power are giving rise to a substantial new body of work. This new thrust includes investigations of portfolio optimisation, asset pricing and market equilibrium. We have selected five of the most exciting presentations on these topics from the conference.

---

[1] Markowitz, H. (1959). *Portfolio Selection: Efficient Diversification of Investments*. New York: Wiley.

- *"Building a Mean Downside Risk Portfolio Frontier"* by G.M. de Athayde presents an algorithm for determining the portfolio with minimum downside risk with respect to a benchmark return. Based on this result, a mean downside risk efficient set is constructed, and its properties are examined. A new, more general approach for the Lower Partial Moment CAPM is presented, which allows for discrete-time observations and the absence of a riskless asset.

- *"Implementing Discrete-time Dynamic Investment Strategies with Downside Risk"* by M. Persson compares returns and risk for two models for optimising portfolios with respect to downside risk, the Dynamic Investment model and the Lower Partial Moments (LPM) model. The models are compared for portfolios containing US T-bills, stocks, long-term bonds and eight international equities markets. Monthly returns data is used in the comparisons, and the portfolios are revised on both a quarterly and annual basis. The main results are that the LPM model provides a good approximation to the dynamic investment model, and that the accuracy improves as the target rate of return for the portfolio increases.

- *"Portfolio Optimisation in a Downside Risk Framework"* by R. Bramante and B. Cazzaniga presents an approach to portfolio optimisation incorporating Value at Risk (VaR). The proposed method is based on maximising the expected return of a portfolio, given that the portfolio must satisfy a VaR limit relative to a specified benchmark portfolio, together with a budget constraint. The authors show that the problem may be reduced to that of maximising a function of the expected portfolio return, the portfolio beta and the quantile of portfolio returns determined by the VaR limit, given the budget constraint. The advantage of this approach is that the optimum portfolio can be determined from the empirical distributions of returns of the individual assets, without using assumptions of normality.

- *"The Three-moment CAPM: Theoretical Foundations and an Asset Pricing Model Comparison in a Unified Framework"* by E. Jurczenko and B. Maillet proposes a theory of asset pricing in the context of a three-moment CAPM that employs expected utility and portfolio choice theory. The authors extend the Sharpe–Lintner–Mossin framework to incorporate the effects of skewness on asset valuation. The paper analyses the properties of the mean–variance–skewness efficient set and discusses the three-moment CAPM market equilibrium. Several hypotheses necessary for multimoment equilibrium capital asset pricing are identified, along with links to other market equilibrium models.

- *"Stress-testing Correlations"* by F. Bourgoin presents methods to stress test portfolios. He motivates the need for extreme event analysis by the Long Term Capital Management crisis of August 1998, and presents a "crisis indicator" that allows the maximum risk of a portfolio to be monitored. The paper builds on the concept of average "implied" correlation, and discusses implications for portfolio risk management. A consistent correlation matrix is needed for accurately calculating VaR and portfolio tracking error. Two methods for stress-testing correlation matrices are presented: one method involves changing the overall level of correlation among the portfolio constituents, while the other allows individual correlations to be altered. The methodologies are applied to the JP Morgan Global Bond Index.

We wish to thank the authors who have contributed to this volume and the members of the scientific and organising committees of Forecasting Financial Markets 2000 and Computational Finance 2000. The papers contained in this collection exemplify key research themes that have figured prominently at both conferences during the past several years, and attest to some of the important and exciting developments emerging in quantitative finance at the turn of the Millennium.

Christian Dunis, Allan Timmermann and John Moody
January 2001

Theme I
Model and Forecast Combinations

—————— 1 ——————

What Exactly Should We Be Optimising? Criterion Risk in Multicomponent and Multimodel Forecasting[1]

A. NEIL BURGESS

ABSTRACT

In this paper we investigate the issue of criterion risk, *i.e.* the additional source of uncertainty, in terms of the ultimate performance measure, which is induced through the use of different optimisation and selection criteria within the modelling process itself. This issue is particularly acute in the case of building trading systems which attempt to exploit small deterministic components in asset price dynamics, because the performance of such systems is in most cases marginal at best. In this paper we investigate two major sources of criterion risk, the first arising from the use of different optimisation criteria at different stages of the modelling process and the second arising from the use of model combination techniques. The first section of this paper provides a review of recent approaches to the problem of optimising trading systems. The second section contains an analysis of the ways in which criterion risk can contribute to the overall success or failure of the modelling process. The third section describes a population-based algorithm which is intended to optimise the joint performance of an overall portfolio of models rather than simply the performance of models on an individual basis. The final part of the paper contains an investigation of the properties of this algorithm, firstly a verification of the algorithm with respect to synthetic data with known properties and secondly an application of the algorithm to the real-world problem of generating a portfolio of statistical arbitrage models.

1.1 INTRODUCTION

In general, the construction and use of predictive models is a multistage process. Although the details may differ depending on the precise methodology adopted, the general phases might be considered to be: selection of the target series, variable selection, specification and estimation of the forecasting model, model selection and combination, decision

---

[1] Neil Burgess conducted this work as a research fellow within the Computational Finance Group of the Decision Technology Centre at London Business School.

Developments in Forecast Combination and Portfolio Choice. Edited by C. Dunis, A. Timmermann and J. Moody.

(trading) rule implementation. Each of these stages involves a number of decisions, choices, inferences or optimisations regarding issues such as: the underlying assumptions, parameter specification/estimation, selection between alternatives, etc.

Whilst ultimately based upon its practical utility, this standard "divide and conquer" approach is nevertheless dangerous in that it introduces a number of inefficiencies to the model search process. In particular, the selections and optimisations performed at previous stages will impose limitations on the options available at later stages. The modelling process can be thought of as a multistage filter with each stage reducing the range of possible models, until ultimately a single model or combination of models has been defined in its entirety. This perspective is illustrated schematically in Figure 1.1.

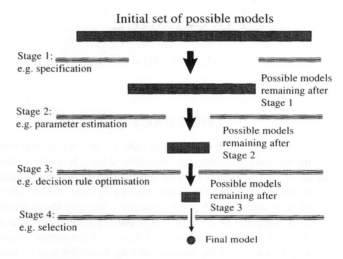

Figure 1.1 Schematic description of the model-building process as a multistage filter. The wide range of possible models is reduced at each stage until the complete model emerges from the final selection stage

Due to the nature of model development, it is generally infeasible to use the same criteria at all stages of the model-building process. For instance, the <u>ultimate</u> objective may be trading performance, but this can only be evaluated in the context of both a predictive model and a decision rule. Thus, whilst trading performance can be used as a criterion at the later stage of optimising the decision rule itself, estimation of the model parameters, and particularly selection of the target variable, are tasks which must be performed before the decision rule is known and hence optimised using alternative criteria. Figure 1.2 illustrates the "forecasting bottleneck" (Moody *et al.*, 1998) which can arise through combining a predictive model with a trading rule.

This problem of multistage modelling has been largely neglected in the literature, with the most common approach being to focus on the statistical accuracy of a forecasting model rather than the trading performance of an entire system. In cases where trading performance is reported, this is typically for the rather naïve case in which a prespecified trading rule is adopted (often for no particular reason other than convenience).

Recent work has moved away from this perspective and recognised the fact that the choice of trading rule can be of comparable importance to the specification of the

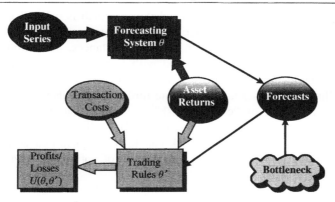

Figure 1.2   Illustration of the "forecasting bottleneck". Separate optimisation of the forecasting system and trading rule means that potentially useful information is ignored in each case; in particular, the forecasts generated by the model are optimised by a different criterion than the trading rule and will for instance fail to take into account transaction costs and other market frictions. Similarly, the information in the input series which represents the current environment is only transmitted to the trading rule in the form of a single forecast, thus losing much information which is potentially important at later stages

forecasting model itself. Given this recognition, the simple "multistage" approach aims to improve system-wide performance by optimising the parameters of a trading rule conditionally upon the properties of a given forecasting model and trading environment (Towers and Burgess, 1999, 2000). An alternative approach is to integrate the two stages of forecasting and trading rule within a single system which is directly optimised with respect to trading performance (Moody and Wu, 1997; Bengio, 1997; Choey and Weigend, 1997). However, for reasons such as model transparency and parsimony, Towers (2000) argues that it is still often preferable to separate the two tasks of forecasting and trading into different modules (for instance model variance can be reduced by partitioning the parameter space between two separate models). In this case an improvement upon the simple multistage approach is to perform joint optimisation of the two (or maybe more) components which make up the model as a whole. A gradient-based iterative algorithm for joint optimisation of forecasting models and trading rules is described by Towers (2000). In this paper we describe an alternative, population-based, algorithm which both evaluates and optimises the entire set of components within a model in terms of the ultimate performance criterion which will be used to measure the performance of the trading system as a whole. An additional advantage of this algorithm is that as well as addressing the issue of jointly optimising the *components* within a *model* it also addresses the issue of optimising the joint performance of a combination of *models* within a portfolio (Burgess, 1997, 1999).

1.2   MODEL COMBINATION AND CRITERION RISK

Given that a set of statistical arbitrage models will be *applied* within a particular context (e.g. a "portfolio of models") it is also preferable to *generate*, *optimise* and *select* models within this context. The motivation for this is to minimise the effect of what we refer to as "criterion risk". The term reflects the performance uncertainty due to the fact that a model, set of models, trading system or whatever, which is optimal with respect to a *particular* selection or performance criterion, will not necessarily be optimal with respect to a *different* criterion. Therefore under ideal circumstances, to minimise this risk, all parameters of a model would be optimised with respect to the ultimate performance criterion. While this ideal is not generally feasible to achieve, it is nevertheless true that standard modelling approaches tend to deviate further from it than is strictly necessary.

We formalise the issue of "criterion risk" by noting that the model and parameters $f_i(\theta_i)$ which maximise a particular criterion M_1 will not necessarily maximise an alternative criterion M_2. The criterion risk can then be quantified as the performance degradation according to M_2 which arises as a result of optimising with respect to some other measure M_1:

$$CR(M_1, M_2, f, \theta) = \max_{f,\theta} M_2[f(\theta)] - M_2[f^{M_1^*}(\theta^{M_1^*})] \geqslant 0 \qquad (1.1)$$

where $f^{M_1^*}(\theta^{M_1^*}) = \arg \max_{f,\theta} M_1[f(\theta)]$.

In this paper we will investigate the sources of criterion risk which arise in the particular context of generating a set of statistical arbitrage models. Our statistical arbitrage models consist of three components which are generated sequentially: a "fair-price model" which generates a linear combination of time series which represents a potentially predictable "statistical mispricing"; a "forecasting model" which predicts the future dynamics of the mispricing; and a "trading rule" which translates the predictions into a trading signal. The details of these models are described in Section 1.5. In fact, our modelling methodology as a whole also contains a fourth stage, namely the combination of the individual models within a portfolio.

Within this context, we potentially suffer from three major sources of criterion risk:

- the criterion for optimising the model weightings within the portfolio;
- the criterion for optimising/selecting the individual *models* within the portfolio;
- the "intermediate" criteria for optimising the various *components* of each model.

The general weaknesses of multistep and individual optimisation of models as opposed to the joint optimisation of the set of models as a whole are discussed in more detail in Burgess (1999). In the particular context of combining a set of statistical arbitrage trading models, the crucial difference between the two approaches is that by optimising models on an individual basis we may undermine the potential advantages which are due to risk diversification across the population of models.

Intriguingly, due to the discrepancy between the criteria used at different stages, the danger of *inefficiency* at the portfolio level is exacerbated by the degree of *efficiency* with which individual models are optimised. The primary danger is that if the set of models "converges" towards the single model which is optimal on an *individual* basis then the opportunities for risk diversification within the *portfolio* are correspondingly restricted. In the limit, where the "convergence" is complete, and all models are identical, then there is no possibility at all of benefiting from risk diversification. In the remainder of this section we demonstrate that the problem of model convergence can be viewed as a particular type of criterion risk, and thus motivate the joint optimisation algorithm which is described in Section 1.3.

1.2.1   Combination in a Portfolio of Models

Irrespective of the statistical rigour of the modelling process, the *future* performance of forecasting models in general, or statistical arbitrage models in particular, will necessarily be uncertain. The fact that model selection criteria are evaluated with respect to a particular finite sample will cause sampling error. This in turn means that the model which is apparently optimal, according to the model selection criteria, will not necessarily be optimal in future. Furthermore, this risk is much increased when the noise content of the data is high and/or the performance may be unstable over time due to the presence of nonstationarities in the underlying data-generating process.

The effect of using small and/or noisy samples is that the sampling error on any in-sample performance estimate will necessarily be large. Similarly, the effect of any time variation in the underlying data-generating process will be to increase the variability of future performance, given a particular level of in-sample performance. This serves to increase the model selection risk, and reduce the probability that the optimal in-sample model will also perform optimally during an out-of-sample period. The model selection risks which arise from the use of finite, noisy and possibly nonstationary datasets are illustrated in Figure 1.3. Note that, whilst the effects of variance are equally likely to be positive as negative, time variation or "nonstationarity" is more likely to lead to performance degradation than to an improvement.

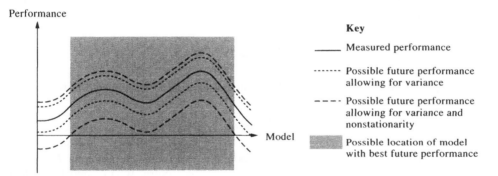

Figure 1.3   Distribution of the possible future performance of a set of models, allowing for both sampling error in the performance statistic and the possible effects of nonstationarity

Additional complications to the model selection procedure are caused by criterion risk and "selection bias". As noted above, criterion risk arises in the case where the metric which is used for model selection is not the same as the metric by which future performance will be evaluated. Selection bias, or "data-snooping", arises because the measured performance of a *selected* model will be positively biased with respect to the true expectation of future performance, due to the fact that:

$$\max(\mu_i) + \mathrm{E}[\varepsilon_i] \leqslant \mathrm{E}[\max(\mu_i + \varepsilon_i)] \leqslant \max(\mu_i) + \max(\varepsilon_i) \tag{1.2}$$

where μ_i is the true in-sample performance of model i and ε_i represents the sampling error of the performance measure. The selection bias is caused by the discrepancy between the first expression, which represents the true expectation of future performance, and the second expression, which is the measured in-sample performance (after correcting for any other biases). The third expression indicates that the maximum possible selection bias is determined by the sample variability of the performance metric.

We believe that the problems posed by model selection risk are not adequately addressed by standard modelling procedures. The majority of model combination techniques are intended not to reduce model **risk** as such but rather to improve model **performance**, in the sense of minimising forecasting error. In finance, however, there is an explicit requirement to take into account not only performance (or expected return) but also risk (or uncertainty in the level of return), with the ultimate measure of utility being some form of "risk-adjusted return".

The methodology which we propose to deal with this issue is an adaptation of the model combination approach in the context of modern portfolio theory (Markowitz, 1959). The core inspiration of Markowitz portfolio theory is that a suitable combination (portfolio) of *assets* may achieve a higher level of risk-adjusted return than any individual asset, due to the ability to diversify risk through a combination of less than perfectly correlated assets. The basis of our model combination methodology is to adapt the Markowitz framework by substituting the profits and losses of statistical arbitrage *models* in place of the returns on individual assets, *i.e.* to create a "portfolio of models".

Given a set of models $\mathbf{m} = \{m_1(\theta_1), m_2(\theta_2), \ldots, m_{n_m}(\theta_{n_m})\}$, (uncertain) performance estimates $\mathbf{r}_M = \{E[r_1] \ E[r_2] \ \cdots \ E[r_2]\}^T$ and inter-relationships between the model performances defined by the covariance matrix $\mathbf{V}_M = E\{[\varepsilon_1 \ \varepsilon_2 \ \cdots \ \varepsilon_{nm}]^T[\varepsilon_1 \ \varepsilon_2 \ \cdots \ \varepsilon_{nm}]\}$, the portfolio of models is given by:

$$P_M = \sum_i w_{M,i} m_i \tag{1.3}$$

and the optimal vector of weights is that which maximises risk-adjusted performance:

$$\mathbf{w}_M^* = \arg \max_w \left\{ \mathbf{w}_M^T \mathbf{r}_M - \frac{1}{T} \mathbf{w}_M^T \mathbf{V}_M \mathbf{w}_M \right\} \tag{1.4}$$

As in the case of standard portfolio optimisation, the risk tolerance parameter T quantifies the desired trade-off between higher levels of expected return, $\mathbf{w}_M^T \mathbf{r}_M$, and lower levels of portfolio risk, represented by the variance term $\mathbf{w}_M^T \mathbf{V}_M \mathbf{w}_M$.

1.2.2 Joint Optimisation of Components Within Models, and Models Within a Population

In this subsection we will describe a methodology which is designed to address two important issues which in fact are facets of the same underlying problem. The first issue is the so-called "forecasting bottleneck" which arises when the performance of a trading rule is conditioned upon the output of a forecasting model. The second issue is that of successful diversification of model risk within the context of the "portfolio of models" approach.

The underlying issue in both cases is the potential inefficiency which is caused by the use of indirect optimisation, by which we mean optimising a model, or a model component, with respect to criteria which are different to those by which the ultimate performance of a model will be judged. This risk is illustrated in Figure 1.4. The model selected according to the criteria of Stage 1 is significantly less than optimal at Stage 2 even though the criteria at each stage are 90% correlated, clearly highlighting the potential inefficiency of indirect optimisation. It is this type of modelling inefficiency which we refer to as "criterion risk".

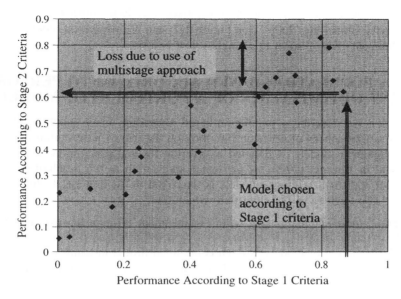

Figure 1.4 Illustration of the potential inefficiency which arises through the use of different criteria at different stages of the modelling process, or when the criteria used during model construction are different to those by which actual performance is measured

The criterion risk which arises in the context of the use of multicomponent models is related to the "forecasting bottleneck" which was described in Section 1.1. For instance, a forecasting model which is optimal with respect to the statistical criteria used during a model estimation procedure will not necessarily lead to optimal performance when used in conjunction with a trading strategy which is optimised independently. In particular, a model which has the most accurate forecasts may not lead to the optimal trading performance if the volatility of the forecasts leads to large numbers of transactions being performed and the profitability being eroded by transaction costs (see Chapter 2).

In the case of diversifying model risk using a portfolio of models approach, the most important form of criterion risk which applies is that models which appear attractive in terms of their *individual* risk-adjusted performance may not necessarily add value to an existing portfolio of models. In particular, models which are highly correlated with other models will offer little opportunity for risk diversification. This is a common problem because the use of model selection criteria which view models on an individual basis will tend to select models which have similar, albeit advantageous, characteristics. In the context of genetic algorithms and similar population-based algorithms this phenomenon is sometimes referred to as "premature convergence".

In the following section, we describe a population-based algorithm which is intended to mitigate the potential inefficiencies which are discussed above. The key elements of the specification of each of the components of our statistical arbitrage models are grouped together as a set of "meta-parameters". The "fitness" of the set of meta-parameters is evaluated in terms of the actual trading performance of the <u>overall</u> model, thus serving to avoid the criterion risk which would arise from separate optimisation of the different model components. This process can be seen as avoiding the forecasting bottleneck by allowing feedback from the trading performance to be passed back to the other model components, thus closing the modelling "loop" (see Figure 1.2) and allowing *joint optimisation* of all model components with respect to a single set of criteria.

1.3   A POPULATION-BASED ALGORITHM TO PERFORM JOINT OPTIMISATION OF A PORTFOLIO OF MODELS

In this section we describe a population-based algorithm which attempts to minimise the adverse consequences of criterion risk through the use of joint optimisation of a set of multi-component models. A detailed motivation for and description of this approach can be found in Burgess (1999). A particular application to the problem of generating a portfolio of statistical arbitrage models is described in Section 1.5. In this section we describe the key features of the algorithm, which are:

- joint optimisation of components within each model through the use of "meta-parameters";
- forced decorrelation of models through <u>conditional</u> fitness measures;
- joint optimisation of the risk-adjusted performance of the "portfolio of models" as a whole.

If we denote a model and its components as $m = (c_1(\theta_1), c_2(\theta_2), \ldots, c_{n_c}(\theta_{n_c}))$, the optimisation criteria at each stage i as M_i and the true "utility" or ultimate performance metric as U, then the optimal model according to the multistage approach is given by:

$$m^{MS} = \left(\max_{\theta_1} M_1(\theta_1), \max_{\theta_2} M_2(\theta_2|\theta_1), \ldots, \max_{\theta_{n_c}} M_{n_c}(\theta_{n_c}|\theta_1, \ldots, \theta_{n_c-1}) \right) \quad (1.5)$$

and the ultimate measure of model performance is given by the utility $U(m^{MS})$.

1.3.1   Meta-parameters

The key danger of the multistage approach is that a set of models will converge to the single optimal solution, thus reducing diversity and unnecessarily restricting the parameter space which is explored by the search procedure. In the evolutionary optimisation community this problem is known as "premature convergence". Furthermore, a model which appears optimal when viewed in isolation will not necessarily be that which has the greatest <u>marginal</u> utility when added to an existing portfolio of models.

Within our population-based algorithm we reduce the "convergence" tendency by means of a hierarchical approach in which a set of meta-parameters $\phi = (\phi_1 \subset \theta_1) \cup \cdots \cup (\phi_{n_c} \subset \theta_{n_c})$ are not conditioned on the previous modelling stages but rather form part of a single high-level model specification. The remaining parameters $\theta \cap \bar{\phi}$ are then optimised according to the standard sequential procedures, but conditioned upon the values of the meta-parameters ϕ:

$$m^H(\phi) = \left(\max_{\theta_1 \cap \overline{\phi_1}} M_1(\theta_1|\phi_1), \max_{\theta_2 \cap \overline{\phi_2}} M_2(\theta_2|\theta_1, \phi_2), \dots, \right.$$

$$\left. \max_{\theta_{n_c} \cap \overline{\phi_{n_c}}} M_{n_c}(\theta_{n_c}|\theta_1, \dots, \theta_{n_c-1}, \phi_{n_c}) \right) \tag{1.6}$$

By partitioning the parameter space in this hierarchical manner, we reduce the dependency both on the indirect optimisation criteria $M_i, \dots, M_{n_c}$ and on the parameter estimation at previous stages, which is replaced by a joint dependency upon the meta-parameters ϕ. The key advantage of this approach is that the utility of the model specification at meta-parameter level can be evaluated as a whole using "conditional" fitness measures which take into account not only the performance of the individual model but also its relationship to the performance of the existing portfolio of models.

1.3.2 Conditional Fitness

Given a candidate model $m^H(\phi_k)$, the standard approach to optimisation would be to compare the fitness of the model to that of the current optimal model, supplanting the existing model in the case where the fitness of the new model exceeds that of the existing solution. The weakness of this approach is that it overlooks any potential advantages which may be obtained through model combination. In the context of a population-based approach, the true choice is not **between** the new and a single old model, but rather whether the new model can **add value** to the existing population of models $P = \bigcup_{i=1,\dots,n_p} m^H(\phi_i)$. In other words, does the new model have a positive marginal utility:

$$mu[m^H(\phi_k)] = U\left[\left(\bigcup_{i \in P} m^H(\phi_i) \right) \cup m^H(\phi_k) \right] - U\left[\bigcup_{i \in P} m^H(\phi_i) \right] \tag{1.7}$$

This expression forms the basis for our solution to the problem of **jointly** optimising a population of models. In the particular case of optimising the risk-adjusted performance of a weighted combination of statistical arbitrage models, one measure of the marginal utility of model m is related to the weight which would be assigned to the new model if added to the existing portfolio:

$$mu[m^H(\phi_m)] = \frac{d}{dw} \left\{ [wr_m + (1-w)r_P] - \frac{1}{T}[w\sigma_m^2 + (1-w)^2\sigma_P^2 \right.$$

$$\left. + 2w(1-w)\sigma_m\sigma_P\rho_{mP}] \right\} \tag{1.8}$$

where r_m, σ_m^2 are the expected return and risk of the new model m; r_P, σ_P^2 are the expected return and risk of the existing portfolio of models; and ρ_{mP} is the correlation of returns between the new model and the existing portfolio. Solving for w in (1.8) gives the optimal combined portfolio with:

$$w = \frac{\frac{T}{2}(r_m - r_P) + (\sigma_P^2 - \sigma_m\sigma_P\rho_{mP})}{\sigma_m^2 + \sigma_P^2 - 2\sigma_m\sigma_P\rho_{mP}} \tag{1.9}$$

A positive value for w indicates that the risk-adjusted performance of the portfolio as a whole can be improved by the addition of the new model m. All other factors being equal, a new model can be assigned a positive weight for any of three reasons: (a) a higher expected return than the current portfolio ($r_m - r_P > 0$); (b) a lower level of risk than the current portfolio ($\sigma_P - \sigma_m > 0$); or (c) a less than perfect correlation with the existing portfolio ($\rho_{mP} < 1$).

This analysis highlights the fact that the value of a model cannot in general be correctly evaluated independently of the existing set of models: whilst r_m and σ_m^2 **can** be computed independently, the correlation ρ_{mP} can only be calculated in the context of the existing portfolio P. Whilst it may seem that correlation plays a less important role than the individual levels of risk and return, this is often far from being the case. For instance, Figure 1.5 illustrates the size of the "niche" w and the marginal utility mu in the case where a new model has equal levels of expected return and risk to the existing portfolio but a varying degree of correlation.

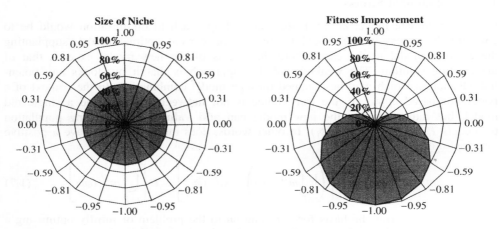

Figure 1.5   The marginal utility of a new model as a function of the **correlation** of its returns with those of a pre-existing portfolio. The correlation is displayed as a function of the angle ($\rho = \cos(\theta)$) with correlation of 1 at zero degrees from vertical, 0 correlation at $\pm 90°$ and -1 correlation at $180°$. The figure on the left indicates the optimal weight w for the new model, whilst the figure on the right indicates the proportional increase in overall utility relative to the old portfolio. The other parameters are $r_m = r_P = 10\%$, $\sigma_m = \sigma_P = 10\%$. The assumed level of risk tolerance T is 20

The figure on the left displays the optimal weighting assigned to the new model, which may be considered as the size of the "ecological niche" which is available for the new model. In this case the fact that the levels of risk and return are equal to those of the existing portfolio creates a symmetry in which the optimal weighting is always 50%. However, the actual *added value* of the new model varies widely as a function of the correlation. At a correlation of +1 the new combination is completely equivalent to the old portfolio and there is zero added value, at the other extreme, a correlation of -1 allows the risk of the old portfolio to be completely cancelled out with a consequent fitness improvement from $10 - (10^2/20) = 5$ for the old portfolio to 10 for the new combination, or a 100% improvement in relative terms.

1.3.3 Population-based Algorithm

We now describe our population-based optimisation algorithm for maximising the combined utility of a set of models. In our case the set of models will represent a portfolio of statistical arbitrage models, although the methodology is equally applicable to other optimisation problems in which the fitness function is risk-averse or contains unknown trade-offs between multiple objectives.

The key feature of our algorithm is that the maximisation is performed jointly on the entire set of models, and is performed with respect to the fitness of the population $P = \bigcup_{i=1,\ldots,n_p} m^H(\phi_i)$ as a whole rather than in terms of the fitness of individual models within the population. The key innovation which allows the optimisation to be performed in this manner is the combination of a meta-parameter representation with the use of conditional fitness functions. The meta-parameters ϕ_i capture the <u>key features</u> of the individual models in a reduced search space, whilst the conditional fitness measures $cf[m^H(\phi_k, P)] = U[P \cup m^H(\phi_k)] - U[P]$ ensure that the evaluation of new models is performed in a manner which accurately represents the <u>added value</u> which they provide to the existing portfolio. The complete algorithm is presented in Figure 1.6.

$$\textit{Initialise population:} \quad \forall_{i=1,\ldots,n_p}: \phi_i = 0, f_i = 0$$

For each population cycle
    Generate candidate models
    For each candidate
        Generate meta-parameters
$$\forall_{i=1,\ldots,n_c}: \phi_{n_p+i} = h\,g(P) + (1-h)\,randvec()$$

        For each model component $k = 1,\ldots,n_c$
          Optimise parameters
$$\theta_k = \phi_{i,k} \cup \max_{\theta_{i,k} \cap \phi_{i,k}} M_k\left(\theta_{i,k}|\theta_{i,1},\ldots,\theta_{i,k-1},\theta_{i,k}\right)$$
        Calculate conditional fitness of model
$$cf[m(\theta_i, P)] = U[P \cup m(\theta_i)] - U[P]$$

    Next model
    Update population
$$P = s\left(\begin{array}{c} P, C = \; Um(\theta_i),\, cf_{1,\ldots,n_p+n_c} \\ {}_{i=n_p+1,\ldots,n_p+n_c} \end{array}\right)$$
Next cycle

Figure 1.6 Details of the population-based algorithm for joint optimisation of a set of models

The application-independent details of the algorithm consist of the "heredity" factor h, the generation function g, and the survival function s. The heredity factor h determines the extent to which new candidates are derived from existing members of the population as opposed to random exploration of the meta-parameter space. For instance, the generation function g for new meta-parameters may act by combining the parameters of a number of "parent" models, in which case the algorithm may be considered a "genetic algorithm" and the term $(1 - h)$ is the "mutation rate". The survival function s governs the manner in which the population base at cycle $t + 1$ is derived from the previous population at time t together with the new candidates. One method is to hold the population size n_p constant, in which case s will act by replacing old members of the population with new candidates which have higher marginal utility with respect to the remainder of the population. Alternatively, we can allow the population to grow and shrink naturally as new candidates with positive marginal utility are discovered, incorporated into the population, and in some cases render existing models obsolete.

The application-dependent aspects of the algorithm will include the utility function U, the model parameterisation $m = (c_1(\theta_1), c_2(\theta_2), \ldots, c_{n_c}(\theta_{n_c}))$, the set of meta-parameters ϕ, and the optimisation criteria for the individual model components M_k. In the following section, we abstract away from these application-dependent aspects to a certain extent, and describe a set of controlled simulation experiments which are designed to highlight the underlying properties of the algorithm in the context of optimising a risk-averse objective function by means of a population of models.

1.4 SIMULATION RESULTS WITH SYNTHETIC DATA

In this section we describe an experiment to verify the properties of the population-based algorithm. The experiment is designed to represent, in an abstracted form, the attempt to identify and exploit "pockets of predictability" in financial market dynamics. The experiment is based upon controlled simulations in which the model parameters relate the performance of the model to a number of underlying "risk factors", which are in turn considered to drive asset prices. The factor sensitivities of the model determine a time series of "returns" which represents a linear combination of the changes in the underlying factors. Some factors have a positive expectation and hence represent systematic *opportunities* for generating profits, other factors have zero expectation and merely represent additional sources of model-dependent *risk*.

An important aspect of the experiment is that it is designed in such a way that there is no **single** combination of parameters which results in an optimal set of factor sensitivities. The performance of the population-based algorithm is compared both to optimising a single model via stochastic hill-climbing, and to a "naïve" population-based algorithm in which fitness is evaluated on an individual rather than conditional basis.

The basis of the controlled simulations is an abstracted form of the general problem of optimising systems for "model-based" trading. The objective is to maximise the quadratic utility of risky returns which are computed as a linear combination of model attributes $x_j(\theta)$ and factor returns $f_j(\psi)$:

$$r(\theta, \psi)_t = \sum_{j=1,\ldots,i} x_j(\theta) f_j(\psi)_t \quad f_j(\psi)_t \sim N(\mu_j, \sigma_j^2) \qquad (1.10)$$

We partition the "risk factors" $f_j(\psi)$ into a set which represents potential sources of excess returns, i.e. $\mu_{j=1,\ldots,i} > 0$, and a second set which merely represents sources of additional uncertainty, i.e. $\mu_{j=i+1,\ldots,i+n} = 0$. Attributes $x_{j=1,\ldots,i}(\theta)$ represent the extent to which the model has successfully captured potential sources of excess return, whilst attributes $x_{j=i+1,\ldots,i+n}(\theta)$ represent the exposure to the additional risks which are associated with trading a particular set of assets, estimating a particular model, etc. The final link in the chain between parameter values θ and model fitness $F(\theta)$ is the parameter attribute mapping. For ease of visualisation we use an abstracted representation in which attributes are represented by two-dimensional Gaussian distributions in parameter space with "centre" $(c_{1,j}, c_{2,j})$ and "spread" s_j.

Table 1.1   The parameters of the risky factors which determine model profits in the simulation experiments

Factor j	Return μ_j	Risk σ_j	Co-ordinates $(c_{1,j}, c_{2,j})$	Spread s_j
1 (F1)	1.0	0.5	(0.25,0.25)	0.25
2 (F2)	0.8	0.5	(0.25,0.75)	0.25
3 (F3)	0.7	0.5	(0.75,0.75)	0.25
4 (F4)	0.6	0.5	(0.75,0.25)	0.25
5, ... , 29 (N1, ... , N25)	0.0	1.0	$(\{0.1, 0.3, 0.5, 0.7, 0.9\}, \{0.1, 0.3, 0.5, 0.7, 0.9\})$	0.2

The actual parameters used for the simulation experiments are reported in Table 1.1. The table indicates that the first four factors (denoted F1, ... , F4) represent potential sources of positive expected returns, *i.e.* $\mu_j > 0$, whilst the remaining factors N1, ... , N25 merely represent additional sources of risk with no associated expectation of excess returns, *i.e.* $\mu_j = 0$.

In this setting then, a model consists of a pair of parameters, which in turn define the factor exposures which represent the "attributes" of the model. These factor exposures are then used to determine the "returns" of the model by acting as weights with which to combine the returns of the underlying risk factors. Finally the model performance is evaluated in terms of the "risk-adjusted return" measure shown in (1.4), with risk tolerance parameter $T = 2$.

For instance, the set of attributes for model (0.5,0.5) is shown in Figure 1.7. This example model, with parameters (0.5,0.5), lies mid-way in parameter space between all four sources of positive returns and also corresponds to the centre of noise factor N13; it is also sensitive to the "nearby" noise factors N7–N9, N12, N14 and N17–N19. The linear combination of factor returns F1, ... , F4 and N1, ... , N25 which is defined by the factor sensitivities in Figure 1.7 has an expected return of 0.42, total risk of 1.62 and risk-adjusted return of $0.42 - (1/2)1.62 = -0.40$.

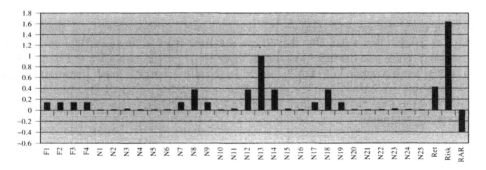

Figure 1.7   Attributes for model (0.5,0.5). The first four columns represent the extent to which the model embodies the four factors which are responsible for generating positive expected returns. The following 25 columns represent the extent to which the model is sensitive to each of the 25 noise factors, which are arranged in an even grid over the parameter space. The final three columns show the combined effect of the attributes in the form of expected return, risk and risk-adjusted return

Even in this relatively simple example, the nonlinearity in the parameter–attribute mapping creates a situation where, viewed from parameter space, the fitness function is both highly nonlinear and multimodal. For this two-dimensional setting, the complete mapping between model parameters and risk-adjusted return is presented in Figure 1.8. A grid search indicates that the optimal (individual) model coincides with the centre of the strongest positive return factor at location (0.25,0.25) and has an expected return of 1.03, risk of 1.82 and risk-adjusted return of 0.12.

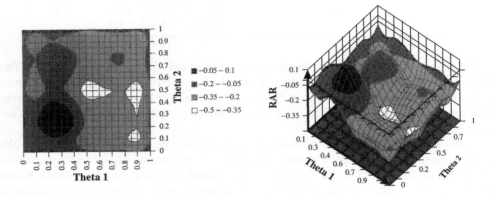

Figure 1.8   Risk-adjusted return as a function of the two model parameters; superior models lie in regions around the centre of each return-generating factor

We now describe a set of controlled simulation experiments, in which synthetic data was used to verify the properties of our population-based algorithm. In particular, the advantages of the portfolio of models approach are demonstrated by comparing its results to those achieved by a standard "stochastic hill-climbing" algorithm used to optimise a single model. Furthermore, the importance of joint optimisation is highlighted by comparing the results of the population-based algorithm in two cases: firstly where traditional "individual" fitness measures are used, and secondly where the population as a whole is jointly optimised through the use of conditional fitness measures.

In each case, the general form of the population-based algorithm is as described in Figure 1.6. In the first case, **P0**, the fitness measure used is an individual measure of risk-adjusted return and the inner loop of the algorithm operates as shown in Figure 1.9. In contrast, the second version of the population-based algorithm, **P1**, uses conditional fitness measures which are based upon the marginal increase in the utility of the population as a whole. The fitness of the population is defined by the solution to the following quadratic programming problem:

$$F(P) = \max_{w} \sum_{f} \mu_f \left(\sum_{m(j) \in P} w_j x_f^{(j)} \right) - \frac{1}{T} \sum_{f} \sigma_f^2 \left(\sum_{m(j) \in P} w_j x_f^{(j)} \right)^2 \qquad (1.11)$$

$$\text{subject to} \quad \sum_{j} w_j = 1; \quad w_j \geqslant 0$$

and the inner loop of algorithm **P1** operates as shown in Figure 1.10.

Generate candidate model: $\theta_1^{(cand)} = rand(\ )$; $\theta_2^{(cand)} = rand(\ )$

Calculate factor exposures: $x_j^{(cand)} = e^{-\left(\frac{(\theta_1^{(cand)} - c_{1,j})^2 + (\theta_2^{(cand)} - c_{2,j})^2}{s_j^2}\right)}$

Calculate individual fitness: $f(cand) = \sum_f \mu_f\, x_f^{(cand)} - \frac{1}{T} \sum_f \sigma_f^2 x_f^{(cand)2}$

Update population: if $\exists_{m(k)\in P} : f(cand) > f(k)$ then replace model k with new model

Figure 1.9 Details of the population-based algorithm P0, in which fitness is evaluated on an individual basis

Generate candidate model: $\theta_1^{(cand)} = rand(\ )$; $\theta_2^{(cand)} = rand(\ )$

Calculate factor exposures: $x_j^{(cand)} = e^{-\left(\frac{(\theta_1^{(cand)} - c_{1,j})^2 + (\theta_2^{(cand)} - c_{2,j})^2}{s_j^2}\right)}$

Calculate conditional fitness: $cf^{(cand)} = \max_{k \in P} F(P - \{m(k)\} \cup \{cand\}) - F(P)$

Update population: if $cf^{(cand)} > 0$ then replace model k with new model

Figure 1.10 Details of population-based algorithm P1, where fitness is evaluated in the context of the current portfolio

Table 1.2 presents a summary of the performance of the final portfolio of models produced by each of the two algorithms, as a function of the population size. The optimisation was conducted with respect to a 1000 observation "in-sample" realisation of the time series of returns $r(\theta, \psi)_t$ and evaluated with respect to a further 1000 observations in an "out-of-sample" set. The same sequence of 1000 candidate models was used for each experiment, and in each case the rate of improvement had slowed almost to zero by this time. Note that the performance with population size 1 is equivalent to that of a traditional single-solution "hill-climbing" approach.

With algorithm P0, there is little benefit from diversification, due to the population **converging** towards the optimal individual model. The results for the algorithm P1 are very different. Viewed on an **individual** basis the quality of the models apparently *deteriorates* with larger population size, however, the *improvement* in **portfolio** performance indicates that the reduced individual return is simply the price of achieving a diversified portfolio of models. The net result is that, with increasing population size, algorithm P1 is able to improve the risk-adjusted return of the portfolio as a whole. Note that in this case the bulk of the diversification can be achieved with only four models, although larger populations create some additional opportunities for diversifying away the "noise" factors.

1.4.1 Learning Trajectories

The key differences between the two approaches are clearly illustrated by considering the way in which the portfolio performance evolves in each case. Figure 1.11 compares the "learning trajectories" of portfolio return, risk and risk-adjusted return for the two

Table 1.2 Performance analysis of the portfolios of models produced by the two algorithms as a function of population size. Algorithm P0 uses a fitness measure based solely on the performance of an individual model. Algorithm P1 uses a conditional fitness measure which is based on "value added" to the existing portfolio. The first three columns of results refer to the average individual fitness, evaluated on the in-sample data. The second set of three columns corresponds to the fitness of the portfolio of models as a whole, again evaluated on the in-sample data. The final three columns of results correspond to the portfolio fitness evaluated against an additional "out-of-sample" set for validation purposes

Population size	Return (indiv.)	Risk (indiv.)	RAR (indiv.)	Port return	Port risk	Port RAR	OS Port return	OS Port risk	OS Port RAR
Algorithm P0 (individual fitness)									
1	0.96	1.77	0.08	0.96	1.77	0.08	0.91	1.83	0.00
4	0.96	1.77	0.08	0.97	1.77	0.08	0.91	1.83	0.00
9	0.96	1.77	0.07	0.94	1.69	0.10	0.89	1.72	0.03
16	0.94	1.75	0.06	0.93	1.65	0.10	0.87	1.68	0.03
25	0.94	1.76	0.05	0.91	1.61	0.11	0.86	1.62	0.05
Algorithm P1 (conditional fitness)									
1	0.96	1.77	0.08	0.96	1.77	0.08	0.91	1.83	0.00
4	0.56	1.40	−0.14	0.75	0.44	0.52	0.73	0.62	0.42
9	0.62	1.59	−0.18	0.82	0.41	0.61	0.80	0.54	0.53
16	0.65	1.59	−0.14	0.82	0.36	0.64	0.80	0.54	0.53
25	0.67	1.55	−0.11	0.84	0.38	0.65	0.82	0.66	0.49

algorithms. In each case, the results refer to a population (portfolio) comprised of 16 individual models.

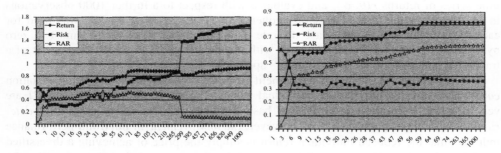

Figure 1.11 Evolution of portfolio risk and return in the case of algorithm P0 on the left (individual fitness) and P1 on the right (conditional fitness). The nonlinear time axis indicates the decreasing rate at which interesting new models are discovered by the random search procedure

In the early stages, new models are discovered which increase the portfolio **return** through higher individual returns and also reduce the **risk** through improved diversification. However, a by-product of the convergence of algorithm P0 towards the individually optimal model is an eventual <u>loss</u> of population diversity and an associated increase in portfolio risk. The "catastrophe" around time 285 corresponds to the loss of the last model which is not in the "cluster" around the *individual* optimum. In contrast, the conditional fitness measure used in the joint optimisation algorithm P1 recognises the value of diversity and achieves a monotonic improvement in the true performance measure of *portfolio* risk-adjusted return.

1.4.2 Portfolio composition

Figure 1.12 presents the composition of the population which is maintained by the different algorithms at various stages of the optimisation procedure. Initially the composition of

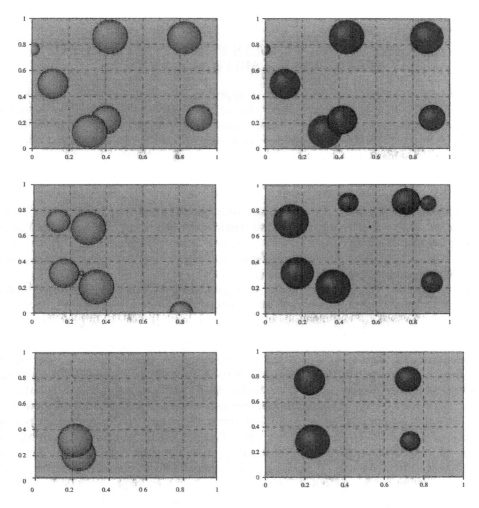

Figure 1.12   Evolution of **portfolio** composition for the two algorithms. Figures on the left-hand side correspond to algorithm P0 and on the right to algorithm P1. The top row is after 10 candidates have been evaluated; the second row is after 30 candidates; the final row is on termination after the evaluation of 1000 candidates. For each sphere, the x-coordinate equals the value of the first model parameter θ_1, the y-coordinate is the second parameter θ_2, and the size of the sphere is the weight allocated to the model within the portfolio

the portfolios is similar. In the case of algorithm P0 there is a clear convergence to a single optimal model, whilst in algorithm P1 the conditional fitness measure leads to only a localised convergence towards each of the sources of (risk-bearing) return.

In this section we have demonstrated that the use of a population-based approach is not sufficient in itself to guarantee that the potential advantages of diversification are realised in practice. In contrast, the joint optimisation algorithm actively encourages diversity by evaluating models in terms of the **added value** which they provide to the existing portfolio. In the following section, we demonstrate the application of the algorithm to the real-world problem of jointly optimising a portfolio of statistical arbitrage models.

1.5   EMPIRICAL RESULTS FOR A PORTFOLIO OF STATISTICAL ARBITRAGE MODELS

In this section we describe the results of applying the population-based algorithm to the problem of joint optimisation of the risk-adjusted return of a portfolio of statistical arbitrage models. Before moving on to the results we first present a brief overview of the models themselves. A detailed discussion of statistical arbitrage in general and our own modelling framework in particular can be found in Burgess (1999).

By analogy with traditional riskless arbitrage strategies, our statistical arbitrage strategies involve three stages:

- identification of statistical fair-price relationships between assets such that the deviations from the relationships can be considered "statistical mispricings" which exhibit a small but consistent regularity (deterministic component) in their dynamics;
- construction of predictive models which capture as much as possible of the deterministic component in the mispricing dynamics;
- implementation of appropriate trading strategies which exploit the predictive information by buying assets (or combinations of assets) which are forecasted to *outperform*, and selling assets (or combinations of assets) which are forecasted to *underperform*.

The first stage addresses the issue of **preprocessing**, which in this case consists of constructing and identifying "statistical mispricings", *i.e.* combinations of time series which contain a predictable component which can potentially be exploited in a statistical arbitrage context. Our approach to constructing these statistical mispricings is based upon the econometric concept of *cointegration*, with extensions to the standard methodology to deal with time-varying parameters and high-dimensional datasets. Individual mispricing models take the form $M_{i,t} = P_{T(i),t} - \sum_j \beta_{i,j,t} P_{C(i,j),t}$, where the mispricing at time t is given by the difference between the price $P_{T(i),t}$ of a particular "target asset" $T(i)$ and a weighted combination $\sum_j \beta_{i,j,t} P_{C(i,j),t}$ of "cointegrating assets" $C(i, j)$. The underlying motivation for this approach is that ideally the combination $\sum_j \beta_{i,j,t} P_{C(i,j),t}$ should represent a "fair price" for asset $T(i)$ and that deviations from this fair price will be mean-reverting. In the simplest case the coefficients $\beta_{i,j,t}$ can be estimated by regressing the target price series onto the set of cointegrating assets. One useful generalisation is to allow the parameters $\beta_{i,j,t}$ to adapt through time, in which case deviations between the target and mispricing series are partly considered to be due to innovations in the mispricing itself (with variance σ_M^2) and partly due to changes in the parameters of the fair-price relationship (with variance σ_B^2). Further details of this methodology are provided in Burgess (1999).

The second component within each statistical arbitrage model consists of a forecasting model which aims to capture the deterministic component of the mispricing dynamics. Depending on the extent to which we are prepared to make *a priori* assumptions regarding the nature of the dynamics, this forecasting model may be based on standard linear modelling techniques. Alternatively, we may choose to exploit the flexibility of nonlinear modelling methodologies such as neural networks, in which case the general model may be expressed in the form $E[\Delta M_{i,t}] = \hat{f}_i(M_{i,t}, \Delta M_{i,t-j}, \mathbf{z}_{i,t}, \theta_i)$, where the expected future change in the mispricing, $E[\Delta M_{i,t}]$, is an arbitrary function $\hat{f}_i()$ of the current mispricing $M_{i,t}$, recent changes in the mispricing, $\Delta M_{i,t-j}$, exogenous variables $\mathbf{z}_{i,t}$ and the model parameters θ_i.

The third component of each model consists of a statistical arbitrage trading rule, which transforms the output of the forecasting model into actual trading positions. Within our methodology we consider two cases of such rules. So-called "Implicit Statistical Arbitrage" (ISA) rules, of the form $ISA(M_t, k)_t = -\text{sign}(M_{t-j})|M_{t-j}|^k$, are designed to exploit an implicit assumption of mean-reverting behaviour in the mispricing time series, without the explicit construction of a forecasting model. A negative mispricing leads to a positive position (implicitly assuming the mispricing will revert upwards towards zero) and a positive mispricing leads to a negative position (exploiting the tendency to revert downwards towards zero). The power parameter k controls the relationship between the magnitude of the mispricing and the size of the position taken (for instance, $k = 0$ corresponds to positions with a fixed magnitude, whilst $k = 1$ corresponds to a linear dependence on the magnitude of the mispricing). In the more general case, the trading position is based upon an explicit forecasting model of the dynamics of the mispricing time series. This leads to so-called "Conditional Statistical Arbitrage" (CSA) rules of the form $CSA(E[\Delta M_t], k)_t = \text{sign}(E[\Delta M_t])|E[\Delta M_t]|^k$, the name in this case reflecting the fact that the positions indicated by the rule are conditioned upon the forecasted change in the mispricing, $E[\Delta M_t]$.

Within the context of the statistical arbitrage models outlined above, the advantage of the population-based algorithm is that it can be used to perform joint optimisation both of the components within each model and of the models themselves. Through this joint optimisation we can thus reflect the fact that the models will not be employed in isolation, but will be combined in the context of a diversified "portfolio of models".

Following the methodology described in Section 1.3, the components within each model are jointly optimised with respect to a conditional fitness measure (marginal utility) by the use of a set of "meta-parameters". The meta-parameters are considered as a high-level "joint specification" of the model, from which the remaining parameters then follow as a natural consequence of the estimation procedure and the sample data. The objective of this approach is to reduce the dimensionality of the joint optimisation process whilst minimising the criterion risk which would otherwise arise through the use of "multi-stage" optimisation procedures. The specific form of the different components within our statistical arbitrage models is presented in Table 1.3, which describes both the meta-parameters which govern the overall nature of the model and the low-level parameters which determine the specific details of each component.

In order to evaluate the performance of the models, we adopt a mean–variance perspective based on standard Markowitz portfolio theory. In this setting, the optimal weights

Table 1.3 Composition of an individual statistical arbitrage model: the meta-parameters are optimised at portfolio level and determine the high-level specification of the model components, in contrast the remaining parameters are estimated from the data and are conditioned upon the values of the meta-parameters

Component	General form	Meta-parameters	Parameters
Statistical Mispricing	$M_{i,t} = P_{T(i),t} - \sum_j \beta_{i,j,t} P_{C(i,j),t}$	$T(i), C(i,j)$	$\beta_{i,j,t}$
	$\beta_{i,j,t} = \beta_{i,j,t-1} + \eta_t$	$q = \sigma_B^2/\sigma_M^2$	
Forecasting Model	$E[\Delta M_{i,t}] = \hat{f}_i(M_{i,t}, \Delta M_{i,t-j}, \mathbf{z}_{i,t}, \theta_i)$	$\hat{f}_i, j, \mathbf{z}_{i,t}$	θ_i
Trading Strategy	$ISA(M_t, k)_t = -\text{sign}(M_{t-j})\|M_{t-j}\|^k$	k	
	$CSA(E[\Delta M_t], k)_t = \text{sign}(E[\Delta M_t])\|E[\Delta M_t]\|^k$	(+smoothing parameters h, θ)	

and expected risk-adjusted return of a portfolio of models are given by:

$$RAR(P) = \max_w \mathbf{rw} - \frac{1}{T}\mathbf{w}^T \mathbf{V} \mathbf{w} \quad \text{subject to} \quad \sum_j w_j = 1; w_j \geqslant 0 \qquad (1.12)$$

where $n_p = |P|$ is the size of the portfolio, $\mathbf{r} = [E(r_1)\ E(r_2)\ \cdots\ E(r_{np})]$ is the vector of expected returns, $\mathbf{V}$ is the $(n_p \times n_p)$ covariance matrix of model returns, $\mathbf{w} = [w_1\ w_2\ \cdots\ w_{n_p}]^T$ is the vector of model weights and T the risk-appetite parameter. Within this context, the "conditional fitness" or marginal utility of a candidate model is simply the increase in risk-adjusted return which is obtained by adding the model to the current portfolio:

$$mu(cand) = RAR(P \cup cand) - RAR(P) \qquad (1.13)$$

In this manner the "fitness" of a candidate model takes into account not only the expected return (in $\mathbf{r}$) and risk of the model (diagonal elements of $\mathbf{V}$) but also the correlations between the various models (off-diagonal elements of $\mathbf{V}$). Straightforward modifications of the algorithm can be used to optimise alternative measures of risk-adjusted return such as the Sharpe Ratio.

1.5.1 Results for Portfolio of Equity Index Models

In this section, we describe the results of applying the population-based algorithm to the problem of jointly optimising a portfolio of statistical arbitrage models based on mispricings between the following set of international equity indices:

Dow Jones Industrial Average, Standard and Poor's 500 Index (US)
FTSE 100 (UK)
DAX 30 (Germany)
CAC 40 (France)
SMI (Switzerland)
IBEX (Spain)
OMX (Sweden)
Hang Seng (Hong Kong)
Nikkei 225 (Japan)

The data used in the experiment were daily closing prices for the period 1st August 1988 to 8th October 1997. From the total of 2419 observations the first 1419 were used for estimation of the parameters of the statistical arbitrage models, the following 500 observations (9th December 1993 to 9th November 1995) were used to perform model selection within the context of the population-based optimisation procedure, and the final 500 observations (10th November 1995 to 8th October 1997) were withheld for an out-of-sample evaluation.

The population-based algorithm was applied to jointly optimise a set of 10 models, each consisting of three components. For the first component, the adaptive form of the statistical mispricing methodology was used, with meta-parameters specifying the target asset, the set of constituent assets, and the degree of adaptivity. The second component consisted of either a linear or neural forecasting model with meta-parameters specifying the functional form of the model together with the explanatory variables (statistical mispricing together with selected lagged innovations in the mispricing). The third group of meta-parameters specifies the sensitivity parameter k and the holding period h for the moving-average form of the CSA trading rule.

Table 1.4 summarises the out-of-sample performance of the individual models within the population, together with two portfolios, one formed from a weighted average (WtAv) and the other from an unweighted average (SimAv) of the individual models.

The wide diversity of the performance of the individual models highlights the high level of risk which is inherent in attempting to choose a single "best" model. The two portfolios constructed by combining the individual models, whether by the weighted average resulting from mean–variance optimisation or a simple unweighted average, both have a similar level of performance—less profitable than the best models, but a long way from making the losses of the worst models, and significantly positive over the out-of-sample period as a whole. The equity curves for the weighted combination of models, together with the individually best- and worst-performing models, are presented in Figure 1.13.

Notice the increased level of risk exhibited by the combined portfolio in the second half of the out-of-sample period. In practice, however, it is unlikely that a single set of models

Table 1.4 Performance of a portfolio of statistical arbitrage models of international equity indices created using the population-based algorithm; the results are subdivided into two equal periods

	Out-of-sample (1–250)			Out-of-sample (251–500)		
	Directional ability	Sharpe Ratio	Total profit	Directional ability	Sharpe Ratio	Total profit
WtAv	**51.2%**	**1.79**	**13.3**	**52.0%**	**0.58**	**8.8**
SimAv	**49.2%**	**1.60**	**11.8**	**49.6%**	**0.29**	**4.7**
Model 1	46.4%	−0.31	−4.5	47.6%	−0.51	−8.4
Model 2	52.4%	3.18	20.4	50.8%	2.17	41.4
Model 3	50.4%	0.57	6.8	55.6%	2.86	39.6
Model 4	50.8%	0.79	21.2	49.6%	0.28	11.6
Model 5	54.8%	1.04	19.8	47.6%	−0.52	−33.8
Model 6	55.2%	2.08	38.8	51.2%	0.35	15.9
Model 7	51.6%	−0.01	−0.1	53.6%	0.00	0.0
Model 8	46.4%	−1.11	−26.3	48.0%	−0.30	−10.1
Model 9	45.6%	−0.06	−0.6	43.6%	−1.53	−59.5
Model 10	53.2%	2.15	42.8	55.2%	1.96	50.3

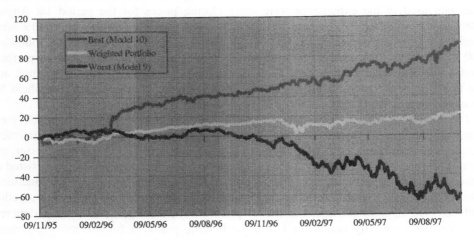

Figure 1.13   Performance of statistical arbitrage models for international equity indices

would be traded in unchanged form for a period of two years. Thus whilst the experiment serves to demonstrate the feasibility, in principle, of using the population-based algorithm to generate a set of trading models, it is a rather crude analysis which neglects the potential for leveraged trading, deselection of underperforming models, periodic refreshing of the portfolio and many other enhancements that would be open to a potential trader of such a system.

In practice statistical arbitrage between international equity markets is conducted not on the spot market index levels themselves, but through the futures markets. Moreover, the different opening and closing times of the different markets mean that the most meaningful way of analysing index futures strategies is through the use of synchronised <u>intraday</u> observations. The following subsection presents results of applying the population-based algorithm in such a context.

1.5.2   Results for Portfolio of Intraday Equity Index Future Models

In this subsection we present the results from an application of the population-based methodology to the task of jointly optimising a portfolio of **intraday** statistical arbitrage models between an international set of equity index futures. In particular, the index futures were the September 1998 contracts on the FTSE 100, DAX 30, CAC 40, S&P 500 and MIB 30 and the July 1998 contract on the Swiss market index. The data consists of hourly samples taken live from a Reuters data-feed from 9 am to 5 pm daily during the period 15/5/98 through to 20/7/98, giving a total of 364 observations.

A population of 10 models was jointly optimised using the first 264 observations and evaluated on the remaining 100 out-of-sample observations. Due to the relatively small sample size, the models used were of the implicit statistical arbitrage type which aims to exploit the mean-reverting component of the mispricing dynamics. The meta-parameters which define each model thus consist of the target asset, the set of constituent assets, the adaptivity parameter for the weights of the fair-price relationship and the trading rule parameters. The performance of both the individual models and unweighted and weighted combinations is shown in Table 1.5, net of transaction costs of 10 basis points.

Table 1.5 Performance analysis of a portfolio of intraday statistical arbitrage models based on a set of international equity index futures. Transaction costs of 10 basis points are included. "Comb" is the performance of an equally weighted combination and "CombWt" a weighted combination of the models

	Weighting	Profit	Sharpe Ratio	Direction
Model 1	0.004	−0.84%	−2.91	47.5%
Model 2	0.055	−0.18%	−0.61	46.5%
Model 3	0.177	1.14%	4.11	55.4%
Model 4	0.084	2.06%	6.71	58.4%
Model 5	0.177	1.76%	5.63	53.5%
Model 6	0.114	−0.57%	−2.39	45.5%
Model 7	0.219	0.90%	3.73	51.5%
Model 8	0.038	1.22%	5.00	54.5%
Model 9	0.110	1.78%	6.10	53.5%
Model 10	0.021	0.69%	2.55	51.5%
Best	—	2.06%	6.71	58.4%
Worst	—	−0.84%	−2.91	45.5%
Comb	—	0.80%	3.60	53.5%
CombWt	—	1.06%	4.57	53.5%

The table demonstrates a wide spread of performance figures across the individual models. Note also that the model which is allocated the highest weight based on **in-sample** performance (Model 7) is far from the best during the **out-of-sample** evaluation. This indicates the danger of using a weighted combination scheme rather than the simpler equally-weighted combination, even though in this case the weighted combination outperforms overall. Even this relatively simple set of models shows useful promise, with the annualised Sharpe Ratio of 4.57 for the weighted portfolio suggesting that the performance is consistent enough to justify a moderate degree of leverage.

1.6 CONCLUSION

In this paper we have described an ambitious approach to the task of creating model-based trading strategies. This approach aims to avoid the risks and inefficiencies which result from the separate optimisation of components within a model, and models within a population.

In our population-based approach, models are jointly optimised by the use of conditional fitness measures which quantify the marginal utility or *added value* which a model provides to the current population. As opposed to the traditional method of evaluating models on an individual basis, this approach actively encourages the generation of a set of well-diversified and hence complementary models. Furthermore, in an attempt to overcome the problem of criterion risk, or the "forecasting bottleneck", the components within each model are also jointly optimised with respect to the marginal utility at the level of a set of "meta-parameters" which can be considered as a high-level specification of the model.

The properties of the algorithm have been verified using controlled simulation, in which the joint optimisation approach was demonstrated to outperform a similar population-based algorithm using a more traditional fitness measure. The algorithm has been applied to the real-world task of optimising a set of statistical arbitrage models within a "portfolio of models" context. Whilst many further improvements are envisaged, even these preliminary results demonstrate the potential to generate profitable strategies at levels of risk which are made tolerable through the strategy of diversification across a portfolio of models.

REFERENCES

Bengio, Y. (1997). "Training a Neural Network with a Financial Criterion rather than a Prediction Criterion", In A. Weigend et al. (eds.), *Decision Technologies for Financial Engineering*. Singapore: World Scientific; 36–48.

Burgess, A.N. (1997)."Asset Allocation across European Equity Indices Using a Portfolio of Dynamic Cointegration Models", In A. Weigend et al. (eds.), *Decision Technologies for Financial Engineering*. Singapore: World Scientific; 276–288.

Burgess, A.N. (1999). "A Computational Methodology for Modelling the Dynamics of Statistical Arbitrage", unpublished Ph.D. thesis, Decision Technology Centre, London Business School.

Choey, M. and A.S. Weigend (1997). "Nonlinear Trading Models through Sharpe Ratio Maximisation". In A. Weigend et al. (eds.), *Decision Technologies for Financial Engineering*. Singapore: World Scientific; 3–22.

Markowitz, H. (1959). *Portfolio Selection: Efficient Diversification of Investments*. New York: Wiley.

Moody, J.E. and L. Wu (1997). "Optimisation of Trading Systems and Portfolios", In A. Weigend et al. (eds.), *Decision Technologies for Financial Engineering*. Singapore: World Scientific; 23–35.

Moody, J.E., L. Wu, Y. Liao and M. Saffell (1998). "Performance Functions and Reinforcement Learning for Trading Systems and Portfolios', *Journal of Forecasting*, **17**, 441–470,

Towers, N. (2000). "Decision Technologies for Trading Predictability in Financial Markets", unpublished Ph.D. thesis, Decision Technology Centre, London Business School.

Towers, N. and A.N. Burgess (1999). A Framework for Applying Reinforcement Learning to Investment Finance, Technical Report, London Business School.

Towers, N. and A.N. Burgess (2000), "Implementing Trading Strategies for Forecasting Models", in Y. Abu-Mostafa et al. (eds.), *Computational Finance*. Cambridge, MA: MIT press.

2

A Meta-parameter Approach to the Construction of Forecasting Models for Trading Systems[1]

NEVILLE TOWERS AND A. NEIL BURGESS

ABSTRACT

Financial forecasting models are commonly constructed using methodologies that have no explicit reference to any associated trading strategy. In general, these methodologies aim to minimise some measure of forecast error, such as squared-error loss, rather than to maximise the economic value of a forecasting model to a particular trading system. In this paper we address this issue by developing a methodology to jointly optimise a trading system consisting of a forecasting model and a parameterised trading strategy. This is achieved by using a "meta-parameter" approach which conditionally optimises the characteristics of the forecasting model, given a specific trading strategy. We demonstrate this framework for trading systems based on a set of 50 "statistical mispricings" within the UK equity market (FTSE 100). In comparison to a naïve approach, our results indicate that joint optimisation can improve trading performance by more effectively compensating for the presence of market frictions such as transaction costs.

2.1 INTRODUCTION

In recent years, substantial research has focused on the controversy of predictability in financial assets which, in turn, has motivated the development of forecasting models which attempt to expose the underlying dynamics of financial markets. The high complexity and almost completely stochastic nature of financial markets has spurred the development of sophisticated forecasting techniques that attempt to capture different deterministic components of market dynamics. This has led to many methodological developments in modelling nonlinear and time-varying relationships in nonstationary, stochastic environments. The potential importance of these techniques has been further highlighted by recent empirical studies which demonstrate that predictable components can exist in financial markets and that sophisticated forecasting models can have predictive power, even after adjusting for "data-snooping" biases (e.g. Lo and MacKinlay, 1995; Burgess, 1999).

[1] Neville Towers conducted this work as a research student in the Decision Technology Centre at London Business School. Neil Burgess conducted this work as a research fellow within the Computational Finance group of the Decision Technology Centre at London Business School.

Developments in Forecast Combination and Portfolio Choice. Edited by C. Dunis, A. Timmermann and J. Moody.
© 2001 John Wiley & Sons Ltd

However, by concentrating on solely improving the accuracy of forecasting, financial modelling research has in some part neglected to consider that ultimately forecasting models must be considered in light of the wider investment context. The complexity involved in developing reliable forecasting models has often led to a decoupling of forecasting from the optimisation of the rest of the decision-making process. In this context, financial forecasting models are commonly constructed using methodologies that have no explicit reference to any associated trading strategy. For example, models are often constructed to minimise some measure of forecast error, such as squared-error loss, rather than to maximise their economic value to a trading strategy. This is demonstrated by many empirical studies which construct forecasting models of asset returns and then subsequently measure performance in terms of the simulated profits generated using simple, *ad hoc* trading rules (e.g. Refenes and Azema-Barac, 1994; Zapranis *et al.*, 1997; Kolias and Metaxas, 1997). This disjointed approach tends to neglect the other elements of the decision-making process such as current inventory (portfolio of asset holdings), transaction costs, investment objectives, constraints and risks. These simplified trading systems should really be considered as "profitability tests" for certain types of predictability rather than realistic methodologies for developing trading systems based upon forecasting models.

In this paper we examine the fact that the active management of predicted asset returns involves the two inter-related modelling tasks of forecasting and decision-making. We emphasise the link between these two tasks by focusing on the "design factors" which condition the estimation of forecasting models. These model design factors may include forecast horizon, statistical loss function, and choice of forecast object as well as the specification of the forecasting method itself. In most forecasting applications, these design factors can be adequately prespecified by conducting a detailed analysis of the decision-making task. For dynamic trading strategies, however, a naïve specification of the forecasting model may indirectly lead to sub-optimal trading performance. This is due to a combination of the highly complex nature of financial markets, the relatively low levels of potential predictability, the typical weakness of *a priori* modelling assumptions and the high sensitivity of trading performance to forecast accuracy.

Thus, a more general, integrated methodology seems appropriate, where the design factors of any forecasting model are optimised for a specific trading strategy. In general this requires a multi-objective optimisation approach which is not part of the traditional approach to constructing forecasting models. We address this problem by the development of a methodology to optimise a trading system as a whole by jointly optimising the two components of the system, namely a forecasting model and a trading strategy. We demonstrate how this may be achieved by using a "meta-parameter" approach which, in essence, optimises particular design factors by considering the importance of different characteristics of the forecasting model in the context of a specific trading strategy. For the purpose of this demonstration we implement the trading strategy using a set of parameterised trading rules (Towers and Burgess, 2000a,b). These have the advantage over heuristic trading rules of taking into account both the prediction ability of the forecasting model and the cost of trading.

In Section 2.2 we discuss the development of forecasting models for trading systems. In particular, we examine the specification of the key model design factors by focusing on the relationship between trading performance and different characteristics of the generated forecasts. We also discuss the design of integrated trading systems that have been developed to exploit predictability. In Section 2.3 we present a synthetic example of a trading system consisting of two modelling stages: firstly an idealised forecasting model and secondly a parameterised trading strategy. We illustrate how one particular design factor, the optimisation criterion, can be optimised with respect to a parameterised trading rule by using a single meta-parameter which reflects a trade-off between two different forecast characteristics (Towers, 2000). In the context of this controlled example we demonstrate that joint optimisation can improve the economic value of a forecasting model. In section 2.4 we extend our analysis to consider how the joint optimisation methodology can be applied to a realistic trading system. We use a set of 50 statistical mispricings from the UK equity market (FTSE 100) as the basis for constructing simple forecasting models which are evaluated in the context of trading strategies to exploit any detectable predictability. We compare in-sample and out-of-sample results for different trading strategies using two heuristic trading rules and three parameterised trading rules (Towers and Burgess, 2000a). Our results indicate that in the presence of transaction costs the joint optimisation approach can achieve a significant improvement in trading performance.

2.2   DEVELOPING FORECASTING MODELS FOR TRADING SYSTEMS

In recent years, advanced financial forecasting models have been developed based on computational and statistical techniques, for example, neural networks (Refenes *et al.*, 1997), adaptive models (Bentz and Connor, 1998) and cointegration (Burgess, 1998). These methods relax some of the assumptions of traditional forecasting methods and allow for nonlinear and time-varying relationships. These methodological advances have been used to demonstrate that forecasting models of the conditional mean and variance of asset (or combinations of asset) returns offer potential for low but significant levels of prediction ability.

In general, these advanced financial forecasting techniques are still derived from traditional model building methodologies which minimise some measure of forecast error, subject to standard model integrity tests. These approaches typically involve constructing a forecasting model using the stages of model identification, estimation and diagnostic evaluation (e.g. Box and Jenkins, 1978). However, these standard approaches tend to construct models without any direct interaction with the trading environment. For trading systems, the economic value of the forecasting model is then often subsequently evaluated by simulating the performance of a trading strategy which uses the predictions from the forecasting model.

The inherent assumption of traditional model building methodologies is that any "higher level" model design factors of the forecasting model must be predefined. Examples of such "design factors" include the object of the forecast (e.g. the specific time series), forecast type (*i.e.* point, interval or density forecast), forecast horizon, optimisation criterion, and the choice of candidate input variables. In most practical situations the process of selecting these factors is achieved by a qualitative assessment of the task. For trading systems the choice of these design factors may significantly influence the prediction (and economic) value of the model and so the traditional *ad hoc* approach may not be sufficient. This is because trading systems typically exhibit a number of properties that are uncommon in other applications. For example, the highly stochastic nature of financial markets limits any realisable prediction ability to relatively low levels and the complexity of financial systems means that forecasting models have a tendency to suffer from weak *a priori* assumptions. In addition, the profitability of trading systems based on forecasting models is unusually sensitive to the accuracy of the predictions when compared to applications of forecasting models in other domains. The combination of these factors means that the usual naïve approach to model construction may indirectly lead to substantially sub-optimal performance.

Thus, for trading systems, a more systematic approach seems essential in order to account for situations where the design attributes of a forecasting model can be optimised with respect to the economic value of the overall trading system. For example, some research has shown that financial forecasting models constructed to minimise mean squared forecasting error, rather than the trading objective, may lead to sub-optimal trading (Satchell and Timmermann, 1995). We adopt a view in which the purpose of the forecasting methodology is to construct a model that produces predictions with a whole set of characteristics which provide the greatest possible opportunities in the context of a given trading strategy.

To formalise this perspective, let us assume that our trading system has an investment utility, U, and a forecasting model that produces predicted returns which can be described by a set of characteristics, denoted by $C_1, C_2, \ldots, C_n$. If we assume that the predicted returns are exploited by a (conditionally) optimal trading strategy, denoted by π^*, then the general relationship between the economic value of the forecasting model and the prediction characteristics takes the form:

$$E[U|\pi^*] = f(C_1, C_2, \ldots, C_n) \tag{2.1}$$

where 'f' is some function of the vector of characteristics, C.

In (2.1) we have related the properties of the forecasting model to the economic value of the trading system, in terms of a controllable set of prediction characteristics. This indicates that any optimisation of a design factor, which affects the characteristics of the model, should ideally be undertaken with respect to an optimal trading strategy. Thus, in principle, the forecasting model and trading strategy should be optimised simultaneously in order to estimate the "best" forecasting model given the optimal trading strategy. If this were possible, then the relationship between the prediction characteristics and expected trading performance could be specified precisely. However, in practice, the two models must be optimised consecutively which, in general, provides no guarantee of joint optimality.

It is interesting to note, however, that the traditional model construction approach fits within the scope of (2.1). For instance, consider the design factors which dictate the choice of optimisation criterion. In the case where the criterion may be correctly specified in terms of a <u>single</u> characteristic, prediction accuracy, the expected value of the trading system is a *monotonically increasing* function of prediction accuracy, *i.e.* higher levels of prediction accuracy are most likely to lead to more profitable trading systems. If the function f in (2.1) could be defined correctly then the expected value of the trading system could be determined for each level of prediction accuracy. This, in turn, would provide a means of assessing the expected economic value of improving the prediction accuracy of a forecasting model. Furthermore, in such a case, the forecasting model could be constructed before optimisation of the trading strategy under the assumption that minimising forecast error would provide the optimal information to the trading strategy. In this way, the two sequential modelling stages automatically implement a joint optimisation over forecasting and trading without explicitly optimising the forecasting model conditionally upon the optimal trading strategy.

However, if <u>multiple</u> characteristics of the forecasting model affect trading performance then the forecasting model cannot be optimised in isolation from the trading strategy. The optimisation of the forecasting model needs to reflect the impact of each characteristic to trading performance, and this cannot be computed without interaction with the optimisation of the trading strategy. For instance, in trading systems for forecasting models, the ultimate objective is to maximise trading performance, but this can only be evaluated after construction of both forecasting and trading systems. Hence, estimation of the forecast model must be performed before the trading policy has been optimised, using some alternative criterion. The separate optimisation of the forecasting system may result in some loss of information which fails to take appropriate account of the trading environment. This effect has been referred to as the "forecasting bottleneck" (Moody *et al.*, 1998).

To avoid this joint optimisation problem, techniques have been developed which use a single model for the trading system rather than taking a modular approach to the two tasks of forecasting and decision-making (e.g. Moody, 1997; Choey and Weigend, 1997). In these systems, explanatory variables act as direct inputs into the decision model, where parameters are optimised to maximise the application-related objective function. This avoids some of the problems associated with separate optimisation of the two-stage process. However, single model systems have potential disadvantages compared to the modular decomposition approach. For instance, the creation of one "large" model may result in a larger number of system states, compared to two "smaller" models, where the combined number of states of the system is additive rather than multiplicative and thus relatively parsimonious (Towers, 2000). Modularisation also allows for greater system transparency and supports the use of integrity checks to assist in the identification of model breakdown or misspecification. It also allows the re-use of existing forecasting models for new applications, reduces the sensitivity to spurious input variables and is less prone to implementation difficulties arising from the need to use nondifferentiable and constrained objective functions.

In light of these issues, we restrict our attention to the two-stage modelling approach and propose a methodology to perform a joint optimisation over the entire trading system. This is achieved by optimising the characteristics of the forecasting model that are assumed to be relevant to trading. In principle, this process has the effect of avoiding the "forecasting bottleneck" because the optimised characteristics ensure that the information produced by the forecasting model is optimally exploitable in terms of overall system performance. We propose that this process be implemented using higher level design parameters to control the modelling strategy and provide information feedback from the trading strategy to re-optimise the forecasting model. The purpose of these higher level parameters, which we refer to as "meta-parameters", is to reflect the value of the different characteristics of the forecast model in the context of a specific trading strategy.

In the next section we present a synthetic example to demonstrate a simple method of controlling the optimisation criterion of a forecasting model which is a function of two prediction characteristics. The use of our meta-parameter approach allows the forecasting model to be optimised with respect to the trading strategy. In particular, we consider the two characteristics of prediction accuracy and prediction smoothness which, under appropriate conditions, have been demonstrated to show a similar magnitude of influence upon trading performance (Towers and Burgess, 1998). For the application of meta-parameters to the optimisation of other design factors, such as forecast horizon and forecast object, see Towers (2000).

2.3   SYNTHETIC EXAMPLE OF THE JOINT OPTIMISATION TECHNIQUE

In this section we investigate a system which trades a single risky asset and which is comprised of two modules addressing the tasks of forecasting and decision-making. The first stage of the modelling process involves constructing a forecasting model in order to generate predicted asset returns, these in turn act as inputs to the decision model. This approach allows control of the trading position on the basis of both the predicted asset returns and also the current state of the system. For the sake of this example we assume that the trading system is influenced solely by the choice of the optimisation criterion which is used to estimate the parameters of the forecasting model. In particular, we consider that the optimisation criterion consists of two prediction characteristics, namely prediction accuracy and prediction smoothness. The second characteristic, prediction smoothness, is included in the optimisation criterion on the basis of evidence that, in the presence of transaction costs, the smoothness of the predicted returns may substantially influence the performance of a trading strategy for exploiting predictability (Towers and Burgess, 1998).

The purpose of this synthetic trading system is to compare two possible optimisation techniques. The first method uses a single optimisation approach which firstly constructs the forecasting model and secondly optimises a decision model to maximise trading performance. This method uses a predefined optimisation criterion for the forecasting model, which we specify as the maximisation of prediction accuracy, measured in terms of predictive correlation. This approach is considered to represent the traditional approach used to optimise a two-stage trading system. The second method we investigate uses a joint optimisation approach which optimises the two prediction characteristics with respect to the current approximation of the optimal trading strategy. This process is achieved using a meta-parameter which represents the trade-off between the two prediction characteristics in order to reach the goal of joint optimality. Later in this section we describe this joint optimisation approach in more detail.

2.3.1   Experimental Set-up

In our simulation experiments we assume an idealised forecasting model which consists of two parameters, θ_1 and θ_2, and has two potentially important prediction characteristics, C_1 and C_2, which take the form:

$$C_1 = g_1(\theta_1, \theta_2) \text{ and } C_2 = g_2(\theta_1, \theta_2) \qquad (2.2)$$

where 'g_1' and 'g_2' are some functions of the two model parameters, θ_1 and θ_2.

This specification provides a means of simulating a generic forecasting model and so allows us to focus on the underlying motivation for our approach without becoming distracted by model-specific details. The only requirement is to specify the two functions, g_1 and g_2, and develop a controllable data-generating process to produce predictions with these two characteristics.

The two characteristics are defined to represent prediction accuracy and prediction smoothness. Prediction accuracy is specified as the correlation between the predicted return and the actual return and prediction smoothness is specified as the first-order prediction autocorrelation. If we suppose that the two characteristics gradually deteriorate around some optimal values in each direction of parameter space then predictive correlation β and prediction autocorrelation φ can be defined as:

$$\beta(\theta_1,\theta_2) = \max\left(0, 0.3 - \left(\frac{\theta_1 - x_1}{\sigma(x_1)}\right)^2 - \left(\frac{\theta_2 - y_1}{\sigma(y_1)}\right)^2\right) \qquad (2.3)$$

$$\varphi(\theta_1,\theta_2) = \max\left(0, 0.9 - \left(\frac{\theta_1 - x_2}{\sigma(x_2)}\right)^2 - \left(\frac{\theta_2 - y_2}{\sigma(y_2)}\right)^2\right) \qquad (2.4)$$

where x and y are the co-ordinates of the centre of the distribution and parameters σ_x and σ_y control the spread of the distribution in each direction.

(2.3) and (2.4) are defined such that the maximum predictive correlation is 30% and the maximum prediction autocorrelation is 90%. We arbitrarily specify parameters which represent both the locations in parameter space at which each characteristic reaches a maximum and the manner in which these characteristics decay in models which fail to achieve these optimal values. The arbitrary parameters used for this experiment are shown in Table 2.1 and displayed graphically in Figure 2.1.

Table 2.1 The function parameters for (2.3) and (2.4) to simulate the two prediction characteristics

Characteristic	x	y	σ_x	σ_y
1. Predictive Correlation	0.2	0.3	1	1
2. Prediction Autocorrelation	0.45	0.6	0.5	0.4

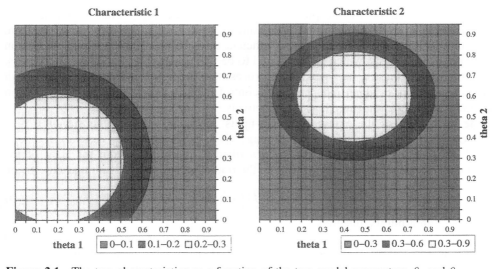

Figure 2.1 The two characteristics as a function of the two model parameters, θ_1 and θ_2

The specification of the two prediction characteristics for a forecasting model with particular parameter values motivates the development of a controllable data-generating process which is capable of producing the appropriate predicted and actual return time series.

To formalise this process, let some asset return Δy be comprised of a deterministic component and a stochastic component represented by variables x_t and ε_t, respectively and defined as

$$\Delta y_t = \beta x_t + \varepsilon_t \qquad \text{where } \varepsilon_t \sim NID(0, \sigma_\varepsilon^2)$$

$$x_t = \varphi x_{t-1} + \eta_t \qquad \text{where } \eta_t \sim NID(0, \sigma_\eta^2)$$

(2.5)

where β and φ are coefficients and ε_t and η_t are two Gaussian processes with variance σ_ε^2 and σ_η^2, respectively.

In (2.5), the coefficient β represents the strength of the deterministic variable x_t, while the coefficient φ introduces autocorrelation into the time series. To specify the variance of the two Gaussian processes, suppose that the variance of the explanatory variable is equal to the variance of the actual asset returns. If we standardise the distributions of the two variables then the variances of the two Gaussian processes are defined as:

$$\sigma_\varepsilon^2 = 1 - \beta^2$$

$$\sigma_\eta^2 = 1 - \varphi^2$$

(2.6)

where the coefficients β and φ are subject to the constraints $\varphi < 1$ and $\beta < 1$.

Using this formulation for the variance of the two processes means that the coefficient φ controls the level of autocorrelation in the explanatory variable x_t and the coefficient β controls the correlation between the asset return and the explanatory variable. Now, if we assume that the deterministic component of the asset return can be completely captured in a statistical forecasting model (*i.e.* the model is maximally predictive), then the predicted return series $\Delta \hat{y}$ is defined as:

$$\Delta \hat{y}_t = \beta x_t$$

(2.7)

Given this formulation for the predicted return, the coefficient β controls the level of correlation between predicted and actual returns, which is considered to be the measure of prediction accuracy. Similarly, the coefficient φ controls the level of autocorrelation in the predicted returns, which is considered to be the measure of prediction smoothness. We have now defined a data-generating process for predicted and actual returns, with parameters β and φ which independently control the two characteristics for prediction accuracy and prediction smoothness, respectively.

The next stage of the experimental set-up is concerned with the construction of a decision model to optimise the trading strategy given predicted returns from a forecasting model. In general, this strategy can be described as a mapping from the state of the system, s, and the predicted return, $\hat{y}_{t+1}$, to the trading position, a_{t+1}, and takes the form:

$$a_{t+1} = f(s_t, \hat{y}_{t+1})$$

(2.8)

where f is an arbitrary function.

For this task we use a method based on parameterised trading rules for predicted returns, as developed in Towers and Burgess (2000a,b). This approach uses moving-average techniques to provide some degree of smoothing to the trading position through time. This provides a means of optimising the trade-off between exploiting the prediction information and minimising the cost of changing the trading position. One parameterised trading rule based on exponential smoothing, with decay rate parameter κ, is defined as:

$$a_{t+1} = m[(1 - \kappa)\hat{y}_{t+1} + \kappa a_t] \tag{2.9}$$

where κ is subject to the constraint $0 \leqslant \kappa \leqslant 1$ and m is a normalisation factor which controls the average trading exposure.

So, for example, if $\kappa = 0$, the trading position is solely determined by the predicted return and is not affected by the previous trades. However, if $\kappa = 1$, the trading position is not affected by the predicted return and remains constant at the previous trading position. Given this definition of the trading position a_{t+1}, we define the investment return r_{t+1} as:

$$r_{t+1} = a_{t+1}y_{t+1} + T|a_{t+1} - a_t| \tag{2.10}$$

where y_{t+1} is the actual asset return and T is a transaction cost parameter, which represents the unit cost of changing the trading position. This is equivalent to a scaled version of the Sharpe Ratio measure (Sharpe, 1996).

In our trading system the decay rate parameter in (2.9), is optimised to maximise some measure of trading performance, which we define as the ratio of expected investment return to the standard deviation of returns. This is equivalent to a scaled version of the Sharpe Ratio measure, which is commonly used throughout the finance industry.

The final stage of the experimental set-up is to define the two methods of optimising the forecasting model, which we refer to as <u>single</u> and <u>joint</u> optimisation. The single optimisation method computes the optimal model parameters, denoted by θ_S^*, by maximising prediction accuracy:

$$\theta_S^* = \arg \max_{\theta} [\beta(\theta_1, \theta_2)] \tag{2.11}$$

The joint optimisation method is more complex and requires the forecasting model to be optimised with respect to the optimal trading strategy. This optimisation problem cannot be completed in a single iterative step and so we define a meta-parameter α to control the design of the optimisation criterion given the current trading strategy. This is achieved by specifying the optimisation criterion as a weighted combination of the two prediction characteristics and so the optimal parameters, denoted by θ_J^*, given a value of α are defined as:

$$\theta_J^* = \arg \max_{\theta} [\alpha\beta(\theta_1, \theta_2) + (1 - \alpha)\varphi(\theta_1, \theta_2)|\alpha] \tag{2.12}$$

where the meta-parameter α is subject to the constraint $0 \leqslant \alpha \leqslant 1$.

Finally, the optimisation of the meta-parameter is achieved by using a gradient-based search algorithm which is defined as:

$$\alpha \leftarrow \alpha + \rho\frac{dU}{d\alpha} \tag{2.13}$$

where ρ is the step size. In this method we estimate the derivative of the investment utility with respect to the meta-parameter using perturbation analysis.

In contrast to single optimisation, the optimisation of the meta-parameter α, in the joint optimisation method, cannot be completed in two stages. It requires the repeated consecutive optimisation of the forecasting model and the decision model to reach the jointly optimal solution. In the next section we develop simulation experiments to highlight the implementation of joint optimisation and compare performance with the single optimisation method.

2.3.2 Simulation Experiments

In this sub-section we conduct simulation experiments to compare the two optimisation techniques for different levels of transaction costs. For the single optimisation approach the forecasting model maximises the prediction accuracy characteristic, which results in optimal model parameters (θ_1, θ_2) of 0.2 and 0.3, irrespective of the level of transaction costs or the trading strategy. For the joint optimisation approach the model parameters are dependent on the trading environment via the meta-parameter. We initialise this approach by setting the step size parameter, given in (2.13), to $\rho = 0.1$ and the initial value of the meta-parameter, $\alpha = 1$, which is equivalent to the single optimisation approach.

On the basis of these parameter settings we used the data-generating process to produce predicted and actual asset returns for 4000 observations. We applied the two optimisation procedures to this artificial trading system with a range of transaction costs from 0 to 0.5, as summarised in Table 2.2. To gain an insight into the optimisation process, we illustrate in Figure 2.2 each iteration of the joint optimisation approach for a transaction cost of 0.2.

Table 2.2 A summary of simulation results over a range of transaction costs from 0 to 0.5 showing the optimisation method, iterations, meta-parameter, statistical loss function, model parameters and characteristics, trading rule parameter (PTR) and trading performance in terms of a scaled version of the Sharpe Ratio

| Transaction costs T | Method | Iteration | Forecasting Model | | | | Characteristics | | PTR | Performance ratio |
			α	Loss function	θ_1	θ_2	β	φ	κ	
0	Single	1	1.0000	0.3000	0.2000	0.3000	0.3000	0.0875	0.0077	0.3015
	Joint	1	1.0000	0.3000	0.2000	0.3000	0.3000	0.0875	0.0077	0.3015
0.05	Single	1	1.0000	0.3000	0.2000	0.3000	0.3000	0.0875	0.1127	0.2526
	Joint	7	0.9723	0.3010	0.2256	0.3454	0.2973	0.2933	0.1132	0.2558
0.1	Single	1	1.0000	0.3000	0.2000	0.3000	0.3000	0.0875	0.2212	0.2060
	Joint	9	0.9246	0.3029	0.2615	0.4013	0.2860	0.5110	0.2680	0.2209
0.15	Single	1	1.0000	0.3000	0.2000	0.3000	0.3000	0.0875	0.3384	0.1622
	Joint	12	0.8809	0.3158	0.2877	0.4373	0.2734	0.6293	0.4129	0.1952
0.2	Single	1	1.0000	0.3000	0.2000	0.3000	0.3000	0.0875	0.4799	0.1223
	Joint	17	0.8455	0.3298	0.3056	0.4550	0.2633	0.6940	0.5150	0.1751
0.25	Single	1	1.0000	0.3000	0.2000	0.3000	0.3000	0.0875	0.6007	0.0870
	Joint	23	0.8171	0.3427	0.3181	0.4749	0.2554	0.7327	0.5822	0.1583
0.3	Single	1	1.0000	0.3000	0.2000	0.3000	0.3000	0.0875	0.7134	0.0565
	Joint	16	0.8004	0.3509	0.3248	0.4827	0.2510	0.7514	0.6237	0.1435
0.35	Single	1	1.0000	0.3000	0.2000	0.3000	0.3000	0.0875	0.7867	0.0303
	Joint	24	0.7770	0.3629	0.3336	0.4926	0.2450	0.7737	0.6606	0.1303
0.4	Single	1	1.0000	0.3000	0.2000	0.3000	0.3000	0.0875	0.8508	0.0079
	Joint	20	0.7624	0.3708	0.3387	0.4982	0.2415	0.7857	0.6889	0.1182
0.45	Single	1	1.0000	0.3000	0.2000	0.3000	0.3000	0.0875	0.9900	−0.0053
	Joint	36	0.7375	0.3846	0.3468	0.5070	0.2356	0.8033	0.7166	0.1072
0.5	Single	1	1.0000	0.3000	0.2000	0.3000	0.3000	0.0875	0.9900	−0.0107
	Joint	32	0.7217	0.3937	0.3517	0.5120	0.2320	0.8130	0.7396	0.0970

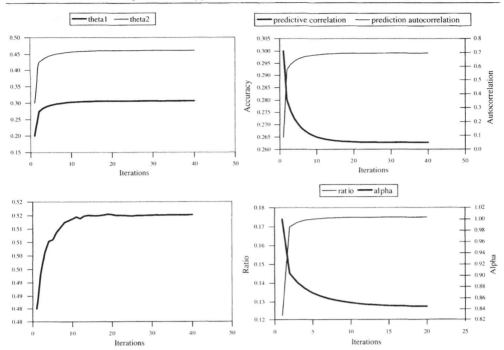

Figure 2.2 The model parameters (top left panel), forecast characteristics (top right panel), smoothing parameter for the trading rule (bottom left panel), meta-parameter α and performance in terms of Sharpe Ratio (bottom right panel)

Given the initial model parameters of (0.2,0.3), the single optimisation method is completed by optimising the trading rule parameter ($\kappa = 0.480$) which gives a trading performance of 0.122. The joint optimisation process starts from this solution and iteratively improves the trading system by modifying the meta-parameter and re-optimising the forecasting model and trading rule. Subsequent iterations show how the meta-parameter is gradually reduced, which changes the optimal forecasting model parameters from (0.2,0.3) to (0.3,0.45). This process has the effect of boosting prediction autocorrelation in the predicted returns at the expense of predictive correlation (top right panel). Our results show that trading performance converges after 17 iterations with an improvement in performance from 0.122 to 0.175, which is an increase of 43%. We validated our joint optimisation procedure by searching for the maximum trading performance across parameter space. Using an exhaustive search procedure we found that the optimal trading and forecasting parameters were a close approximation (to within four significant digits) of the parameters found using the joint optimisation procedure. This indicated that the joint optimisation process had converged to the optimal solution.

Further experiments were conducted for a range of transaction costs as summarised in Table 2.2.

For zero transaction costs, our results show that joint optimisation has no advantage over the single optimisation approach, with equal trading performance of 0.301. Increasing trading costs has the effect of gradually reducing trading performance as expected, with the trading rule parameter increasing in order to boost the smoothness of the trading position through time. For all nonzero transaction costs, joint optimisation outperforms single optimisation as the prediction smoothness becomes an increasingly significant factor in the design of the forecasting model. For this example, the percentage performance difference between joint and single optimisation is shown in Figure 2.3.

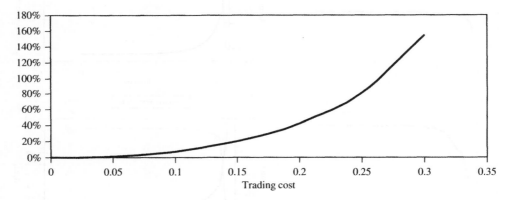

Figure 2.3   The percentage difference between joint and single optimisation over a range of the transaction cost parameter

Our results indicate that joint optimisation can provide a significant increase in performance for trading systems with nonzero transaction costs. In this particular experiment, the percentage improvement in performance increases almost exponentially with transaction costs. This indicates how the joint optimisation methodology could be expected to improve real-world trading systems, which suffer from performance degradation due to the cost of trading. In the next section we demonstrate how our joint optimisation methodology may be applied to a realistic trading system which is based on statistical arbitrage trading.

2.4   APPLICATION TO STATISTICAL ARBITRAGE TRADING

2.4.1   Statistical Arbitrage Trading

In this subsection we apply our joint optimisation methodology to the development of two-stage trading systems based on statistical arbitrage trading strategies for forecasting models. We build upon the methodology developed by Burgess (1999) for modelling the dynamics of statistical arbitrage which identifies and predicts statistical mispricings from amongst groups of assets. In this form of statistical arbitrage, modelling techniques are used to develop trading strategies based on identifying and exploiting statistical regularities in asset price dynamics. The development of these statistical arbitrage models involves three components:

1.   identify an appropriate combination of assets;
2.   develop a forecasting model to predict the statistical mispricing returns;
3.   optimise a trading strategy to exploit the predictions.

The first stage of the modelling process involves constructing the set of statistical mispricings which can be implemented using a cointegration framework and described as follows (Burgess, 1999):

- specify the universe of assets, the time period over which the cointegration analysis will be performed, and the number of constituent assets;
- take each asset in turn as the target asset and perform a stepwise regression to identify the constituent assets, that form a combination that most closely tracks the price movements of the target asset;
- generate the synthetic asset price and the mispricing;
- repeat this process for each target asset before moving on to build the forecasting models.

The second and third stages of the modelling process can be considered as a two-stage trading system for the tasks of forecasting and trading. This forms a suitable trading system to test the performance of our joint optimisation methodology. For demonstration purposes, we specified the forecasting model using simple exponential smoothing, which only requires one model parameter, denoted by θ, and for a statistical mispricing time series y_t is defined as:

$$\hat{y}_{t+1} = \theta y_t + (1 - \theta)\hat{y}_t \tag{2.14}$$

The statistical mispricing return is then computed as the difference between the current and predicted mispricing.

We specified the trading strategy using a set of five trading rules which consisted of two widely used heuristic trading rules and three parameterised trading rules, described below, which take into account the cost of trading by using different techniques to smooth the trading position through time (Towers, 2000).

The first heuristic rule, denoted H1, buys a fixed amount of the asset if the predicted return is positive and sells an equal amount if the prediction is negative, and is defined as:

$$\begin{aligned} a_{t+1} &= m & \text{if } \hat{y}_{t+1} \geqslant 0 \\ &= -m & \text{if } \hat{y}_{t+1} < 0 \end{aligned} \tag{2.15}$$

where $\hat{y}_{t+1}$ is the predicted return, a_{t+1} is the trading position and m is a normalisation factor, controlling the average absolute size of the trading position.

The second heuristic rule, denoted H2, buys (sells) the synthetic asset, which describes the statistical mispricing, so that the trading position is linearly proportional to the predicted return, and is defined as:

$$a_{t+1} = m\hat{y}_{t+1} \tag{2.16}$$

The first parameterised trading rule, denoted PTR1, is based on a simple exponential smoothing of the trading position through time, and is defined in (2.9). The second parameterised trading rule, PTR2, is based on a simple moving average of the trading position, and is defined as:

$$a_{t+1} = \frac{m}{h}\left[\sum_{j=0}^{h-1} \hat{y}_{t+1-j}\right] \tag{2.17}$$

where h is a rolling window parameter controlling the number of past observations with constraint $h \geqslant 1$ and m is the normalisation factor. For example, if $h = 1$ no smoothing is applied to the trading position and increasing h produces a higher degree of smoothing.

The third parameterised trading rule, PTR3, uses a "noise-tolerant" approach which attempts to decrease overall trading costs by reducing the number of relatively "small" changes in the trading position, operates by only trading if the proposed change is significantly large, and is defined as:

$$a_{t+1} = m\hat{y}_{t+1} \quad \text{if } |m\hat{y}_{t+1} - a_t| > \lambda$$
$$= a_t \qquad \text{otherwise}$$
(2.18)

where λ is the tolerance parameter with constraint $\lambda \geqslant 0$, and again m is the normalisation factor. For example, if $\lambda = 0$, the trading position is solely determined by the predicted return while larger values of λ introduce some degree of smoothing by reducing the turnover of the trading position.

2.4.2   Empirical Evaluation

In this subsection we present the results of applying our methodology to a problem of exploiting statistical mispricings from within the UK equity market (FTSE 100). The dataset consists of 1100 observations of hourly prices collected from a live Reuters data-feed from 9 am to 4 pm daily during a period from 15th May 1998 to 4th December 1998. The data was split into three parts. The first set of 300 observations was used to detect any statistical mispricings. The second set of 600 observations was used to optimise the parameters of the forecasting model and parameterised trading rules. The third set of 200 observations was kept for out-of-sample evaluation.

The cointegration-based framework, described in the previous subsection, was used to construct and test for significant statistical mispricings. Using this method, 50 statistical mispricings were selected on the basis of the degree of mean-reverting behaviour, which was tested against random walk hypothesis using the Variance Ratio statistic (Burgess, 1999). The construction of 50 models has the advantage of producing a combined out-of-sample period of 10,000 observations for conducting extensive empirical analysis. For each statistical mispricing we applied our joint optimisation methodology to construct a simple forecasting model and a trading strategy to exploit any detectable predictability. For these experiments we specified the optimisation criterion for the trading system to be the annualised Sharpe Ratio, which we considered to be representative of the goals of risk-adverse trading strategies.

For example, one of the selected statistical mispricings was defined as:

$$y_t = NAM - 63.334 - 0.182^*GLXO + 0.206^*HFX - 0.238^*UU$$
(2.19)

where NAM, GLXO, HFX and UU represent the price of stock in Nycomed Amersham, Glaxo plc., Halifax Group and United Utilities, respectively. A graph of this statistical mispricing is shown in Figure 2.4.

The graph shows the time series for the statistical mispricing specified in (2.19). Significant mean-reversion was identified in the first 300 observations, even after compensating for the bias induced through forming the cointegrating vector. To exploit this identified predictability, trading systems were optimised using the five trading rules in combination

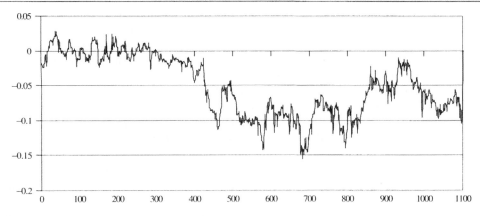

Figure 2.4   The statistical mispricing for the assets defined in (2.19)

Table 2.3   Summary of the results of applying different trading systems to the statistical mispricing, described in (2.19), with transaction costs of 0.2%

Rule	Method	Model parameters		Performance			
				In-sample		Out-of-sample	
		Forecast	Trading	Profit	SR	Profit	SR
H1	Single	0.610	—	−13.17%	−1.460	1.51%	0.431
H2	Single	0.610	—	8.51%	0.425	39.07%	4.123
PTR1	Single	0.610	0.950	35.07%	2.519	16.68%	3.534
	Joint	0.050	0.100	39.45%	2.747	22.61%	4.180
PTR2	Single	0.610	10	18.18%	1.324	10.38%	2.693
	Joint	0.050	1	39.62%	2.717	23.96%	4.252
PTR3	Single	0.610	0.009	28.62%	2.930	43.71%	8.064
	Joint	0.550	0.008	54.31%	4.013	42.89%	6.930

with both single and joint optimisation methods over the next 600 observations. The final 200 observations were held back for out-of-sample testing. A summary of the results for trading systems constructed for this statistical mispricing is given in Table 2.3.

For all trading systems, the single optimisation approach produces the same forecasting model parameter ($\theta = 0.610$) which gives an in-sample predictive correlation of 23.8% and prediction autocorrelation of 14.8%. For the joint optimisation approach the model parameter θ drops to 0.05 and 0.55, depending on the parameterised trading rule, which has the effect of reducing predictive correlation from 23.8% to 14.3% and 23.7%, respectively. However, for these two forecasting models the prediction autocorrelation increases from 14.8% to 88.6% and 20.2%. This has the effect of reducing the optimal values of the three trading rule parameters from 0.95, 10 and 0.009 to 0.1, 1 and 0.008, respectively. For this example, we can see that joint optimisation has the effect of boosting prediction autocorrelation at the expense of reducing predictive correlation and trading position smoothness.

The trading results for the single optimisation approach show that over the in-sample period the two heuristic trading rules give poor in-sample performance with Sharpe

Ratios of −1.460 and 0.425. As expected, the three parameterised trading rules give higher in-sample performance with Sharpe Ratios of 2.519, 1.324 and 2.930, respectively. Joint optimisation further increases performance with in-sample Sharpe Ratios of 2.747, 2.717 and 4.013. The out-of-sample results are less conclusive, although the two heuristic rules give an average Sharpe Ratio of 2.28 compared to the average performance of single and joint optimisation, for the three parameterised trading rules, of 4.76 and 5.12, respectively. For this example, we estimate that the parameterised trading rules increase average performance by 88% and joint optimisation provides an additional 8%. However, these results primarily serve to demonstrate the potential value of using parameterised trading rules and joint optimisation. For a more comprehensive study we generated trading systems for a set of 50 statistical mispricings in order to get reliable estimates of the potential advantages of these techniques. A summary of these results is given in Table 2.4.

In these results the three parameterised trading rules produce positive performance both in-sample and out-of-sample compared to negative returns from the two heuristic rules. In addition, joint optimisation outperforms single optimisation for all three parameterised trading rules with average out-of-sample Sharpe Ratios increasing from 0.89, 0.18 and 0.69 to 1.54, 1.21 and 0.88, respectively. Across the three parameterised trading rules, joint and single optimisation methods give out-of-sample performance, in terms of average Sharpe Ratio, of 1.21 and 0.59, respectively. These results indicate the advantage of our parameterised trading rules and joint optimisation methodology. Further experiments were conducted to analyse the influence of the level of transaction costs, with results summarised in Table 2.5. These results show the average Sharpe Ratio for the out-of-sample period over all 50 trading models for the set of five trading rules in combination with both single and joint optimisation methods. For zero trading costs, the parameterised trading rules do not provide any significant improvement over the heuristic rules. In this case, joint optimisation also provides no benefit over the single optimisation approach. As transaction costs increase, however, trading performance deteriorates across all trading strategies with the parameterised trading rules significantly outperforming heuristic trading rules for costs as low as 10 basis points. At this transaction cost level, average performance of the heuristic rules is −0.97 compared to 1.35 for parameterised trading rules in combination with single optimisation. Performance is further enhanced using joint optimisation

Table 2.4 Comparison of the performance, in terms of both cumulative profit and annualised Sharpe Ratio, of the five different trading rules in combination with the two optimisation methods across all models with transaction cost of 0.2%

	Performance							
	Single optimisation				Joint optimisation			
	In-sample		Out-of-sample		In-sample		Out-of-sample	
Trading rule	Profit	SR	Profit	SR	Profit	SR	Profit	SR
H1	−33.3%	−4.58	−13.7%	−5.24	—	—	—	—
H2	−20.3%	−1.67	−17.3%	−3.63	—	—	—	—
PTR1	22.8%	1.17	0.03%	0.89	32.7%	1.87	0.06%	1.54
PTR2	12.7%	0.49	0.01%	0.18	30.3%	1.71	0.04%	1.21
PTR3	36.5%	2.15	0.07%	0.69	51.9%	3.57	0.03%	0.88

Table 2.5 Comparison of the performance of the two optimisation methods and the three parameterised trading rules across all models for transaction costs up to 70 basis points

	Performance (Sharpe Ratio)							
	Single optimisation					Joint optimisation		
Transaction Costs (bp)	H1	H2	PTR1	PTR2	PTR3	PTR1	PTR2	PTR3
0	3.11	4.09	3.86	3.83	3.71	3.44	3.25	2.82
10	−1.18	0.21	1.60	1.11	1.34	1.85	1.54	1.01
20	−5.23	−3.63	0.89	0.18	0.69	1.54	1.21	0.88
30	−8.81	−7.30	−0.26	−1.60	0.05	1.00	0.52	0.21
40	−11.84	−10.69	−1.23	−3.09	−0.52	1.00	0.80	−0.01
50	−14.32	−13.74	−2.23	−4.61	−1.12	0.99	0.72	−0.37
60	−16.33	−16.46	−3.24	−6.01	−1.49	0.80	0.57	−0.48
70	−17.95	−18.85	−4.31	−7.30	−1.98	0.72	0.53	−0.58

with average Sharpe Ratios increasing from 1.35 to 1.47, which is an 8.9% increase. These results demonstrate that joint optimisation can significantly improve performance for nonzero transaction costs.

2.5 CONCLUSIONS

In this paper we have developed a joint optimisation methodology for a trading system consisting of a pair of forecasting and decision models. We have applied our methodology to trading systems for exploiting statistical mispricings from among groups of assets.

We have conducted simulation experiments for an artificial trading system consisting of an idealised forecasting model and a parameterised trading rule. We compared two optimisation techniques: a single and a joint optimisation approach. The single optimisation approach optimises the forecasting model to minimise forecast error (solely) and then optimises the trading strategy to maximise trading performance. In contrast, the joint optimisation method allows the optimisation criterion for the forecasting model to take into account two relevant forecast characteristics, namely prediction accuracy and prediction smoothness. A meta-parameter is used to represent the trade-off between the two characteristics which allows us to jointly optimise the forecasting model and the trading strategy. Our simulation results demonstrate that in the presence of transaction costs the joint optimisation approach outperforms the standard, single optimisation approach.

We have extended this analysis by conducting extensive empirical evaluations on a set of 50 "statistical mispricings" which are identified using hourly data from the UK equity market (FTSE 100). We assumed stable transaction costs and used a simple exponential smoothing model to forecast the one-step-ahead change in each statistical mispricing. For comparison purposes, five different trading strategies were implemented using two heuristic rules, based simply on the "sign" and "magnitude" of the predicted return, and three parameterised trading rules. The parameters of the forecasting model and the trading strategy were then optimised using two optimisation methods.

Overall, the results show that trading strategies can be developed for statistical mispricings that lead to promising trading performance. As expected, profitability is influenced by transaction costs, with an increased level of costs leading to a deterioration in trading performance. However, the three-path dependent trading rules consistently outperform the two heuristic trading rules with additional performance improvements gained from utilising the joint optimisation methodology. For realistic transaction costs of 10 basis points, the average Sharpe Ratio is increased from -0.97 to 1.35 by using parameterised trading rules, with the joint optimisation approach allowing an additional increase in performance of 8.9% to give a Sharpe Ratio of 1.47.

In this paper we have raised a number of issues which are important in the development of reliable trading systems for exploiting predictability in financial markets. Firstly, we have only just begun to explore the interaction between forecasting and decision-making in trading systems and the implications of model design factors on overall trading performance. Secondly, there are further opportunities to apply the meta-parameter approach to the optimisation of other model design factors, such as forecast horizon, and also to more advanced forecasting and decision modelling techniques. Finally, there is the empirical issue of exploiting trading opportunities within different sets of financial instruments and over different time scales which could also involve the application of our joint optimisation method to more complex trading systems.

REFERENCES

Box, G.P.E. and G.M. Jenkins (1978). *Time Series Analysis: Forecasting and Control*, revised ed. San Francisco: Holden Day.

Bentz, Y. and J.T. Connor (1998). "Unconstrained and Constrained Time-Varying Factor Sensitivities in Equity Investment Management." In A.-P.N. Refenes *et al.* (eds.), *Decision Technologies for Computational Finance*. Dordrecht: Kluwer Academic.

Burgess, A.N. (1998). "Controlling Nonstationarity in Statistical Arbitrage Using a Portfolio of Cointegration Models". In A.-P.N. Refenes *et al.* (eds.), *Decision Technologies for Computational Finance*. Dordrecht: Kluwer Academic.

Burgess, A.N. (1999). "*A Computational Methodology for Modelling the Dynamics of Statistical Arbitrage*", Ph.d. thesis, Decision Technology Centre, London Business School.

Choey, M. and A.S. Weigend (1997). "Nonlinear Trading Models through Sharpe Ratio Maximisation". In A. Weigend *et al.* (eds.) *Decision Technologies for Financial Engineering*. Singapore: World Scientific; 3–22.

Kolias, C. and K. Metaxas (1997). "Selecting Relative Value Stocks with Nonlinear Cointegration". In A. Weigend *et al.* (eds.), *Decision Technologies for Financial Engineering*. Singapore: World Scientific.

Lo, A.W. and A.C. MacKinlay (1995). *Maximizing Predictability in the Stock and Bond Markets*. National Bureau for Economic Research.

Moody, J. (1997). "Optimisation of Trading Systems and Portfolios". In A. Weigend *et al.* (eds.), *Decision Technologies for Financial Engineering*. Singapore: World Scientific.

Moody, J., L. Wu, Y. Liao and M. Saffell (1998). "Performance Functions and Reinforcement Learning for Trading Systems and Portfolios". *Journal of Forecasting* **17**, 441–470.

Refenes, A.-P.N. and M. Azema-Barac (1994). "Neural Network Applications in Financial Asset Management", *Neural Computing and Applications* **2**, 13–39.

Refenes, A.-P.N., A.N. Burgess and Y. Bentz (1997). "Neural Networks in Financial Engineering: A Study of Methodology", *IEEE Transactions on Neural Networks* **8**(6), 1222–1267.

Satchell S. and A. Timmermann (1995). "An Assessment of the Economic Value of Nonlinear Foreign Exchange Rate Forecasts", *Journal of Forecasting* **14**(6), 477–498.

Sharpe, W.F. (1966). "Mutual Fund Performance", *Journal of Business* **39**(1), 119–138.

Towers, N. (2000). "Decision Technologies for Trading Predictability in Financial Markets", Ph.D. thesis, Decision Technology Centre, London Business School.

Towers, N. and A.N. Burgess (1998). "Optimisation of Trading Strategies Using Parameterised Decision Rules". In L. Xu *et al.* (eds.), *Intelligent Data Engineering and Learning*. Singapore: Springer-Verlag; 163–170.

Towers, N. and A.N. Burgess (2000a). "Implementing Trading Strategies for Forecasting Models". *In Computational Finance 1999*. Cambridge, MA: MIT Press.

Towers, N. and A.N. Burgess (2000b). "Learning Trading Strategies for Imperfect Markets", Technical Report, London Business School.

Zapranis, A.D., J. Utans and A.-P.N. Refenes (1997). "Specification Tests for Neural Networks: A Case Study in Tactical Asset Allocation". In A. Weigend *et al.* (eds.), *Decision Technologies for Financial Engineering*. Singapore: World Scientific.

3

The Use of Market Data and Model Combination to Improve Forecast Accuracy[1]

CHRISTIAN L. DUNIS, JASON LAWS AND
STÉPHANE CHAUVIN

ABSTRACT

In this paper, we examine the medium-term forecasting ability of several alternative models of currency volatility. The data period covers more than eight years of daily observations, January 1991–March 1999, for the spot exchange rate, 1- and 3-month volatility of the DEM/JPY, GBP/DEM, GBP/USD, USD/CHF, USD/DEM and USD/JPY. Comparing with the results of 'pure' time series models, we investigate whether the inclusion of market implied volatility data into time series models can add value in terms of medium-term forecasting accuracy. We do this using data directly available from the marketplace in order to avoid the potential biases arising from "backing out" volatility from a specific option pricing model. On the basis of the over 34,000 out-of-sample forecasts produced, evidence tends to indicate that, although no single volatility model emerges as an overall winner in terms of forecasting accuracy, the "mixed" models incorporating market data for currency volatility perform best most of the time. We are also vindicated in considering a number of model combinations and find when applied to this databank that they produce the "best" forecast almost one quarter of the time.

3.1 INTRODUCTION

Measuring the risks associated with participating in financial markets has become the focus of interest since the beginning of the 1990s. Advances in time series modelling such as, amongst others, ARCH/GARCH and/or stochastic volatility models have made it possible to integrate the time-varying nature of volatility and correlation and thus to relax such embarrassing assumptions as constant volatilities (in the field of risk management) and constant correlations (in the field of portfolio diversification).

Although risk management encompasses both "short-term" and more "medium-term" risks (such as, respectively, trading risk and credit risk), necessitating both short-term and medium-term volatility forecasts (*i.e.* 1-day or 1-week out versus 1-month or 3-month out),

---

[1] The opinions expressed herein are not necessarily those of Girobank.

Developments in Forecast Combination and Portfolio Choice. Edited by C. Dunis, A. Timmermann and J. Moody.
© 2001 John Wiley & Sons Ltd

portfolio optimisation remains a medium-term process even if portfolio management has undoubtedly moved towards more "high frequency" trading over the past few years.

Consequently, in this paper, we choose to focus on the medium-term forecasting ability of different volatility models with an application to the foreign exchange market, as it has the advantage of providing volatility data directly observable on the marketplace.

We first review the predictive power of several time series models of currency volatility (homoskedastic, ARMA, GARCH and stochastic volatility) using daily data from January 1991 through March 1999 for six major exchange rates: DEM/JPY, GBP/DEM, GBP/USD, USD/CHF, USD/DEM and USD/JPY.[2] We carry on to check whether market implied volatility data can add value in terms of forecasting accuracy.

Although this has been done in the past in the context of tests of market efficiency (see, for instance, Day and Lewis, 1992 or Dunis and Keller, 1995) or in a forecasting context using a specific option pricing model to "back out" *ex post* implied standard deviations (see Kroner *et al.*, 1995 for instance), this is the first time to our knowledge that such a forecasting exercise has been conducted using data directly available from the marketplace in order to avoid the potential biases from the "backing out" procedure. This original approach seems further warranted by current market practice, whereby brokers and market makers in currency options deal in fact in volatility terms and no longer in terms of option premiums.

We compare the out-of-sample forecasting accuracy of our time series models with that of the "mixed" models incorporating market data for currency volatility and conclude by combining these forecasts using a simple averaging procedure as a benchmark against the Granger–Ramanathan (1984) approach and the novel SOFI algorithm of data fusion by Chauvin *et al.* (1997, 1999).

Accordingly, following this Introduction, Section 3.2 presents our data, giving their statistical description; Section 3.3 examines the different models that we estimate, giving the precise definition of both the time series models and the "mixed" models investigated, documenting the estimation procedure that we use. Section 3.4 presents the estimation results for all our volatility models, focusing on out-of-sample results as they constitute the acid test of forecasting efficiency. Finally, Section 3.5 closes this paper with a summary of our conclusions.

3.2 THE EXCHANGE RATE AND VOLATILITY DATA

We present in turn the two databanks we have used for this study and the modifications to the original series we have made where appropriate.

3.2.1 The Exchange Rate Series Databank

The return series we use for the six major exchange rates selected, DEM/JPY, GBP/DEM, GBP/USD, USD/CHF, USD/DEM and USD/JPY, were extracted from a historical exchange rate database provided by Datastream. Logarithmic returns, defined as $\log(P_t / P_{t-1})$, are calculated for each exchange rate on a daily frequency basis. We

---

[2] We use the notation of the International Organisation for Standardisation (IOS), respectively DEM/JPY for the Deutsche Mark against the Japanese Yen, GBP/DEM and GBP/USD for the Deutsche Mark and the US Dollar against the Pound Sterling, USD/CHF, USD/DEM and USD/JPY for the Swiss Franc, Deutsche Mark and Japanese Yen against the US Dollar.

multiply these returns by 100, so that we end up with percentage changes in the exchange rates considered, *i.e.* $s_t = 100 \log(P_t/P_{t-1})$.

Our exchange rate databank spans from 3rd September 1990 to 7th May 1999 giving 2197 datapoints per currency. We use a restricted sample from 2nd January 1991 to 31st December 1998 corresponding to the range of our volatility databank, which leaves us with 2019 datapoints and also allows us sufficient observations to compute out-of-sample volatility estimates. Some summary statistics for the daily returns over this restricted sample are shown in Table 3.1.

In line with the findings of many earlier studies on exchange rate changes (see, amongst others, Baillie and Bollerslev, 1989; Engle and Bollerslev, 1986; West and Cho, 1995), the above statistics clearly show that our currency returns are non-normally distributed and heavily fat-tailed. They also show that mean returns are not statistically different from zero. Further standard tests of autocorrelation, nonstationarity and heteroskedasticity (not reported here in order to conserve space) show that logarithmic returns are all stationary and heteroskedastic. They are also noncorrelated, although some evidence of autocorrelation exists for the GBP/USD and USD/JPY return series.

The fact that our currency returns have zero unconditional mean enables us to use *squared returns* as a measure of their variance and *absolute returns* as a measure of their standard deviation or volatility.[3] The standard tests of autocorrelation, nonstationarity and heteroskedasticity (again not reported here in order to conserve space) show that squared and absolute currency returns series for the period 2nd January 1991 to 31st December 1998 are all non-normally distributed, stationary, heteroskedastic and autocorrelated with means that are statistically different from zero.[4]

Still, as we are interested in analysing whether market implied volatility data can add value in terms of forecasting realised currency volatility, we must adjust our statistical computation of volatility to take into account the fact that, even if it is only the matter of a constant, in currency options markets, volatility is quoted in annualised terms. As we also wish to focus on medium-term volatility forecasts (*i.e.* 1- and 3-month out), taking, as is usual practice, a 252-day trading year (and consequently a 21-day trading month and a 63-day trading quarter), we compute the 1-month and 3-month volatility as the moving annualised standard deviation of our logarithmic returns and end up with the following

Table 3.1 Summary statistics of daily logarithmic returns (2nd January 1991–31st December 1998)

	DEM/JPY	GBP/DEM	GBP/USD	USD/CHF	USD/DEM	USD/JPY
Mean	0.015	−0.002	−0.008	0.004	0.006	−0.010
Std. Dev.[a]	0.742	0.482	0.602	0.749	0.680	0.738
Skewness	1.278	−0.460	−0.164	−0.202	−0.019	−0.779
Kurtosis	16.379	7.714	6.117	5.292	4.967	8.696
Jarque–Bera	15,608.33	1940.40	826.46	455.70	325.56	2933.66
Probability	0.00	0.00	0.00	0.00	0.00	0.00

[a] Heteroskedasticity-consistent standard deviations.

---

[3] Although the unconditional mean is zero, it is of course possible that the conditional mean may vary over time.

[4] As an exception, squared GBP/DEM returns were found to be homoskedastic.

historical volatility measures for the 1-month and 3-month horizons:

$$HVOL21_t = \frac{1}{21} \sum_{t-20}^{t} (\sqrt{252}\,|s_t|)$$

and

$$HVOL63_t = \frac{1}{63} \sum_{t-62}^{t} (\sqrt{252}\,|s_t|)$$

where $|s_t|$ is the absolute currency return.[5] $HVOL21_t$ and $HVOL63_t$ are the realised 1-month and 3-month currency volatilities that we are interested in forecasting as accurately as possible, either for risk management or portfolio management purposes. Some summary statistics for these series over the restricted sample are shown in Tables 3.2 and 3.3.

As we can see from Tables 3.2 and 3.3, all series are non-normally distributed and often fat-tailed. Further statistical tests of autocorrelation, heteroskedasticity and nonstationarity (again not reported here in order to conserve space) show that all 1-month and 3-month historical volatility series exhibit strong autocorrelation and heteroskedasticity but, whereas all 1-month volatilities are stationary in levels, all 3-month volatilities are only stationary when first differenced.[6]

Table 3.2 Summary statistics of 1-month historical volatility (2nd January 1991–31st December 1998)

	DEM/JPY	GBP/DEM	GBP/USD	USD/CHF	USD/DEM	USD/JPY
Mean	8.353	5.449	6.697	8.812	7.972	8.113
Std. Dev.[a]	3.543	2.522	2.846	2.850	2.802	3.394
Skewness	1.845	1.479	1.213	1.104	1.125	1.800
Kurtosis	8.982	7.208	4.841	4.518	4.754	7.355
Jarque–Bera	4155.66	2225.60	779.94	603.86	685.01	2685.84
Probability	0.00	0.00	0.00	0.00	0.00	0.00

[a] Heteroskedasticity-consistent standard deviations.

Table 3.3 Summary statistics of 3-month historical volatility (2nd January 1991–31 December 1998)

	DEM/JPY	GBP/DEM	GBP/USD	USD/CHF	USD/DEM	USD/JPY
Mean	8.312	5.432	6.702	8.794	7.968	8.080
Std. Dev.[a]	2.809	2.062	2.454	2.319	2.260	2.728
Skewness	1.338	0.634	0.931	0.926	0.674	1.543
Kurtosis	5.466	3.128	3.252	3.577	3.164	6.128
Jarque–Bera	1113.64	136.82	296.91	316.72	155.31	1624.60
Probability	0.00	0.00	0.00	0.00	0.00	0.00

[a] Heteroskedasticity-consistent standard deviations.

[5] The use of absolute returns (rather than their squared value) is justified by the fact that with zero unconditional mean, averaging absolute returns gives a measure of standard deviation.

[6] A possible explanation of the acceptance of the null hypothesis of a unit root in the 3-month volatilities may be due to the fact that by construction they are 62nd order moving averages. This clearly induces serial correlation into the returns series and causes a decline in the finite-sample power of the unit root test.

Having presented our exchange rate series databank and explained how we computed from these original series our historical volatilities (so that they are in a format comparable to that which prevails in the currency options market), we now turn our attention to the implied volatility databank that we have used.

3.2.2 The Implied Volatility Series Databank

As mentioned above, volatility has now become an observable and traded quantity in financial markets, and particularly so in the currency markets. So far, most studies dealing with implied volatilities have used volatilities backed out from historical premium data on traded options rather than over-the-counter (OTC) volatility data (see, amongst others, Chiras and Manaster, 1978; Kroner *et al.*, 1995; Lamoureux and Lastrapes, 1993; Latane and Rendleman, 1976; Xu and Taylor, 1996).

The problem in using exchange data is that call and put prices are only available for given strike levels. The corresponding implied volatility series must therefore be *backed out* using a specific option pricing model. This procedure generates two sorts of potential biases: material errors or mismatches can affect the variables that are needed for solving the pricing model, e.g. the forward points or the spot rate, and, more importantly, the very specification of the pricing model that is chosen can have a crucial impact on the final "backed out" implied volatility series. For instance, the choice of an arbitrary interest rate for the foreign risk-free rate of the theoretical option pricing model is a source of potential bias in deriving implied standard deviations. Following O'Brien and Kennedy (1982), this problem has been recognised and a line of research has developed which solves for the implied volatility and an implied risk-free rate *simultaneously*, with contributions, amongst others, by Martin and French (1987) and Pedersen (1998). Nevertheless, as noted by Pedersen (1998), it appears that solving for two implied variables yields less information than solving for implied volatility alone, which suggests that, in trying to reduce the potential bias linked to the unknown risk-free rate, one may in fact be introducing a larger source of error.

This is the reason why, in this paper, we use *data directly observable on the marketplace*. This original approach seems further warranted by current market practice whereby brokers and market makers in currency options deal in fact *in volatility terms* and not in option premium terms any more.[7] The volatility time series we use for the six major exchange rates selected, DEM/JPY, GBP/DEM, GBP/USD, USD/CHF, USD/DEM and USD/JPY, were extracted from a *market quoted implied volatilities* database provided by Chemical Bank for data until end-1996, and updated from Reuters "Ric" codes subsequently. These at-the-money forward, market-quoted volatilities are in fact obtained from brokers by Reuters on a daily basis, at the close of business in London. Some summary statistics for these implied volatility series over the restricted sample are shown in Tables 3.4 and 3.5.

As we can see from Tables 3.4 and 3.5, all series are non-normally distributed and often fat-tailed. Further statistical tests of autocorrelation and heteroskedasticity (again

---

[7] The market data that we use are *at-the-money forward volatilities*, as the use of either in-the-money or out-of-the-money volatilities would introduce a significant bias in our analysis due to the so-called "smile effect", *i.e.* the fact that volatility is "priced" higher for strike levels which are not at-the-money. It should be made clear that these implied volatilities are not simply backed out of an option pricing model, but are instead directly quoted from brokers. Due to arbitrage they cannot diverge too far from the theoretical level.

Table 3.4 Summary statistics of 1-month implied volatility (2nd January 1991–31st December 1998)

	DEM/JPY	GBP/DEM	GBP/USD	USD/CHF	USD/DEM	USD/JPY
Mean	11.007	7.426	10.079	11.964	11.229	11.263
Std. Dev.[a]	2.808	2.577	2.983	2.529	2.487	3.119
Skewness	0.865	0.332	0.646	0.913	0.715	1.355
Kurtosis	5.437	2.769	3.538	4.415	4.123	7.249
Jarque–Bera	751.32	41.63	164.57	448.67	278.13	2136.56
Probability	0.00	0.00	0.00	0.00	0.00	0.00

[a] Heteroskedasticity-consistent standard deviations.

Table 3.5 Summary statistics of 3-month implied volatility (2nd January 1991–31st December 1998)

	DEM/JPY	GBP/DEM	GBP/USD	USD/CHF	USD/DEM	USD/JPY
Mean	11.043	7.277	10.346	12.018	11.307	11.435
Std. Dev.[a]	2.212	2.255	2.434	1.879	1.911	2.562
Skewness	0.593	−0.120	0.260	0.482	0.171	1.154
Kurtosis	3.971	2.262	2.608	3.325	2.933	5.247
Jarque–Bera	197.65	50.63	35.70	86.97	10.22	872.83
Probability	0.00	0.00	0.00	0.00	0.01	0.00

[a] Heteroskedasticity-consistent standard deviations.

not reported here in order to conserve space) show that all 1-month and 3-month implied volatility series exhibit strong autocorrelation and heteroskedasticity. Unit root tests show a much more mixed picture: at the 1-month horizon, DEM/JPY, GBP/DEM and GBP/USD implied volatilities are stationary at the 5% significance level only, whereas USD/CHF, USD/DEM and USD/JPY are stationary at the 1% significance level; nevertheless, at the 3-month horizon, DEM/JPY, GBP/DEM, GBP/USD and USD/JPY implied volatilities are all nonstationary in level,[8] whereas USD/CHF implied volatility is stationary at the 1% significance level and USD/DEM implied volatility is stationary at the 5% level.

Certainly, the most interesting feature from Tables 3.4 and 3.5 is the mean level of implied volatilities which, for all currencies and both time horizons, are well above, sometimes by more than three percentage points, average historical volatility levels (see Tables 3.2 and 3.3).[9] This tendency of the currency options market to overestimate actual volatility is further documented by Figures A3.1 to A3.6 in Appendix 3.1, which show 1-month actual and implied volatilities for the DEM/JPY, GBP/DEM, GBP/USD, USD/CHF, USD/DEM and USD/JPY exchange rates.[10] Still, it is pretty obvious that, for each currency concerned, actual and implied volatilities are moving rather closely together: in fact, for all currencies and both time horizons during our restricted sample period 2nd

[8] All nonstationary series in level terms are stationary when first differenced.

[9] A possible explanation of implied volatility being higher than historical counterparts may be due to the fact that market makers are generally options sellers (whereas end-users are more often option buyers); there is probably a tendency among option writers to include a "risk premium" when pricing volatility.

[10] Here again, in order to conserve space, we only show 1-month volatilities but the message conveyed by 3-month volatilities is basically identical.

January 1991–31st December 1998, the instantaneous correlation coefficient lies in the range 81–87%, except for 3-month USD/CHF volatilities where it stands at 78.1%.

It should therefore come as no surprise if implied volatility data directly available from the marketplace were to prove helpful in forecasting actual realised volatility more accurately.

3.3 THE VOLATILITY MODELS AND ESTIMATION PROCEDURE

As mentioned in the Introduction, we intend to review the predictive power of several time series models of currency volatility (homoskedastic, ARMA, GARCH and stochastic volatility) and to see whether market implied volatility data can add value in terms of forecasting accuracy.

Table 3.6 gives a list of the 13 different models, both linear and nonlinear, that we have estimated for each time horizon considered.[11] Each original time series model is complemented by a "mixed" version counterpart integrating the added information provided by the relevant implied volatility data.

We present below the actual analytical formulae for the one-step-ahead and the n-step-ahead conditional variance forecasts: if much of the literature on volatility forecasting

Table 3.6 List of volatility models

Model 1	GARCH(1,1) based on variance of log-returns (21-day)
Model 2	GARCH(1,1) based on variance of log-returns+implied I30 volatility (21-day)
Model 3	GARCH(1,1) based on variance of log-returns (63-day)
Model 4	GARCH(1,1) based on variance of log-returns+implied I90 volatility (63-day)
Model 5	AR(10) based on squared log-returns (21-day)
Model 6	AR(10) based on squared log-returns+implied I30 (21-day)
Model 7	AR(10) based on squared log-returns (63-day)
Model 8	AR(10) based on squared log-returns+implied I90 (63-day)
Model 9	AR(10) based on absolute log-returns (21-day)
Model 10	AR(10) based on absolute log-returns (63-day)
Model 11	AR(10) based on absolute log-returns+implied I30 (21-day)
Model 12	AR(10) based on absolute log-returns+implied I90 (63-day)
Model 13	SV(1) based on squared log-returns (21-day)
Model 14	SV(1) based on squared log-returns (63-day)
Model 15	SV(1) based on squared log-returns+implied I30 (21-day)
Model 16	SV(1) based on squared log-returns+implied I90 (63-day)
Model 17	Actual annualised historical volatility (21-day)
Model 18	Actual annualised historical volatility (63-day)
Model 19	Implied volatility I30 (21-day)
Model 20	Implied volatility I90 (63-day)
Model 21	Average of all previous 21-day models
Model 22	Average of all previous 63-day models
Model 23	Regression-weighted average of all previous 21-day models
Model 24	Regression-weighted average of all previous 63-day models
Model 25	Average of all previous 21-day models except "worst" model
Model 26	Average of all previous 63-day models except "worst" model

---

[11] The exact specification of each model is provided in Appendix 3.2.

deals with the former, our interest clearly lies with the latter, as we are concerned with medium-term volatility forecasts.

As most of the retained modelling approaches are well documented in the literature, we just present each model very briefly, starting with the popular GARCH model.

3.3.1 The GARCH(1,1) Time Series and "Mixed" Models

The Generalised Autoregressive Conditional Heteroskedastic (GARCH) model was originally devised by Bollerslev (1986) and Taylor (1986) and has now become widely used, in various forms, by both academics and practitioners to model conditional variance: it basically states that the conditional variance of asset returns in any given period depends upon a constant, the previous period's squared random component of the return *and* the previous period's variance.

In other words, if we denote by h_t the conditional variance of the return in time t and ε_{t-1}^2 the squared random component of the return in the previous period, for a standard GARCH(1,1) process we have:

$$h_t = \omega + \alpha\varepsilon_{t-1}^2 + \beta h_{t-1} \tag{3.1}$$

(3.1) yields immediately the one-step-ahead volatility forecast and, using recursive substitution, Engle and Bollerslev (1986) and Baillie and Bollerslev (1992) give the n-step-ahead forecast for a GARCH(1,1) process:

$$h_{t+n} = \omega[1 + (\alpha + \beta) + \cdots + (\alpha + \beta)^{n-2}] + \omega + \alpha\varepsilon_t^2 + \beta h_t \tag{3.2}$$

This is the formula that we use to compute our GARCH(1,1) n-step-ahead out-of-sample forecast.

In fact, we tried several alternative GARCH specifications in our in-sample period (2nd January 1991–2nd March 1998), but no other specification managed to consistently outperform the more standard GARCH(1,1) specification.[12]

The "mixed" version counterpart of the GARCH(1,1) integrating implied volatility data yields the following formulation for the conditional variance (see, for instance, Kroner *et al.*, 1995):

$$h_t = \omega + \alpha\varepsilon_{t-1}^2 + \beta h_{t-1} + \gamma IMP_{t-1} \tag{3.3}$$

Following the recursive procedure above and taking into account the fact that, in order to compute a truly out-of-sample forecast, the last information on implied volatility available at time t is IMP_t, the "mixed" GARCH(1,1) model n-step-ahead forecast becomes:

$$h_{t+n} = \omega[1 + (\alpha + \beta) + \cdots + (\alpha + \beta)^{n-2}] + \omega + \alpha\varepsilon_t^2 + \beta h_t + \gamma IMP_t \tag{3.4}$$

All these models are estimated by maximum likelihood assuming conditional normality and using the standard Marquardt optimisation algorithm and a small convergence criterion as recommended by Zumbach (2000) in order to avoid the usual pitfalls in fitting GARCH models. In line with the descriptive statistics of our mean and squared returns (see Section 3.2.1), we set mean returns to zero and use a heteroskedasticity-consistent covariance matrix as suggested by Bollerslev and Wooldridge (1992). We estimate models 1 to 4 with the GARCH(1,1) procedure (see Table 3.6).

---

[12] Again, these computations are not reported here in order to conserve space.

3.3.2 The AR(p) Time Series and "Mixed" Models

In our analysis of currency returns in Section 3.2.1, we found that squared returns could be used as a measure of their variance and absolute returns as a measure of their standard deviation. Furthermore, we mentioned that squared and absolute currency returns were all non-normally distributed, stationary, heteroskedastic (except for squared GBP/DEM returns) and autocorrelated with means statistically different from zero.

This stationarity allows us to apply the traditional ARMA estimation procedure to our squared and absolute currency return series, provided we make good for the presence of both heteroskedasticity and autocorrelation.[13]

Because, on the one hand, any MA process can be represented in autoregressive form as an infinite AR process and, on the other hand, practical out-of-sample n-step-ahead forecasting with MA terms is not tractable, we restrict ourselves to AR(p) processes. In practice, we use standard nonlinear least squares estimation and correct for heteroskedasticity with the heteroskedasticity-consistent covariance estimation proposed by White (1980). For autocorrelation, based on the AIC criterion and the standard error of the estimation, we select in the end an AR(10) process for both squared and absolute returns of all currencies concerned, both for the sake of simplicity and harmonisation and also because it represents a "round" horizon of two trading weeks.[14]

In the circumstances, we model the conditional variance as:

$$h_t = \omega + \sum_{i=1}^{10} \alpha_i s_{t-i}^2 + \varepsilon_t \tag{3.5}$$

or

$$h_t = \omega + \sum_{i=1}^{10} \alpha_i |s_{t-i}| + \varepsilon_t \tag{3.6}$$

The n-step-ahead forecast for our AR(10) models becomes, respectively:

$$h_{t+n} = \omega + \sum_{i=1}^{10} \alpha_i s_{t+n-i}^2 \tag{3.7}$$

and

$$h_t = \omega + \sum_{i=1}^{10} \alpha_i |s_{t+n-i}| \tag{3.8}$$

The "mixed" version counterparts of the AR(10) models integrating implied volatility data are then:

$$h_t = \omega + \sum_{i=1}^{10} \alpha_i s_{t-i}^2 + \gamma IMP_{t-1} + \varepsilon_t \tag{3.9}$$

and

$$h_t = \omega + \sum_{i=1}^{10} \alpha_i |s_{t-i}| + \gamma IMP_{t-1} + \varepsilon_t \tag{3.10}$$

---

[13] A further reason noted by Bollerslev (1986) is that GARCH models imply ARMA processes for squared returns.

[14] Again, in order to conserve space, we do not report our detailed experiments here.

Taking into account the fact that, in order to compute a truly out-of-sample forecast, the last information on implied volatility available at time t is IMP_t, the "mixed" AR(10) model n-step-ahead forecast becomes:

$$h_{t+n} = \omega + \sum_{i=1}^{10} \alpha_i s_{t+n-i}^2 + \gamma IMP_t \qquad (3.11)$$

and

$$h_{t+n} = \omega + \sum_{i=1}^{10} \alpha_i |s_{t+n-1}| + \gamma IMP_t \qquad (3.12)$$

We estimate models 5 to 12 with the AR(10) procedure (see Table 3.6).

3.3.3   The Stochastic Variance SV(1) Time Series and "Mixed" Models

The seminal works of Harvey (1989) and Hamilton (1994) have underlined the advantages of using state space modelling for representing dynamic systems where unobserved variables (the so-called "state" variables) can be integrated within an "observable" model.

Among other applications of the state space modelling procedure, stochastic volatility models have become more popular in recent years, if not among market practitioners, at least in academic circles: intuitively, there is a clear attraction with the idea that volatility and its time-varying nature could be stochastic rather than the result of some deterministic function.

Following, amongst other contributions, Harvey and Shepherd (1993) and Harvey et al. (1994), it is thus possible to model volatility in state space form as a time-varying parameter model. We tried several alternative specifications (again not reported here in order to conserve space) and selected our preferred approach on the basis of the resulting log-likelihood and the standard error of the observation equation. The selected specification came out as the best one for all variances in our in-sample period, except for DEM/JPY and USD/DEM variances where it came as a very close second: for the sake of simplicity and harmonisation, we therefore adopted the same specification for all currencies concerned.

In the end, we chose to model the logarithm of the conditional variance as a random walk plus noise.[15] We further made the assumption that our random coefficient (our "state" variable) was best modelled as an AR(1) process with a constant mean, implying that shocks would show some persistence, but that the random coefficient would eventually return to its mean level, an assumption compatible with the behaviour of currency volatility.

Calling our time-varying coefficient SV_t, we have the following system:

$$\log h_t = \omega + SV_t + \varepsilon_t$$

$$SV_t = \delta SV_{t-1} + v_t \quad \text{with E}\,(\varepsilon_t, v_t) = 0 \qquad (3.13)$$

The "mixed" version counterpart of this system that integrates implied volatility data is then straightforwardly:

---

[15] Working in logarithms ensures that h_t is always positive.

$$\log h_t = \omega + SV_t + \gamma \log IMP_{t-1} + \varepsilon_t$$
$$SV_t = \delta SV_{t-1} + v_t \quad \text{with } E(\varepsilon_t, v_t) = 0 \tag{3.14}$$

In order to derive the n-step-ahead forecast for system (3.13), we must compute $E(SV_{t+n}|I_t)$, with I_t the information set available at time t. It is clear from (3.13) that we have:

$$E(SV_{t+1}|I_t) = \delta E(SV_t) = \delta^2 SV_{t-1} \tag{3.15}$$

By iterating (3.15), we can therefore compute $E(SV_{t+n}|I_t)$:

$$E(SV_{t+n}|I_t) = \delta^n SV_t \tag{3.16}$$

We can now compute the n-step-ahead forecast for the logarithm of squared returns as:

$$\log h_{t+n} = \omega + SV_{t+n}$$
$$SV_{t+n} = \delta^n SV_t \tag{3.17}$$

Similarly, taking into account the fact that, in order to compute a truly out-of-sample forecast, the last information on implied volatility available at time t is IMP_t, the "mixed" system n-step-ahead forecast becomes:

$$\log h_{t+n} = \omega + SV_{t+n} + \gamma \log IMP_t$$
$$SV_{t+n} = \delta^n SV_t \tag{3.18}$$

All these models are estimated by quasi-maximum likelihood assuming conditional normality. As noted by Hamilton (1994), state space model estimation can often be quite cumbersome. Thus, for efficiency reasons, we constrain the covariance matrix of the error terms in both the observation and state equations to be an identity matrix (implying that the error terms are uncorrelated and have unit variance) and use the Berndt–Hall–Hall–Hausman optimisation algorithm (which proved more efficient than the standard Marquardt algorithm) and a small convergence criterion.[16] We estimate models 13 to 16 with the state space SV(1) procedure (see Table 3.6).

3.3.4 The "Naïve" Random Walk Models

We proceed to "estimate" two alternative types of "naïve" random walk models, one which simply states that the best n-step-ahead forecast of the conditional variance is its current past n-day average and the other which sets the n-step-ahead forecast of the conditional variance at the current n-day implied volatility level.

Consequently, the first type of "naïve" model based on historical volatility yields the following n-step-ahead forecast:

$$h_{t+n} = (1/\sqrt{252})HVOL_{i,t}^2 \tag{3.19}$$

---

[16] Other specifications of the covariance matrix of the error terms slowed the convergence process significantly; similarly, the Marquardt algorithm either converged very slowly or even failed to converge in some cases: with 218 out-of-sample forecasts per model and currency volatility (*i.e.* 5232 system estimations in total), efficiency was a clear constraint on the overall system estimation.

where $HVOL_{i,t}$ is the realised 1-month or 3-month historical volatility as defined in Section 3.2.1. The second type of "naïve" model is based on market quoted implied volatility and yields the following n-step-ahead forecast:

$$h_{t+n} = (1/\sqrt{252})IMP_{i,t}^2 \tag{3.20}$$

where $IMP_{i,t}$ is the 1-month or 3-month implied volatility prevailing at time t.

Models 17 to 20 are "estimated" according to (3.19) and (3.20) for the two time horizons considered (see Table 3.6).

3.3.5   The Combined Time Series and "Mixed" Models

In his well-known survey of the literature on forecast combinations, Clemen (1989) noted that such combinations outperform individual forecasts, particularly for longer term horizons, a remark consistent with earlier findings by Makridakis et al. (1982).

Accordingly, we compute three different model combinations. The first one is a simple average, for the 1-month and the 3-month horizons, of the previous 10 time series and "mixed" models n-step-ahead forecasts. We thus have:

$$h_{t+n} = (1/10) \sum_{i=1}^{10} h_{i,t+n}^{[n=(21,63)]} \tag{3.21}$$

where $h_{i,t+n}$ represents the forecast of each previous forecasting model for time $t + n$. Models 21 and 22 are estimated according to (3.21) for the two time horizons considered (see Table 3.6).

The second forecast combination uses the linear regression weighting approach suggested by Granger and Ramanathan (1984), which yields:

$$h_{t+n} = (1/10) \sum_{i=1}^{10} \alpha_i h_{i,t+n}^{[n=(21,63)]} \tag{3.22}$$

where $\alpha_i h_{i,t+n}$ represents the regression-weighted forecast of each single forecasting model for time $t + n$.[17] Models 23 and 24 are estimated according to (3.22) for the two time horizons considered (see Table 3.6).

Finally, the third forecast combination we retain is the simple average, for the 1-month and the 3-month horizons, of each single forecasting model for time $t + n$, minus the stochastic variance model which generally performs worst in-sample for each time horizon. We thus have:

$$h_{t+n} = (1/9) \sum_{i=1}^{9} h_{i,t+n}^{[n=(21,63)]} \tag{3.23}$$

where $h_{i,t+n}$ represents the forecast of each single forecasting model except the worst performing one for time $t + n$. Models 25 and 26 are estimated according to (3.23) for the two time horizons considered (see Table 3.6).

---

[17] The parameter α_i was determined using the first 50 days of the forecasting period. However, the forecast accuracy of this model was computed using the remaining 168 forecasts.

3.3.6 The Out-of-sample Estimation Procedure

We have now presented the 13 models that we estimate for the two time horizons considered and documented the estimation procedure particular to each model. As mentioned in the Introduction, in this paper, we choose to gauge the medium-term forecasting ability of these alternative currency volatility models, focusing on their out-of-sample results as they constitute the acid test of forecasting efficiency.

Our in-sample period for model estimation covers the period 2nd January 1991–27th February 1998 (1801 data points), which leaves the last 218 observations of our restricted sample, from 2nd March 1998 to 31st December 1998, for out-of-sample forecasting.[18]

This choice of 2nd March 1998 to start our forecasting exercise is arbitrary: we just picked a trading day which was the beginning of a month and would give us enough data points for in-sample model estimation, but still leave over 10% of our restricted sample for the evaluation of the forecasting ability of our models.

Another issue concerns the nature of the sample to be used for our forecasting exercise beyond the first out-of-sample forecast on 2nd March 1998. This is a very important practical issue in actual investment management, as underlined by Bentz (1999).

Should we retain a rolling 1801 data points sample (adding one extra observation each trading day and deleting the oldest observation at each new forecasting step) or should we choose an expanding sample (by just adding each new observation to our original in-sample dataset)?

Rolling samples are generally preferred in the presence of nonstationarity, but, as we have seen from the statistical description of our data in Section 3.2.1, this is not the case here and we could therefore adopt an expanding sample procedure.

Still, with 20,928 models to estimate,[19] not to mention the subsequent 7848 forecast combinations, a choice had to be made to keep the project manageable. This is why, taking into account the respectable size of our in-sample dataset, we decided in the end to choose a rolling 1801 data window.

3.4 THE OUT-OF-SAMPLE ESTIMATION RESULTS

Having documented the 13 different models that we estimate for the two time horizons considered and our general out-of-sample estimation procedure, we need to present the measures of forecasting accuracy that we use.

3.4.1 The Measures of Forecasting Accuracy

To start with, we must remember from Section 3.2.1 above that, as volatility is quoted in annualised terms in currency options markets, we had to adjust our statistical computation of historical volatility to take this factor into account and make our historical volatility measures comparable with market implied volatility data.

---

[18] Because of the forward-looking nature of this exercise, we need to be able to compare our 3-month out forecasts on 31st December 1998 with the actual outcome 3 months later, which explains that our exchange rate databank extends beyond that date well into 1999.

[19] That is: eight time series and "mixed" models times two forecasting horizons times six currency volatilities times 218 forecasting steps.

Similarly, although this is a straightforward transformation, we must adjust the results of our forecasting models (which give us either a conditional variance forecast or the forecast of its logarithm) to give us an annualised volatility forecast.[20]

As is standard in the economic literature, we then compute the Root Mean Squared Error (RMSE), the Mean Absolute Error (MAE), the Mean Absolute Percentage Error (MAPE) and the Theil U-statistic (Theil-U). These measures have already been presented in detail by, amongst others, Makridakis et al. (1983), Pindyck and Rubinfeld (1981) and Theil (1966).

If we call the actual volatility at time τ, σ and the forecast volatility at time τ, $\hat{\sigma}$, with a forecast period going from $t + 1$ to $t + n$, the forecast error statistics are respectively:

$$RMSE = \sqrt{(1/n) \sum_{\tau=t+1}^{t+n} (\hat{\sigma}_\tau - \sigma_\tau)^2}$$

$$MAE = (1/n) \sum_{\tau=t+1}^{t+n} |\hat{\sigma}_\tau - \sigma_\tau|$$

$$MAPE = (1/n) \sum_{\tau=t+1}^{t+n} |(\hat{\sigma}_\tau - \sigma_\tau)/\sigma_\tau|$$

$$\text{Theil-}U = \sqrt{(1/n) \sum_{\tau=t+1}^{t+n} (\hat{\sigma}_\tau - \sigma_\tau)^2} \Bigg/ \left[\sqrt{(1/n) \sum_{\tau=t+1}^{t+n} \hat{\sigma}_\tau^2} + \sqrt{(1/n) \sum_{\tau=t+1}^{t+n} \sigma_\tau^2} \right]$$

The RMSE and the MAE statistics are scale-dependent measures, but give us a basis to compare our volatility forecasts across the different models that we use.

The MAPE and the Theil-U statistics are independent of the scale of the variables. In particular, the Theil-U statistic is constructed in such a way that it necessarily lies between zero and one, with zero indicating a perfect fit.

For the four error statistics retained, the lower the output, the better the forecasting accuracy of the model concerned.

Finally, we also compute a Correct Directional Change (CDC) index to check whether the direction given by the forecast (i.e. the direction of change implied by the forecast at time t for time $t + n$ compared with the volatility level prevailing at time t) is the same as the actual change which has subsequently occurred between time t and time $t + n$. We have:

$$CDC = (100/n) \sum_{\tau=t+1}^{t+n} D_\tau$$

where

$$D_\tau = 1 \text{ if } (\sigma_\tau - \sigma_{\tau-1})(\hat{\sigma}_\tau - \sigma_{\tau-1}) > 0, \text{ else } D_\tau = 0$$

---

[20] This is easily done by taking the square root of the conditional variance forecast and multiplying it by $\sqrt{252}$; in the case of the stochastic variance forecasts, it is further necessary to begin taking the exponential of the respective model's forecast after having adjusted it by the log-forecast variance (we used the variance from the observation equation over the in-sample period since, in a true out-of-sample forecasting process, one does not know ex ante what the forecast error is going to be) to account for the transformation to "anti-log" the forecasts.

3.4.2   The Out-of-sample Forecasting Results

Having documented the error measures that we use to gauge the forecasting accuracy of our different models, we now turn to the analysis of our out-of-sample empirical results. We basically wish to be able to answer the following questions:

(i)   How do our models fit out-of-sample and is there, currency by currency (in fact, we should say volatility by volatility), a (or several) better forecasting model(s)?

(ii)   Do market implied volatility data and model combination each add value in terms of forecasting accuracy?

(iii)   Finally, are some currency volatilities "easier" to forecast than others?

We start with the 1-month out forecasts and concentrate first on error *levels*. As can be seen from Table 3.7, these results are quite mixed.[21] True, if our volatility models have indeed a forecasting power, as shown for instance by the Theil-U statistic, the errors remain important as evidenced by the MAPE measure amongst others. Nevertheless, if one compares the MAE figures of the best models in Table 3.7 with the standard deviation of 1-month historical volatilities in Table 3.2, one can see that the forecasting errors we make are on average significantly lower than the actual volatility of the time series concerned,[22] with the exception of DEM/JPY volatility: yet, one needs to qualify this result with the fact that the volatility of the DEM/JPY has been particularly high during the out-of-sample period, the actual standard deviation of the DEM/JPY volatility reaching 5.29% during that period. Figures A3.7 to A3.12 in Appendix 3.4 depict the results of the forecasting exercise at the 1-month horizon graphically. For each of the six currencies the forecasts from the best two performing models are shown alongside the realised volatility.

For DEM/JPY volatility, model 2, the "mixed" GARCH(1,1) seems to perform best overall, although model 17, the "naïve" model based on historical volatility, performs best on the MAPE measure, and model 19 which uses only the current level quoted on the market comes as a not too distant second on the other measures.

For GBP/DEM volatility, model 17 comes as the "best model" on all measures, although model 23, our regression-weighted average forecast, comes as a close contender.

For GBP/USD volatility, model 11, the AR(10) "mixed" model based on absolute log-returns, and model 17 again come as the best models.

For USD/CHF volatility, model 11 and model 21, the average of all 21-day models, perform best depending on the chosen criterion, while model 6, the AR(10) "mixed" model based on squared log-returns, performs well also.

For USD/DEM volatility, model 11 is again the best model, although model 17 comes as a close second.

Finally, for USD/JPY volatility, model 21 and model 2 perform best, although model 11 again gives rather good results.

Continuing with the 3-month out forecasts and still concentrating first on error *levels*, as can be seen from Table 3.8, our empirical results confirm that volatility models have indeed a forecasting power: if anything, it seems that, with the exception of the USD/CHF volatility, they manage to forecast better at a 3-month than at a 1-month horizon, as shown

---

[21] Some further tests of the statistical significance of the forecasting accuracy are reported in Appendix 3.3.

[22] This is also true when taking, more appropriately, the in-sample period until 27th February 1998 that we use: these calculations are not reported here in order to conserve space.

Table 3.7 Out-of-sample volatility forecast performance (1-month)

	Model 1	Model 2	Model 5	Model 6	Model 9	Model 11	Model 13	Model 15	Model 17	Model 19	Model 21	Model 23	Model 25	Min.	Best model
DEM/JPY															
RMSE	9.12	5.38	16.29	13.52	7.83	7.92	10.24	8.29	6.63	5.62	6.55	10.97	7.93	5.38	Model 2
MAE	6.40	4.58	6.65	8.70	6.79	6.44	8.68	6.48	5.16	4.97	4.92	8.20	6.05	4.58	Model 2
MAPE	0.54	0.41	0.59	0.79	0.67	0.60	0.63	0.45	0.39	0.45	0.41	0.53	0.54	0.39	Model 17
THEIL-U	0.29	0.19	0.44	0.37	0.24	0.25	0.57	0.41	0.24	0.19	0.23	0.48	0.25	0.19	Model 2
GBP/DEM															
RMSE	2.67	2.79	5.62	5.80	7.28	3.19	3.31	2.35	1.44	3.43	2.69	1.81	3.82	1.44	Model 17
MAE	2.21	2.54	5.48	5.56	7.16	2.83	3.05	2.03	1.17	3.10	2.42	1.32	3.58	1.17	Model 17
MAPE	0.42	0.49	1.04	1.04	1.34	0.54	0.51	0.34	0.20	0.59	0.47	0.20	0.68	0.20	Model 17
THEIL-U	0.19	0.20	0.33	0.33	0.39	0.22	0.39	0.24	0.12	0.23	0.19	0.16	0.25	0.12	Model 17
GBP/USD															
RMSE	2.63	3.05	7.85	3.35	7.87	1.42	2.10	2.62	1.50	3.57	2.57	1.81	3.59	1.42	Model 11
MAE	2.37	2.75	7.77	2.72	7.77	1.16	1.82	2.37	1.15	3.22	2.28	1.54	3.35	1.15	Model 17
MAPE	0.53	0.61	1.66	0.59	1.66	0.24	0.34	0.46	0.23	0.70	0.51	0.28	0.73	0.23	Model 17
THEIL-U	0.21	0.24	0.44	0.26	0.44	0.14	0.25	0.34	0.15	0.27	0.21	0.19	0.27	0.14	Model 11
USD/CHF															
RMSE	3.52	2.44	7.06	2.35	6.79	2.09	4.22	4.58	2.48	2.54	2.19	2.96	2.99	2.09	Model 11
MAE	3.24	2.18	6.65	1.92	6.37	1.52	3.30	4.16	1.94	2.25	1.96	2.23	2.73	1.52	Model 11
MAPE	0.45	0.30	0.95	0.24	0.91	0.17	0.35	0.49	0.22	0.31	0.26	0.22	0.38	0.17	Model 11
THEIL-U	0.18	0.13	0.30	0.13	0.29	0.13	0.31	0.35	0.15	0.13	0.12	0.18	0.15	0.12	Model 21
USD/DEM															
RMSE	3.06	2.89	7.47	3.13	7.81	1.61	2.64	2.99	1.78	3.48	2.52	3.33	3.57	1.61	Model 11
MAE	2.70	2.59	7.30	2.65	7.61	1.28	2.16	2.73	1.48	3.14	2.22	2.86	3.32	1.28	Model 11
MAPE	0.47	0.44	1.23	0.44	1.28	0.22	0.30	0.40	0.23	0.52	0.39	0.39	0.57	0.22	Model 11
THEIL-U	0.19	0.18	0.36	0.19	0.37	0.11	0.24	0.28	0.13	0.21	0.16	0.29	0.21	0.11	Model 11
USD/JPY															
RMSE	6.22	5.06	5.72	7.26	5.54	5.49	10.51	8.01	6.38	5.92	5.06	19.41	5.59	5.06	Model 21
MAE	5.17	4.67	5.16	6.26	5.08	4.43	9.20	6.30	4.97	5.31	4.24	11.38	4.98	4.24	Model 21
MAPE	0.42	0.40	0.46	0.56	0.45	0.33	0.64	0.41	0.37	0.47	0.32	0.79	0.42	0.32	Model 21
THEIL-U	0.21	0.17	0.19	0.22	0.18	0.19	0.56	0.37	0.22	0.19	0.18	0.53	0.19	0.17	Model 2

Table 3.8 Out-of-sample volatility forecast performance (3-month)

	Model 3	Model 4	Model 7	Model 8	Model 10	Model 12	Model 14	Model 16	Model 18	Model 20	Model 22	Model 24	Model 26	Min.	Best model
DEM/JPY															
RMSE	7.77	5.18	58.62	10.08	7.71	9.21	9.56	7.59	5.14	3.93	8.26	158.20	10.57	3.93	Model 20
MAE	4.78	3.82	8.15	7.47	6.60	7.59	8.95	6.78	4.44	3.53	4.15	23.28	5.37	3.53	Model 20
MAPE	0.38	0.31	0.68	0.66	0.60	0.67	0.67	0.50	0.33	0.30	0.33	1.80	0.46	0.30	Model 20
THEIL-U	0.26	0.18	0.78	0.29	0.23	0.27	0.55	0.39	0.20	0.14	0.28	0.91	0.32	0.14	Model 20
GDP/DEM															
RMSE	2.95	2.71	6.24	6.67	9.87	4.92	3.26	2.40	1.50	3.07	3.19	1.59	4.51	1.50	Model 18
MAE	2.42	2.45	6.16	6.46	9.81	4.64	3.13	2.07	1.22	2.75	2.94	1.32	4.32	1.22	Model 18
MAPE	0.45	0.46	1.11	1.17	1.76	0.84	0.53	0.34	0.20	0.51	0.54	0.20	0.79	0.20	Model 18
THEIL-U	0.21	0.19	0.35	0.37	0.46	0.30	0.38	0.25	0.13	0.21	0.22	0.15	0.28	0.13	Model 18
GBP/USD															
RMSE	2.70	2.70	8.64	3.33	9.54	1.53	1.96	2.68	1.03	3.55	2.74	1.08	3.91	1.03	Model 18
MAE	2.54	2.52	8.61	2.85	9.50	1.24	1.87	2.58	0.90	3.35	2.58	0.97	3.78	0.90	Model 18
MAPE	0.52	0.52	1.74	0.59	1.92	0.26	0.36	0.50	0.19	0.69	0.53	0.18	0.78	0.18	Model 24
THEIL-U	0.21	0.21	0.46	0.26	0.49	0.14	0.24	0.36	0.10	0.26	0.22	0.11	0.28	0.10	Model 18
USD/CHF															
RMSE	3.40	2.53	7.20	3.27	7.54	2.44	3.97	4.96	2.71	2.74	2.38	3.03	3.26	2.38	Model 22
MAE	3.00	2.25	6.94	2.78	7.24	1.88	3.43	4.55	2.29	2.49	2.15	2.56	2.94	1.88	Model 12
MAPE	0.41	0.29	0.92	0.33	0.96	0.21	0.37	0.52	0.26	0.33	0.28	0.26	0.40	0.21	Model 12
THEIL-U	0.17	0.14	0.30	0.18	0.31	0.15	0.29	0.39	0.16	0.15	0.13	0.19	0.17	0.13	Model 22
USD/DEM															
RMSE	3.05	2.59	7.91	3.47	9.27	2.41	2.47	3.27	1.51	3.28	2.71	1.36	3.90	1.36	Model 24
MAE	2.79	2.34	7.83	3.07	9.15	2.17	2.24	3.07	1.34	2.99	2.45	1.05	3.68	1.05	Model 24
MAPE	0.45	0.37	1.22	0.48	1.43	0.34	0.32	0.45	0.20	0.47	0.39	0.14	0.58	0.14	Model 24
THEIL-U	0.19	0.16	0.37	0.21	0.41	0.16	0.22	0.31	0.11	0.20	0.17	0.10	0.23	0.10	Model 24
USD/JPY															
RMSE	4.55	3.43	3.88	6.91	4.57	5.34	10.01	7.49	4.54	4.11	3.60	8.45	4.27	3.43	Model 4
MAE	3.52	2.80	3.19	5.23	3.70	4.00	9.58	6.82	4.14	3.21	3.08	5.64	3.43	2.80	Model 4
MAPE	0.26	0.22	0.26	0.43	0.30	0.31	0.68	0.47	0.30	0.26	0.23	0.38	0.27	0.22	Model 4
THEIL-U	0.16	0.12	0.13	0.21	0.15	0.17	0.55	0.35	0.17	0.14	0.13	0.27	0.14	0.12	Model 4

for instance by the relative MAPE measures of the best models in Table 3.7 and 3.8. Still, this time around, comparing the MAE figures of the best models in Table 3.8 with the standard deviation of 3-month historical volatilities in Table 3.3, the forecasting errors we make are on average significantly lower than the actual volatility of the time series concerned in four out of six cases only, with DEM/JPY and USD/JY volatilities being the exceptions.[23]

For DEM/JPY volatility, model 20, the current 3-month volatility level quoted on the market, gives the best prediction, followed by model 4, the "mixed" GARCH(1,1) model.

For GBP/DEM volatility, as for the 1-month horizon, model 18 which is only based on past historical volatility comes as the "best model" on all measures, although model 24, the regression-weighted average forecast, comes as a close second best.

For GBP/USD volatility, model 18 and model 24 come again as the best models depending on the chosen criterion.

For USD/CHF volatility, model 12, the AR(10) "mixed" model based on absolute log-returns, and model 22, the average of all 63-day models, perform best depending on the error measure selected.

For USD/DEM volatility, model 24 is the best, followed by model 18.

Finally, for USD/JPY volatility, model 4 gives the best forecasts, followed by model 22 and model 7, the AR(10) time series model based on squared log-returns.

In the end, looking at the level of out-of-sample forecast errors of our models for both horizons, and whether one concentrates on the hard-and-fast rule of picking the best models in the last column of Tables 3.7 and 3.8 or tries to conduct a finer analysis as we have attempted just above, a few conclusions can already be drawn.

(i) Some of the forecasting models retained have indeed a good forecasting power, but the lagged historical volatility and current market data for volatility provide a tough benchmark to beat (they come first, respectively 22.9 and 8.3% of the time, in the "best model" classification of Tables 3.7 and 3.8).

(ii) Market implied volatility data and model combination do indeed add value in terms of forecasting accuracy. Concerning implied volatility, "mixed" AR(10) based on squared log-returns with the appropriate implied volatility series appears first 22.9% of the time, while mixed GARCH(1,1) models come first in 16.3% of the cases considered. It is interesting to note that AR(10) models correcting for heteroskedasticity appear to be an efficient (and simpler) alternative for the more complex GARCH(1,1) model, whereas stochastic variance models generally appear as relatively poor performers, perhaps justifying *ex-post* that very few applications of this modelling technology in the literature have been benchmarked against competing approaches. Concerning model combinations, they also come first 22.9% of the time in one form or another, mostly at the 3-month horizon; a demonstration of the fact that such combinations can indeed sometimes outperform individual forecasts. It is worth noting that, in seven cases out of 12 for both time horizons, the simple average of the other forecasting models outperforms the regression-weighted average procedure. This is most likely due to the deterioration of the out-of-sample performance of the GR procedure of model combination.

(iii) Finally, it does seem that some currency volatilities are harder to forecast than others, as evidenced by the much bigger errors recorded by the DEM/JPY and

---

[23] The remark in footnote 22 applies here too.

USD/JPY forecasts, even if, as mentioned before, this is not surprising in view of the very sharp volatility experienced by the Japanese currency at the end of 1998 and in early 1999, *i.e.* the time of our out-of-sample forecasting exercise. It should be noted that the simple average of forecasts is found to be best for the USD/JPY at the 1-month horizon, suggesting that such an approach is desirable during periods of turbulence.

We now turn to the analysis of the *direction* of our forecasts using the results for the CDC index in Table 3.9.

If minimising the retained error measures, RMSE, MAE, MAPE and Theil-U statistics, is indeed important in order to gauge the forecasting ability of our models, correctly predicting the direction of the next move is also critical: for instance, if one is to use the forecast to make a one-off or several scattered decisions on the opportunity to initiate specific volatility hedges.

A first general remark is that our forecasting models do not predict directional change with great accuracy as the best level achieved is only 57.6%: this is reached by model 11, the "mixed" AR(10) model based on absolute log-returns, for USD/DEM volatility at the 1-month horizon. At the other end of the spectrum, for USD/JPY volatility at the 1-month horizon, none of our models are able to predict the directional change in volatility even 50% of the time!

Some models perform rather poorly in terms of the CDC index: this is the case of the stochastic variance models (models 13 and 15 at the 1-month horizon and models 14 and 16 at the 3-month horizon) as they only manage to predict the direction of volatility changes correctly more than 50% of the time for one exchange rate out of six.

This is also the case for model 17, the "naïve" model based on past historical volatility, at the 1-month horizon, and model 18, its 3-month horizon counterpart, is hardly any better.

It also appears that directional forecasting is more accurate at the 1-month horizon where the models produce an overall CDC index above 50% in 41 cases out of the 78 surveyed (52.6% of the time). At the 3-month horizon, they only achieve a CDC index above 50% in 37 cases (47.4% of the time).

In other words, if the analysis of the error measures conducted above, particularly for "mixed" models and model combinations, leads to a favourable conclusion in terms of the out-of-sample forecasting accuracy of some volatility models, their ability to predict directional change consistently is more questionable.

Admittedly, with 34,008 out-of-sample forecasts in total,[24] it may reasonably be argued that average error and correct directional change measures constitute a serious reduction of dimensionality in a true assessment of the medium-term forecasting accuracy of the models concerned. Accordingly, we resort to the most recent data mining technique of data fusion to gauge the quality of these out-of-sample forecasts.

3.4.3 The Out-of-sample Forecasts Fusion

The System Optimisation by Fusion of Information (SOFI) is a new analytical data mining method merging a cross-sectional database with temporal characteristics with the results

---

[24] That is: 13 volatility models times two forecasting horizons times six currency volatilities times 218 forecasting steps.

Table 3.9 Correct directional change index out-of-sample performance

21-day	Model 1	Model 2	Model 5	Model 6	Model 9	Model 11	Model 13	Model 15	Model 17	Model 19	Model 21	Model 23	Model 25	Best level	Best models
DEM/JPY	45.16	48.39	47.93	48.85	50.69	47.93	50.23	50.23	45.16	47.93	46.54	52.10	47.00	52.10	Model 23
GBP/DEM	53.00	53.00	53.46	53.46	53.46	52.53	46.54	47.93	47.93	53.46	53.00	49.70	53.46	53.46	Models 5, 6, 19, 25
GBP/USD	51.61	50.69	50.69	49.77	50.69	50.23	49.31	49.77	47.47	50.69	51.61	49.70	50.69	51.61	Models 1, 21
USD/CHF	51.61	52.07	53.46	50.23	53.00	51.61	48.39	47.93	47.00	52.07	50.69	53.29	52.07	53.46	Model 5
USD/DEM	53.92	52.53	52.07	52.53	52.07	57.60	47.93	47.93	51.61	52.07	52.53	49.70	52.07	57.60	Model 11
USD/JPY	47.47	47.47	47.47	48.85	48.39	49.31	48.39	48.85	44.70	49.77	46.54	49.70	48.39	49.77	Model 19

63-day	Model 3	Model 4	Model 7	Model 8	Model 10	Model 12	Model 14	Model 16	Model 18	Model 20	Model 22	Model 24	Model 26	Best level	Best models
dem/jpy	49.77	53.00	55.76	51.15	51.61	53.92	46.54	46.54	48.85	53.92	53.92	52.10	51.15	55.76	Model 7
GBP/DEM	54.38	53.46	53.46	53.46	53.46	53.46	46.54	44.24	53.46	53.46	53.46	49.10	53.46	54.38	Model 3
GBP/USD	48.85	48.85	48.85	49.31	48.85	46.54	51.15	51.15	47.47	48.85	48.85	53.29	48.85	53.29	Model 24
USD/CHF	50.23	45.62	53.00	43.32	53.00	47.00	47.00	47.00	45.62	46.54	48.39	49.70	48.39	53.00	Models 7, 10
USD/DEM	52.53	51.61	53.00	50.69	53.00	49.77	47.00	47.00	51.15	52.07	51.15	52.10	53.00	53.00	Models 7, 10, 26
USD/JPY	41.01	50.23	49.31	51.15	47.93	46.54	44.70	44.70	46.08	51.15	48.39	44.91	43.78	51.15	Models 8, 20

Note: The CDC indices for models 23 and 24 are based on the last 168 forecasts as these were derived using coefficients obtained using the first 50 observations.

of a classification and/or segmentation of the data. It is essentially a nonparametric unsupervised multidimensional classifier (see Chavin and Jañez Escalada, 1997; Chauvin *et al.*, 1999; Dunis *et al.*, 2000).

The SOFI Methodology

We resort to data mining tools to classify the 156 volatility models (denoted VM), as we try to identify those VMs that minimise volatility estimation errors and/or volatility trend estimation errors.[25] To allow for a comparison, the 156 VMs are normalised by the estimation error $E_{1,t}$ and the trend estimation error $E_{2,t}$. We have:

$$E^m_{1,t} = HVOLn_{t+n} - h_{t+n}$$

$$E^m_{2,t} = \tfrac{1}{2}[(HVOLn_{t+1+n} - HVOLn_{t-1+n}) - (h_{t+1+n} - h_{t-1+n})]$$

with $m = \{1, \ldots, 78\}$ (for each VM at the 21-day or 63-day horizon), $t = \{1, \ldots, 218\}$ (for each out-of-sample forecasting step) and $n = \{21, 63\}$ (for each forecasting horizon).

We then look for the set M_{opt} of the VMs which minimise the range of values for $E^m_{1,t}$ and $E^m_{2,t}$ and maximise the confidence interval:[26]

$$M_{\text{opt}} = \{M = \{m \in VM\}|\ \min_M [\max_{t=1,\ldots,218, m \in M} E^m_{j,t} - \min_{t=1,\ldots,218, m \in M} E^m_{j,t}]\}$$

where $j = \{1, 2\}$.

The analysis of our dataset is done using the SOFI approach which derives from the application of Bayesian networks (see, amongst others, Jensen, 1996 and Becker and Naïm, 1999).

SOFI's originality is to assess a set of solutions combining some *a priori* knowledge on a given application and the results of data mining analyses conducted on the original dataset.[27] It is a model of numerical fusion conducted on the basis of combinations of "experts" which links the informational content of the databank to the *a priori* knowledge provided by an "expert user".

For our application, we use the following *priors*.

(i)   The 13 models are first classified into three categories: five models using "little information", *i.e.* the time series models and the "naïve" models based on past historical volatility, which are denoted "*lower*" (models 1, 3, 5, 7, 9, 10, 13, 14, 17 and 18 for both forecasting horizons), five models using more information, *i.e.* the implied volatility data, which are denoted "*upper*" (models 2, 4, 6, 8, 11, 12, 15, 16, 19 and 20 for both forecasting horizons) and, finally, the three model combinations which average in some way the results of the previous models and therefore encapsulate even more information, and which are denoted "*sup*" (models 21, 22, 23, 24, 25 and 26 for both forecasting horizons). We then create three "experts": "*ExpertInfo*" analyses the VMs according to the classification described just above, "*Expert-Money*" analyses the VMs according to the exchange rate volatility concerned and "*ExpertModel*" analyses the VMs on a model-by-model basis.

---

[25] We have 13 volatility models times six currency volatilities, *i.e.* 78 VMs per forecasting horizon.

[26] We also use several other "intermediate" variables, such as the variance of these errors, their absolute value, etc.

[27] For our particular application, we use the decision tree software ALICE™ of ISoft.

(ii)   The statistical measures RMSE, MAE, MAPE and Theil-U are optimal in terms
       of forecasting accuracy if they are close to zero (see Section 3.4.1). Accordingly,
       we create another two "experts": "*ExpertAlice1*" uses a decision tree to classify
       the VMs according to these statistical measures, while "*ExpertAlice2*" classifies the
       VMs on the basis of these measures and the error measures $E_{1,t}^m$ and $E_{2,t}^m$ which we
       introduced earlier in this section.

With a logical labelling of the resulting classes, SOFI allows for a methodical search of
the knowledge hidden in the data. This knowledge is evaluated by a Bayesian network
acting as a multidimensional classifier which measures the informational quality brought
in by each "expert" used.

The SOFI Results

Analysing the quality of each "expert", the fusion model extracts and evaluates the variables that determine the resulting classification. We look in turn at each "expert" and
summarise the results.

  (i)   For "*ExpertInfo*", there is a reduction in the range of the errors $E_{1,t}$ the more
        complex, in terms of informational content, the model gets: at the 21-day horizon
        (respectively 63-day), the error $E_{1,t}$ for the "*sup*" VMs is kept within the range
        $[-6.21;3.57]$ (respectively $[-1.96;5.06]$); for the "*upper*" VMs, that range is
        $[-6.47;7.05]$ (respectively $[-6.78;7.52]$); for the "*lower*" VMs, it is $[-9.19;7.76]$
        (respectively $[-9.54;9.81]$).
  (ii) For "*ExpertMoney*", not surprisingly, the fusion model detects the particular
        behaviour of the DEM/JPY and USD/JPY volatilities, to the point that it isolates
        JPY-related volatilities in a separate class at the 21-day horizon.
  (iii) For "*ExpertModel*", the "*lower*" VMs 17 and 18, the "naïve" models based on past
        historical volatility, have the overall lowest range for the error $E_{1,t}$ with a range
        of $[-0.41;-0.01]$ at the 21-day horizon and $[-1.05;0.11]$ at the 63-day horizon.
        Again, the worst performing models appear to be the stochastic variance models
        which systematically underestimate currency volatilities even if, here again, the
        "mixed" models show better results.
  (iv) For "*ExpertAlice1*", the VMs are discriminated into seven classes at the 21-day
        horizon and into five classes at the 63-day horizon, according to the distance of the
        RMSE, MAE, MAPE and Theil-U statistics from their optimal value.
  (v)   Finally, for "*ExpertAlice2*", the VMs are separated into five classes at the 21-
        day horizon and into six classes at the 63-day horizon, according to the combined
        distance of the previous measures and the error measures $E_{1,t}^m$ and $E_{2,t}^m$ from their
        optimal value.

The actual fusion process then involves combining these different analyses in order to
obtain a new classification optimised in terms of the quality of the composite results from
the five "experts".
    The fusion model produces five classes at the 21-day horizon and four classes at the
63-day horizon, with the "experts" "*ExpertAlice1*" and "*ExpertAlice2*" mostly responsible
for the optimised solution. Table 3.10 describes the classes for each forecasting horizon

Table 3.10   VM classification after data fusion

	21-Day horizon	63-Day horizon
Class 1		
Meaning	Good trend and level estimation	Good trend and level estimation
Volatilities	GBP/DEM, GBP/USD, USD/CHF, USD/DEM	GBP/DEM, GBP/USD, USD/CHF, USD/DEM
Models	9 Models: "*Sup*" 21 and 23; "*Lower*" 17; "*Upper*" 11	11 Models: "*Sup*" 22 and 24; "*Lower*" 18; "*Upper*" 12 and 5
Class 2		
Meaning	Good trend, poor level estimation	Relatively good trend and level estimation
Volatilities	GBP/DEM, GBP/USD, USD/CHF, USD/DEM	GBP/DEM, GBP/USD, USD/CHF, USD/DEM, USD/JPY
Models	34 Models: "*Lower*" 1, 13 and 14; "*Upper*" 2, 6, 11 and 19; "*Sup*" 25, 23 and 21	27 Models: "*Lower*" 3; "*Upper*" 4, 8, 12, 15, 16 and 20; "*Sup*" 26, 24 and 22
Class 3		
Meaning	Poor statistics, good trend estimation	Large error estimation on E1 and E2
Volatilities	GBP/DEM, USD/CHF	GBP/DEM, GBP/USD, USD/DEM, USD/JPY, USD/JPY, DEM/JPY
Models	4 Models: "*Lower*" 5 and 9; "*Upper*" 6	9 Models: "*Lower*" 7, 10 and 14; "*Sup*" 24
Class 4		
Meaning	Large error estimation on E1 and E2	Poor statistical measures (RMSE, etc.)
Volatilities	GBP/DEM, GBP/USD, USD/DEM	All volatilities
Models	5 Models: "*Lower*" 5 and 9; "*Upper*" 6	31 Models: "*Upper*" 15, 16 and 20; "*Sup*" 26; 24 JPY volatility models
Class 5		
Meaning	All JPY volatilities	
Volatilities	USD/JPY, DEM/JPY	
Models	26 Models: All JPY volatility models	

in descending order of both "symbolic meaning" and numerical error measures. It also gives the volatilities and models concerned on a class-by-class basis. Table 3.11 further documents the fusion results with a classification of the models according to the currency volatility and forecast horizon concerned, with the best models in bold characters.

Class 1 and class 2 group models that respectively give good estimates of both the level and the trend of currency volatilities (*i.e.* with values of $E_{1,t}^m$ and $E_{2,t}^m$ around zero) and models which give good estimates of the trend only (*i.e.* with values of $E_{2,t}^m$ around zero). Figures 3.1 and 3.2 clearly show that the range of errors for class 1 is lower than that for class 2.

Whatever the chosen forecast horizon, both tables show that the following models minimise the estimation error for the GBP/DEM, GBP/USD, USD/CHF and USD/DEM volatilities: models 11 and 12 (the "mixed" AR(10) models based on absolute returns and implied volatility data), models 17 and 18 (the models based on past historical

Table 3.11 Volatility models classification (21-day and 63-day horizon)

	GARCH Model 1 / Model 3 "Lower" / "Upper"	GARCH Model 2 / Model 4 "Upper" / "Upper"	AR Sq. Model 5 / Model 7 "Lower" / "Lower"	AR Sq. Model 6 / Model 8 "Upper" / "Upper"	AR Abs. Model 9 / Model 10 "Lower" / "Lower"	AR Abs. Model 11 / Model 12 "Upper" / "Upper"	SV Model 13 / Model 14 "Lower" / "Lower"	SV Model 15 / Model 16 "Upper" / "Upper"	Hist. vol. Model 17 / Model 18 "Lower" / "Lower"	Imp. vol. Model 19 / Model 20 "Upper" / "Upper"	Average 1 Model 21 / Model 22 "Sup" / "Sup"	Regression Model 23 / Model 24 "Sup" / "Sup"	Average 2 Model 25 / Model 26 "Sup" / "Sup"	Best model
DEM/JPY 21-day	Class 5	Class 5	Class 5	Class 5	Class 5	Class 5	Class 5	Class 5	Class 5	Class 5	Class 5	Class 5	Class 5	None
63-day	Class 4	Class 4	Class 3	Class 4	Class 4	Class 4	Class 3	Class 4	Class 4	Class 4	Class 4	Class 3	Class 4	7, 15, 24
GBP/DEM 21-day	Class 2	Class 2	Class 3	Class 3	Class 4	Class 2	Class 2	Class 2	**Class 1**	Class 2	**Class 1**	**Class 1**	Class 2	**17, 21, 23**
63-day	Class 2	Class 2	Class 4	Class 4	Class 3	Class 4	Class 2	Class 2	**Class 1**	Class 2	**Class 1**	**Class 1**	Class 4	**18, 24**
GBP/USD 21-day	Class 2	Class 2	Class 4	Class 2	Class 4	**Class 1**	Class 2	Class 2	**Class 1**	Class 2	**Class 1**	**Class 1**	Class 4	**17, 21, 23**
63-day	Class 2	Class 2	Class 3	Class 2	Class 3	**Class 1**	**Class 1**	Class 2	**Class 1**	Class 4	**Class 1**	**Class 1**	Class 4	**18, 22, 24**
USD/CHF 21-day	Class 2	Class 2	Class 3	Class 2	Class 4	Class 2	Class 2	Class 2	Class 2	Class 2	**Class 1**	Class 2	Class 2	**21**
63-day	Class 2	Class 2	Class 4	Class 2	Class 4	Class 2	Class 4	Class 4	Class 2	Class 2	**Class 1**	Class 2	Class 2	**22**
USD/DEM 21-day	Class 2	Class 2	Class 4	Class 2	Class 4	Class 2	Class 2	Class 2	**Class 1**	Class 2	**Class 1**	Class 2	Class 2	**21**
63-day	Class 2	Class 2	Class 3	Class 2	Class 3	Class 2	Class 2	Class 2	Class 5	Class 2	**Class 1**	**Class 1**	Class 4	**18, 22, 24**
USD/JPY 21-day	Class 5	Class 5	Class 5	Class 5	Class 5	Class 5	Class 5	Class 5	Class 5	Class 5	Class 5	Class 5	Class 5	None
63-day	Class 4	Class 4	Class 4	Class 4	Class 4	Class 5	Class 3	Class 4	Class 4	Class 4	Class 2	Class 4	Class 4	22
Majority class 21-day	Class 2	Class 2	Class 3–4	Class 2	Class 3	**Class 1–2**	Class 2	Class 2	**Class 1–2**	Class 2	**Class 1**	**Class 1–2**	Class 2	
63-day	Class 2	Class 2	Class 3–4	Class 2	Class 3	**Class 1–4**	Class 1–3	Class 2–4	**Class 1–4**	Class 2–4	**Class 1–2**	**Class 1–2**	Class 2–4	

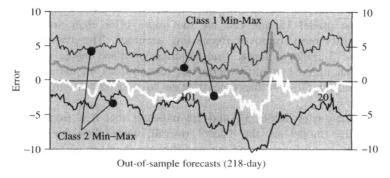

Figure 3.1   Estimation error E1 (21-day)

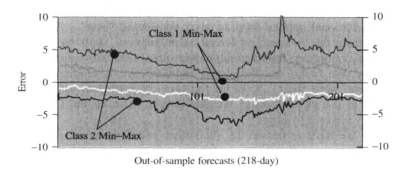

Figure 3.2   Estimation error E1 (63-day)

volatility), models 21 and 22 (the average of all previous models) and models 23 and 24 (the regression-weighted average of all previous models). It is also worth noting that GARCH(1,1) time series and "mixed" models always give a good estimation of volatility trends (see Table 3.11). Models considered by SOFI as poor forecasting models are grouped in classes 3 and 4 of Table 3.10, with high values of the error measures. These include models 5 and 7 (the time series AR(10) models based on squared log-returns) and models 9 and 10 (the time series AR(10) models based on absolute log-returns).

As mentioned before, the level and trend of DEM/JPY and USD/JPY volatilities are not well estimated. At the 21-day horizon, class 5 is a specific class for all 26 JPY volatility models while, at the 63-day horizon, class 4 groups, amongst others, all 13 DEM/JPY volatility models and 11 USD/JPY volatility models out of 13.

3.5   CONCLUSION

An objective of this study was to investigate whether the inclusion of market implied volatility data in pure time series models can improve forecasting accuracy at the 1- and 3-month horizons. Consideration of Tables 3.7 and 3.8 indicates this to be true. For example, if one considers, at the 1-month horizon, the forecasting performance of model 1 against model 2, model 5 against model 6, model 9 against model 11 and model 13 against model 15 one can see that more often than not the inclusion of an implied volatility term improves forecasting accuracy. The evidence is even more supportive at the 3-month horizon. Consideration of these tables also indicates that the addition of an implied volatility term has least impact on the stochastic variance models where indeed 50% of the time it leads to a deterioration of the forecasting accuracy.

Further examination of Tables 3.7 and 3.8 indicates that it is impossible to identify a single volatility model as the "best" overall. Depending on the horizon, the currency volatility being forecast and the performance measure being used, the "mixed" GARCH(1,1) model, the "mixed" AR(10) on absolute log-returns, the models based on past historical volatility or the current level of implied volatility are all, at one time or another, considered "best". This also indicates that the GARCH(1,1) and both AR(10) models without the implied term are never considered "best". It is also interesting to note that the most computationally intensive model, the stochastic variance model with or without the additional implied term, is never considered "best".

As expected from the literature on forecast combinations, we were also able to show that, in this application too, model combination often does add value in terms of forecasting accuracy. We found that the model combinations, depending on the choice of accuracy measure, were "best" 22.9% of the time. Nevertheless, on balance, it seems that it is better to use equal forecast weights than to estimate the forecast weights by regression.

In this study we have estimated 13 alternative volatility models and produced 218 out-of-sample forecasts at two horizons for six currencies, a total of 34,008 forecasts. With such an amount of data, average error measures clearly constitute an important reduction of dimensionality in assessing the medium-term forecasting accuracy of the models concerned. This is why we chose to use the System Optimisation by Fusion of Information (SOFI) to gauge the quality of these out-of-sample forecasts. The SOFI results in Tables 3.10 and 3.11 confirm that market implied volatility data and model combination do indeed add value in terms of forecasting accuracy.

Finally, it should be stressed that, in order to keep the project manageable, the time series and "mixed" models were selected on the basis of providing the best fit for all currencies concerned over the in-sample dataset. The specification of the volatility models was then kept constant during the entire forecast period. We have therefore not allowed for the specification to be adjusted on a currency-by-currency basis and/or during the course of our forecasting exercise. Given the evidence above supporting the inclusion of the implied volatility term in our time series models, we can also infer that respecifying the model during the forecast period and/or on a currency-by-currency basis would lead to an increase in forecasting accuracy.

REFERENCES

Baillie, R.T. and T. Bollerslev (1989). "The Message in Daily Exchange Rates: A Conditional Variance Tale", *Journal of Business and Economic Statistics* **7**, 297–305.

Baillie, R.T. and T. Bollerslev (1992). "Prediction in Dynamic Models with Time-Dependent Conditional Variances", *Journal of Econometrics* **52**, 91–113.

Becker, A. and P. Naïm (1999). "Les Réseaux Bayésiens: Modèles Graphiques de Connaissance", Eyrolles, Paris.

Bentz, Y. (1999). "Identifying and Modelling Conditional Factor Sensitivities: an Application to Equity Investment Management", Ph.D. dissertation, London Business School.

Bollerslev, T. (1986). "Generalised Autoregressive Conditional Heteroskedasticity", *Journal of Econometrics* **31**, 307–327.

Bollerslev, T. and J. Wooldridge (1992). "Quasi-Maximum Likelihood Estimation and Inference in Dynamic Models with Time Varying Covariances, *Econometric Reviews* **11**, 143–172.

Chauvin, S. and L. Jañez Escalada (1997). "Tracking Knowledge Data Bases: Fusion of Data Software, International Conference on Model Recognising Shape", MRF Research Document, C.I.R.M., Marseille, November (www.itc.ucm.es/proyectos/tracksofi/track_so.html).

Chauvin, S., L. Jañez Escalada and D. Martínez (1999). "Fusion de Données Numériques par l'A Priori des Données Symboliques", RFIA 2000, Paris (forthcoming).

Chiras, D.P. and S. Manaster (1978). "The Information Content of Option Prices and a Test of Market Efficiency", *Journal of Financial Economics* **6**, 213–234.

Clemen, R.T. (1989). "Combining Forecasts: A Review and Annotated Bibliography", *International Journal of Forecasting* **5**, 559–583.

Day, T.E. and C.M. Lewis (1992). "Stock Market Volatility and the Information Content of Stock Index Options", *Journal of Econometrics* **52**, 267–287.

Dunis, C. and A. Keller (1995). "Efficiency Tests with Overlapping Data: An Application to the Currency Options Market", *European Journal of Finance* **1**, 345–366.

Dunis, C., J. Laws and S. Chauvin (2000). "FX Volatility Forecasts: A Fusion-Optimisation Approach", *Neural Network World* **10**(1/2), 187–202.

Engle, R.F. and T. Bollerslev (1986). "Modelling the Persistence of Conditional Variances", *Econometric Reviews* **5**, 1–50.

Granger, C.W. and R. Ramanathan (1984). "Improved Methods of Combining Forecasts", *Journal of Forecasting* **3**, 197–204.

Hamilton, J. (1994). *Time Series Analysis*. Princeton, NJ: Princeton University Press.

Harvey, A.C. (1989). *Forecasting Structural Time Series Models and the Kalman Filter*. Cambridge: Cambridge University Press.

Harvey, A.C. and N. Shepherd (1993). "The Econometrics of Stochastic Volatility", LSE discussion paper, no. 166.

Harvey, A.C., E. Ruiz and N. Shepherd (1994). "Multivariate Stochastic Variance Models", *Review of Economic Studies* **61**, 247–264.

Jensen, F.V. (1996). *An Introduction to Bayesian Networks*. London: UCL Press.

Kroner, K.F., K.P. Kneafsey and S. Claessens (1995). "Forecasting Volatility in Commodity Markets", *Journal of Forecasting* **14**, 77–95.

Lamoureux, C.G. and W.D. Lastrapes (1993). "Forecasting Stock-Return Variances: Toward an Understanding of Stochastic Implied Volatilities", *Review of Financial Studies* **6**, 293–326.

Latane, H.A. and R.J. Rendleman (1976). "Standard Deviations of Stock Price Ratios Implied in Option Prices", *Journal of Finance* **31**, 369–381.

Makridakis, S., A. Andersen, R. Carbone, R. Fildes, M. Hibon, R. Lewandwski, J. Newton, E. Parzen and R. Winkler (1982). "The Accuracy of Time Series (Extrapolative) Methods: Results of a Forecasting Competition", *Journal of Forecasting* **1**, 111–153.

Makridakis, S., S.C. Wheelwright and V.E. McGee (1983). *Forecasting: Methods and Applications*. New York: Wiley.

Martin, D.W. and D.W. French (1987). "The Characteristics of Interest Rates and Stock Variances Implied in Option Prices", *Journal of Economics and Business* **39**, 279–288.

O'Brien, T.J. and W.F. Kennedy (1982). "Simultaneous Option and Stock Prices: Another Look at the Black-Scholes Model", *Financial Review* **17**, 219–227.

Pedersen, W.R. (1998). "Capturing All the Information in Foreign Currency Options: Solving for One Versus Two Implied Variables", *Applied Economics* **30**, 1679–1683.

Pindyck, R.S. and D.L. Rubinfeld (1981). *Econometric Models and Economic Forecasts*. Auckland: McGraw-Hill.

Taylor, S.J. (1986). *Modelling Financial Time Series*. Chichester: Wiley.

Theil, H. (1966). *Applied Economic Forecasting*, Amsterdam: North-Holland.

West, K.D. and D. Cho (1995). "The Predictive Ability of Several Models of Exchange Rate Volatility", *Journal of Econometrics* **69**, 367–391.

White, H. (1980). "A Heteroskedasticity-Consistent Covariance Matrix Estimator and a Direct Test for Heteroskedasticity", *Econometrica* **48**, 817–838.

Xu, X. and S.J. Taylor (1996). "Conditional Volatility and the Informational Efficiency of the PHLX Currency Options Market" in C. Dunis (ed.), *Forecasting Financial Markets*. Chichester: Wiley; 181–200.

Zumbach, G. (2000). "The Pitfalls in Fitting GARCH Processes" in C. Dunis (ed.), *Advances in Quantitative Asset Management*. Boston: Kluwer Academic.

APPENDIX 3.1

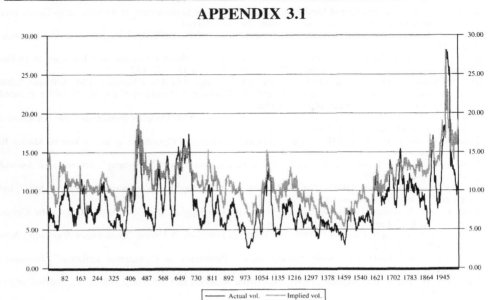

Figure A3.1   DEM/JPY 1-month volatility

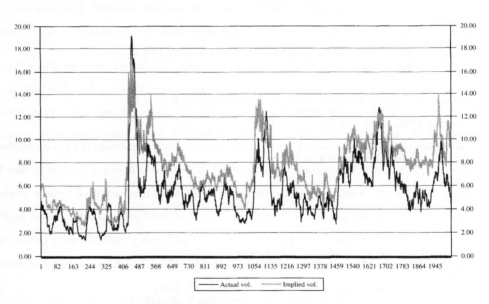

Figure A3.2   GBP/DEM 1-month volatility

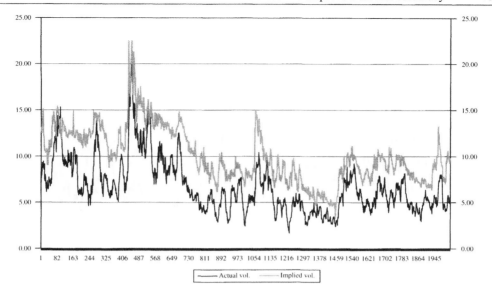

Figure A3.3   GBP/USD 1-month volatility

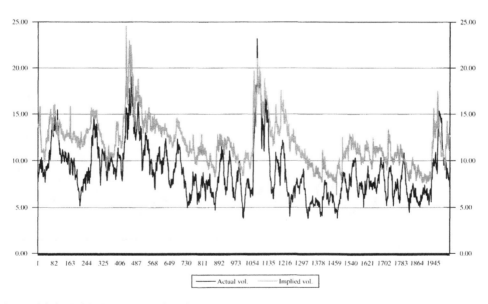

Figure A3.4   USD/CHF 1-month volatility

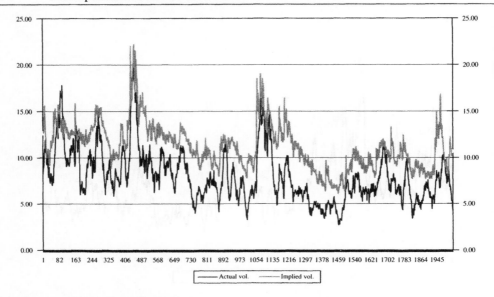

Figure A3.5   USD/DEM 1-month volatility

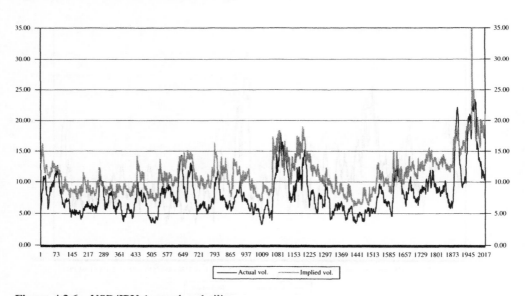

Figure A3.6   USD/JPY 1-month volatility

APPENDIX 3.2

Table A3.1 Different models estimated and formulas used for n-step-ahead conditional variance

Type of model	Model number	Formula for h_t	Value of n	Formula for h_{t+n}
GARCH(1,1)	Model 1	$h_t = \omega + \alpha\varepsilon_{t-1}^2 + \beta h_{t-1}$	$n = 21$	$h_{t+n} = \omega[1 + (\alpha+\beta) + \cdots + (\alpha+\beta)^{n-2}] + \omega + \alpha\varepsilon_t^2 + \beta h_t$
	Model 2	$h_t = \omega + \alpha\varepsilon_{t-1}^2 + \beta h_{t-1} + \gamma IMP_{t-1}$	$n = 21$	$h_{t+n} = \omega[1 + (\alpha+\beta) + \cdots + (\alpha+\beta)^{n-2}] + \omega + \alpha\varepsilon_t^2 + \beta h_t + \gamma IMP_t$
	Model 3	$h_t = \omega + \alpha\varepsilon_{t-1}^2 + \beta h_{t-1}$	$n = 63$	$h_{t+n} = \omega[1 + (\alpha+\beta) + \cdots + (\alpha+\beta)^{n-2}] + \omega + \alpha\varepsilon_t^2 + \beta h_t$
	Model 4	$h_t = \omega + \alpha\varepsilon_{t-1}^2 + \beta h_{t-1} + \gamma IMP_{t-1}$	$n = 63$	$h_{t+n} = \omega[1 + (\alpha+\beta) + \cdots + (\alpha+\beta)^{n-2}] + \omega + \alpha\varepsilon_t^2 + \beta h_t + \gamma IMP_t$
AR(10) in s_t^2	Model 5	$h_t = \omega + \sum_{i=1}^{10} \alpha_i s_{t-i}^2$	$n = 21$	$h_{t+n} = \omega + \sum_{i=1}^{10} \alpha_i s_{t+n-i}^2$
	Model 6	$h_t = \omega + \sum_{i=1}^{10} \alpha_i s_{t-i}^2 + \gamma IMP_{t-1}$	$n = 21$	$h_{t+n} = \omega + \sum_{i=1}^{10} \alpha_i s_{t+n-i}^2 + \gamma IMP_t$
	Model 7	$h_t = \omega + \sum_{i=1}^{10} \alpha_i s_{t-i}^2$	$n = 63$	$h_{t+n} = \omega + \sum_{i=1}^{10} \alpha_i s_{t+n-i}^2$
	Model 8	$h_t = \omega + \sum_{i=1}^{10} \alpha_i s_{t-i}^2 + \gamma IMP_{t-1}$	$n = 63$	$h_{t+n} = \omega + \sum_{i=1}^{10} \alpha_i s_{t+n-i}^2 + \gamma IMP_t$
AR(10) in $|s_t|$	Model 9	$h_t = \omega + \sum_{i=1}^{10} \alpha_i |s_{t-i}|$	$n = 21$	$h_{t+n} = \omega + \sum_{i=1}^{10} \alpha_i |s_{t+n-i}|$
	Model 10	$h_t = \omega + \sum_{i=1}^{10} \alpha_i |s_{t-i}| + \gamma IMP_{t-1}$	$n = 21$	$h_{t+n} = \omega + \sum_{i=1}^{10} \alpha_i |s_{t+n-i}| + \gamma IMP_t$

(continued overleaf)

Table A3.1 (*continued*)

Type of model	Model number	Formula for h_t	Value of n	Formula for h_{t+n}
	Model 11	$h_t = \omega + \sum_{i=1}^{10} \alpha_i \lvert s_{t-i} \rvert$	$n = 63$	$h_{t+n} = \omega + \sum_{i=1}^{10} \alpha_i \lvert s_{t+n-i} \rvert$
	Model 12	$h_t = \omega + \sum_{i=1}^{10} \alpha_i \lvert s_{t+n-i} \rvert + \gamma IMP_{t-1}$	$n = 63$	$h_{t+n} = \omega + \sum_{i=1}^{10} \alpha_i \lvert s_{t+n-i} \rvert + \gamma IMP_t$
Stochastic variance	Model 13	$\log h_t = \omega + SV_t$ $SV_t = \delta SV_{t-1}$	$n = 21$	$\log h_{t+n} = \omega + SV_{t+n}$ $SV_{t+n} = \delta^n SV_t$
	Model 14	$\log h_t = \omega + SV_t + \gamma IMP_{t-1}$ $SV_t = \delta SV_{t-1}$	$n = 21$	$\log h_{t+n} = \omega + SV_{t+n} + \gamma IMP_t$ $SV_{t+n} = \delta^n SV_t$
	Model 15	$\log h_t = \omega + SV_t$ $SV_t = \delta SV_{t-1}$	$n = 63$	$\log h_{t+n} = \omega + SV_{t+n}$ $SV_{t+n} = \delta^n SV_t$
	Model 16	$\log h_t = \omega + SV_t + \gamma IMP_{t-1}$ $SV_t = \delta SV_{t-1}$	$n = 63$	$\log h_{t+n} = \omega + SV_{t+n} + \gamma IMP_t$ $SV_{t+n} = \delta^n SV_t$
Historical volatility	Model 17	$h_t = (1/\sqrt{252}) HVOL21_t^2$	$n = 21$	$h_{t+n} = (1/\sqrt{252}) HVOL21_t^2$
	Model 18	$h_t = (1/\sqrt{252}) HVOL63_t^2$	$n = 63$	$h_{t+n} = (1/\sqrt{252}) HVOL63_t^2$
Implied volatility[a]	Model 19	$h_t = (1/\sqrt{252}) IMP_t^2$	$n = 21$	$h_{t+n} = (1/\sqrt{252}) IMP_t^2$
	Model 20	$h_t = (1/\sqrt{252}) IMP_t^2$	$n = 63$	$h_{t+n} = (1/\sqrt{252}) IMP_t^2$

Average combination	Model 21	$h_t = (1/10)\sum_{i=1}^{10} h_{i,t}^{[n=21]}$	$n = 21$ $h_{t+n} = (1/10)\sum_{i=1}^{10} h_{i,t+n}^{[n=21]}$
	Model 22	$h_t = (1/10)\sum_{i=1}^{10} h_{i,t}^{[n=63]}$	$n = 63$ $h_{t+n} = (1/10)\sum_{i=1}^{10} h_{i,t+n}^{[n=63]}$
Weighted combination[b]	Model 23	$h_t = (1/10)\sum_{i=1}^{10} \alpha_i h_{i,t}^{[n=21]}$	$n = 21$ $h_{t+n} = (1/10)\sum_{i=1}^{10} \alpha_i h_{i,t+n}^{[n=21]}$
	Model 24	$h_t = (1/10)\sum_{i=1}^{10} \alpha_i h_{i,t}^{[n=63]}$	$n = 63$ $h_{t+n} = (1/10)\sum_{i=1}^{10} \alpha_i h_{i,t+n}^{[n=63]}$
Modified combination[c]	Model 25	$h_t = (1/9)\sum_{i=1}^{9} h_{i,t}^{[n=21]}$	$n = 21$ $h_{t+n} = (1/9)\sum_{i=1}^{9} h_{i,t+n}^{[n=21]}$
	Model 26	$h_t = (1/9)\sum_{i=1}^{9} h_{i,t}^{[n=63]}$	$n = 63$ $h_{t+n} = (1/9)\sum_{i=1}^{9} h_{i,t+n}^{[n=63]}$

[a] The IMP_t variable is the 1-month implied volatility where $n = 21$ and the 3-month implied volatility where $n = 63$.

[b] The weighting coefficients α_i are obtained by regressing the actual historical volatility on the set of respectively 1- and 3-month volatility forecasts of models 1–20.

[c] Models 25 and 26 differ from models 21 and 22 in so far as the former exclude the least accurate respectively 1- and 3-month model among models 1–20.

APPENDIX 3.3

Table A3.2 T-test and F-test of models, out-of-sample forecasting performance[a]

	21-Day T-test	21-Day F-test	63-Day T-test	63-Day F-test
DEM/JPY	Models 17, 21	Models 11, 17, 25	Models 7[b], 18[b], 24	Model 18
GBP/DEM	Model 17	Models 11, 17, 19, 23	Model 18	Models 16, 18, 20, 26
GBP/USD	Model 17	Models 2, 11, 17	None	Models 3, 24
USD/CHF	Model 17	Model 17	None	Models 12, 18
USD/DEM	Model 17	Models 2, 11, 17	Model 18	Models 3, 4, 7, 18, 26
USD/JPY	Models 11, 17, 21	Models 1, 6, 17	Models 3, 22, 24	Models 10, 20, 22, 26

[a]Unless mentioned otherwise, results are significant at the 99% level.
[b]Result significant at the 95% level.

If a forecasting model is "good", its average forecast over the 218-day out-of-sample forecast period should be close to the actual volatility over that period. Accordingly, on top of the measures of forecasting accuracy reported in the text, we also performed a T-test between our models average forecast volatility and the actual historical volatility average over the out-of-sample forecast period with the null hypothesis that the difference between both averages is zero.

Similarly, we also tested the null hypothesis that the variance ratio between both series is equal to one. This statistic is distributed as a Fisher-Snedecor with (217,217) degrees of freedom.

APPENDIX 3.4

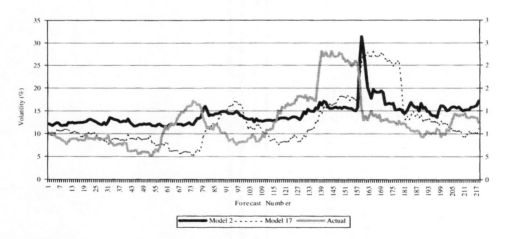

Figure A3.7   1-Month volatility forecasts for DEM/JPY

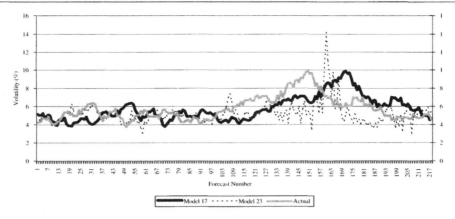

Figure A3.8   1-Month volatility forecasts for GBP/DEM

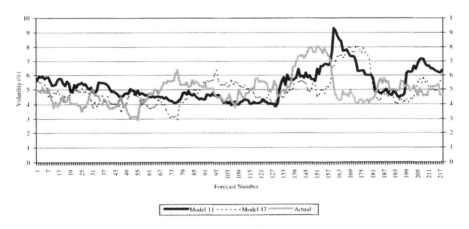

Figure A3.9   1-Month volatility forecasts for GBP/USD

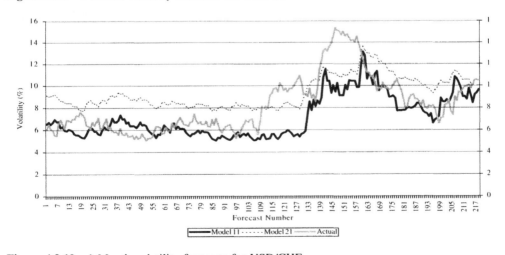

Figure A3.10   1-Month volatility forecasts for USD/CHF

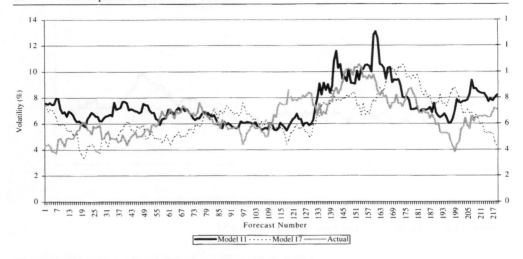

Figure A3.11   1-Month volatility forecasts for USD/DEM

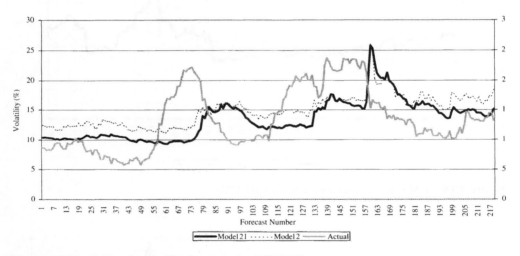

Figure A3.12   1-Month volatility forecasts for USD/JPY

4

21 Nonlinear Ways to Beat the Market[1]

GEORGE T. ALBANIS AND ROY A. BATCHELOR

ABSTRACT

This paper investigates the relative power of three information sets—lagged accounting data, lagged economic data and the combined dataset—in discriminating between high and low performing shares. The information is presented to five statistical classifiers, one linear and four nonlinear, and to two rules for pooling their results based on majority and unanimous voting. All 21 (information set × classification model) pairs have statistically and economically significant predictive power. The most powerful results come from the unanimous voting rule, using the best variables from both accounting and nonaccounting information sets. This not only makes efficient use of information, but economises on trading costs by focusing on a small set of particularly promising investments.

Keywords: Forecasting; Stock Market; Combining Forecasts; Statistical Classification; Discriminant Analysis; Recursive Partitioning; Probabilistic Neural Network

4.1 INTRODUCTION

In Albanis and Batchelor (1999b) we introduced a set of linear and nonlinear statistical classifiers, and tested their performance in identifying high-performing shares on the London Stock Exchange in the years 1993–1997 using accounting ratios as inputs. In the present paper we extend this earlier work in two ways. We investigate the benefits of combining the output from different classifiers. And we investigate the benefits of extending the inputs to include economic data and information on the history of the share price.

This paper adds to the substantial number of empirical studies in the literature that find predictability in stock returns. Typical studies are Chen *et al.* (1986), Campbell (1987), Fama and French (1988, 1989), Balvers *et al.* (1990), Ferson and Harvey (1993), Glosten *et al.* (1993) and Pesaran and Timmermann (1994, 1995). Some of these suggest several "fundamental" variables that might be able to explain the cross-section of expected returns—firm size (Banz, 1981), earnings yield (Basu, 1983), dividend yield (Fama and French, 1988), leverage (Bhandari, 1988) and the ratio of the firm's book-to-market equity (Fama and French, 1992). Other empirical studies suggest that stock returns can be predicted by means of general environmental "economic" information—the level of

---

[1] The opinions expressed herein are not necessary those of Enron.

Developments in Forecast Combination and Portfolio Choice. Edited by C. Dunis, A. Timmermann and J. Moody.
© 2001 John Wiley & Sons Ltd

interest rates and the yield spread, economic growth and inflation, recent trends in the stock market, trends about the state of the economy or about recent trends in the stock market (Chen *et al.*, 1986; Campbell, 1987; Brock *et al.*, 1992).

As trading rules based on these findings have been implemented, some further general truths about stock price behaviour have emerged. First, these relationships change over time, so a rule developed from the distant past cannot be expected to work in the current market. The correlation between the dividend yield and market returns, for example, was strong and positive in the 1980s, but has vanished in the late 1990s (Pesaran and Timmerman, 2000). Second, the relationships may be complex, involving nonlinear interactions among the variables (Hinich and Patterson, 1985; Pesaran and Timmermann, 1994; Abhyankar *et al.*, 1997). The gearing of stock returns to firm size, for example, depends on the phase of the business cycle. Third, statistical predictability need not imply financial profitability. Trading costs can eat severely into returns if the model predicts many turning points. Even in the absence of trading costs, profits in practice depend on the identification of a few "big hits". Qi and Maddala (1999) provide evidence that a neural network model can improve upon the linear regression model in terms of predictability but not in terms of profitability.

For these reasons we advocate a "robust" approach to "statistical arbitrage" (identifying outperforming shares). Rather than make point prediction, we aim only to classify shares as potentially high-performing. We use only recent (past two year's) data. We use a nontheoretical model which utilises a variety of inputs. And we allow these to be combined in a nonlinear way, using a set of (mostly) nonlinear statistical classification techniques. Specifically, as described in Albanis and Batchelor (1999b,d), we apply five statistical classification methods, namely: Linear Discriminant Analysis (LDA); Probabilistic Neural Network (PNN); Learning Vector Quantisation (LVQ); Oblique Classifier (OC1); and RIPPER Rule Induction (RRI) algorithm, plus two majority (MV) and unanimous (UV) voting rules based on their predictions.

This paper focuses on the relative value of "fundamental" accounting and nonfundamental inputs into this system. It can be regarded as a test of the incremental value of accounting data, over and above the data which is freely available to traders in the history of share prices, interest rates and monthly economic data releases. The (5 + 2 combined =) 7 classifiers × the 3 input datasets (accounting, nonaccounting and both) = 21 implementations of the system all prove to "beat the market".

The paper is organised as follows. In Section 4.2, we discuss the data and trading rules that we used in our study. In Section 4.3, we describe the classification methods that we used in our study. In Section 4.4, we discuss the methodology that we used to implement the classification methods. In Section 4.5 we report the results of experimentation and discuss the economic implications of our findings. In the final section of the paper, we discuss the practical implications of our study and the possibilities for further improvements in our methodology.

4.2   DATA AND TRADING RULES

Our target data are total returns for around 700 shares traded on the London Stock Exchange in the years 1993–1997. We calculated the share returns on an annual basis using end-month price data adjusted for dividends received during the year. The price data were collected in the month of publication of the company's annual report, with different companies having different reporting cycles. The predictions were made for the performance of these companies' shares over 1-year holding periods during the years 1993–1997. Using the price data, we calculated excess returns for each share by subtracting the corresponding total return on an equally-weighted index of all sampled shares from the individual share return.

The central task of our classification methods is to predict whether or not a share will be a high- or low-performing share in the out-of-sample years 1993–1997. The distinction between high- and low-performing shares was based on the excess returns of the shares over an equally-weighted benchmark index. Shares with excess returns in the top 25% in a given year were marked as high-performing shares (H), whereas shares in the bottom 75% in the same year were marked as low-performing shares (L).

To predict whether a particular share will be H or L in a given year, we collected previous years' accounting information published in the annual accounts of the companies and calculated 38 accounting indicators. In addition, we collected 17 economic indicators, 6-month, 1-year, 2-year and 3-year past total share and index returns information as well as information about the industrial classification of the companies. A detailed list of the variables that were selected to implement the classification methods in order to classify a new observation as H performing or L performing share over 1-year holding periods is given in Table 4.1. The company data were collected from the EXTEL service, whereas the share prices, the economic data and the industrial classification information were collected from the DATASTREAM service.

The idea of collecting the variables listed in Table 4.1 in the month of publication of the company's annual report was to develop a trading system that will be able to incorporate the impact of the public announcement of the accounting information to the share return and examine the interaction of this information with economic information, past share and index returns information, as well as information about the industrial classification of the companies. We included information about the industrial classification of the companies in our sample because we expected some relation between share returns and the nature of the activities of the company. For example, one of the most important trends in the UK economy is the continuing shift of activity to services. The service sector accounted for around 60% of the UK output in 1998 compared to 50% in 1950. On the other hand, the manufacturing sector accounted for less than 25% of the UK output in 1998 compared to 33% in 1950. Another important trend concerns the profitability of UK industrial sectors. The net rate of return on capital (NROC) for service companies was 14.0% in 1998 compared to 14.5% in 1990. On the other hand, the NROC for manufacturing companies was 11.0% in 1998 compared to 7.0% in 1990 (Warton, 1999). Including an indication of the industrial classification of the companies, we might be able to identify if these and other relevant industrial trends affect the share returns that we included in our sample. The companies that were included in our sample come from six separate sectors, namely services (S), manufacturing (M), property (P), utility (U), extractive (E) and financial (F).

Table 4.1 Initial list of the accounting and nonaccounting variables

Accounting variables	Economic variables	Past share and index returns variables	Industrial classification
Return on Capital	UK Industrial Production (UIP)	6-Month Aggregate Return (6MAR)	Manufacture (M)
PBT/TA	UK Effective Exchange Rate Index (UEERI)	6-Month All Share Index Return (6MASIR)	Financial (F)
PBT/TCE	UK Retail Price Index (URPI)	1-Year Aggregate Return (1YAR)	Service (S)
NI/TCE	UK Import Price Index (UIPI)	1-Year All Share Index Return (1YASIR)	Extractive (E)
CF/TA	UK Export Price Index (UEPI)	2-Year Aggregate Return (2YAR)	Utility (U)
CF/TCE	UK Volume of Retail Sales (UVRS)	2-Year All Share Index Return (2YASIR)	Property (P)
	UK Average Earnings Index (UAEI)	3-Year Aggregate Return (3YAR)	
Profitability	UK Unemployment Rate (UUR)	3-Year All Share Index Return (3YASIR)	
PBT/SR			
PAT/SR			
NI/SR	UK 10 Year Government Bond Yield (U10YGBY)		
CF/SR	UK Corporate Bond Yield (UCBY)		
PAT/EQ	UK Gross Reduced Yield on 20 Year Gilts (UGRY20YG)		
CF/MKBD			
	UK 3-M Discounted Treasury Bill Rate (U3MDTBR)		
Financial Leverage	UK 3-M Discounted Bank Bill Rate (U3MDBBR)		
DEBT/EQ			
DEBT/TCE	Fuel Oil Prices (Pounds/Gallon) (FOP)		
DEBT/TA			
TL/EQ	US $ TO UK £Exchange Rate (US/UKER)		
TA/EQ	German Mark to UK £Exchange Rate (GM/UKER)		
BA/MKBD	Japanese Yen to UK £Exchange Rate (JY/UKER)		
Investment			
P/E			
DY			
EY			
BE/ME			

Growth (%)
TA
PAT
PBT
EPS
MKBD
SR
Short-term
  Liquidity
CA/CL
CL/TA
CL/EQ
Return on
  Investment
NI/TA
PAT/TA
Efficiency
SR/TA
DRS/SR
Risk
PBT/CL
PAT/CL
NI/CL
CF/CL

Notes: PBT, Profit Before Taxes; TA, Total Assets; TCE, Total Capital Employed; CF, Cash Flow; PAT, Profit after Taxes; SR, Sales Revenue; NI, Net Income; EQ, Shareholders' Equity; MKBD, Market Capitalisation at Balance Sheet Date; DEBT, Debt; TL, Total Liabilities; BA, Book Assets; P/E, Price/Earnings Ratio; EY, Earnings Yield; DY, Dividend Yield; BE, Book Equity; ME, Market Equity; EPS, Earnings Per Share; CA, Current Assets; CL, Current Liabilities; DRS, Debtors.

Based on the variables presented in Table 4.1, we aimed to find rules that classify a particular share as H or L performing share using the two previous years' data to predict the next year. For example, to predict relative excess returns for 1993, we first trained the classification methods on the two preceding years 1991, 1992 and tested them on the data available on 1993. We then moved the implementation one year ahead and used information available from 1992, 1993 to predict 1994, and so on. We use only two previous years of data to predict relative excess returns for the next year because we believe that only recent accounting and nonaccounting historical information may be relevant to predict relative excess returns in the next year.

4.3   CLASSIFICATION METHODS

One consequence of the rapid development of computer power in the 1980s was the development of computer-intensive classification algorithms. These include among others neural networks, recursive partitioning methods and rule induction techniques. Computer-intensive methods can be used to address the problem of stock predictability in the form of statistical classification. Statistical classification is also well known as supervised learning. Supervised learning is a form of learning from a sample of previously known objects. Each object is described by a set of observations and a class label. Given that the objects are known to come from one of C_{jt} distinct classes ($j = 1, 2, \ldots, k$) of observations, we wish to find functions of these observations that will distinguish the classes, and that will enable us to assign a new object to one of these classes on the basis of m measured characteristics, x, associated with this object.

In our application, we are particularly interested in whether a particular share will be classified as H or L excess return share based on accounting information, economic variables, past share and index returns information as well as information about the industrial classification of the companies included in the sample. Let us assume that y_{it} is the 1-year-ahead excess return on some share i bought at time t, and x_{it} is the i vector of information attributes known at time t. The idea is to apply a classification method to assign y_{it} to one of the two classes C_{jt} ($j =$ H, L) depending on whether or not this return is above or below the 25% threshold percentile that has been decided after ranking the returns in excess of an equally-weighted index. The model input is the vector x_{it} of variables that represent useful information. It is obvious that there are two distinct objectives here: first, class separation; and second, classification of future shares as H or L. The class separation is handled through the use of a discriminant function. On the other hand, the classification of future shares is handled through a classification rule.

Advances in theory and computing power over the past decades have led to a large number of classification methods. For this study, we chose five heterogeneous classifiers as representatives of five different model families. These classifiers are: LDA, PNN, LVQ, RRI and OC1. These classifiers are described in more detail below.

4.3.1   Linear Discriminant Analysis

According to the LDA algorithm, linear combinations of the independent variables can be formed and used as a basis for classifying patterns into one of the classes. In the case of two classes H and L, we use a linear combination of the observations, and choose the coefficients so that the ratio of the difference of the means of the linear combination in the two classes to the variance is maximised. Let us denote the linear combination $F = \alpha'x$. If we assume that the covariance matrices in the two classes are equal so that $C_H = C_L = C$ and $\overline{x}_H, \overline{x}_L, S$ denote the sample means and the sample standard deviation S in H, L, respectively, then we have to choose α to maximise (Lachenbruch, 1975):

$$\phi = \frac{(\alpha'\overline{x}_H - \alpha'\overline{x}_L)^2}{\alpha'S\alpha} \tag{4.1}$$

Differentiating ϕ with respect to α we get $\alpha = kS^{-1}(\overline{x}_H - \overline{x}_L)$ for an arbitrary constant multiplying factor k which is usually taken as one (Lachenbruch, 1975). According to this algorithm, we assign an individual to H if $F = (\overline{x}_H - \overline{x}_L)'S^{-1}x$ is closer to $\overline{F}_H = (\overline{x}_H - \overline{x}_L)'S^{-1}\overline{x}_H$ and to L if F is closer to $\overline{F}_L = (\overline{x}_H - \overline{x}_L)'S^{-1}\overline{x}_L$. The midpoint of the interval between $\overline{F}_H$ and $\overline{F}_L$ is given as follows (Lachenbruch, 1975):

$$\frac{(\overline{F}_H + \overline{F}_L)}{2} = \frac{1}{2}(\overline{x}_H - \overline{x}_L)'S^{-1}(\overline{x}_H + \overline{x}_L) \tag{4.2}$$

F is closer to $\overline{F}_H$ if $|F - \overline{F}_H| < |F - \overline{F}_L|$ which occurs if $F > \frac{1}{2}(\overline{F}_H + \overline{F}_L)$ since $\overline{F}_H > \overline{F}_L$.

Figure 4.1 illustrates the LDA algorithm for the case of two predictor variables: Price–Earnings (P/E) ratio and Book Equity to Market Equity (BE/ME) ratio. As we can see, the LDA imposes two elliptical distributions over the means of the two classes. The line connecting points of equal distance from the two neighbouring means defines a linear partition of the space into H and L regions (Albanis and Batchelor 1999c,d).

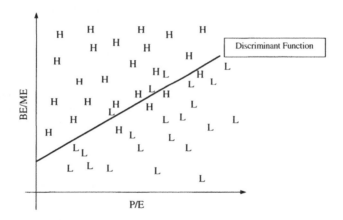

Figure 4.1 Linear Discriminant Analysis

The LDA model has been applied successfully in a wide variety of applications including financial distress prediction (Altman, 1968), bond ratings prediction (Kaplan and Urwitz, 1979), etc. Generally, this algorithm is favoured if there are linearities in the data. However, the LDA model has been criticised extensively in the literature because the validity of its results hinges on restrictive assumptions (Pinches, 1980). One assumption that is particularly important for LDA analysis is that the independent variables, in our case financial ratios, must have a multivariate normal distribution. This requirement, however, has frequently been violated. Empirical evidence seems to indicate that most ratio distributions are either highly skewed, flat and/or dominated by outliers (Deakin, 1976). On the other hand, remedial measures taken to improve the multivariate normality are often inadequate (Lachenbruch *et al.*, 1973). Despite these criticisms, however, this algorithm is still used in a variety of applications because it offers statistical simplicity and an easy interpretation (Albanis and Batchelor, 1999b).

4.3.2   Probabilistic Neural Network

The PNN algorithm is a well-known representative of the family of nonlinear models. The algorithm starts by positioning a separate distribution over each individual data point. Therefore, we can see the algorithm as a generalisation of the LDA algorithm that imposes two elliptical distributions around the means of the two groups. According to the PNN algorithm, we classify x into class H if $p_H c_H d_H(x) > p_L c_L d_L(x)$ where $p_H (p_L)$ is the prior probability of membership in the class H (L), $c_H (c_L)$ is the cost of misclassification into class H (L), and $d_H(x)[d_L(x)]$ is the Probability Density Function (PDF) of class H (L), respectively. Parzen (1962) developed a nonparametric technique for estimating a univariate PDF from a random sample. Cacoullos (1966) extended Parzen's method to the multivariate case.

Let us assume that we have to assign a new observation x_{it} to one of the classes H or L. The distance of x_{it} from H is the average of distances from all individual members x_{jt-i} that belong to class H. If we assume that m_H is the number of members in class H, then the average of distances of x_{it} from all x_{jt-i} can be represented as a superposition of potential functions $f(x_{it}, x_{jt-i})$ over samples of $d_H(x)$ as follows (Albanis and Batchelor 1999d,e):

$$d_H(x_{it}) = \frac{1}{m_H} \sum_{j=1}^{m_H} f(x_{it}, x_{jt-i}) \tag{4.3}$$

Although there is considerable freedom in choosing the potential function, the function most often employed is the Gaussian function that has desirable computational properties. Using the Gaussian function, we can represent the density function as follows (Albanis and Batchelor 1999d,e):

$$d_H(x_{it}) = \frac{1}{\sqrt{2\pi}\sigma m_H} \sum_{j=1}^{m_H} \exp\left(-\frac{\|x_{it} - x_{jt-i}\|^2}{2\sigma^2}\right) \tag{4.4}$$

The potential function shows the decreasing influence of a sample point x_{it} upon a point x_{jt-i} as the distance $d(x_{it}, x_{jt-i})$ between the points increases. The average of these potentials from samples of class H at a point x_{it} constitutes a measure of the degree of membership of point x_{it} in class H. The scaling parameter σ defines the width of the area of influence and should decrease as the sample size increases (Meisel, 1972). It is obvious that the selection of the smoothing parameter σ can be crucial for the positioning of a mixture of identical Gaussian distributions at each of the training sample points. If the value of σ is too small, then individual training cases may exert too much influence, thus eliminating the gain of aggregate information. On the other hand, if the value of σ

is too large, then the excess blurring may distort the density estimate because important details of the density are lost (Masters, 1995).

The original PNN architecture was proposed by Specht (1990). Specht showed that the algorithm could be split into a large number of simple processes each of which has its own dedicated task and most of which could run in parallel. A graphical illustration of the PNN architecture is given in Figure 4.2. As we can see in Figure 4.2, the network consists of four layers: an input layer, a pattern layer, a summation layer and an output layer. The input layer has as many neurons as the inputs. The pattern layer has one neuron for each training case. Each pattern neuron computes a distance measure between the input and the training case represented by that neuron and then subjects that measure to the neuron's activation function. The summation layer has one neuron for each class. Each summation neuron sums the pattern layer neurons corresponding to numbers of that summation neuron's class and estimates the density functions for classes H and L, respectively. The output neuron is a discriminator that decides which of its inputs from the summation units is the maximum (Masters, 1995).

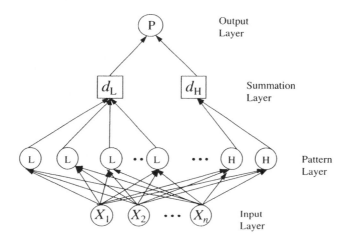

Figure 4.2 Probabilistic Neural Network

The PNN has been proposed in the literature as an alternative technique to LDA for a variety of real-world applications, including financial distress, bond ratings and stock selection (Albanis, 1998a,b; Albanis and Batchelor, 1999a–c). As opposed to LDA, the PNN does not suffer from departures from multivariate normality and equality of the group covariance matrices. However, the PNN has some other drawbacks: first, the performance of the network depends on having a thorough and representative training set due to the way it uses the potential functions around clusters of the training data; second, the entire training set must be stored each time an unknown case is classified (Masters, 1995). This results in large memory requirements and considerably slows the execution speed; and third, the success of the PNN paradigm is at a cost: an inherent inability to explain in a comprehensible form the process by which a given decision or output generated by the model has been reached. These criticisms, however, are not relevant for our application because the size as well as the dimensionality of the data ensure a thorough and representative training set that does not particularly slow the execution speed. On the other hand, the main concern for our application is classification accuracy and profitability rather than explanation of the decision generated by the model.

4.3.3 Learning Vector Quantisation

The LVQ algorithm assumes that a mixture of distributions rather than a single elliptical distribution can approximate the distribution of each class. Therefore, we can see this algorithm as a generalisation of the LDA algorithm that imposes two elliptical distributions around the means of the two groups and maybe as a special case of the PNN that imposes a number of distributions equal to the training sample size. This idea is illustrated in Figure 4.3 for the case of two predictor variables: P/E and BE/ME. As we can see in Figure 4.3, the data points are centred on distinct clusters of observations corresponding to H and L performing shares. The points around the centre of each cluster have equal likelihood in that cluster. If we connect the points with equal distance from the neighbouring means we have a nonlinear partition of the space into H and L regions (Albanis and Batchelor, 1999d,e).

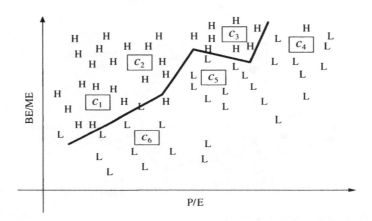

Figure 4.3   Learning Vector Quantisation

According to the LVQ algorithm, a finite number of prototypes are chosen in the input space. During the learning process each sample is compared to all prototypes and the nearest one is selected. If the class of the selected prototype is the same as the class of the input sample, then the selected prototype is moved in the direction of the input sample. On the other hand, if the class of the selected prototype is not the same as the class of the input sample, then the selected prototype is moved in the opposite direction. During the test phase there is no modification of the location of the prototype selection. The class label of the selected prototype gives the class of the input sample (Albanis and Batchelor, 1999a).

Let p_i be a number of free parameter vectors that are placed in the input space to approximate various domains of the input vector x_{it} by their quantised values. According to the LVQ algorithm, the x_{it} is decided to belong to the same class to which the nearest

p_i belongs. Let us denote the nearest p_i to x_{it} by p_n. This can be written as follows (Kohonen *et al.*, 1995):

$$n = \arg \min_{it} \{\|x_{it} - p_i\|\} \qquad (4.5)$$

The values for the p_i that minimise the misclassification errors in the above classification rule can be found as asymptotic values in the following learning process (Kohonen *et al.*, 1995):

$$p_{n(t+1)} = p_{nt} + \alpha_t[x_{it} - p_{nt}] \quad \text{if } x_{it} \text{ and } p_n \text{ belong to the same class}$$

$$p_{n(t+1)} = p_{nt} - \alpha_t[x_{it} - p_{nt}] \quad \text{if } x_{it} \text{ and } p_n \text{ belong to different classes} \qquad (4.6)$$

$$p_{i(t+1)} = p_{it} \qquad\qquad\qquad \text{for } i \neq n$$

where x_{it} is the input sample, p_{it} are sequences of the p_i in the discrete-time domain and α_t is a parameter that may be a constant or decrease monotonically with time.

The algorithm described in (4.6) is known as the LVQ1 algorithm. Kohonen proposed the optimised LVQ1 (oLVQ1) algorithm in such a way that an individual learning rate α_{it} is assigned to each p_i. Taking into account this modification, we can write (4.6) as follows (Kohonen *et al.*, 1995):

$$p_{n(t+1)} = [1 - h_t \alpha_{nt}]p_{nt} + h_t \alpha_{nt} x_{it} \qquad (4.7)$$

where $h_t = +1$ if the classification is correct and $h_t = -1$ if the classification is incorrect.

According to Kohonen *et al.* (1995), the optimal value of α_{nt} is determined by the following recursion:

$$\alpha_{nt} = \frac{\alpha_{n(t-1)}}{1 + h_t \alpha_{n(t-1)}} \qquad (4.8)$$

Although the LVQ1 algorithm performs both a quantisation and a classification task, neither of them is optimal. Specifically, the vector quantisation is better if the classification task is not achieved and the boundaries between classes do not approximate the optimal Bayes boundary. In order to overcome this problem, Kohonen *et al.* (1995) suggested two improved versions of the LVQ1 algorithm, named LVQ2 and LVQ3. We have to mention, however, that our preliminary results suggest that there are no significant differences in the classification performance of the LVQ1, LVQ2 and LVQ3 algorithms. More significant improvements in classification performance may result after implementing the optimised oLVQ1 version of the algorithm.

4.3.4 Oblique Classifier

Decision trees are hierarchical classification structures that recursively partition a set of observations. They represent a way to describe rules underlying data. A decision tree is induced on a training set that consists of examples. Each example can be described by a set of predictor variables and a class label. The concept underlying the data is the true mapping between the predictor variables and the class label (Murthy, 1997). A new example x_{it} is classified by passing it through the tree starting at the root node. Each time, a test is applied to the attributes of x_{it} on the tree. The result of this test determines the next edge on the tree where this example should be placed. The label at the leaf node at which x_{it} ends up is outputted as its classification (Hand, 1997). The tree misclassifies the new example if the predicted classification is not the same as the example's class label.

Figure 4.4 gives a graphical illustration of a decision tree that classifies shares into H and L classes for the case of two predictor variables: P/E and BE/ME. A hypothetical sequential representation of this tree is given in Figure 4.5. To classify a new share at the top or root of the tree, we first test whether the P/E ratio is greater than 0.2. If the P/E ratio is not greater than 0.2, then the share is H. If the P/E ratio is greater than 0.2, then we note whether the BE/ME is less than 0.7. If the BE/ME is greater than 0.7, then the share is H. If it is less than 0.7, then we note whether the linear combination BE/ME-3(P/E) is less than 0.2, and so on. Following this path, we work down the tree, recursively testing conditions of the predictor variables at the nodes of the tree, and decide which

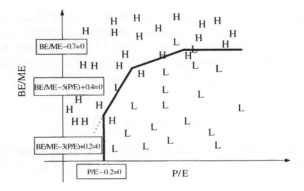

Figure 4.4   An imaginary decision tree with oblique splits

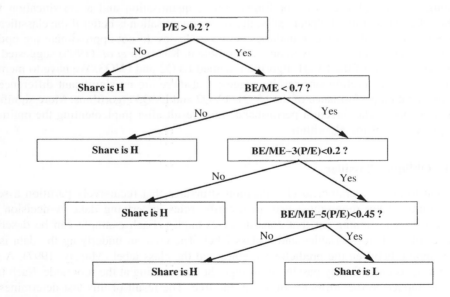

Figure 4.5   A sequential representation of a decision tree with oblique splits

path to follow depending on whether or not the conditions of the predictor variables are satisfied. As we can see in the tree structure presented in Figure 4.5, each nonterminal node is associated with a single variable and a partition of that variable into two classes determines which path a new example should follow.

When building a tree, we have to decide the partitioning criteria that determine which variable should be used at each internal node, which internal node should be split and what would be the nature of the split. The usual approach to solve these problems is to use an "impurity" index at each node of the tree. The "impurity" index is a measure of the differences between the probabilities of belonging to each class. For example, let us assume there are 20 examples at an internal node and that 10 of these examples are from class H while the other 10 examples are from class L. Furthermore, let us assume that all examples from class H have P/E values less than 0.2, whereas all examples from class L have P/E values greater than 0.2. It is obvious that this node is relatively impure because it has equal numbers from each of the two classes. However, if we decide to split this node and build the tree further by splitting this node using P/E at the value 0.2, then we have two offspring nodes that are perfectly pure since one would have only class H examples and the other would have only class L examples (Hand, 1997).

Several impurity measures have been suggested in the literature. These include among others the Information Index, the Gini Index, Max Minority, Sum Minority, Sum of Variances, etc. A very effective impurity index is also the Twoing Rule that was proposed by Breiman *et al.* (1994). This impurity index is given as follows:

$$TV = \left(\frac{|N_L|}{n}\right)\left(\frac{|N_R|}{n}\right)\left(\sum_{i=1}^{k}\left|\frac{CL_L}{|N_L|} - \frac{CR_H}{|N_R|}\right|\right)^2 \tag{4.9}$$

where TV is the Twoing value, $|N_L|$ is the number of examples on the left of a split at node v, $|N_R|$ is the number of examples on the right of a split at node v, n is the total number of examples at node v, CL_L is the number of examples in category L on the left of the split and CR_H is the number of examples in category H on the right of the split.

Many variants of decision trees have been introduced in the last decade. Two well-known variants of decision trees that have been proposed in the literature are axis parallel trees and oblique decision trees. Axis parallel trees use tests at each internal node of the form $x_{it} > k$, where x_{it} is one of the attributes and k is a constant. These tests are equivalent to axis-parallel hyperplanes in the attribute space. On the other hand, oblique decision trees use tests at each internal node of the form (Murthy, 1997):

$$\sum_{i=1}^{m}\alpha_{it}x_{it} + \alpha_{m+1} = 0 \tag{4.10}$$

where m is the number of attributes and α_{it} are real-valued coefficients. These tests are equivalent to hyperplanes at an oblique orientation of the axis.

A very popular decision tree algorithm is the oblique classifier (OC1) of Murthy (1997). This algorithm finds first the best axis-parallel split at a node before looking for an oblique split. It uses the oblique split only if it improves the best axis-parallel split. The equation of the current hyperplane Y at a node of a decision tree is equivalent to (4.10). If we substitute a point T_{jt} from the training set into the equation for Y, we get (Murthy, 1997):

$$\sum_{i=1}^{m} \alpha_{it} x_{it} + \alpha_{m+1} = G_{jt} \qquad (4.11)$$

The sign of G_{jt} tells us whether the point T_{jt} is above or below the hyperplane. If $G_{jt} > 0$ then T_{jt} is above Y. If Y splits the training set perfectly, then all points belonging to the same category will have the same sign for T_{jt}. OC1 adjusts the coefficients of Y by treating the coefficient α_{mt} as a variable and all the other coefficients as constants. Then, T_{jt} can be viewed as a function of α_{mt}. The condition that T_{jt} is above Y is equivalent to (Murthy, 1997):

$$G_{jt} > 0, \quad \alpha_{mt} > \frac{\alpha_{mt} - G_{jt}}{x_{jm}} = F_{jt} \qquad (4.12)$$

According to this definition for F_{jt}, the point T_{jt} is above Y if $\alpha_{mt} > F_{jt}$ and below otherwise. The problem with this approach, however, is to find a value for α_{mt} that satisfies as many of the constraints as possible. A very effective solution to this problem is provided by Murthy (1997).

Decision tree algorithms have a number of desirable properties: first, they can model a wide range of data distributions since only a few assumptions are made about the model and the data distribution; second, they are based on the hierarchical decomposition which implies better use of available features and computational efficiency in classification; third, they are very able to handle complex interactions between variables; fourth, they perform classification by a sequence of simple, easy to understand, tests whose semantics are intuitively clear to domain experts; fifth, they reduce the volume of data by transforming them in a more compact form which preserves the essential characteristics and provides an accurate summary. However, the main disadvantage of decision trees is that they tend to grow very large for realistic applications and are thus difficult to interpret by humans. Hence, there has been some research in transforming decision trees into other representations.

4.3.5 Ripper Rule Induction

Rule induction algorithms have been an important area of research in the Artificial Intelligence (AI) science. Although a variety of other representations have also been used in machine learning, a great deal of research has focused on rule induction for the following reasons: first, rules are often easier for people to understand; second, certain types of prior knowledge can be easily incorporated in the learning process; and third, rule induction techniques overcome the use of the limited-knowledge propositional logic formalism and they can be easily extended to the first order logic (Cohen, 1995). This property should be considered particularly important because one of the well-established findings of AI and machine learning is that the use of domain knowledge is essential for achieving intelligent behaviour.

Most of the rule induction algorithms use an overfit-and-simplify learning strategy to handle noisy data. According to this strategy a hypothesis is formed by first growing a rule set which overfits the data and then simplifying or pruning the rule set. A variety of methods have been proposed in the literature to prune rule sets. One well-studied method is known as Reduced Error Pruning (REP), proposed by Pagallo and Haussler (1990) and Brunk and Pazzani (1991). According to this method the training data is split into a growing set and a pruning set and a rule set is formed that overfits the growing set using some heuristic method. The rule set is then simplified at successive stages by applying pruning operators that reduce the error on the pruning set. This process terminates when applying any pruning operator would increase the error on the pruning set.

Empirical evidence suggests that REP improves generalisation performance on noisy data. Cohen (1993, 1995), on the other hand, showed that REP is computationally expensive for large datasets. He proposed instead an alternative method called Grow. Applying this method to a set of benchmark problems, he showed that Grow is competitive with REP with respect to error rates and is an order of magnitude faster. A different finding, however, was reported by Cameron-Jones (1994) who showed that Grow systematically overfits the target concept on noisy data and this has an adverse effect on Grow's time complexity.

Furnkranz and Widmer (1994) proposed a novel learning algorithm called Incremental Reduced Error Pruning (IREP). According to this algorithm a rule set is built in a greedy fashion, one rule at a time. After a rule is found, all examples covered by the rule are deleted. This process terminates when no positive examples exist or when the rule found by IREP has a large error rate.

Cohen (1995) implemented the IREP algorithm by randomly partitioning the uncovered examples into a growing set and a pruning set. The process of building a rule begins by greedily adding conditions to an empty conjunction of conditions and considers adding to this any condition of the form $x_{it} \leqslant \theta$ or $x_{it} \geqslant \theta$ where x_{it} is a continuous variable and θ is some value for x_{it} that exists in the training data. The building of the rule is continued until all positive examples are covered in the growing dataset. After the rule is grown, it is then simplified by deleting any final sequence of conditions from the rule so as to improve its performance on the pruning dataset. During this phase of pruning, *ad hoc* heuristic measures are used to guide the greedy search for new conditions and simplifications. The set of rules can be interpreted as a disjunction of conjunctions that formulate the testable hypothesis as follows: a stock is considered to be H if and only if

$$(x_{it1} \leqslant 0.8 \quad \text{and} \quad x_{it2} \geqslant 0.8) \quad \text{or}$$

$$(x_{it1} \geqslant 0.2 \quad \text{and} \quad x_{it2} \leqslant 0.4, \dots, x_{itm} \leqslant 0.6) \quad \text{or}$$

$$(x_{it3} \leqslant 0.7 \quad \text{and} \quad x_{it4} \geqslant 0.1)$$

Once the rule set is complete, it is then optimised through multiple passes so as to reduce its size and improve its fit to the training data. Each optimisation pass involves constructing for each rule R_i two alternative rules: a replacement rule and a revision rule. The replacement rule can be formed by growing and then pruning R_i so as to minimise error of the entire rule set on the pruning data. The revision rule can be formed in a similar fashion as the replacement rule, the only difference is to add conditions to R_i greedily rather than the empty rule. After both the replacement and the revised rule are formed, a decision can be made as to whether the final theory should include the revised rule, the replacement rule or the original rule. This decision can be taken by inserting a variant of R_i into the rule set and then starting to delete rules that decrease the Total Description Length (TDL) of the rules and examples. The TDL of the examples and the simplified rule set can then be used to compare variants of R_i. Finally, rules can be added to cover any remaining positive examples. Cohen called the new algorithm RIPPER.

Figure 4.6 gives an example of rules developed by the RRI algorithm. It should be mentioned that, despite the fact that rule induction techniques offer interpretable rules, they are not expert systems. The knowledge engineer has still a substantial amount of work to perform in order to generate rules that perform well and are also sensible so that they can enhance the knowledge of domain experts. Despite this weakness, however, rule induction systems result in simple rules that are preferable to other machine learning representations.

Initial Hypothesis:
1. High: **EPS(%)**>=11.19, **DEBT/TA**<=13.91, **PAT(%)**<=34.44, **DEBT/TA**>=3.16, **PBT/TA**>=8.51, **NI/TCE**<=19.55
2. High: **P/E**<=888.65, **D/Y**>=6.16, **CF/TA**<=1.36, **CF/TA**>=- 2.48
3. High: **CF/TA**>=8.88, **EPS(%)**>=8.66, **TA(%)**<=12.56
4. High: **PBT/CL**<=-14.55
5. High: **CF/MKBD**>=7.50, **P/E**>=931.05, **MKBD(%)**>=94.63, **CA/CL**<=208.08
6. High: **EY**>=7.56, **EPS(%)**<=-33.96
7. High: **EY**>=7.51, **MKBD(%)**>=31.50,**TA(%)**<=10.48, **P/E**>=1260.3
8. High: **EPS(%)**>=26.83, **SR/TA**>=152.56, **CF/SR**<=1.55
9. High: **PBT/CL**>=23.66, **PAT/TA**<=6.82, **CL/EQ**>=47.67, **SR/TA**<=105.26
10. High: **CF/TCE**>=3.20, **NI/TCE**>=6.89, **PAT/TA**>=4.68
11. High: **PBT/CL**<=6.60, **PAT/TA**>=1.18, **TA(%)**<=-0.69
12. High: **MKBD(%)**<=-30.54, **PBT/TA**<=0.47, **EPS(%)**>=-106.9, **DEBT/TA**>=13.05
13. High: **PBT/CL**>=33.22, **CL/EQ**>=48.37, **PBT/CL**>=63.04, **BE/ME**>=26.32
14. High: **DEBT/EQ**<=16.26, **EY**>=8.33, **PAT/TA**<=7.53, **SR(%)**>=2.94
15. High: **SR(%)**<=-4.76, **NI/TCE**>=10.28, **NI/TCE**<=11.30
16. High: **PAT/SR**<=3.01, **PBT/CL**>=13.12, **EPS(%)**<=-32.56
17. High: **CF/TA**>=10.45, **TA/EQ**>=272.77, **TA(%)**<=5.78
18. Low: True

Figure 4.6   Rules developed by RRI

4.4   IMPLEMENTATION

One problem in practical applications of classification methods concerns the normalisation of the inputs. For some classification methods such as PNN, the input variables must be normalised so as to be commensurate with the loss function practical limits. Although normalisation is not always a necessary prerequisite for LDA and RRI, we decided that the comparison of the models might be more fair after applying the same data preprocessing technique for each individual classification method. On the other hand, our preliminary results suggested that normalisation of the data does not affect the discriminating power of methods such as LDA and RRI whose loss function does not depend necessarily upon normalisation. On the opposite side, we found some evidence of improvements in accuracy after normalising the data for RRI. Therefore, the accounting data were normalised in the range $(0,1)$.

To make the classification methods more robust and smooth the effect of outliers, we also applied data winsorisation and trigonometric transformations of the variables. We winsorised the input variables by ranking all observations on each individual variable in a given year, and setting values in the lower and upper 5% tails equal to the 5th and 95th percentile values. Then, we transformed the data by applying trigonometric transformations of the variables. A more detailed description of these transformations can be found in Acton (1970). These transformations were applied to the predictor variables but not in the target data. It is obvious that the same transformations were applied in the training and test sets.

One of the desirable end products of discriminant analysis is the identification of good predictor variables. A standard methodology that has been applied in the literature to identify an optimal subset of ratios for the LDA model is based on a stepwise variable selection algorithm using criteria which eliminate overfitting of variables, thereby improving the model's classification of out-of-sample cases and its robustness over time. The most commonly used criterion for stepwise variable selection is minimisation of Wilk's lambda. *Lambda* is the ratio of the within-groups sum of squares to the total sum of squares. Values of *lambda* close to 1 indicate that group means do not appear to be different. On the other hand, values of *lambda* close to 0 indicate that group means do appear to be different. The significance of the change in *Wilk's lambda* when a variable is entered or removed by the model is based on the F statistic. The variable with the largest F (or smallest value of Wilk's lambda) enters the model. The F value for the change in *Wilk's lambda* when the second variable is added to the model is given as follows:

$$F = \left(\frac{n - g - m}{g - 1} \right) \left(\frac{1 - \lambda_{m+1}/\lambda_m}{\lambda_{m+1}/\lambda_m} \right) \tag{4.13}$$

where m = number of independent variables, n = total number of cases, g = number of groups, λ_m = Wilk's lambda before adding the variable, λ_{m+1} = Wilk's lambda after including the variable.

There are no equivalent standard procedures for avoiding overfitting in the PNN, LVQ, RRI and OC1 algorithms. In these cases, we follow the methodology suggested by Tyree and Long (1996) and Albanis and Batchelor (1998a,b). That is, the algorithms are implemented using all 38 ratios and the misclassification rate is recorded. A single variable is then removed and the algorithms are implemented again. If the misclassification rate is lower, the variable is removed permanently. Otherwise, it is returned back to the pool of variables to be included in the final model. This procedure is repeated for each individual variable.

We applied this methodology given the different types of information we used to implement our classification methods. For example, if the implementation was based on either accounting or nonaccounting information only, we selected the best subset of variables as follows: initially, we implemented the classification methods to predict the out-of-sample year 1993 using either all accounting variables or all nonaccounting variables at the same time and we recorded the misclassification rate. In the next step, we removed a single variable and we implemented the classification methods again. If the misclassification rate was lower, we removed the variable permanently; otherwise, we returned this variable back to the pool of variables to be included in the final model. Then, we repeated this procedure for each individual variable. We used the selected best subset of variables to predict the next target years 1994–1997 while rolling the model one year ahead and using two previous years' data to predict the next out-of-sample year.

However, if the implementation of the classification methods was based on mixing accounting and nonaccounting variables at the same time, we thought that the above selection procedure might not be efficient because the large number of variables from both subsets of information might affect the selection of variables due to excessive overfitting. Therefore, we adapted this methodology as follows: after selecting the best accounting variables using a complete selection procedure, we added to them all the nonaccounting variables and we implemented the classification methods to predict 1993. We then removed one variable from the nonaccounting variables and we implemented the classification methods again. If the misclassification rate was lower, the nonaccounting variable was removed permanently as before. Otherwise, this variable was returned back to the pool of the variables to be included in the final model. This procedure was then repeated for each individual nonaccounting variable. As before, we used the selected best subset of variables to predict the next out-of-sample years 1994–1997 while rolling the model one year ahead and using two previous years' of data to predict the next out-of-sample year. We implemented the above variable selection procedures for all five classification methods to make the comparisons of the models equal. We have to mention, however, that the opposite experiment of selecting the best subset of nonaccounting variables first, and then adding to them the accounting variables and repeating the variable selection procedure, was also attempted but the models were not proven robust.

After selecting an optimal subset of variables for each particular classifier, we implemented them separately using two years of data to predict the next year. For example, to predict relative excess returns for 1993, we first trained the classification methods on the two preceding years 1991, 1992 using cross-validation procedures to find the optimal values of parameters for each individual classifier. After selecting optimal parameters for each individual classifier, we applied them to predict the out-of-sample year 1993. We then moved the implementation one year ahead and used information available from 1992, 1993 to predict 1994, and so on.

The cross-validation procedures that we applied to select optimal parameters for each particular classifier include the leave-one-out method and other similar rotation procedures. According to the leave-one-out method, a single element is held out from the training set and the remaining $n - 1$ elements are used to build the classification rule which is then used to classify the element that was left out. In the next step, this single element is returned into the training set and a different element is removed. The classifier is then retrained using the remaining $n - 1$ elements and tested on the new element that was left out. By repeating this process for any individual element in the training set, every known element is used to both train and test. The proportion of elements misclassified from each class gives a direct estimate of the actual error rate in that class. A close relative of the leave-one-out method is the rotation method. According to this method, a number m of mutually exclusive subsets are defined. The $m - 1$ subsets are used to build the classification rule which is then used to classify the subset that was left out. Repeating this procedure m times, all observations are tested out-of-sample.

After implementing the models, we found that all classifiers were more accurate to classify L performing shares than H performing shares. In order to increase the classification accuracy for H performing shares, we changed the loss functions to incorporate prior probabilities and misclassification costs. For example, in the case of the PNN classifier we classified an unknown share with measurement vector x_{it} as a H performing share if the following inequality was true:

$$\left(\frac{p_H}{p_L}\right)\left(\frac{c_H}{c_L}\right) \tilde{f}^H(x) > \tilde{f}^L(x) \tag{4.14}$$

where p_H is the prior probability for H performing shares, p_L is the prior probability for L performing shares, c_H is the cost of misclassification for H performing shares and c_L is the cost of misclassification for L performing shares. A tactic more or less similar to the above was followed for the other classifiers as well. The prior probabilities and misclassification costs for each particular classifier were determined after implementing the classifiers in the training set.

We also investigate two voting schemes to combine component classifiers: the MV and UV schemes. In both cases, the voters have equal weight in their predictions. Assuming that we have g_{it} $(i = 5)$ classifiers and C_{jt} $(j = H, L)$ classes, we assign a share to the H class if the following conditions hold:

$$V_t = \sum_{i=1}^{5} w_{it} g_{it}^{H} \geqslant V_t^* \tag{4.15}$$

$$w_{it} \geqslant 0, \quad \sum_{i=1}^{n} w_{it} = 1 \tag{4.16}$$

where w_{it} are weights on each prediction, g_{it}^{H} is the estimate of classifier i for class H and V_{it}^* is a threshold value: $V_{it}^* = 3$ if the MV rule is applied, whereas $V_{it}^* = 5$ if the UV rule is applied. If (4.15) does not hold, then we assign a share to class L. As there is no *a priori* reason to favour one voter over another, weights are taken as equal, $w_j = 1/5$. This is simple voting. In this experiment, we have not applied weighted voting schemes because the in-sample performance of the classifiers was broadly similar.

Skalak (1997) proposed three design criteria for building composite classifiers: accuracy, diversity and efficiency. A brief explanation of these criteria is given below.

(1) The accuracy criterion ensures that the component classifiers that are used to build the composite classifier are also accurate when applied individually to make predictions. If the predictions of the component classifiers that are being combined are not accurate, then the ultimate prediction of the composite classifier might not be highly accurate.
(2) The diversity criterion ensures that the component classifiers make diverse errors when applied individually to make predictions. If the predictions of the component classifiers are exactly the same, then a combination of these predictions will not improve the predictive accuracy of the composite classifier. On the other hand, if the individual components make some different predictions, then there is a hope that combining their predictions using the appropriate mechanisms might improve the predictive accuracy of the composite architecture.
(3) As far as concerns the efficiency of the composite classifier, two principles should be taken into account: first, we have to prefer fewer component classifiers over more; and second, we have to prefer computationally inexpensive ones over expensive ones. These principles ensure that the composite classifier is not only accurate but also fast in reaching the ultimate prediction.

Taking into account these criteria, we combined the five classifiers, namely LDA, PNN, LVQ, OC1 and RRI, to predict high-performing shares for three main reasons: first, all classifiers were found accurate when they were applied individually; second, these classifiers are representatives of different model families and this ensures diverse component models in our composite architecture; and third, we prefer fewer components over more to keep the computational complexity as low as possible. Furthermore, we used the MV and

UV schemes to combine the five classifiers because they are simple and can be applied with no cost.

We compared and contrasted the classifiers in terms of classification accuracy, profitability and trading volume. To evaluate the profitability of the classification methods, we calculated average returns and excess returns over the index for the portfolios of actual H and L shares in our data in all the 12-month holding periods starting each year, and then compared them with the respective averages for the portfolios of H and L shares predicted by the classification methods. On the other hand, to examine if transaction costs can have an important impact in our trading system, we also compared the classification methods for the number of shares which each individual classification method suggested should be traded for the out-of-sample years 1993–1997. It is obvious that this is the number of actual H performing shares that were correctly predicted as H by each individual classification method as well as the number of actual L performing shares that were incorrectly predicted as H. We also considered the trade-off between predicted returns and risk. According to our trading system, if a share is classified as H, we buy equal amounts of this share at the end of the reporting month and we hold it for one year. The profitability of each classification method is therefore calculated by the cumulative profits generated by the resulting portfolio of H performing shares. The benefit of this approach is that it minimises transaction costs while it is not affected by price fluctuations around the reporting date. Each share is traded at most once per year and trades can be done at the end of the month in a basket of no more than 13–16 shares bought and sold in the ideal trading strategy. On average, the H performing portfolio will turn over 1/12 of its constituents each month.

4.5   RESULTS

In this section, we summarise the results of our experimentation. We compare the five algorithms, namely LDA, PNN, LVQ, OC1 and RRI, and our two voting methodologies, namely MV and UV, in terms of classification accuracy, profitability, risk and trading volume for the test out-of-sample year 1993—on which the input dimensionality reduction was conducted—and for the genuine out-of-sample years 1994–1997.

We implemented the five classifiers and the two voting methodologies using three different sets of information: first, using accounting information only (AI); second, using economic information, past share and index returns information and information about the industrial classification of the companies only (ERIIC); and third, using all the available information (ALL).

The full results are shown in Appendix 4.1. In the text we show only summary tables.

Table A4.1 shows the classification results after implementing the classifiers and the voting methodologies using accounting information only. These results are also presented in Figure A4.1. As we can see, the UV methodology outperforms significantly the MV and the individual classifiers for the test out-of-sample year 1993 as well as for the genuine out-of-sample years 1994–1997. The PNN and the LDA also produce very good results for the target year 1993, but it seems that their classification performance deteriorates for the next years compared to the other classifiers. As we can see, the MV voting is the second best classifier for the target year 1994, with a very balanced predictive accuracy for both H and L performing shares. On the other hand, the OC1 classifier is the best classifier for the target year 1995, even though its classification accuracy seems to favour more L performing shares against H performing shares compared to LDA, PNN and RRI, that favour more H performing shares against L performing shares. The PNN is again the second best classifier for the target year 1996, but it seems that the MV predicts more accurately than the PNN H performing shares. The pattern is slightly different for the target year 1997, where the LVQ and the MV have the second best classification performance and achieve a very good predictive accuracy for both H and L performing shares.

Table A4.2 shows the classification results after implementing the classifiers and the voting methodologies using economic, past share and index returns information, as well as information about the sectoral classification of the companies. These results are also presented in Figure A4.2. As we can see, the UV outperforms clearly the other classifiers for the test out-of-sample year 1993, as well as for the genuine out-of-sample years 1994–1997. The RRI is the second best classifier for the target year 1993, whereas the PNN is the second best classifier for the target year 1994. The classification performance of the PNN is also good for the target year 1995, but the LVQ and the MV are very close to the PNN and produce very favourable results. Although the pattern remains the same for the target year 1996 with PNN, LVQ and MV sharing the second best classification performance, we have to notice that the RRI classifier predicts more accurately H performing shares compared to PNN, LVQ and MV. The pattern will change slightly for the target year 1997. The PNN is the second best classifier in terms of overall classification accuracy for 1997, whereas the LDA, OC1, RRI and MV predict more accurately than the PNN H performing shares that particular year.

Table A4.3 shows the classification results after implementing the classifiers and voting methodologies using all the available information. Figure A4.3 gives the graphical presentation of the results. As we can see, the UV once more outperforms significantly the other classifiers for the test out-of-sample year 1993, as well as for the genuine out-of-sample years 1994–1997. The PNN is the second best classifier for the target year 1993, whereas MV is the second best classification rule for the target years 1994 and 1995. The OC1 classifier has the second best classification accuracy for the target year 1996, but the MV predicts more accurately than OC1 H performing shares for this year. However, the same will not happen the next target year 1997, where MV is the second best classification rule in terms of overall classification accuracy but not in terms of predictive accuracy for H performing shares since PNN and LDA produce more favourable results for H performing shares that year.

The results are brought together in Table 4.2. Note that if any model has no predictive skill the proportion of shares predicted to be H which are actually H would be 25%. In all cases, the models comfortably outperform the benchmark as we can see in Table 4.2. Overall, the classification results suggest that the UV outperforms significantly the other classification methods for the target years 1993–1997. PNN and LDA favour the use of either accounting or nonaccounting subsets of information for the target years 1993–1996, whereas they favour more the use of all available information for the latest target year 1997. LVQ, OC1, RRI and MV follow a different pattern than LDA and PNN. Their classification performance is as good or even better after using all available information rather than using either accounting or nonaccounting subsets of information in most out-of-sample years. However, the improvements in classification accuracy using all available information seem to be more significant for LVQ and OC1 rather than RRI and MV. On the other hand, UV seems to follow a more inconsistent pattern and it is more difficult

Table 4.2 Accuracy of models × information sets

	Model predictions													
	LDA		PNN		LVQ		OC1		RRI		MV		UV	
Information set	H	L	H	L	H	L	H	L	H	L	H	L	H	L
Accounting Variables														
Actual H	468	355	468	355	468	355	456	355	454	367	489	334	158	665
L	898	1561	887	1572	937	1522	966	1522	1017	1493	873	1586	218	2241
% Correct overall	61.8%		62.2%		60.6%		59.4%		57.8%		63.2%		73.1%	
% Actual high/predicted high	34.3%		34.5%		33.3%		32.1%		30.9%		35.9%		42.0%	
Nonaccounting Variables														
Actual H	468	355	470	353	449	353	441	374	485	338	473	350	155	668
L	1068	1391	935	1524	951	1524	1001	1508	1055	1404	969	1490	214	2245
% Correct overall	56.6%		60.8%		59.6%		57.9%		57.6%		59.8%		73.1%	
% Actual high/predicted high	30.5%		33.5%		32.1%		30.6%		31.5%		32.8%		42.0%	
All Variables														
Actual H	465	358	469	354	446	354	456	377	459	364	469	354	156	667
L	963	1496	891	1568	880	1568	900	1559	982	1477	810	1649	146	2313
% Correct overall	59.8%		62.1%		61.7%		61.4%		59.0%		64.5%		75.2%	
% Actual high/predicted high	32.6%		34.5%		33.6%		33.6%		31.9%		36.7%		51.7%	

to extract a general conclusion about the relationship between type of information and classification performance for this particular methodology.

Although the classification performance is a very important factor to evaluate a particular classifier, it is not the primary concern for this particular application. The ultimate purpose of our trading system is profitability. We therefore compared the average returns and excess returns over the index of the portfolios of actual H and L shares in our data in all the 12-month holding periods starting each year, with the respective average returns and excess returns of the portfolios of H and L shares predicted by the classifiers and voting methodologies.

Table A4.4 shows the financial returns and excess returns over the index of the portfolios of actual H and L shares in all the 12-month holding periods starting in each year, with the financial returns and excess returns of the portfolios of H and L shares predicted by the classifiers and voting methodologies using accounting information only. These results are also presented in Figures A4.4, A4.5, A4.6, and A4.7 for H returns and excess returns and for L returns and excess returns, respectively. As we can see, all the classifiers and voting methodologies produce positive returns and excess returns. However, the UV methodology outperforms significantly the other classifiers for the test out-of-sample year 1993, as well as for the genuine out-of-sample years 1994–1997 and produces the highest financial results. We recall that the financial results for the UV methodology represent the returns of actual H performing shares that correctly classified as H based on a unanimous decision from the five classification methods as well as the number of L performing shares that incorrectly classified as H based on a unanimous decision from the five classification methods as well. As far as the other classifiers are concerned, PNN and LDA produce very good results for the target year 1993. On the other hand, it seems that the financial returns deteriorate for the next target year 1994, even though all classifiers and voting methodologies produce positive results. As we can see, there are only minor differences between the MV, which is the second most profitable classification rule that year, and the other classifiers that produce slightly lower financial returns. The next target year 1995 is a year of high profitability for all classifiers and voting methodologies. The UV produces the highest financial results that year, whereas there are only minor differences in the financial results between the other classifiers. This pattern will not change significantly for the next target years 1996 and 1997 which are years of positive financial returns as well. The PNN is the second most profitable classifier for the target year 1996, whereas LVQ is the second most profitable classifier for the target year 1997.

Table A4.5 shows the financial returns and excess returns over the index of the portfolios of actual H and L shares in all the 12-month holding periods starting in each year, with the financial returns and excess returns of the portfolios of H and L shares predicted by the classifiers and voting methodologies using economic, past share and index returns information, as well as information about the sectoral classification of the companies. These results are also presented in Figures A4.8, A4.9, A4.10, and A4.11 for H returns and excess returns and for L returns and excess returns, respectively. As we can see, the UV methodology outperforms significantly the MV and the individual classifiers for the test out-of-sample year 1993, as well as for the genuine out-of-sample years 1994–1997 and produces impressive financial results. The RRI is the second most profitable classifier for the target year 1993, but the profitability of MV and the other classifiers is also high as well. The next target year 1994 is a year of very high profitability for UV and its predicted high return (20.3%) and high excess return (14.8%) are almost twice the respective returns of the PNN, which is the second most profitable classifier. The other classifiers produce lower but still positive results for the target year 1994. The profitability increases significantly for the target year 1995 and deteriorates slightly for the latest target years 1996 and 1997. However, the UV still produces very impressive financial returns for these years, whereas there are only minor differences in the financial returns predicted by the other classifiers.

Table A4.6 shows the financial returns and excess returns over the index for the portfolios of actual H and L shares in all the 12-month holding periods starting in each year, with the financial returns and excess returns of the portfolios of H and L shares predicted by the classifiers and voting methodologies using all the available information. These results are also presented in Figures A4.12, A4.13 and A4.14, A4.15 for H returns and excess returns and for L returns and excess returns, respectively. As we can see, the UV methodology once more outperforms significantly the other classifiers for the test out-of-sample year 1993, as well as for the genuine out-of-sample years 1994–1997 and produces impressive financial results. The MV and PNN are the second most profitable classification rules for the target year 1993, whereas the other classifiers also produce impressive financial results. The next target year 1994 is a year of very high profitability for UV, whereas the other classifiers produce lower but positive financial returns. As we can see, UV outperforms significantly the other classifiers and its financial return (30.9%) is almost twice the return of the LVQ (12.1%), which is the second most profitable classifier for the target year 1994. However, even more impressive is the excess return produced by UV (26.1%) that is four times higher than the excess return produced by MV and LVQ (6.2%), which are the second most profitable classifiers in excess returns. The next target year 1995 is a year of high profitability for all classifiers and voting methodologies. The UV is still the most profitable methodology for this year, whereas there are only minor differences in financial returns among the other classifiers. The profitability deteriorates for the target 1996 but the financial returns are still positive for all classifiers and voting methodologies. The UV clearly outperforms the other classifiers, whereas there are only minor differences in the financial returns among the other classifiers. The UV will produce very impressive results for the last target year 1997 with impressive high return (41.4%) and excess return (29.3%) almost twice the respective returns of MV and PNN, which are the second most profitable classifiers.

The trading performance results are collected in Table 4.3. Overall, the predicted financial returns suggest that UV outperforms significantly the other classification methods for the target years 1993–1997. PNN and LDA seem to prefer the use of either accounting or nonaccounting subsets of information for the target years 1993–1996, whereas they favour more the use of all available information for the target year 1997. If we compare these results with the classification performance of the algorithms we might notice some degree of correlation between classification accuracy and profitability. LVQ, OC1, RRI follow a different pattern than LDA and PNN and their financial returns are as good or even better after using all available information rather than using either accounting or nonaccounting subsets of information for specific out-of-sample years. However, the improvements in financial returns using all available information are less obvious for LVQ and RRI rather than OC1. On the other hand, MV and UV seem to favour the use of all available information rather than the use of specific subsets of information for most out-of-sample years.

Table 4.3 Returns from models × information sets

	Model predictions													
	LDA		PNN		LVQ		OC1		RRI		MV		UV	
Information set	H	L	H	L	H	L	H	L	H	L	H	L	H	L
Accounting Variables														
Annual % Return	26.0%	8.6%	26.6	8.1%	23.4	9.6%	21.6%	10.9%	20.0%	11.9%	25.9%	8.3%	37.7%	6.5%
Annual % Excess Return	10.7%	−7.1%	11.0%	−7.4%	8.0%	−6.0%	6.2%	−4.7%	4.8%	−3.9%	10.5%	−7.3%	21.7%	−9.3%
Betas (High Portfolio)	1.38		1.31		1.32		1.24		1.13		1.39		1.51	
Nonaccounting Variables														
Annual % Return	21.3%	10.4%	23.9%	9.4%	21.8%	10.9%	21.4%	10.9%	21.7%	10.4%	23.0%	9.8%	30.8%	4.9%
Annual % Excess Return	5.7%	−5.0%	8.0%	−5.9%	6.5%	−4.8%	5.0%	−3.9%	6.6%	−5.5%	7.3%	−5.6%	15.5%	−10.6%
Betas (High Portfolio)	1.07		1.07		1.12		1.06		1.08		1.11		1.17	
All Variables														
Annual % Return	23.5%	9.5%	26.2%	8.4%	23.1%	10.4%	22.4%	10.5%	21.9%	10.7%	26.9%	8.5%	42.0%	5.6%
Annual % Excess Return	7.5%	−5.7%	10.3%	−6.8%	7.2%	−4.9%	7.2%	−5.1%	6.3%	−4.8%	11.3%	−7.0%	25.4%	−9.4%
Betas (High Portfolio)	1.32		1.16		1.22		1.35		1.16		1.37		1.43	

Although the financial returns are a primary factor to evaluate a particular trading system, there are several other aspects that we have to consider in evaluating the quality of our trading system. One important aspect is the transaction costs involved in trading the number of shares predicted by the classification methods. For this purpose, we calculated the predicted number of shares included in the portfolios of H performing shares that are traded for the test out-of-sample year 1993 as well as for the genuine out-of-sample years 1994–1997. It is obvious that this is the number of actual H performing shares correctly predicted as H by the classification methods as well as the number of actual L performing shares incorrectly predicted as H. Tables A4.7–A4.9 compare the classification methods for the number of shares predicted to be H in all the 12-month holding periods for the test out-of-sample year as well as for the genuine out-of-sample years 1994–1997 using accounting information, nonaccounting information, as well as using all available information. As we can see, the UV produces the smallest trading volume for the target years 1993–1997 and outperforms significantly the other classification methods under all three different types of information.

Another important aspect in evaluating the importance of our trading system is the trade-off between predicted returns and risk. To examine this trade-off, we regressed the returns of the classifiers and voting methodologies of the H class shares on the index for the genuine out-of-sample years 1994–1997. These results are presented in Table A4.10 under the three different types of information, and the resulting beta estimates are also listed in Table 4.3. As we can see, the actual H portfolio does have a high beta, around 1.62. The first two columns of Table A4.10 show the predicted H returns and estimated betas after implementing the five classifiers and the two voting methodologies using accounting information. As we can see, the predicted H portfolios by the first four classifiers produce high returns but have higher betas than the RRI that produces lower returns than the other classifiers. The two voting methodologies produce higher returns than the individual classifiers but have higher betas as well. The next two columns of Table A4.10 show the predicted high returns and estimated betas after implementing the five classifiers and the two voting methodologies using nonaccounting information. As we can see, the predicted H portfolios by the five classifiers and the two voting methodologies produce a very good trade-off between predicted returns and risk. All betas are very close to 1, whereas their predicted returns are very similar to the returns predicted by the same classifiers and voting methodologies after using accounting information. The last two columns of Table A4.10 show the predicted H returns and estimated betas after implementing the five classifiers and the two voting methodologies using all available information. As we can see, the predicted H portfolios from PNN, LVQ and RRI achieve a very good trade-off between predicted returns and betas, whereas the other classification methods have higher betas. Once again, the MV and UV methodologies produce higher returns than the five individual classifiers but have accordingly higher betas.

Overall, the results in Table A4.10 and Table 4.3 seem to support the hypothesis that high returns are associated with high risk. The predicted H portfolios by the voting methodologies that produce the higher returns have similarly higher betas. More interestingly, the predicted H portfolios by the five individual classifiers and the two voting methodologies that result after using nonaccounting information produce a very good trade-off between predicted returns and risk. All betas are very close to 1, whereas the predicted returns are very similar to the returns predicted by the same classifiers and voting methodologies after using accounting information. On the other hand, we have to recognise that the actual H portfolios and to a lesser degree the predicted H portfolios contain a disproportionate number of small capitalisation stocks. This may impose additional risk if we consider that the market in these shares is relatively illiquid. Despite these considerations, however, we have to emphasise that the strong advantage of our trading system is that all classification methods produce returns and excess returns on a consistent basis during the target years 1993–1997, even though some of the theoretical measures of risk make the results vulnerable to the accusation that higher returns are achieved at the expense of higher risk.

4.6   CONCLUSION

In this paper, we applied five statistical classification methods from different model families to identify H and L performing shares in the period 1993–1997 and examined the possibility of combining their forecasts using majority and unanimity voting principles. The model inputs we used were accounting information, economic information, past share and index returns information as well as information about the sectoral classification of around 700 companies. We implemented the models using accounting and nonaccounting subsets of information separately, as well as using all the available information.

We found that all classification methods produce consistent excess returns. However, greater gains result from UV where a share is not classified as H performing unless all classifiers agree. The UV principle not only produces significantly greater returns than the other methods, but also results in substantial reductions in the number of shares traded.

The results also suggest that there are substantial gains in using all available information rather than using subsets of information only. Much greater gains result for RRI, OC1 and LVQ due to the way they explore the search space. These results are of course conditional on the information sets that we have used, the way we have implemented the various models and the trading rules we have assumed.

Our work in this paper confirms previous studies that report predictable patterns in stock returns using firm specific variables, economic variables, as well as past share and index returns information. However, our findings extend previous research that examined the predictability of share returns mostly under restricted forms of linear and nonlinear models. Our results provide evidence for the ability of nonlinear classification methods over the linear model to identify high performing shares. Nonlinear models are more flexible to deal with the complex relationships that are evident in financial data compared to the linear model that is able to handle more simple linear patterns. The main advantage of our methodology is model flexibility that is essential for the complex financial processes that are volatile and inconsistent in the time scale.

Our results also confirm the findings of previous studies that combinations of individual forecasts improve forecasting accuracy. In response to previous studies that support combinations of homogeneous component classifiers rather than heterogeneous classifiers, we provide substantial evidence that a combination of heterogeneous classifiers using the unanimous voting scheme is also successful and produces impressive results over the individual component classifiers. The benefit of applying voting procedures to combine the individual component classifiers is that combining can be done with little or no increase in cost.

The practical importance of our trading system is obvious if we consider the nature of our application and the financial results we achieved after testing the models. Considering previous studies that used either linear models or restricted forms of nonlinear models to predict stock returns, we can easily understand that most of the existing financial theory concerning stock return predictability has been built around a given model that was applied for a particular application. On the other hand, if a more general nonlinear model is more successful than the linear models to predict stock returns, then this implies that the previous financial theory in stock return predictability is not necessarily valid. However, we have to consider that it is very difficult to assess the contribution of each individual variable in our composite architectures given the type of models we have used for this particular application. Although this does not affect the practical importance of our financial results, it makes the theoretical analysis of the model rather difficult.

ACKNOWLEDGEMENTS

We are indebted for comments on an earlier draft of this paper to participants in the Computational Finance 2000/International Conference on Forecasting Financial Markets: Interest Rates, Exchange Rates and Asset Management, London, June 2000.

REFERENCES

Abhyankar, A., L.S. Copeland and W. Wong (1997). "Uncovering Non-Linear Structure in Real-Time Stock Market Indexes: The S&P 500, the DAX, the Nikkei 225, and the FTSE-100", *Journal of Business and Economic Statistics* **15**, 1–14.

Acton, S.F. (1970). *Numerical Methods that Work (Usually)*. New York: Harper & Row.

Albanis, G.T. (1998a). "Using Rule Induction Techniques to Predict Long-Term Bond Ratings", paper presented at the BNP Forecasting Financial Markets: Advances for Exchange Rates, Interest Rates and Asset Management Conference, London.

Albanis, G.T. (1998b). "Using Probabilistic Neural Networks and Rule Induction Techniques to Predict Long-Term Bond Ratings", paper presented at the Second World Multiconference on Systemics, Cybernetics and Informatics and the Fourth International Conference on Information Systems, Analysis and Synthesis (SCI'98/ISAS'98), Orlando, FL.

Albanis, G.T. and R.A. Batchelor (1999a). "Assessing the Long-Term Credit Standing Using Dimensionality Reduction Techniques Based on Neural Networks—An Alternative to Overfitting", paper presented at the Third World Multiconference on Systemics, Cybernetics and Informatics and the Fifth International Conference on Information Systems, Analysis and Synthesis (SCI'99/ISAS'99), Orlando, FL.

Albanis, G.T. and R.A. Batchelor (1999b). "Five Algorithms to Predict High Performance Stocks", paper presented at the Sixth Forecasting Financial Markets: Advances for Exchange Rates, Interest Rates and Asset Management International Conference, London.

Albanis, G.T. and R.A. Batchelor (1999c). "Combining Heterogeneous Experts to Predict High Performance Stocks", working paper, City University Business School, London.

Albanis, G.T. and R.A. Batchelor (1999d). "Five Classification Algorithms to Predict High Performance Stocks". In C. Dunis (ed.), *Advances in Quantitative Asset Management*, Boston: Kluwer Academic; 295–318.

Albanis, G.T. and R.A. Batchelor (1999e). "Combining Nonlinear Classifiers for Stock Selection", paper presented at the Forecasting Financial Markets 2000/Computational Finance 2000 Conference (CF'2000/FFM'2000), London.

Altman, E.I. (1968). "Financial Ratios, Discriminant Analysis and the Prediction of Corporation Bankruptcy", *Journal of Finance* **23**, 589–609.

Balvers, R.J., T.F. Cosimano and B. McDonald (1990). "Predicting Stock Returns in an Efficient Market", *Journal of Finance* **55**, 1109–1128.

Banz, R.W. (1981). "The Relationship Between Return and Market Value of Common Stocks", *Journal of Financial Economics* **9**, 3–18.

Basu, S. (1983). "The Relationship Between Earning's Yield, Market Value, and the Returns for NYSE Common Stocks: Further Evidence", *Journal of Financial Economics* **12**, 129–156.

Bhandari, L.C. (1988). "Debt/Equity Ratio and Expected Common Stock Returns: Empirical Evidence", *Journal of Finance* **43**, 507–528.

Breiman, L., J.H. Friedman, E.A. Olshen and C.J. Stone (1994). *Classification and Regression Trees*. New York: Chapman & Hall.

Brock, W.A., B. LeBaron and J. Lakonisshok (1992). "Simple Technical Trading Rules and the Stochastic Properties of Stock Returns", *Journal of Finance* **47**, 1731–1764.

Brunk, C. and M. Pazzani (1991). "Noise-Tolerant Relational Concept Learning Algorithms", paper presented at the Eighth International Workshop on Machine Learning, Ithaca, NY.

Cacoullos, T. (1966). "Estimation of a Multivariate Density", *Annals of the Institute of Statistical Mathematics* **18**(2), 179–189.

Cameron-Jones, M. (1994). "The Complexity of Cohen's Grow Method", unpublished manuscript, University of Edinburgh, UK.

Campbell, J.Y. (1987). "Stock Returns and the Term Structure", *Journal of Financial Economics* **18**, 373–399.

Chen, N.F., R. Roll and S.A. Ross (1986). "Economic Forces and the Stock Market", *Journal of Business* **59**, 383–403.

Cohen, W.W. (1993). "Efficient Pruning Methods for Separate-and-Conquer Rule Learning Systems", paper presented at the Thirteenth International Joint Conference on Artificial Intelligence, Chambéry, France.

Cohen, W.W. (1995). "Fast Effective Rule Induction", paper presented at the Twelfth International Conference on Machine Learning, Lake Tahoe, CA.

Deakin, E.B. (1976). "Distributions of Financial Accounting Ratios: Some Empirical Evidence", *The Accounting Review* **January**, 90–96.

Fama, E.F. and K.R. French (1988). "Dividend Yields and Expected Stock Returns", *Journal of Financial Economics* **22**, 3–25.

Fama, E.F. and K.R. French (1989). "Business Conditions and Expected Returns on Stocks and Bonds", *Journal of Financial Economics* **25**, 23–49.

Fama, E.F. and K.R. French (1992). "The Cross-Section of Expected Stock Returns", *Journal of Finance* **47**, 427–465.

Ferson, W.E. and C.R. Harvey (1993). "The Risk and Predictability of International Equity Returns", *Review of Financial Studies* **6**, 527–566.

Furnkranz, J. and G. Widmer (1994). "Incremental Reduced Error Pruning", paper presented at the Eleventh Annual Conference in Machine Learning, New Brunswick, NJ.

Glosten, C.R., R. Jagannathan and D.E. Runkle (1993). "On the Relation Between the Expected Value and the Volatility of the Nominal Excess Returns on Stocks", *Journal of Finance* **48**, 1779–1802.

Hand, D.J. (1997). Construction and Assessment of Classification Rules, Chichester: Wiley.

Hinich, M.J. and D.M. Patterson (1985). "Evidence of Non-Linearity in Daily Stock Returns", *Journal of Business and Economic Statistics* **3**, 69–77.

Kaplan, S.R. and G. Urwitz (1979). "Statistical Models of Bond Ratings: A Methodological Inquiry", *Journal of Business* **52**(2), 231–261.

Kohonen, fnmT., J. Hynninen, J. Kangas, J. Laaksonnen and K. Torkkola (1995). LVQ_PAK—The Learning Vector Quantisation Programme Package, Version 3.1, LVQ Programming Team, Helsinki University of Technology, Laboratory of Computer and Information Science, Finland.

Lachenbruch, P.A., C. Sneeringer and L.T. Revo (1973). "Robustness of the Linear and Quadratic Discriminant Function to Certain Types of Nonnormality", *Communication Statistics* **1**, 39–56.

Lachenbruch, P.A. (1975). Discriminant Analysis, New York: Sage Publications.

Masters, T. (1995). *Advanced Algorithms for Neural Networks*. New York: Academic Press.

Meisel, W. (1972). *Computer-Oriented Approaches to Pattern Recognition*. New York: Academic Press.

Murthy, K.V.S. (1997), "On Growing Better Decision Trees from Data", Ph.D. thesis, John Hopkins University, Baltimore, MD.

Paggallo, G. and D. Hausler (1990). "Boolean Feature Discovery in Empirical Learning" *Machine Learning* **5**(1), 71–101.

Parzen, E. (1962). "On Estimation of a Probability Density Function and Mode", *Annals of Mathematics and Statistics* **33**, 1065–1076.

Pesaran, M.H. and A. Timmermann (1994). "Forecasting Stock Returns, An Examination of Stock Market Trading in the Presence of Transaction Costs", *Journal of Forecasting* **13**, 335–367.

Pesaran, M.H. and A. Timmermann (1995). "Predictability of Stock Returns: Robustness and Economic Significance", *Journal of Finance* **50**, 1201–1228.

Pesaran, M.H. and A. Timmerman (2000). "A Recursive Approach to Predicting UK Stock Returns", *Economic Journal* **110**, 159–191.

Pinches, R.A. (1980). "Pitfalls in the Application of Discriminant Analysis in Business, Finance, and Economics", *Journal of Finance* **3**, 875–900.

Qi, M. and G.S. Maddala (1999). "Economic Factors and the Stock Market: A New Perspective", *Journal of Forecasting* **18**, 151–166.

Skalak, D.B. (1997). "Prototype Selection for Composite Nearest Neighbor Classifiers", Ph.D. thesis, University of Massachusetts, Amherst, MA.

Specht, D. (1990). "Probabilistic Neural Networks", *Neural Networks* **3**, 109–118.

Tyree, E. and J.A. Long (1996). "Assessing Financial Distress with Probabilistic Neural Networks", paper presented at the Third International Conference on Neural Networks in the Capital Markets, London.

Warton, R. (1999). "Company Profitability and Finance", unpublished manuscript, Office of National Statistics, London.

APPENDIX 4.1

Table A4.1 Out-of-sample classification results of LDA, PNN, LVQ, OC1, RRI, MV and UV for 1993–1997 using accounting information to predict high and low performing shares

		Predicted class membership													
		LDA		PNN		LVQ		OC1		RRI		MV		UV	
Actual class	Patterns	H	L	H	L	H	L	H	L	H	L	H	L	H	L
1993															
H	157	95	62	95	62	95	62	95	62	98	59	99	58	36	121
L	469	116	353	121	348	180	289	180	289	173	296	139	330	25	444
Overall (%)		**71.57%**		**70.77%**		**61.34%**		**61.34%**		**62.94%**		**68.53%**		**76.68%**	
1994															
H	155	83	72	84	71	83	72	83	72	80	75	88	67	25	130
L	463	193	270	183	280	188	275	199	264	201	262	178	285	52	411
Overall (%)		**57.12%**		**58.90%**		**57.93%**		**56.15 %**		**55.34%**		**60.36%**		**70.55 %**	
1995															
H	160	90	70	90	70	82	78	88	72	92	68	91	69	31	129
L	479	183	296	185	294	177	302	168	311	225	254	177	302	65	414
Overall (%)		**60.41%**		**60.09%**		**60.09%**		**62.44%**		**54.15%**		**61.50%**		**69.64%**	
1996															
H	171	94	77	93	78	98	73	93	78	88	83	99	72	34	137
L	510	195	315	189	321	212	298	219	291	188	322	197	313	37	473
Overall (%)		**60.06%**		**60.79%**		**58.15%**		**56.39%**		**60.21%**		**60.50%**		**74.45%**	
1997															
H	180	106	74	106	74	110	70	97	83	96	84	112	68	32	148
L	538	211	327	209	329	180	358	200	338	230	308	182	356	39	499
Overall (%)		**60.31%**		**60.58%**		**65.18%**		**60.58%**		**56.27%**		**65.18%**		**73.96%**	

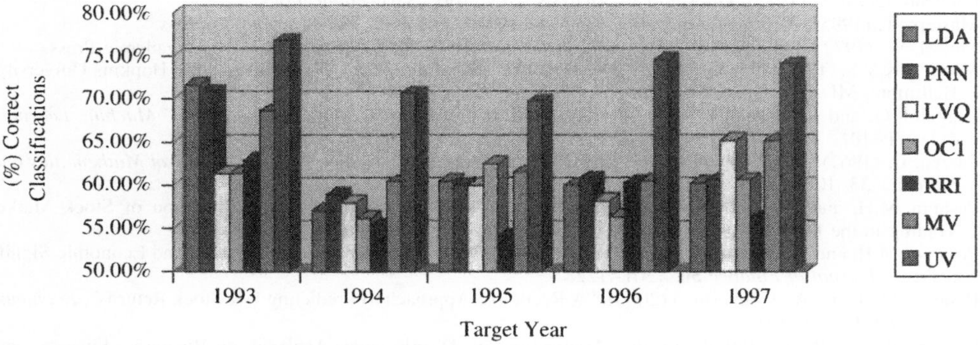

Figure A4.1 Out-of-sample classification results of LDA, PNN, LVQ, OC1, RRI, MV and UV for 1993–1997 using accounting information to predict high and low performing shares

Table A4.2 Out-of-sample classification results of LDA, PNN, LVQ, OC1, RRI, MV and UV for 1993–1997 using nonaccounting information to predict high and low performing shares

Actual class	Patterns	LDA		PNN		LVQ		OC1		RRI		MV		UV	
		H	L	H	L	H	L	H	L	H	L	H	L	H	L
1993															
H	157	94	63	90	67	81	76	81	76	93	64	85	72	37	120
L	469	199	270	162	307	170	299	173	296	153	316	148	321	15	454
Overall (%)		58.15%		63.42%		60.70%		60.22%		65.34%		64.86%		78.43%	
1994															
H	155	85	70	87	68	83	72	86	69	88	67	84	71	27	128
L	463	208	255	175	288	174	289	191	272	198	265	187	276	36	427
Overall (%)		55.02%		60.68%		60.19%		57.93%		57.12%		58.25%		73.46%	
1995															
H	160	89	71	100	60	98	62	84	76	93	67	102	58	30	130
L	479	188	291	188	291	191	288	179	300	213	266	191	288	44	435
Overall (%)		59.47%		61.19%		60.41%		60.09%		56.18%		61.03%		72.77%	
1996															
H	171	95	76	94	77	91	80	86	85	105	66	94	77	22	149
L	510	226	284	209	301	204	306	210	300	240	270	204	306	45	465
Overall (%)		55.65%		58.00%		58.30%		56.68%		55.07%		58.74%		71.51%	
1997															
H	180	105	75	99	81	96	84	104	76	106	74	108	72	39	141
L	538	247	291	201	337	212	326	248	290	251	287	239	299	74	464
Overall (%)		55.15%		60.72%		58.77%		54.87%		54.74%		56.69%		70.06%	

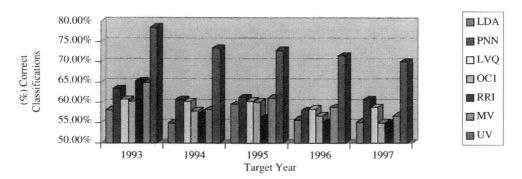

Figure A4.2 Out-of-sample classification results of LDA, PNN, LVQ, OC1, RRI, MV and UV for 1993–1997 using nonaccounting information to predict high and low performing shares

Table A4.3 Out-of-sample classification results of LDA, PNN, LVQ, OC1, RRI, MV and UV for 1993–1997 using all available information to predict high and low performing shares

		Predicted class membership												
		LDA		PNN		LVQ		OC1		RRI		MV		UV	
Actual class	Patterns	H	L	H	L	H	L	H	L	H	L	H	L	H	L
1993															
H	157	95	62	93	64	83	74	91	66	94	63	89	68	44	113
L	469	162	307	119	350	157	312	179	290	152	317	125	344	28	441
Overall (%)		64.22%		70.77%		63.10%		60.86%		65.65%		69.17%		77.48%	
1994															
H	155	82	73	84	71	81	74	90	65	85	70	91	64	21	134
L	463	197	266	195	268	172	291	197	266	177	286	181	282	25	438
Overall (%)		56.31%		56.96%		60.19%		57.61%		60.03%		60.36%		74.27%	
1995															
H	160	90	70	91	69	96	64	89	71	86	74	100	60	16	144
L	479	201	278	180	299	166	313	152	327	206	273	156	323	26	453
Overall (%)		57.59%		61.03%		64.01%		65.10%		56.18%		66.20%		73.40%	
1996															
H	171	93	78	94	77	89	82	86	85	92	79	90	81	31	140
L	510	213	297	214	296	190	320	175	335	218	292	182	328	35	475
Overall (%)		57.27%		57.27%		60.06%		61.82%		56.39%		61.38%		74.30%	
1997															
H	180	105	75	107	73	97	83	100	80	102	78	99	81	44	136
L	538	190	348	183	355	195	343	197	341	229	309	166	372	32	506
Overall (%)		63.09%		64.35%		61.28%		61.42%		57.24%		65.60%		76.60%	

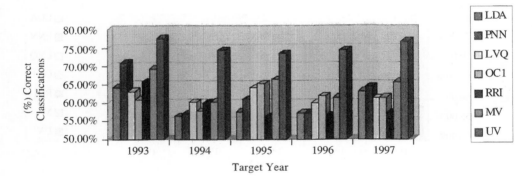

Figure A4.3 Out-of-sample classification results of LDA, PNN, LVQ, OC1, RRI, MV and UV for 1993–1997 using all available information to predict high and low performing shares

Table A4.4 Out-of-sample returns and excess returns of LDA, PNN, LVQ, OC1, RRI, MV and UV for 1993–1997 using accounting information to predict high and low performing shares

		Predicted returns and excess returns												
		LDA		PNN		LVQ		OC1		RRI		MV		UV	
	Index	H	L	H	L	H	L	H	L	H	L	H	L	H	L
1993															
Actual Return															
H = 90.1 L = 9.8	H = 31.1	55.9	16.7	57.1	15.6	41.7	20.7	41.2	21.1	40.0	22.3	50.2	17.5	79.1	13.3
Actual Excess Return															
H = 59.0 L = −19.8	L = 29.6	24.5	−12.5	24.8	−13.1	11.1	−8.7	9.8	−7.7	10.0	−7.6	19.1	−11.7	44.7	−14.7
1994															
Actual Return															
H = 44.2 L = −7.7	H = 5.5	9.6	1.9	10.5	1.4	8.7	2.7	8.1	3.0	7.6	3.5	11.2	0.9	15.1	2.4
Actual Excess Return															
H = 38.7 L = −12.9	L = 5.2	5.1	−4.1	5.7	−4.3	4.1	−3.2	3.1	−2.6	2.7	−2.2	6.5	−4.9	11.4	−3.5
1995															
Actual Return															
H = 78.8 L = 7.6	H = 25.1	37.2	16.7	35.0	18.2	33.8	19.8	34.7	19.2	30.4	20.6	35.5	18.2	42.5	12.9
Actual Excess Return															
H = 53.7 L = −17.9	L = 25.5	11.3	−8.4	9.4	−7.2	8.0	−5.5	9.2	−6.2	4.8	−4.7	9.9	−7.1	16.0	−12.1
1996															
Actual Return															
H = 50.5 L = −4.4	H = 9.1	16.8	3.9	17.1	3.9	15.6	4.1	12.5	6.8	13.6	6.5	16.6	3.8	27.0	2.1
Actual Excess Return															
H = 41.44 L = −13.9	L = 9.5	7.6	−5.6	7.7	−5.4	6.3	−5.3	3.1	−2.6	4.2	−2.9	7.2	−5.5	16.5	−8.1
1997															
Actual Return															
H = 58.8 L = −6.9	H = 9.7	15.9	4.6	18.7	2.4	20.3	2.3	15.1	5.7	11.5	8.0	20.0	2.3	32.5	2.4
Actual Excess Return															
H = 49.1 L = −16.4	L = 9.5	5.9	−4.7	8.5	−6.7	10.5	−7.1	5.8	−4.1	2.4	−2.0	10.1	−7.0	22.5	−7.5

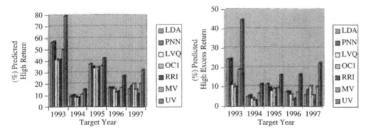

Figures A4.4, A4.5 Out-of-sample high returns and excess returns of LDA, PNN, LVQ, OC1, RRI, MV and UV for 1993–1997 using accounting information to predict high and low performing shares

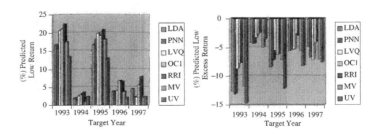

Figures A4.6, A4.7 Out-of-sample low returns and excess returns of LDA, PNN, LVQ, OC1, RRI, MV and UV for 1993–1997 using accounting information to predict high and low performing shares

Table A4.5 Out-of-sample returns and excess returns of LDA, PNN, LVQ, OC1, RRI, MV and UV for 1993–97 using nonaccounting information to predict high and low performing shares

		Predicted returns and excess returns													
		LDA		PNN		LVQ		OC1		RRI		MV		UV	
	Index	H	L	H	L	H	L	H	L	H	L	H	L	H	L
1993															
Actual Return															
H = 90.1 L = 9.8	H = 31.1	39.1	21.8	41.8	22.0	39.0	23.9	38.1	24.4	44.9	20.3	42.5	22.5	53.6	15.2
Actual Excess Ret															
H = 59.0 L = −19.8	L = 29.6	7.5	−6.6	9.7	−6.6	8.4	−5.7	5.2	−3.6	12.7	−8.2	10.2	−6.0	18.4	−13.8
1994															
Actual Return															
H = 44.2 L = −7.7	H = 5.5	7.6	3.3	12.3	0.3	10.9	1.4	10.4	1.2	8.7	2.4	10.6	1.2	20.3	−2.0
Actual Excess Ret															
H = 38.7 L = −12.9	L = 5.2	2.1	−1.9	6.6	−4.9	4.7	−3.4	4.4	−3.5	4.2	−3.6	5.2	−4.1	14.8	−6.4
1995															
Actual Return															
H = 78.8 L = 7.6	H = 25.1	32.5	20.1	32.8	19.4	32.4	19.7	31.8	21.0	31.5	19.9	32.9	19.1	43.5	13.5
Actual Excess Ret															
H = 53.7 L = −17.9	L = 25.5	7.2	−5.5	7.6	−6.2	7.6	−6.3	5.8	−4.1	5.5	−5.1	7.7	−6.5	17.0	−11.9
1996															
Actual Return															
H = 50.5 L = −4.4	H = 9.1	14.0	5.2	15.8	4.2	13.3	6.4	13.1	6.5	13.9	4.7	15.7	4.5	18.6	0.1
Actual Excess Ret															
H = 41.44 L = −13.9	L = 9.5	5.8	−5.1	6.5	−5.2	4.9	−3.7	5.1	−3.9	5.3	−5.5	6.9	−5.4	14.5	−10.8
1997															
Actual Return															
H = 58.8 L = −6.9	H = 9.7	16.3	3.1	19.1	2.7	16.0	4.8	15.8	3.6	13.1	6.1	16.0	3.6	21.9	−0.9
Actual Excess Ret															
H = 49.1 L = −16.4	L = 9.5	5.9	−5.7	9.5	−6.8	6.8	−5.1	4.4	−4.2	5.3	−5.2	6.7	−6.2	12.8	−9.9

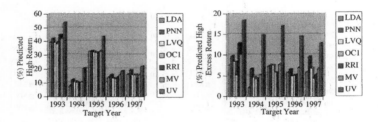

Figures A4.8, A4.9 Out-of-sample high returns and excess returns of LDA, PNN, LVQ, OC1, RRI, MV and UV for 1993–1997 using nonaccounting information to predict high and low performing shares

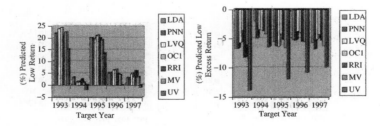

Figures A4.10, A4.11 Out-of-sample low returns and excess returns of LDA, PNN, LVQ, OC1, RRI, MV and UV for 1993–1997 using nonaccounting information to predict high and low performing shares

Table A4.6 Out-of-sample returns and excess returns of LDA, PNN, LVQ, OC1, RRI, MV and UV for 1993–1997 using all available information to predict high and low performing shares

		Predicted returns and excess returns												
		LDA		PNN		LVQ		OC1		RRI		MV		UV	
	Index	H	L	H	L	H	L	H	L	H	L	H	L	H	L
1993															
Actual Return															
H = 90.1 L = 9.8	H = 31.1	48.0	17.3	53.0	18.1	41.0	23.0	44.6	18.8	45.1	20.1	52.3	18.3	77.1	10.5
Actual Excess Return															
H = 59.0 L = −19.8	L = 29.6	13.8	−9.6	21.0	−10.7	7.1	−4.4	11.2	−8.5	12.6	−8.2	18.3	−9.5	42.3	−13.5
1994															
Actual Return															
H = 44.2 L = −7.7	H = 5.5	9.4	2.0	10.3	1.3	12.1	0.6	9.0	2.2	9.4	2.4	11.7	0.4	30.9	1.1
Actual Excess Return															
H = 38.7 L = −12.9	L = 5.2	3.3	−2.7	4.5	−3.7	6.2	−4.3	4.3	−3.7	4.4	−3.2	6.2	−4.9	26.1	−3.2
1995															
Actual Return															
H = 78.8 L = 7.6	H = 25.1	32.3	19.7	35.0	18.4	35.3	18.6	34.5	19.9	30.6	21.1	37.5	17.4	41.5	12.9
Actual Excess Return															
H = 53.7 L = −17.9	L = 25.5	7.7	−6.4	8.5	−6.3	9.9	−6.9	10.2	−6.2	5.3	−4.4	12.4	−8.3	14.3	−13.6
1996															
Actual Return															
H = 50.5 L = −4.4	H = 9.1	12.8	6.6	15.4	4.4	11.8	7.7	10.7	8.5	13.4	6.0	15.1	5.6	24.5	2.6
Actual Excess Return															
H = 41.44 L = −13.9	L = 9.5	5.8	−4.7	6.2	−5.1	4.4	−3.0	4.1	−2.5	4.1	−3.4	8.0	−5.3	16.8	−9.5
1997															
Actual Return															
H = 58.8 L = −6.9	H = 9.7	18.9	3.1	21.9	1.2	18.4	3.6	17.1	4.3	14.7	5.2	22.2	2.2	41.4	1.4
Actual Excess Return															
H = 49.1 L = −16.4	L = 9.5	7.3	−5.1	12.1	−8.2	8.6	−5.9	6.5	−4.6	5.2	−4.5	12.0	−7.0	29.3	−6.9

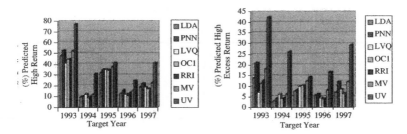

Figures A4.12, A4.13 Out-of-sample high returns and excess returns of LDA, PNN, LVQ, OC1, RRI, MV and UV for 1993–1997 using all available information to predict high and low performing shares

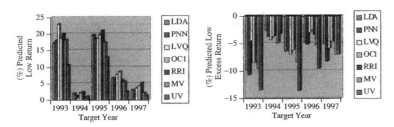

Figures A4.14, A4.15 Out-of-sample low returns and excess returns of LDA, PNN, LVQ, OC1, RRI, MV and UV for 1993–1997 using all available information to predict high and low performing shares

Table A4.7   Out-of-sample trading volume of LDA, PNN, LVQ, OC1, RRI, MV and UV for 1993–1997 using accounting information to predict high and low performing shares

Target year	Predicted trading volume						
	PNN	LDA	LVQ	OC1	RRI	MV	UV
1993	216	211	275	275	271	238	61
1994	267	276	271	282	281	266	77
1995	275	273	259	256	317	268	96
1996	282	289	310	312	276	296	71
1997	315	317	290	297	326	294	71

Table A4.8   Out-of-sample trading volume of LDA, PNN, LVQ, OC1, RRI, MV and UV for 1993–1997 using nonaccounting information to predict high and low performing shares

Target year	Predicted trading volume						
	PNN	LDA	LVQ	OC1	RRI	MV	UV
1993	252	293	251	254	246	233	90
1994	262	293	257	277	286	271	63
1995	288	277	289	263	306	293	74
1996	303	321	295	296	345	298	67
1997	300	352	308	352	357	347	113

Table A4.9   Out-of-sample trading volume of LDA, PNN, LVQ, OC1, RRI, MV and UV for 1993–1997 using all available information to predict high and low performing shares

Target year	Predicted trading volume						
	PNN	LDA	LVQ	OC1	RRI	MV	UV
1993	212	257	240	270	246	214	72
1994	279	279	253	287	262	272	46
1995	271	291	262	241	292	256	42
1996	308	306	279	261	310	272	66
1997	290	295	292	297	331	265	76

Table A4.10   Betas of predicted high portfolios for the out-of-sample years 1994–1997

	Accounting information		Nonaccounting information		All available information	
	Return	Beta	Return	Beta	Return	Beta
Actual	58.1	1.62	58.1	1.62	58.1	1.62
Predicted						
LDA	19.9	1.38	17.3	1.07	18.4	1.32
PNN	20.3	1.31	20.0	1.07	20.4	1.16
LVQ	19.6	1.32	18.3	1.12	19.3	1.22
OC1	17.0	1.24	17.4	1.06	17.3	1.35
RRI	16.1	1.13	16.7	1.08	17.1	1.16
MV	20.7	1.39	18.8	1.11	21.6	1.37
UV	29.3	1.51	25.9	1.17	34.5	1.43

5

Predicting High Performance Stocks Using Dimensionality Reduction Techniques Based on Neural Networks[1]

GEORGE T. ALBANIS AND ROY A. BATCHELOR

ABSTRACT

Dimensionality reduction is important to avoid overfitting in highly parameterised fore-casting models. Standard methods include variable elimination and Principal Components Analysis (PCA). In this paper, we introduce and test more general techniques based on a neural network representation of the input data. These are illustrated using a set of company accounting ratios. We find that neural network implementations of neural network linear and nonlinear PCA (NN-PCA and NN-NLPCA) explain a higher proportion of the variation in the data than conventional PCA. The resulting Principal Components (PCs) retain important discriminating power in a number of statistical classification models aimed at forecasting outperforming shares.

Keywords: Principal Components; Neural Networks; Nonlinear Principal Components; Forecasting; Stock Market; Statistical Classification

5.1 INTRODUCTION

Dimensionality reduction is widely advocated as an important step in preprocessing data input to highly parameterised nonlinear forecasting models. In this paper we compare the performance of three dimensionality reduction techniques as preprocessors of data input into a system for predicting outperforming shares. The techniques are linear Principal Components Analysis (PCA), neural-network linear PCA (NN-PCA), and neural network nonlinear PCA (NN-NLPCA). The forecasting model is a set of linear and nonlinear statistical classifiers, and the forecasts themselves are year-ahead predictions for the relative performance of some 700 equities traded on the London Stock Exchange in each of the years 1993–1997.

This paper brings together two elements of our earlier research. One is the development of a methodology for avoiding overfitting in complex models by applying linear and

---

[1] The opinions expressed herein are not necessarily those of Enron.

Developments in Forecast Combination and Portfolio Choice. Edited by C. Dunis, A. Timmermann and J. Moody.
© 2001 John Wiley & Sons Ltd

nonlinear dimensionality reduction techniques based on neural networks. In Albanis and Batchelor (1999) we applied this to the problem of predicting bond credit ratings. The other element is our work on predicting outperforming shares by combining classifiers. The effectiveness of combining these models is demonstrated in Albanis and Batchelor (2000a,b, 2001).

We start in Section 5.2 with a short description and critique of linear PCA. We then present the NN-PCA technique (Section 5.3), and the NN-NLPCA technique (Section 5.4). In Section 5.5, we discuss the data and the forecasting methodology that was used in this study. Our target data are total returns on all shares traded on the London Stock Exchange in the years 1993–1997, for which a set of 38 accounting ratios was published—around 700 shares each year. Our forecasting models are Linear Discriminant Analysis (LDA), Learning Vector Quantisation (LVQ), a Probabilistic Neural Network (PNN), an Oblique Recursive Classifier (OC1), and the RIPPER Rule Induction Technique (RRI).

After experimentation (Section 5.6), we find that NN-PCA and NN-NLPCA explain a higher proportion of variation in the original set of variables than the common PCA methodology. Moreover, the resulting PCs retain important discriminating power to identify which shares are likely to have exceptional returns in the future. On the other hand, we found that the resulting PCs are easier to interpret if extracted from homogeneous groups of financial ratios. In Section 5.7, we summarise the results and discuss some practical implications of our study.

5.2 PRINCIPAL COMPONENTS ANALYSIS

Various dimensionality reduction techniques have been proposed in the literature over the past decades, the best known being PCA. The central idea of PCA is to reduce the dimensionality of a dataset which consists of a large number of inter-related variables, by transforming it into a substantially smaller set of uncorrelated variables, which nonetheless contains a substantial proportion of the information in the original set of variables. A small set of uncorrelated variables is much easier to understand and use in further analyses than a larger set of correlated variables (Dong and McAvoy, 1995; Albanis, 1998).

PCA approximates n points in m dimensions by fitting a p-dimensional ($p < m$) plane through the middle of the points so that the sum of the distances between the points and their projections onto the plane is minimised. Formally, let X_t be an $n \times m$ data matrix that is centred about the mean so that the column totals are zero. The variance–covariance matrix of X_t can be estimated as $V_t = X_t' X_t /(n - 1)$. If we assume that α_{it} and x_{it} are $m \times 1$ data vectors, then any linear combination $\alpha_{it}' x_{it}$ has an estimated variance $\alpha_{it}' V_t \alpha_{it}$. Following Jolliffe (1986), the PCs can be derived by solving:

$$\frac{\partial}{\partial \alpha_{it}} (\alpha_{it}' V_t \alpha_{it} - l_{it} \alpha_{it}' \alpha_{it} = 0) \tag{5.1}$$

where l_{it} is the Langrange multiplier so that $V_t \alpha_{it} = l_{it} \alpha_{it}$.

The values of l_{it} are the m eigenvalues of V_t and to each of these eigenvalues $l_{1t}, l_{2t}, \ldots, l_{mt}$ [$l_{it} > l_{jt}$ ($i > j$)] corresponds an eigenvector so that the variance of $\alpha_{it}' x_{it}$ is equal to l_{it}. The vectors $\alpha_{it}' x_{it}$ are the PCs. The vector α_{it} contains the coefficients of the ith PC and $X_t \alpha_{it}$ gives the scores of the n elements on the ith PC. It is obvious that $\alpha'_{it} \alpha_{it} = 1$ and $\alpha'_{it} \alpha_{jt} = 0$, $i \neq j$.

Alternatively, PCA can be viewed as an optimal transformation of X_t into two matrices: a scores matrix and a loadings matrix. Let S_t be the $n \times p$ scores matrix, F_t the $m \times p$ loadings matrix, and E_t the $n \times m$ matrix of residuals. Then, we can write the following expression (Kramer, 1991; Albanis, 1998; Albanis and Batchelor, 1999):

$$X_t = S_t F'_t + E_t \qquad (5.2)$$

where p is the number of first PCs ($p < m$). The condition of optimality on the factorisation is that the Euclidean norm of the residual matrix E_t, must be minimised for a given number of PCs. This criterion is satisfied if the columns of F_t are the eigenvectors corresponding to the p largest eigenvalues of the covariance matrix of X_t.

The spectral or Jordan decomposition of the square symmetric matrix X_t can be written as $X'_t X_t = F_t L_t F'_t$, where the columns of F_t are the unit-length eigenvectors of $X'_t X_t$, and the diagonal elements of $L_t = \mathrm{diag}(l_{1t}, l_{2t}, \ldots, l_{mt})$ are the eigenvalues of $X'_t X_t$ [$l_{it} > l_{jt}/(i > j)$]. The eigenvectors form a basis for $\mathbb{R}^m$ and the coordinates of X_t relative to the eigenbasis are the PC scores. Therefore, we can write $S_t = X_t F_t$.

PCA approximates X_t by projecting X_t onto the subspace spanned by a subset of the eigenvectors given by the columns of F_t. If F_{pt} is a matrix of the first $p < m$ columns of F, then the approximation of matrix X_t is

$$X'_{it} = \mathrm{Pr}_{X_{it} \longrightarrow F_{pt}} = S_{pt} F'_{pt} \qquad (5.3)$$

where S_{pt} is the matrix of PC scores. The loadings of matrix F_t are the coefficients of the linear transformation. The information lost in this projection (Malthouse, 1996) is:

$$E_{pt} = X_t - \mathrm{Pr}_{X_{it} \longrightarrow F_{pt}} \qquad (5.4)$$

where E_{pt} is the matrix of errors.

The variances of the various PCs provide an indication of how well they account for the variability in the data. The relative sizes of the elements in a variable weight vector associated with a particular PC indicate the relative contribution of the variable to the variance of the PC. Indeed, the patterns of variable weights for a particular PC are sometimes used to "interpret" the PC. But when more than a few variables have a significant contribution to the variance of a particular PC, intuitive interpretation of the PC becomes problematical.

The main attractions of PCA are first, that PCA can be shown to be the optimal linear technique in terms of mean square error when compressing a set of high-dimensional vectors into lower dimensions, and when decompressing. Second, the model parameters can be computed directly by diagonalising the sample covariance matrix of the data set. Compressing and decompressing are then easy operations to perform because they require only matrix multiplications given the model parameters.

However, PCA has several disadvantages. The method is not suitable for extremely high-dimensional data. If we try to diagonalise a sample covariance matrix of n data vectors in a space of p dimensions when n and p are several hundreds or thousands, then difficulties can arise in the form of data scarcity. We may simply not have enough data in high dimensions for the sample covariance matrix to be full rank, and at the very least direct diagonalisation of a symmetric matrix thousands of rows in size can be an extremely costly operation (Rowies, 1997).

PCA can be used as a dimensionality reduction technique within some other type of procedure such as discriminant analysis, cluster analysis, or canonical correlation analysis. We would for example typically apply PCA in discriminant analysis by replacing the original set of independent variables by their principal components, and using a (hopefully small and high variance) subset of these in the derivation of a discriminant rule, thus reducing the dimensionality of the problem. However, a common assumption in many forms of discriminant analysis is that the covariance matrix is the same for all groups, and the PCA is therefore made using an estimate of this common within-group covariance matrix. Jolliffe (1986) argues that this procedure may be unsatisfactory for two reasons. First, the within-group covariance matrix may be different for different groups. Second, there is no guarantee that the separation between groups will be in the direction of the high-variance PCs. Chang (1983) shows with a real example that low variance PCs can be important discriminators in practice. He also demonstrates that a change in scaling of the variables can change the relative importance of the PCs.

Finally, we note that PCA is a linear technique, while most real-world problems are at least potentially nonlinear. It has been shown that if PCA is applied in nonlinear problems, minor components might contain important information. We therefore move to a discussion of NLPCA, which in principle should deal with these problems. NLPCA aims to uncover both linear and nonlinear correlations among variables without restriction on the character of the nonlinearities presented in the data (Kramer, 1991; Dong and McAvoy, 1995; Albanis, 1998).

5.3   NEURAL NETWORK LINEAR PRINCIPAL COMPONENTS ANALYSIS

It is well known that many meaningful information processing operations can be done by simple neural networks whose input–output mappings become linear after learning. Oja (1992) suggests several of the unsupervised learning algorithms of such networks can be regarded as neural realisations of PCA.

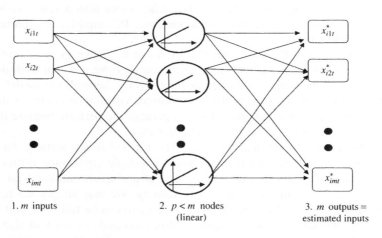

1. m inputs   2. $p < m$ nodes   3. m outputs =
                          (linear)   estimated inputs

Figure 5.1   NN-PCA architecture

For example, consider a multilayer perceptron of the form shown in Figure 5.1, having m neurons in the input layer, m neurons in the output layer and p neurons in the hidden layer, with $p < m$. This network can be used to map vectors x_{it}^n in an m-dimensional space $(x_{i1t}, x_{i2t}, \ldots, x_{imt})$ onto vectors s_{it}^n in a p-dimensional space $(s_{i1t}, s_{i2t}, \ldots, s_{ipt})$ where $p < m$. The targets used to train the network are simply the inputs themselves. Therefore, the network is trained to map each input vector onto itself. The activation functions for all nodes are linear and there are no direct connections between input and output nodes. The hidden layer is sometimes called a bottleneck layer because the m-dimensional inputs must pass through this $p < m$-dimensional layer before again producing the inputs. As the terminology suggests, data compression occurs in the bottleneck layer (Bishop 1995; Malthouse 1996; Albanis, 1998; Albanis and Batchelor, 1999).

If we assume a whole data set of N vectors x^n, then the network can be trained to minimise the objective function (Malthouse, 1996),

$$E = \min \sum_{i=1}^{n} \sum_{i=1}^{m} (x_{ijt} - \tilde{x}_{ijt})^2 \qquad (5.5)$$

Bourland and Kamp (1988) and Baldi and Hornik (1989) showed that if the hidden units have **_linear activation functions_** then the error function has a unique global minimum. Moreover, at this minimum the network performs a projection onto the p-dimensional subspace which is spanned by the first p principal components of the data. The weight vectors between the input and the bottleneck layers span the same subspace as the p eigenvectors in PCA.

PCA networks are useful in optimal feature extraction and data compression, and they have a number of possible applications in different areas. However, they have an important limitation that makes them less attractive from a neural network point of view. Linear PCA networks are able to perform only linear input–output mappings. A more subtle point is that the outputs of standard PCA networks are not usually independent, though this would be more desirable in many cases.

We might think that this limitation of the linear PCA network could be overcome if we used nonlinear activation functions for the hidden units in Figure 5.1. However, Bourland and Kamp (1988) showed that nonlinear activation functions in the hidden layer make no difference and that the minimum error solution is again given by the projection onto the principal component subspace.

On the other hand, the results would be different if additional hidden layers with nonlinear activation functions were permitted into the network. In that case, we could have a genuinely nonlinear PCA network, which might succeed in increasing the independence of the outputs, so that the original signals might be separated from their mixture.

5.4   NEURAL NETWORK NONLINEAR PRINCIPAL COMPONENTS ANALYSIS

The NN-NLPCA is a general purpose feature extraction algorithm producing features that retain the maximum possible amount of information from the original dataset. The main difference between PCA and NLPCA is that the former involves linear mappings between the original and reduced dimension spaces, whereas the latter involves nonlinear mappings. If nonlinear correlations between variables exist and sufficient data to support the formulation between more complex mapping functions are available, then NLPCA will describe the data with greater accuracy than PCA and by fewer PCs. Advocates of nonlinear PCA networks include Baldi and Hornik (1989), Kramer (1991), Karhunen and Joutsensalo (1994) and Dong and McAvoy (1995).

Following Kramer (1991), let x_{it} represent a row of the X_t, a single data vector, and s_{it} represent a row of the scores matrix, S_t. By applying NLPCA, we seek a mapping in the form:

$$s_{it} = \phi_i(x_{it}) \tag{5.6}$$

where ϕ is a nonlinear vector function, composed of p individual nonlinear functions $\phi = (\phi_1, \phi_2, \ldots, \phi_p)$ analogous to the columns of the loadings matrix, F_t. The information lost in this mapping can be assessed by reconstruction of the measurement vector by reversing the projection back to $\mathbb{R}^m$ as:

$$x'_{jt} = \theta_j(s_{it}) \tag{5.7}$$

where $\theta_j = (\theta_1, \theta_2, \ldots, \theta_m)$ is a second nonlinear function. The loss of information is then measured by $E_{it} = X_{it} - X'_{jt}$.

The functions ϕ_i and θ_j are selected to minimise $|E_{it}|$ for individual measurement vectors, or $|E_t|$ for the whole dataset, and can be modelled by fitting functions of the form:

$$v_k = \sum_{j=1}^{M_2} w_{jk2}\sigma\left(\sum_{i=1}^{M_1} w_{ij1}\varepsilon_i + \zeta_{j1}\right) \tag{5.8}$$

where $\sigma(x_{it})$ is a continuous monotonically increasing function so $\sigma(x_{it}) \rightarrow 1$ as $x_{it} \rightarrow +\infty$, and $\sigma(x_{it}) \rightarrow 0$ as $x_{it} \rightarrow -\infty$ (Cybenko, 1989). But if $\sigma(x_{it})$ is some sigmoid function, then (5.8) simply describes a feedforward neural network with M_1 inputs, a hidden layer with M_2 nodes and sigmoidal transfer functions, and a linear output node for each k. The w_{ijk} is the weight on the connection from node i in layer k to node j in layer $k + 1$, and the ζ are nodal biases that are treated as adjustable parameters like the weights.

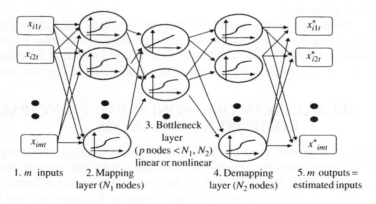

Figure 5.2 NN-NLPCA architecture

Kramer (1991) combines the two networks that represent functions ϕ and θ as shown in Figure 5.2. Intuitively, the neural networks that represent ϕ and θ can be described as follows. The neural network that represents the function ϕ operates on the rows of the $n \times m$ data matrix X_t and has m inputs. The hidden layer of this network is a mapping layer that contains N_1 nodes with sigmoidal transfer functions so that $N_1 > p$. The output of the network is then a projection of the input vector into feature space and therefore has p nodes with linear or sigmoidal activation functions. The function ϕ_i is the ith nonlinear factor that is defined by the weights and biases of the connections from the input to the ith output. On the other hand, the network that represents the inverse mapping function θ_i takes the rows of the scores matrix S_t as inputs and therefore has p inputs. The hidden layer of this network is a demapping layer that contains N_2 nodes with sigmoidal transfer functions so that $N_2 > p$. The output layer of the network contains m nodes that can be linear or sigmoidal and give the reconstructed data matrix X'_t. The function θ_i is defined by the weights and biases that connect the inputs to the ith output node.

Hence the architecture presented in Figure 5.2 has five layers—an input layer (1), a mapping layer (2), a bottleneck layer (3), a demapping layer (4), and an output layer (5). This five-layer NLPCA architecture has m nodes in the input layer, p nodes in the bottleneck layer and m nodes in the output layer. The mapping and demapping layers of the network have **sigmoidal activation functions**. The bottleneck and output layers have linear activation functions. Direct connections are allowed between layers 1 and 3 and between layers 3 and 5, but direct connections are not allowed to cross bottleneck layer 3 (Malthouse, 1996). The bottleneck layer has fewer nodes than the input or output layer.

The network is trained to perform the identity mapping, where the input is approximated at the output layer. Because the dimension of the bottleneck layer is smaller than both the input and output layers, the network is forced to develop a compact representation of the input data. If network training finds an acceptable solution, a good representation of the input must exist in the bottleneck layer. This implies that data compression caused by the bottleneck layer may force hidden units to represent significant features in data. The outputs of the bottleneck layer therefore represent the nonlinear PCs.

NLPCA effectively reduces the dimension of the inputs by fitting a curved surface through the data. The first three layers of the network project the original data onto this surface, and the activation values of the bottleneck layer, called scores, give the location of the projection. The last three layers (3, 4 and 5) define the surface.

Efficient estimation of the parameters (weights) of networks of this kind is not trivial. Let $s_f : \mathbb{R}^m \to \mathbb{R}^p$ denote the function modelled by layers 1, 2 and 3, and let $f : \mathbb{R}^p \to \mathbb{R}^m$ denote the function modelled by layers 3, 4 and 5. The weights in the autoassociative NLPCA network are determined by the following objective function (Malthouse, 1996):

$$\min_{f, s_f} \sum_{i=1}^{n} \|x_{it} - f[s_f(x_{it})]\|^2 \tag{5.9}$$

Many methods have been proposed in the literature to minimise smooth nonlinear functions $f : \mathbb{R}^m \to \mathbb{R}$ if the number of variables m is large. These methods include among others Newton's method, variations of Newton's method, the partitioned quasi-Newton method, the conjugate gradient method, the limited memory quasi-Newton method (L-BFGS), and methods that combine cycles of BFGS and conjugate gradient steps.

Numerical tests performed on medium-size problems show that L-BFGS methods require fewer function evaluations than conjugate gradient methods, even when little additional storage is added. In addition, empirical evidence suggests that L-BFGS methods are faster than methods that combine cycles of BFGS and conjugate gradient steps, and they are better able to use additional storage to accelerate convergence. However, evidence also suggests that partitioned quasi-Newton methods are better than L-BFGS methods for problems where the user is able to supply the information on the objective function that the method requires. It is also good for problems where the element functions depend on less than three or four variables. On the other hand, L-BFGS methods are better than quasi-Newton methods for problems where the element functions depend on more than three or four variables. This is because they are very simple to implement, are faster and require only function and gradient values and no other information about the problem (Liu and Nocedal, 1989).

Limited memory quasi-Newton methods can be viewed as extensions of the conjugate gradient methods. They are more suitable for large-scale problems because the amount of storage to be used can be controlled by the user. On the other hand, L-BFGS methods can be viewed as implementations of quasi-Newton methods in which storage is restricted. The main advantage of L-BFGS methods is that they do not require knowledge of the sparsity structure of the Hessian.

Following the notation of Liu and Nocedal (1989), let us denote the iterates by x_k and define $\sigma_k = x_{k+1} - x_k$ and $\gamma = g_{k+1} - g_k$. The L-BFGS methods use the inverse BFGS formula in the form $H_{k+1} = B_k^\tau H_k B_k + r_k \sigma_k \sigma_k^\tau$ where $r_k = 1/\gamma_k^\tau \sigma_k$ and $B_k = 1 - r_k \gamma_k \sigma_k^\tau$. The L-BFGS algorithm which we use can be described as follows.

Step 1: Choose x_0, μ and θ, θ' so that $0 < \theta' < \frac{1}{2}$ and $\theta' < \theta < 1$. In addition, choose a symmetric and positive definite starting matrix H_0 and set $k = 0$.

Step 2: Compute $\delta_k = -H_k g_k$ and $x_{k+1} = x_k + \alpha_k \delta_k$ where α_k satisfies the Wolfe conditions: $f(x_k + \alpha_k \delta_k) \leqslant f(x_k) + \theta \alpha_k g_k^\tau \delta_k$ and $g(x_k + \alpha_k \delta_k)^\tau \delta_k \geqslant \theta g_k^\tau \delta_k$.

Step 3: Let $\tilde{\mu} = \min(k, \mu - 1)$. Update $H_0 \tilde{\mu} + 1$ times using the pairs $[\gamma_j, \sigma_j]_{j=k-\tilde{\mu}}^k$. In that case $H_{k+1} = (B_k^\tau, \ldots, B_{k-\tilde{\mu}}^\tau) H_0 (B_{k-\tilde{\mu}}, \ldots, B_k) + r_{k-\tilde{\mu}}(B_k^\tau, \ldots, B_{k-\tilde{\mu}+1}^\tau)\sigma_{k-\tilde{\mu}}\sigma_{k-\tilde{\mu}}^\tau (B_{k-\tilde{\mu}+1}^\tau, \ldots, B_k) + \cdots + r_k \sigma_k \sigma_k^\tau$

Step 4: Set $k := k + 1$ and go to step 2.

Note that the matrices H_k are not formed explicitly, but the previous values of γ_j and σ_j are stored separately.

5.5 DATA AND FORECAST METHODOLOGY

The data and classification methods used in our study have been fully described elsewhere (Albanis and Batchelor, 2000a,b, 2001). Here we describe them only briefly, since our focus is on the effectiveness of the alternative dimensionality reduction methods.

For each year 1993–1997 we identify companies listed on the London Stock Exchange which have comprehensive annual accounts data on the EXTEL database for the two preceding years (around 700 companies each year). The returns made by investors in these shares in the 12 months following the publication of the annual accounts are measured using share price information from DATASTREAM. The central task of our classification methods is to predict whether or not a share will be a high- or low-performing share in the out-of-sample years 1993–1997. The distinction between high- and low-performing shares is based on the excess returns of the shares over an equally-weighted benchmark index. Shares with excess returns in the top 25% in a given year are marked as high-performing shares (H), whereas shares in the bottom 75% in the same year are marked as low-performing shares (L). The 25% cut-off point between H and L performing shares is decided so as to achieve a reasonable difference in the mean returns on the H and L classes, and at the same time ensure a reasonably large sample size for these classes.

To help discriminate between the H and L classes, we have for each company a set of 38 accounting ratios which are commonly recorded and used by accounts and investment analysts. As shown in Table 5.1, these fall naturally into nine groups, each measuring different aspects of the company's financial performance—profitability, growth, liquidity and so on.

We use five statistical classifiers to discriminate between H and L shares on the basis of these ratios.

- *Linear Discriminant Analysis* (LDA): this searches for the single hyperplane which best separates H and L classes into two clusters in the space spanned by the features vectors.
- *Learning Vector Quantisation* (LVQ): this identifies a small number of promising clusters of H and L shares, and progressively refines this clustering.
- *Probabilistic Neural Network* (PNN): this effectively identifies each sample observation as the centroid of a H or L cluster, and assigns new observations on the basis of a "nearest neighbour" rule.
- *Oblique Classifier* (OC1): a decision tree technique, which considers firstly "axis-parallel" rules involving only one feature, and then simple "oblique" rules involving linear combinations of features.
- *RIPPER Rule Induction* (RRI): an expert system similar to OC1, but which starts from the most comprehensive conjugate rules involving many features, and then moves to simpler rules to classify the remaining data points.

The 38 accounting ratios are not input directly to these classifiers. This would almost certainly result in "overfitting"—a highly parameterised model which performs well in describing the sample data, but which is not robust in forecasting applications. The dimensionality of the input vector is first reduced using two procedures—the techniques described above, and a more conventional benchmarking data reduction method.

Table 5.1 Accounting variables used in classification models

Return on Capital	PBT/TA, PBT/TCE, NI/TCE, CF/TA, CF/TCE
Profitability	PBT/SR, PAT/SR, NI/SR, CF/SR, PAT/EQ, CF/MKBD
Financial Leverage	DEBT/EQ, DEBT/TCE, DEBT/TA, TL/EQ, TA/EQ, BA/MKBD
Investment	P/E, DY, EY, BE/ME
Growth (%)	TA, PAT, PBT, EPS, MKBD, SR
Short-term Liquidity	CA/CL, CL/TA, CL/EQ
Return on Investment	NI/TA, PAT/TA
Efficiency	SR/TA, DRS/SR
Risk	PBT/CL, PAT/CL, NI/CL, CF/CL

Notes: PBT, Profit Before Taxes; TA, Total Assets; TCE, Total Capital Employed; CF, Cash Flow; PAT, Profit after Taxes; SR, Sales Revenue; NI, Net Income; EQ, Shareholders' Equity; MKBD, Market Capitalisation at Balance Sheet Date; DEBT, Debt; TL, Total Liabilities; BA, Book Assets; P/E, Price/Earnings Ratio; EY, Earnings Yield; DY, Dividend Yield; BE, Book Equity; ME, Market Equity; EPS, Earnings Per Share; CA, Current Assets; CL, Current Liabilities; DRS, Debtors.

In the first case, we apply PCA, NN-PCA and NN-NLPCA to each of the nine groups of ratios separately. From each group we then extract one principal component. Applying this methodology, we achieve two benefits: first, we reduce the possibility of overfitting; and second, we can easily interpret the PCs since they are extracted from homogeneous groups of ratios.

The data used for the implementation of the NN-PCA and NN-NLPCA are normalised within the range (0,1). We minimised the objective functions presented in (5.5) and (5.9) by applying the L-BFGS optimisation routine as suggested by Liu and Nocedal (1989) and Malthouse (1996).

The most widely used criterion for assessing the performance of a particular classification method is the misclassification rate or error rate. The misclassification rate or error rate indicates the proportion of objects classified incorrectly after applying a particular classification rule.

To assess the effectiveness of the PCA, NN-PCA and NN-NLPCA dimensionality reduction techniques, we alternatively reduce the dimensionality of the data by applying stepwise variable elimination procedures. This is a standard methodology for identifying an optimal subset of variables for an LDA model. According to this method, the first variable included in the analysis has the largest acceptable value for some selection criterion. After the first variable is entered, the value of the criterion is re-evaluated for all variables not in the model, and the variable with the largest acceptable criterion value is entered next. At this point, the variable entered first is re-evaluated to determine whether it meets the removal criterion. If it does, it is removed from the model. Variable selection terminates when no more variables meet entry or removal criteria. The criterion used for selecting the best subset of variables for the LDA was minimisation of *Wilk's lambda*. A detailed description of this criterion can be found in Albanis and Batchelor (2001).

There are no equivalent standard procedures for avoiding overfitting in the PNN, LVQ, RRI and OC1 algorithms. In these cases, we follow the methodology suggested by Tyree and Long (1996). That is, the algorithms are implemented using all 38 ratios and the misclassification rate is recorded. A single variable is then removed and the algorithms are implemented again. If the misclassification rate is lower, the variable is removed permanently. Otherwise, it is returned back to the pool of variables to be included in the final model. This procedure is repeated for each individual variable.

One general drawback of these *ad hoc* variable elimination procedures is that the selection of the variables may be dependent on the choice of the model parameters rather than the discriminating power of the variables. For example, a specific variable may be found significant for a given setting of model parameters, whereas the same variable may be found insignificant for a different setting of parameters. Searching all possible combinations of parameters for each individual variable might be an expensive task in terms of computational resources. Another drawback of this approach is that it might be time-consuming if the dataset is large because we have to implement the same procedure for each individual variable.

After selecting an optimal subset of variables for each particular classifier, we implemented them separately using two years of data to predict the next year. For example, to predict relative excess returns for 1993, we first trained the classification methods on the two preceding years 1991 and 1992 using cross-validation procedures to find the optimal values of parameters for each individual classifier. After selecting optimal parameters for each individual classifier, we applied them to predict the out-of-sample year 1993. We then moved the implementation one year ahead and used information available from 1992 and 1993 to predict 1994, and so on. The cross-validation procedures that we applied to select optimal parameters for each particular classifier include the leave-one-out method and other similar rotation procedures. A detailed description of these procedures can be found in Hand (1997).

To evaluate the profitability of the five classifiers and the two voting methodologies, we calculated average returns and excess returns over an equally-weighted benchmark index for the portfolios of actual H and L shares in our data in all the 12-month holding periods starting each year, and then compared them with the respective averages for the portfolios of H and L shares predicted by the classification methods.

5.6   RESULTS

The critical questions are:

- Do the PC techniques produce classifications which are close to those using (subsets of) the original variables?
- Do the nonlinear PC techniques perform better than the linear PCA?

Table 5.2 shows the Percentage of Variance Explained (PVE) by PCA, NN-PCA and NN-NLPCA if the 38 ratios are grouped into homogeneous groups of ratios based on conceptual clustering, one architecture is applied for each group, and only one PC is extracted from each group for the years 1993–1997.

Table 5.2   Percentage of variance explained by PCA, NN-PCA and NN-NLPCA

Groups	Initial dimension	PCs extracted	PCA	NN-PCA	NN-NLPCA
			Percentage of variance explained		
1993					
RCAP	5	1	46.76%	64.99%	76.05%
PROF	6	1	46.37%	53.56%	79.75%
FLEV	6	1	39.96%	37.90%	85.24%
INV	4	1	29.81%	69.72%	87.50%
GRT	6	1	29.34%	57.58%	80.78%
ST-LIQ	3	1	44.75%	75.20%	95.90%
ROI	2	1	88.42%	94.53%	99.61%
EFF	2	1	59.34%	70.08%	98.80%
RISK	4	1	72.66%	79.51%	80.82%
1994					
RCAP	5	1	43.12%	39.43%	78.22%
PROF	6	1	51.14%	52.67%	78.27%
FLEV	6	1	42.62%	41.38%	81.47%
INV	4	1	30.69%	62.96%	85.85%
GRT	6	1	28.79%	45.67%	80.82%
ST-LIQ	3	1	44.32%	76.69%	95.08%
ROI	2	1	99.92%	99.93%	99.93%
EFF	2	1	59.43%	69.94%	98.74%
RISK	4	1	74.55%	90.43%	94.95%

Table 5.2   (*continued*)

Groups	Initial dimension	PCs extracted	Percentage of variance explained		
			PCA	NN-PCA	NN-NLPCA
1995					
RCAP	5	1	40.79%	47.18%	87.30%
PROF	6	1	52.03%	56.36%	95.27%
FLEV	6	1	36.78%	62.11%	71.63%
INV	4	1	29.00%	83.04%	90.09%
GRT	6	1	27.24%	45.82%	78.27%
ST-LIQ	3	1	41.83%	84.69%	95.80%
ROI	2	1	99.85%	99.85%	99.85%
EFF	2	1	59.14%	76.71%	99.02%
RISK	4	1	74.10%	85.68%	91.18%
1996					
RCAP	5	1	41.78%	44.91%	88.04%
PROF	6	1	50.94%	48.83%	94.79%
FLEV	6	1	42.78%	43.89%	92.14%
INV	4	1	27.56%	31.84%	72.46%
GRT	6	1	34.15%	39.95%	75.71%
ST-LIQ	3	1	41.97%	83.18%	97.12%
ROI	2	1	99.86%	99.86%	99.86%
EFF	2	1	58.10%	80.05%	99.27%
RISK	4	1	74.13%	73.47%	84.18%
1997					
RCAP	5	1	58.15%	54.89%	77.71%
PROF	6	1	50.23%	51.61%	80.07%
FLEV	6	1	41.98%	79.00%	95.74%
INV	4	1	28.11%	37.42%	76.24%
GRT	6	1	37.34%	56.41%	76.05%
ST-LIQ	3	1	45.18%	87.29%	97.37%
ROI	2	1	99.97%	99.97%	99.97%
EFF	2	1	57.90%	82.81%	99.45%
RISK	4	1	75.07%	92.75%	97.80%
Average PVE for the whole period 1993–1997					
RCAP	5	1	46.12%	50.28%	81.46%
PROF	6	1	50.14%	52.61%	85.63%
FLEV	6	1	40.82%	52.86%	85.24%
INV	4	1	29.03%	57.00%	82.43%
GRT	6	1	31.37%	49.09%	78.33%
ST-LIQ	3	1	43.61%	81.41%	96.25%
ROI	2	1	97.60%	98.83%	99.84%
EFF	2	1	58.78%	75.92%	99.06%
RISK	4	1	74.10%	84.37%	89.79%

The PVE by the individual PCs was found after implementing the architectures for every two successive years. For example, the PVE by the individual PCs for 1993 was found after implementing the architectures using the data for 1992 and 1993. The bottom part of Table 5.2 shows the average PVE by the individual PCs for the period 1993–1997. As we can see, the PCs extracted from NN-NLPCA explain a greater proportion of variance in the original dataset than the other dimensionality reduction techniques. These results indicate the existence of strong nonlinearities in the original dataset.

To determine whether the average PVE by the different architectures is equal, we performed formal statistical tests. First, we tested the NN-PCA against the PCA, and then we tested the NN-NLPCA against the NN-PCA. In the former case, the null hypothesis is that the average PVE by PCA is greater than or equal to the average PVE by NN-PCA. In the latter case, the null hypothesis is that the average PVE by NN-PCA is greater than or equal to the average PVE by NN-NLPCA. To perform these tests, we applied the following statistics:

$$Z_1 = \frac{(\tilde{P}_{\text{NN-PCA}} - \tilde{P}_{\text{PCA}}) - 0}{\left(\dfrac{\tilde{P}_{\text{NN-PCA}} \tilde{Q}_{\text{NN-PCA}} + \tilde{P}_{\text{PCA}} \tilde{Q}_{\text{PCA}}}{n} \right)^{\frac{1}{2}}}$$

$$Z_2 = \frac{(\tilde{P}_{\text{NN-NLPCA}} - \tilde{P}_{\text{NN-PCA}}) - 0}{\left(\dfrac{\tilde{P}_{\text{NN-NLPCA}} \tilde{Q}_{\text{NN-NLPCA}} + \tilde{P}_{\text{NN-PCA}} \tilde{Q}_{\text{NN-PCA}}}{n} \right)^{\frac{1}{2}}}$$

where $\tilde{P}$ is the Average Percentage of Variance Explained (APVE), $\tilde{Q}$ is the Percentage of Variance Unexplained (APNU), and n is the average number of companies.

As we can see from the p-values presented in Table 5.3, the null hypothesis is rejected for eight out of nine Z_1 tests and is rejected also for all Z_2 tests at the 5% level of significance. These results suggest that the average PVE by NN-PCA is significantly greater than the PVE by PCA, whereas the PVE by NN-NLPCA is significantly greater than the PVE by NN-PCA and therefore by PCA.

The full results for the classification accuracy of the five classifiers are rather lengthy, and they have been gathered together in Appendix 5.1. Table A5.1 and Figure A5.1, for example, assess the classification performance of LDA for the out-of-sample years 1993–1997 using five different sets of inputs:

1. using all variables;
2. using the best subset of variables that we found after variable reduction;
3. using PCA for each homogeneous group of ratios and then using the resulting PCs as independent variables;

Table 5.3 One-tail Z test for differences between percentages of variance explained

	n	PCA	NN-PCA	NN-NLPCA	Z_1	p-Value	Z_2	p-Value
RCAP	1378	46.12%	50.28%	81.46%	2.19*	0.0143	18.28*	0.0000
PROF	1378	50.14%	52.61%	85.63%	1.30	0.0968	20.09*	0.0000
FLEV	1378	40.82%	52.86%	85.24%	6.38*	0.0000	19.63*	0.0000
INV	1378	29.03%	57.00%	82.43%	15.46*	0.0000	15.12*	0.0000
GRT	1378	31.37%	49.09%	78.33%	9.64*	0.0000	16.76*	0.0000
ST-LIQ	1378	43.61%	81.41%	96.25%	22.26*	0.0000	12.72*	0.0000
ROI	1378	97.60%	98.83%	99.84%	2.44*	0.0073	3.27*	0.0007
EFF	1378	58.78%	75.92%	99.06%	9.76*	0.0000	19.60*	0.0000
RISK	1378	74.10%	84.37%	89.79%	6.70*	0.0000	4.26*	0.0000

Note: *Denotes significance at the 5% level.

4. using NN-PCA for each homogeneous group of ratios and then using the resulting
    PCs as independent variables;
5. using NN-NLPCA for each homogeneous group of ratios and then using the resulting
    PCs as independent variables.

As we can see, the classification performance of LDA is better after using the best
subset of variables for the out-of-sample year 1993. On the other hand, the classification
performance of LDA is more unstable after using the PCs from the PCA methodology
for the out-of-sample years 1994–1997, whereas there are only minor inconsistencies in
the performance of this classifier after applying the other four dimensionality reduction
techniques over the same period.

Table A5.2 shows the classification performance of the PNN for the out-of-sample years
1993–1997 after applying the five dimensionality reduction techniques. These results are
also summarised in Figure A5.2. The classification performance of the PNN is better after
using the best subset of variables for the out-of-sample years 1993 and 1994. On the other
hand, the classification performance of PNN seems to be more unstable after using the
PCs from the PCA methodology for the out-of-sample years 1995–1997, whereas there
are only minor inconsistencies in the performance of this classifier after using the other
dimensionality reduction techniques over the same period.

Table A5.3 shows the classification performance of LVQ for the out-of-sample years
1993–1997 after applying the five dimensionality reduction techniques. These results are
also illustrated in Figure A5.3. The classification performance of LVQ is significantly
better after using the best subset of variables for the out-of-sample year 1993, whereas it
is significantly better after using the PCs from NN-NLPCA for the out-of-sample years
1994, 1995 and 1997. On the other hand, there are only minor inconsistencies in the
performance of this classifier for the out-of-sample year 1996 under all five dimensionality
reduction techniques.

Table A5.4 shows the classification performance of OC1 for the out-of-sample years
1993–1997 after applying the five dimensionality reduction techniques. These results are
also presented in Figure A5.4. The classification performance of OC1 is significantly
better after using the PCs from NN-NLPCA as well as after using the best subset of
variables for the out-of-sample years 1993–1997. On the other hand, the classification
performance of OC1 is affected significantly after using all variables as well as after using
the PCs from PCA and NN-PCA over the same period.

Table A5.5 shows the classification performance of RRI for the out-of-sample years
1993–1997 after applying the five dimensionality reduction techniques. These results are
also presented in Figure A5.5. There are large inconsistencies in the classification performance of RRI after applying the five procedures. The results suggest that the classification
performance of RRI is significantly better after using the best subset of variables for the
out-of-sample year 1993, whereas it is significantly better after using all variables for
the out-of-sample year 1994. On the other hand, the classification performance of RRI
is significantly better after using the PCs from PCA for the out-of-sample years 1995
and 1997, whereas the NN-PCA and NN-NLPCA outperform the other techniques for the
out-of-sample year 1996.

Table 5.4 shows the average total percentage of correct classifications of the classification methods for the whole out-of-sample period 1993–1997. These results are also
illustrated in Figure 5.3. The common feature of all the results is the relatively weak
performance of linear PCA. The classification performance of LDA, PNN, LVQ and OC1

Table 5.4 Classification performance under alternative dimensionality reduction techniques, average 1993–1997

Classifier	All variables	Best subset	PCA	NN-PCA	NN-NLPCA
LDA	57.67%	60.34%	56.24%	59.76%	59.26%
PNN	61.12%	61.33%	57.93%	60.91%	59.95%
LVQ	55.47%	60.71%	54.83%	56.01%	61.41%
OC1	54.16%	61.13%	55.40%	52.61%	59.45%
RRI	57.34%	58.00%	56.97%	56.73%	56.22%

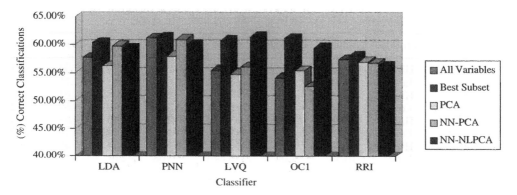

Figure 5.3 Classification performance under alternative dimensionality reduction techniques, average 1993–1997

Table 5.5 Annual percentage returns to predicted high and low portfolios, 1993–1997

Variables	Portfolio	Actual	Predicted	LDA	PNN	LVQ	OC1	RRI
All	High	65.62	High	22.63	25.72	18.97	18.95	21.37
	Low	−0.76	Low	10.12	9.29	13.17	12.98	11.36
Best Subset	High	65.62	High	25.23	25.94	23.72	22.57	21.51
	Low	−0.76	Low	9.35	9.37	10.60	11.13	11.6
PCA	High	65.62	High	21.67	22.31	21.51	20.79	21.54
	Low	−0.76	Low	12.22	11.61	10.59	11.38	11.16
NN-PCA	High	65.62	High	24.05	24.90	19.11	16.26	21.09
	Low	−0.76	Low	9.79	9.98	13.26	15.44	11.27
NN-NLPCA	High	65.62	High	23.62	24.24	25.15	23.30	20.77
	Low	−0.76	Low	9.95	10.42	9.88	10.19	12.02

is affected seriously after applying the PCA methodology. Another common feature is that the NN-NLPCA is generally better than the NN-PCA. It is also clear that the NN-NLPCA outperforms the best subset implementation with the LVQ classifier, whereas it is marginally worse than the best subset with some other classifiers such as LDA, PNN and OC1. The LDA and PNN, for example, classify on average better after using the best subset of variables, and fairly well using the PCs from NN-PCA and the PCs from NN-NLPCA.

Table 5.5 (and Appendix Table A5.6 and Figure A5.6) bring us closer to the interests of traders, and show the average actual H and L returns, and the H and L returns predicted by the classifiers for the out-of-sample years 1993–1997, under each dimensionality reduction technique. It is known that in general the relative accuracy of competing point forecasts of financial market variables may be only weakly correlated with the financial returns made from trading on these forecasts. In the case of directional forecasts like those investigated here, the correlation is likely to be closer. Looking across the information sets used in implementing the LDA, for example, the most accurate is the best subset, followed by the NN-PCA, NN-NLPCA and full input set. The ranking by relative profitability of the H portfolio is exactly the same. Similarly, looking across the relative profitability of different classifiers using the NN-NLPCA inputs, the most accurate is the LVQ, followed

Table 5.6 Annual percentage excess returns to predicted high and low portfolios, 1993–1997

Variables	Portfolio	Actual	Predicted	LDA	PNN	LVQ	OC1	RRI
All	High	49.48	High	10.63	9.62	3.02	2.93	5.21
	Low	−16.54	Low	−5.622	−6.462	−2.6	−2.75	−4.26
Best subset	High	49.48	High	9.23	9.84	7.61	6.61	5.45
	Low	−16.54	Low	−6.474	−6.4	−5.13	−4.69	−4.12
PCA	High	49.48	High	5.35	6.19	5.35	4.63	5.54
	Low	−16.54	Low	−3.358	−4.12	−4.98	−4.19	−4.59
NN-PCA	High	49.48	High	7.81	8.72	3.25	0.46	5.08
	Low	−16.54	Low	−5.846	−5.768	−2.6	−0.48	−4.5
NN-NLPCA	High	49.48	High	7.34	8.09	9.15	7.12	4.72
	Low	−16.54	Low	−5.642	−5.342	−5.86	−5.43	−3.74

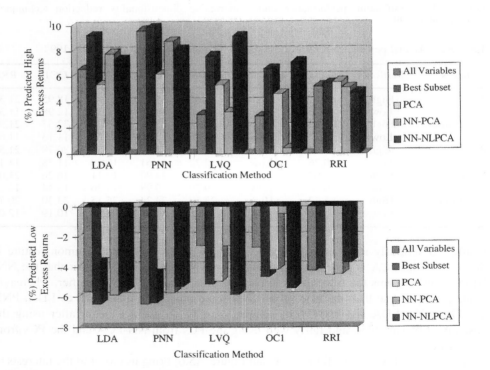

Figure 5.4 Average excess returns to predicted high and low performing shares

by the PNN, LDA, OC1 and RRI. Again the profitability ranking for the portfolio of high-performing shares is identical. The conclusions for L returns are similar.

Table 5.6 (and Appendix Table A5.7) and Figure 5.4 report the average actual H and L excess returns and the respective average H and L excess returns over the index predicted by the classifiers for the out-of-sample target years 1993–1997 after applying the five dimensionality reduction techniques. These results confirm that the PNN predicts more accurately H excess returns after using the best subset of variables. The LVQ and OC1 predict more accurately H excess returns after applying the NN-NLPCA dimensionality reduction technique. The LDA predicts more accurately H excess returns after using the best subset of variables, whereas the RRI produces very similar and generally inferior results under all five dimensionality reduction techniques.

5.7   CONCLUSION

In this paper, we have introduced and investigated ways of reducing the dimensionality of our data other than *ad hoc* stepwise variable elimination procedures. The alternative methods we investigated are linear principal components analysis and linear and nonlinear techniques based on neural networks. The techniques have been illustrated using one data set, but a variety of linear and nonlinear statistical classifiers.

The most striking feature of the results is the loss of information from using linear principal components. As a dimensionality reduction technique this generally fares worse than simple variable deletion and both the neural network-based feature extraction methods. As between the linear and nonlinear neural network PCA methods, the nonlinear approach usually dominates, particularly when used in the context of the more powerful classification methods (PNN and LVQ).

Taken together, these results suggest that there are discoverable patterns relating fundamental data on the published financial performance of companies and their subsequent share price performance. But these patterns are nonlinear, and are more likely to be detected using nonlinear classifiers with nonlinear data preprocessing.

ACKNOWLEDGEMENTS

We are indebted for comments on an earlier draft of this paper to participants in the Computational Finance 2000/International Conference on Forecasting Financial Markets: Interest Rates, Exchange Rates and Asset Management, London, June 2000.

REFERENCES

Albanis, G.T. (1998). "Combining Heterogeneous Classifiers for Stock Selection", Ph.D. transfer panel thesis, City University Business School, London.

Albanis, G.T. and R.A. Batchelor (1999). "Assessing the Long-Term Credit Standing of Bond Issuers Using Dimensionality Reduction Techniques Based on Neural Networks—An Alternative to Overfitting", paper presented at the Third World Multiconference on Systemics, Cybernetics and Informatics and the Fifth International Conference on Information Systems, Analysis and Synthesis (SCI'99/ISAS'99), Orlando, FL.

Albanis, G.T. and R.A. Batchelor (2000a). "Five Classification Algorithms to Predict High Performance Stocks". In C. Dunis (ed.), Advances in Quantitative Asset Management. Boston: Kluwer Academic, 295–318.

Albanis, G.T. and R.A. Batchelor (2000b). "Combining Nonlinear Classifiers for Stock Selection", paper presented at the *Forecasting Financial Markets 2000/Computational Finance 2000* Conference (CF'2000/FFM'2000), London.

Albanis, G.T. and R.A. Batchelor (2001). "21 Nonlinear Ways to Beat the Market", this volume.

Baldi, P. and K. Hornik (1989). "Neural Networks and Principal Component Analysis: Learning from Examples without Local Minima", Neural Networks, **2**, 53–58.

Bishop, M.C. (1995). *Neural Networks for Pattern Recognition*. Oxford: Oxford University Press.

Bourland, H. and Y. Kamp (1988). "Auto-Association by Multilayer Perceptrons and Singular Value Decomposition", *Biological Cybernetics* **59**, 291–294.

Chang, W.C. (1983). "On Using Principal Components Before Separating a Mixture of Two Multivariate Normal Distributions", *Applied Statistics* **32**, 267–275.

Cybenko, G. (1989). "Approximation by Superpositions of a Sigmoidal Function, *Mathematics of Control, Signal, and Systems* **2**, 303–314.

Dong, D. and T.J. McAvoy (1995). "Non-Linear Principal Component Analysis Based on Principal Curves and Neural Networks", *Computer Chemical Engineering* **20**(1), 65–78.

Hand, D.J. (1997). *Construction and Assessment of Classification Rules*. Chichester: Wiley.

Jolliffee, I.T. (1986). *Principal Component Analysis*. New York: Springer-Verlag.

Karhunen, J. and J. Joutsensalo (1994). "Representation and Separation of Signals Using Non-Linear PCA Type Learning", *Neural Networks* **7**(1), 113–127.

Kramer, A.M. (1991). "Non-Linear Principal Component Analysis Using Autoassociative Neural Networks", *American Institute of Chemical Engineers Journal* **37**(21), 233–243.

Liu, D.C. and J. Nocedal (1989). "On the Limited Memory BFGS Method for Large Scale Optimisation", *Mathematical Programming* **45**, 503–528.

Malthouse, C. (1996). "Non-Linear Partial Least Squares", Ph.D. thesis, Northwestern University, Graduate School of Management.

Oja, E. (1992). "Principal Components, Minor Components, and Linear Neural Networks", *Neural Networks* **5**, 927–935.

Rowies, S. (1997). "Algorithms for PCA and SPCA", *Neural Information Processing Systems* **10**, 626–632.

Tyree, E. and J.A. Long (1996). "Assessing Financial Distress with Probabilistic Neural Networks", paper presented at the Third International Conference on Neural Networks in the Capital Markets, London Business School, London.

APPENDIX 5.1

Table A5.1   Classification performance of LDA for 1993–1997

		Predicted Class Membership								
		All Variables		12 Variables		PCA		NN-PCA		NN-NLCA	
Actual Class	Patterns	H	L	H	L	H	L	H	L	H	L
1993											
H	163	107	56	98	65	97	66	102	61	105	58
L	488	176	312	128	360	145	343	152	336	153	335
Total (%)		64.36%		70.35%		67.59%		67.28%		67.59%	
1994											
H	163	89	74	92	71	88	75	87	76	88	75
L	488	212	276	212	276	242	246	212	276	214	274
Total (%)		56.07%		56.53%		51.31%		55.76%		55.61%	
1995											
H	173	109	64	106	67	85	88	107	66	108	65
L	519	211	308	208	311	295	224	200	319	209	310
Total (%)		60.26%		60.26%		44.65%		61.56%		60.40%	
1996											
H	188	107	81	106	82	101	87	103	85	100	88
L	561	278	283	262	299	241	320	255	306	257	304
Total (%)		52.07%		54.07%		56.21%		54.61%		53.94%	
1997											
H	188	109	79	105	83	103	85	108	80	107	81
L	564	255	309	214	350	205	359	224	340	229	335
Total (%)		55.59%		60.51%		61.44%		59.57%		58.78%	

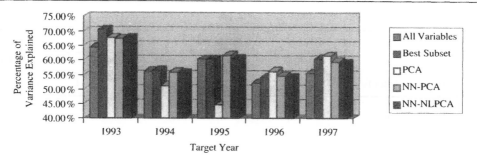

Figure A5.1   Classification performance of LDA for 1993–1997

Table A5.2   Classification performance of PNN for 1993–1997

Actual Class	Patterns	All Variables		17 Variables		PCA		NN-PCA		NN-NLPCA	
		H	L	H	L	H	L	H	L	H	L
1993											
H	163	94	69	96	67	90	73	93	70	93	70
L	488	138	350	123	365	136	352	130	358	138	350
Total (%)		68.20%		70.81%		67.90%		69.28%		68.05%	
1994											
H	163	83	80	84	79	89	74	83	80	83	80
L	488	221	267	199	289	221	267	218	270	229	259
Total (%)		53.76%		57.30%		54.69%		54.22%		52.53%	
1995											
H	173	104	69	103	70	84	89	106	67	96	77
L	519	192	327	193	326	264	255	187	332	182	337
Total (%)		62.28%		61.99%		48.99%		63.29%		62.57%	
1996											
H	188	99	89	100	88	98	90	96	92	96	92
L	561	223	338	254	307	238	323	236	325	236	325
Total (%)		58.34%		54.34%		56.21%		56.21%		56.21%	
1997											
H	188	102	86	103	85	102	86	102	86	102	86
L	564	192	372	199	365	201	363	203	361	212	352
Total (%)		63.03%		2.23%		61.84%		61.57%		60.37%	

Predicted Class Membership

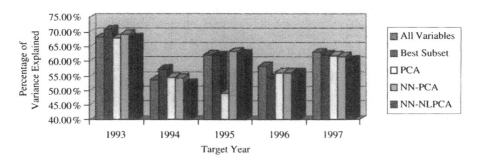

Figure A5.2   Classification performance of PNN for 1993–1997

Table A5.3   Classification performance of LVQ for 1993–1997

		Predicted Class Membership								
		All Variables		19 Variables		PCA		NN-PCA		NN-NLCA	
Actual Class	Patterns	H	L	H	L	H	L	H	L	H	L
1993											
H	163	84	79	90	73	91	72	88	75	90	73
L	488	210	278	154	334	233	255	205	283	187	301
Total (%)		55.61%		65.13%		53.15%		56.99%		60.06%	
1994											
H	163	87	76	84	79	82	81	83	80	84	79
L	488	227	261	206	282	218	270	219	269	181	307
Total (%)		53.46%		56.22%		54.07%		54.07%		60.06%	
1995											
H	173	98	75	90	83	98	75	89	84	85	88
L	519	239	280	188	331	231	288	227	292	155	364
Total (%)		54.62%		60.84%		55.78%		55.06%		64.88%	
1996											
H	188	99	89	105	83	101	87	99	89	96	92
L	561	221	340	216	345	229	332	207	354	207	354
Total (%)		58.61%		60.08%		57.81%		60.48%		60.08%	
1997											
H	188	106	82	100	88	118	70	95	93	103	85
L	564	256	308	203	361	281	283	257	307	201	363
Total (%)		55.05%		61.30%		53.32%		53.46%		61.97%	

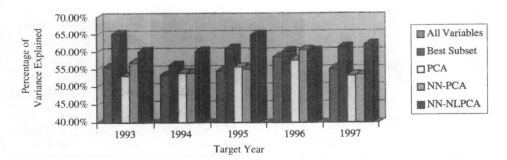

Figure A5.3   Classification performance of LVQ for 1993–1997

Table A5.4   Classification performance of OC1 for 1993–1997

		All Variables		21 Variables		PCA		NN-PCA		NN-NLPCA	
		Predicted Class Membership									
Actual Class	Patterns	H	L	H	L	H	L	H	L	H	L
1993											
H	163	92	71	88	75	98	65	87	76	95	68
L	488	227	261	163	325	236	252	241	247	174	314
Total (%)		54.22%		63.44%		53.76%		51.31%		62.83%	
1994											
H	163	83	80	99	64	78	85	77	86	83	80
L	488	200	288	193	295	229	259	223	265	196	292
Total (%)		56.99%		60.52%		51.77%		52.53%		57.60%	
1995											
H	173	87	86	98	75	95	78	87	86	97	56
L	519	228	291	183	336	220	299	254	265	214	305
Total (%)		54.62%		62.72%		56.99%		50.87%		58.09%	
1996											
H	188	106	82	96	92	99	89	106	82	100	88
L	561	279	282	216	345	233	328	264	297	222	339
Total (%)		51.80%		58.88%		57.01%		53.81%		58.61%	
1997											
H	188	111	77	100	88	114	74	97	91	109	79
L	564	275	289	212	352	246	318	251	313	221	343
Total (%)		53.19%		60.11%		57.45%		54.52%		60.11%	

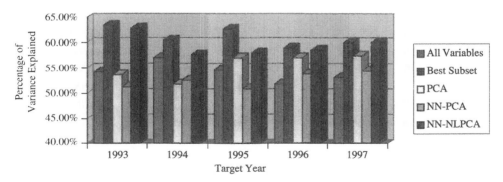

Figure A5.4   Classification performance of OC1 for 1993–1997

Table A5.5   Classification performance of RRI for 1993–1997

Actual Class	Patterns	All Variables		35 Variables		PCA		NN-PCA		NN-NLCA	
		H	L	H	L	H	L	H	L	H	L
1993											
H	163	93	70	91	72	90	73	95	68	88	75
L	488	189	299	149	339	216	272	188	300	176	312
Total (%)		60.22%		66.05%		55.61%		60.68%		61.44%	
1994											
H	163	88	75	94	69	90	73	88	75	89	74
L	488	197	291	233	255	226	262	217	271	228	260
Total (%)		58.22%		53.61%		54.07%		55.15%		53.61%	
1995											
H	173	97	76	99	74	104	69	105	68	95	78
L	519	225	294	233	286	212	307	251	268	246	273
Total (%)		56.50%		55.64%		59.39%		53.90%		53.18%	
1996											
H	188	99	89	113	75	97	91	101	87	97	91
L	561	261	300	253	308	246	315	229	332	226	335
Total (%)		53.27%		56.21%		55.01%		57.81%		57.68%	
1997											
H	188	102	86	96	92	101	87	104	84	99	89
L	564	226	338	220	344	208	356	246	318	248	316
Total (%)		58.51%		58.51%		60.77%		56.12%		55.19%	

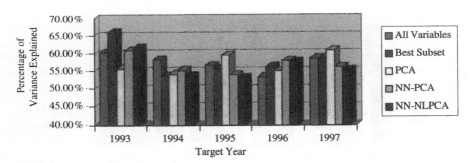

Figure A5.5   Classification performance of RRI for 1993–1997

Table A5.6 Annual actual and predicted returns

Year	Inputs	Actual returns		Predicted returns for the target years 1993–1997				
				LDA	PNN	LVQ	OCI	RRI
1993								
	All	High	89.98	High	44.36	47.62	34	33.15	37.36
		Low	9.22	Low	17.97	19.38	25.68	25.88	23.39
	Best subset	High	89.98	High	50.86	51.77	42.49	35.87	43.31
		Low	9.22	Low	18.06	18.12	21.62	25.41	21.34
	PCA	High	89.98	High	48.17	45.82	35.14	34.87	36.42
		Low	9.22	Low	18.36	20.73	23.8	23.73	23.25
	NN-PCA	High	89.98	High	47.36	49.2	31.32	30.3	38.94
		Low	9.22	Low	17.98	19.15	27.9	28.57	22.14
	NN-NLPCA	High	89.98	High	47.68	48.06	39.37	41.03	42.06
		Low	9.22	Low	17.47	19.2	22.09	21.28	20.84
1994								
	All	High	45.48	High	6.73	7.5	6.28	9.13	9.67
		Low	−7.61	Low	4.76	4.07	5.11	3.01	2.56
	Best subset	High	45.48	High	8.05	9.06	6.62	10.5	8.17
		Low	−7.61	Low	3.59	3.07	4.91	1.75	3.15
	PCA	High	45.48	High	5.46	8.76	9.59	7.37	8.52
		Low	−7.61	Low	5.89	2.87	2.33	4.16	2.99
	NN-PCA	High	45.48	High	6.67	8.56	9.62	6.04	8.43
		Low	−7.61	Low	4.83	3.19	2.26	5.36	3.24
	NN-NLPCA	High	45.48	High	7.11	6.96	10.23	7.97	6.83
		Low	−7.61	Low	4.43	4.49	2.54	3.95	4.57
1995								
	All	High	79.78	High	36.97	39.77	29.48	28.64	31.03
		Low	7.12	Low	15.24	14.46	21.31	22.49	20.29
	Best subset	High	79.78	High	37.81	38.7	36.04	35.4	29.93
		Low	7.12	Low	14.89	15.26	18.06	18.37	21.01
	PCA	High	79.78	High	23.79	26.39	33.48	31.69	34.36
		Low	7.12	Low	27.11	24.17	17.86	19.94	17.66
	NN-PCA	High	79.78	High	37.61	36.89	28.76	22.41	31.6
		Low	7.12	Low	15.46	16.77	22.37	28.09	18.6
	NN-NLPCA	High	79.78	High	34.5	35.49	41.78	32.93	28.64
		Low	7.12	Low	17.5	18.44	16.53	19.05	22.03
1996								
	All	High	54.45	High	12.05	15.93	14	11.05	13.09
		Low	−5.34	Low	7.12	4.92	6.41	8.18	6.48
	Best subset	High	54.45	High	13.15	13.21	16.35	15.32	14.16
		Low	−5.34	Low	6.28	6.47	4.63	5.61	5.36
	PCA	High	54.45	High	14.11	13.94	15.71	14.07	11.16
		Low	−5.34	Low	5.91	6.17	4.89	6.14	8.38
	NN-PCA	High	54.45	High	12.7	13.32	15.71	13.34	12.09
		Low	−5.34	Low	6.87	6.64	5.47	6.06	7.74
	NN-NLPCA	High	54.45	High	13.23	13.83	16.24	16.47	12.8
		Low	−5.34	Low	6.4	6.34	5.18	4.51	7.27
1997								
	All	High	58.44	High	13.07	17.81	11.13	12.8	15.74
		Low	−7.23	Low	5.53	3.64	7.36	5.36	4.1
	Best subset	High	58.44	High	16.29	17	17.13	15.76	12
		Low	−7.23	Low	3.94	3.93	3.81	4.51	7.14
	PCA	High	58.44	High	16.84	16.66	13.67	15.98	17.27
		Low	−7.23	Low	3.87	4.134	4.1	2.94	3.53
	NN-PCA	High	58.44	High	15.94	16.54	10.14	9.22	14.41
		Low	−7.23	Low	3.83	4.15	8.34	9.14	4.63
	NN-NLPCA	High	58.44	High	15.62	16.88	18.17	18.12	13.55
		Low	−7.23	Low	3.98	3.66	3.08	2.18	5.43

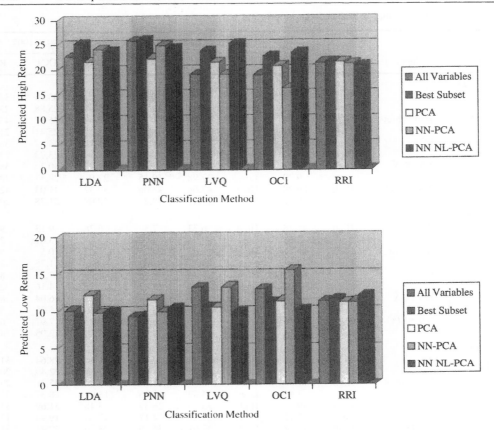

Figure A5.6   Average returns to predicted high and low performing shares

Table A5.7   Annual excess returns to predicted high and low performing shares

Year	Variables	Actual Excess Returns			Classifier: LDA	PNN	LVQ	OC1	RRI
1993	All	High	58.65	High	13.73	16.93	4.97	2.98	8.17
		Low	−19.53	Low	−10.48	−9.3	−4.01	−2.77	−6.17
	Best subset	High	58.65	High	20.4	20.77	11.61	5.46	12.94
		Low	−19.53	Low	−10.78	−10.46	−6.89	−3.35	−7.49
	PCA	High	58.65	High	16.66	15	5.13	4.67	5.94
		Low	−19.53	Low	−9.79	−7.9	−4.99	−4.83	−5.19
	NN-PCA	High	58.65	High	15.53	17.6	2.09	0.58	7.94
		Low	−19.53	Low	−9.86	−9.1	−1.63	−0.5	−6.03
	NN-NLPCA	High	58.65	High	16.03	16.79	8.64	10.53	11.45
		Low	−19.53	Low	−10.45	−9.17	−6.32	−7.34	−7.74
1994	All	High	39.67	High	1.98	2.85	0.29	3.42	3.12
		Low	−13.24	Low	−1.7	−2.5	−0.27	−2.62	−2.42
	Best subset	High	39.67	High	3.08	4.37	1.77	5.54	1.73
		Low	−13.24	Low	−2.7	−3.36	−1.42	−4.5	−1.75
	PCA	High	39.67	High	0.8	4.58	3.42	1.17	3.4
		Low	−13.24	Low	−0.82	−4.16	−2.92	−1.04	−3.21
	NN-PCA	High	39.67	High	1.68	3.86	3.66	0.37	3.66
		Low	−13.24	Low	−1.42	−3.31	−3.16	−0.31	−3.22
	NN-NLPCA	High	39.67	High	2.24	2.3	5.65	2.95	2.2
		Low	−13.24	Low	−1.94	−2.12	−3.87	−2.21	−2.09
1995	All	High	54.89	High	11.72	14.14	4.18	2.99	5.73
		Low	−18.3	Low	−10.09	−10.58	−3.98	−2.51	−5
	Best subset	High	54.89	High	12.61	13.27	10.86	10.17	4.67
		Low	−18.3	Low	−10.49	−9.93	−7.3	−6.96	−4.32
	PCA	High	54.89	High	−2.15	0.21	7.97	6.39	9.17
		Low	−18.3	Low	2.6	−0.23	−7.23	−5.35	−7.72
	NN-PCA	High	54.89	High	12.29	11.51	3.61	−2.55	6.3
		Low	−18.3	Low	−9.81	−8.46	−3.04	2.47	−6.69
	NN-NLPCA	High	54.89	High	9.09	10.08	16.49	7.25	3.29
		Low	−18.3	Low	−7.7	−6.78	−8.76	−5.93	−3.21
1996	All	High	44.84	High	2.42	6.14	4.08	1.83	3.22
		Low	−15.1	Low	−2.69	−4.74	−3.15	−2.06	−3.1
	Best subset	High	44.84	High	3.41	3.53	6.8	5.58	4.73
		Low	−15.1	Low	−3.41	−3.28	−5.21	−4.09	−4.64
	PCA	High	44.84	High	4.21	4.04	5.96	4.53	1.14
		Low	−15.1	Low	−3.65	−3.4	−4.8	−3.72	−1.07
	NN-PCA	High	44.84	High	3.03	3.48	6	3.88	2.27
		Low	−15.1	Low	−2.89	−2.97	−4.24	−3.91	−1.9
	NN-NLPCA	High	44.84	High	3.44	4.22	6.47	6.79	2.99
		Low	−15.1	Low	−3.25	−3.47	−4.5	−5.22	−2.37
1997	All	High	49.37	High	3.23	7.93	1.58	3.45	5.81
		Low	−16.54	Low	−3.15	−5.19	−1.59	−3.78	−4.61
	Best subset	High	49.37	High	6.63	7.25	7	6.29	3.18
		Low	−16.54	Low	−4.99	−4.97	−4.83	−4.57	−2.42
	PCA	High	49.37	High	7.25	7.12	4.25	6.39	8.07
		Low	−16.54	Low	−5.13	−4.91	−4.94	−5.99	−5.74
	NN-PCA	High	49.37	High	6.5	7.17	0.9	0.01	5.24
		Low	−16.54	Low	−5.25	−5	−0.91	−0.13	−4.68
	NN-NLPCA	High	49.37	High	5.88	7.06	8.49	8.1	3.69
		Low	−16.54	Low	−4.87	−5.17	−5.87	−6.45	−3.28

Theme II
Structural Change and Long Memory

6

Structural Change and Long Memory in Volatility: New Evidence from Daily Exchange Rates

MICHEL BEINE AND SÉBASTIEN LAURENT

ABSTRACT

Using a Markov Switching Fractionally Integrated GARCH model of a daily exchange rate (DEM/USD), we provide clear evidence in favour of a strong interaction between structural change and long memory in the variance. It is however found that these features are "imperfect substitutes" in the sense that both are required to capture all of the observed persistence in the volatility.

Keywords: Structural Change; FIGARCH; Persistence in Volatility; Daily Exchange Rate Returns

6.1 INTRODUCTION

Recent developments in time series econometrics have been concerned with the interaction between structural change and long-range dependence in the first two moments of financial series. Diebold and Inoue (1999) show that, under some conditions, stochastic regime switching is observationally equivalent to long memory, both asymptotically and in finite samples. Granger and Hyung (1999) emphasise a positive relationship between occasional structural break and the fractional degree of integration. Mikosch and Starica (1999) argue that structural change in asset returns could be responsible for the long memory in the volatility. Quite recently, focusing on the first two moments, Timmemann (2000) showed analytically that for some parameters, the Markov switching models yield volatility clustering and persistence as well as structural breaks. Furthermore, empirical analysis, mostly based on stock exchange returns, documents the much lower estimated persistence obtained when accounting for structural change, either in the conditional mean or in the conditional variance. Granger and Hyung (1999) show that there is much less evidence of long memory in the absolute and squared S&P 500 daily returns when adjusting for breaks. On 30 stocks and two indexes, Kim and Kon (1999) also showed that the persistence captured in a GARCH model is strongly reduced when including previously identified structural shifts in the variance.

Developments in Forecast Combination and Portfolio Choice. Edited by C. Dunis, A. Timmermann and J. Moody.
© 2001 John Wiley & Sons Ltd

In this paper, we provide further evidence of the strong interaction between structural change and long memory in the field of exchange rate volatility. The choice of exchange rate is quite important since previous analysis (Baillie *et al.*, 1996; Bollerslev and Mikkelsen, 1996; Tse, 1998; Beine *et al.*, 2000) have used exchange rate returns to provide strong evidence in favour of the Fractionally Integrated GARCH (FIGARCH) model. Simultaneously, some evidence in favour of structural change in the conditional variance of exchange rate returns has been proposed by Bollen *et al.* (2000) through a Markov switching analysis. To allow for both structural change and long memory, we estimate a new model, the Markov switching FIGARCH model, that jointly integrates both features.[1] This contrasts with previously mentioned empirical contributions which rely on a two-step procedure, *i.e.* identification of the structural breaks followed by the estimation of break-filtered models.

Basically, the advantage of our approach is threefold. The first advantage is of course related to efficiency in the estimation of the final model parameters. A one-step estimation allows us to control for the interaction between parameters thought to capture long memory and those related to structural change. The second advantage is related to the data-generating process that the researcher has in mind. Earlier studies assume that structural change occurs and is correctly detected; in this case, this allows us to investigate the impact of its presence on the estimated persistence of shocks. Nevertheless, as Granger and Hyung (1999) show, if the true process is $I(d)$, spurious breaks will be detected.[2] By allowing for long memory and structural changes, our integrated approach is less subject to these biases. Third, as suggested by Timmermann (2000), combining (G)ARCH-type models and Markov switching is necessary since pure Markov switching models with constant variance within each regime yield only limited persistence in the second moment. Our highly flexible FIGARCH framework shows that this may still be insufficient to reproduce the high persistence of volatility shocks observed for the high-frequency financial series.

This paper is organised as follows. Section 6.2 provides preliminary evidence both in favour of structural changes and long memory in the volatility of exchange rates. Section 6.3 presents the FIGARCH model that extends the basic GARCH by introducing a fractional integration parameter aimed at capturing the long run persistence. This model may be seen as limited in the sense that it does not account for sudden changes in the conditional variance. Thus, Section 6.4 is devoted to the presentation and estimation of a new model, the Markov switching FIGARCH model, that integrates both long memory and structural changes.

6.2   PRELIMINARY EVIDENCE

In this paper, we focus on daily nominal exchange rate returns (denoted r_t) of the Deutsche Mark (DEM) against the US Dollar (USD) obtained from the Federal Reserve Bank. Our

---

[1] A similar approach including both FIGARCH and regime switching features has simultaneously and independently been proposed by Hsieh *et al.* (1999). Comparing their analysis with ours, one may identify several main differences. First, their analysis is applied on stock returns (S&P 500). Second, on the methodological side, only the scale parameter is made dependent on the regime. Finally, the main conclusions are quite different: by contrast to these authors, we conclude that long memory in volatility is still present within at least one regime.

[2] By contrast, when the dates of breaks are supposed to be known, dummy variables can be directly included and Likelihood Ratio Tests (LRT) conducted to assess the occurrence of structural change. See Beine and Laurent (2000) for an illustration.

estimation period ranges from 1st January 1980 to 31st December 1998 and involves 4739 data points. Figure 6.1 plots the returns over the full period.

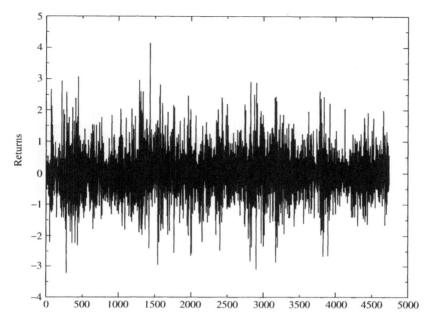

Figure 6.1   Daily exchange rate returns: DEM/USD, 1980–1998

Unsurprisingly, this series exhibits the traditional volatility clustering observed for high-frequency financial data. In turn, such a pattern justifies a GARCH-type model as a preliminary model used to analyse the dynamics of the conditional volatility.

Although some evidence has been provided in favour of long memory and structural change for particular financial series like stock returns, it may be useful to focus on the dynamics of the volatility of r_t. Figure 6.2 plots the autocorrelations computed from the traditional autocorrelogram (ACF) for the absolute returns ($|r_t|$) as a proxy for the variance. This ACF reveals two interesting features of the dynamics of the exchange rate volatility.

First, the autocorrelations decrease at a hyperbolic rate (rather than at an exponential rate), which is often considered as strong evidence of a long memory process (see for instance Baillie *et al.*, 1996). Figure 6.2 shows that the time dependence of volatility shocks may last at least for more than 3 months. This time dependence is obviously the major justification of the rejection of the GARCH model to the extent that this model implies that the effect of volatility shocks dies out quite rapidly. Furthermore, the persistence of these shocks is not infinite, which rules out the use of an IGARCH process. This is the main purpose of the FIGARCH model, to provide additional flexibility between the GARCH and the IGARCH model.

The second feature is that the decrease of this persistence is far from being linear and smoothed, as suggested by the "wave" movements observed in the autocorrelations at lags between 200 and 400, 400 and 600 and so on. Such evidence is consistent with some recent

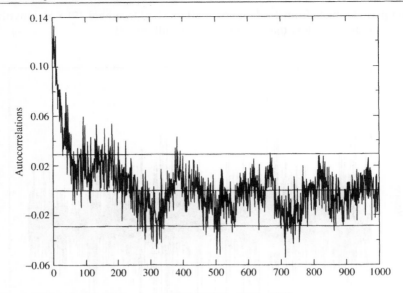

Figure 6.2   ACF for the absolute returns: DEM/USD, 1980–1998

studies on exchange rate volatility, including Andersen *et al.* (1999) for instance. These authors document several characteristics of realised volatility, including clear evidence of long memory but also temporal variation in exchange rate volatilities. This last point and the wave effects observed in the ACF of $|r_t|$ suggest that a "pure" long memory process for capturing the volatility dynamics may not be completely satisfying. In turn, this opens the door for extending the FIGARCH model.

6.3   THE SINGLE-REGIME FIGARCH MODEL

As a starting point, one can estimate the FIGARCH(p, d, q) model introduced by Baillie *et al.* (1996) that accounts for a long run dependence in the conditional variance:

$$r_t = \mu + \varepsilon_t, \varepsilon_t | \Omega_t \sim N(0, \sigma_t^2) \tag{6.1}$$

$$\sigma_t^2 = \omega + \beta(L)\sigma_t^2 + [1 - \beta(L) - \varphi(L)(1 - L)^d]\varepsilon_t^2 \tag{6.2}$$

where μ is the mean of the process and Ω_t is the information set at time t. $\beta(L) = \beta_1 L + \cdots + \beta_p L^p$ and $\varphi(L) = 1 - \varphi_1 L - \cdots - \varphi_p L^p$ are the lag polynomials of respective orders p and q of which all roots lie outside the unit circle. μ, ω, β, φ and d are parameters to be estimated, with d being the fractional integration parameter[3] and finally, L is the lag operator.[4] Approximate quasi-maximum likelihood estimation results of the

---

[3] We follow Baillie *et al.* (1996) and truncate the infinite Taylor approximation of $(1 - L)^d$ at a number of lags equal to 1000. Chung (1999) proposes an alternative specification of the FIGARCH due to the strong relationship between ω and the truncation order. We do not tackle this issue in this paper because the parameter of interest is d which is not affected by this choice. Moreover, the results related to the Chung specification (not reported here to save space) are almost identical.

[4] In the case of a FIGARCH(1,d,0) model, $\varphi_1 = \varphi_2 = \cdots = \varphi_q = 0$.

Table 6.1   FIGARCH and MS-(FI)GARCH models for the DEM/USD exchange rate

	FIGARCH(1,d,0)	MS-GARCH(1,1) (restricted)	MS-FIGARCH(1,d,0) (unrestricted)	MS-FIGARCH(1,d,0) (restricted)
$\mu\vert\mu_1$	−0.0061	0.0303	0.0457	0.0571
	(0.0092)	(0.0298)	(0.0391)	(0.0400)
μ_2	—	−0.0148	−0.0197	−0.0193
	—	(0.0123)	(0.0113)	(0.0106)
$\omega\vert\omega_1$	0.0724	0.8794	0.7313	1.0150
	(0.0135)	(0.0702)	(0.2322)	(0.0940)
$\beta\vert\beta_{1,1}$	0.2060	—	0.0314	—
	(0.0501)		(0.0639)	
$d\vert d_1$	0.2754	—	0.0538	—
	(0.0360)		(0.0493)	
ω_2	—	0.1772	0.0717	0.0770
		(0.0415)	(0.0353)	(0.0255)
$\beta_{1,2}$	—	0.2280	0.1114	0.1109
		(0.1315)	(0.0358)	(0.342)
$\phi_{1,2}$	—	−0.0069	—	—
		(0.0193)		
d_2	—	—	0.0900	0.0958
			(0.0221)	(0.0204)
p_{11}	—	0.9617	0.9228	0.9227
		(0.0152)	(0.0408)	(0.0326)
p_{22}		0.9794	0.9681	0.9747
		(0.0084)	(0.0202)	(0.0104)
AIC	2.0114	1.9890	1.9823	1.9820
SBIC	2.0169	2.0003	1.9961	1.9930
$Q^2(20)$	26.4796	19.6910	25.5198	22.9882
$Q^2(50)$	58.6737	55.2263	61.6184	59.1267
Log L	−4762.0911	−4705.0643	−4687.2872	−4688.5829

Note: Asymptotic standard errors are in parenthesis. AIC = Akaike information criterion. SBIC = Schwarz Bayesian information criterion. $Q^2(k)$ = Ljung–Box statistic on squared residuals at lag k. Log L = Log-likelihood.
Data Source: Federal Reserve Statistical Release H.10.

FIGARCH(1,d,0) are reported in column 2 of Table 6.1.[5] As found by Baillie *et al.* (1996) and Tse (1998), the estimate for d suggests that the stable GARCH ($d = 0$) or the integrated GARCH ($d = 1$) models are rejected in favour of a long memory in the conditional variance. Therefore, the statistical inference up to now confirms the preliminary analysis drawn from Figure 6.2.

6.4   THE MARKOV SWITCHING FIGARCH MODEL

6.4.1   Long Memory and Structural Change

Recently, Diebold and Inoue (1999) proved that, under some conditions, changes in regimes are observationally equivalent to long memory both asymptotically and in finite samples. Let $\{s_t\}_{t=1}^{T}$ be a latent variable which takes the value 0 or 1 and which is

---

[5] An Ox package devoted to the estimation of a single-regime ARCH-type model (with a friendly interface) is available upon request from the second author.

governed by a first-order Markov chain with transition matrix $P = \begin{bmatrix} p_{11} & 1 - p_{22} \\ 1 - p_{11} & p_{22} \end{bmatrix}$,
$y_t = \mu_{s_t} + \varepsilon_t$, with $\varepsilon_t \sim i.i.d. \ N(0, \sigma_{s_t}^2)$ and $E(s_t, \varepsilon_t) = 0 \ \forall t, \tau$. Diebold and Inoue (1999) demonstrate that, if $\mu_0 \neq \mu_1$, $p_{11} = 1 - c_1 T^{-\delta_1}$, $p_{22} = 1 - c_2 T^{-\delta_2}$, $0 < c_1, c_2 < 1$ and $\delta_1, \delta_2 > 0$, then y_t is integrated of order equal to the minimum of δ_1 and δ_2, i.e. $y_t = I[\min(\delta_1, \delta_2)]$.

Basically, the idea of Diebold and Inoue (1999) is that if we let the probability of a break decrease with the sample size, the series may exhibit long memory. In a finite sample, regardless of the sample size, if the series has only a few breaks, it can also display some long memory. In a quite similar perspective, Mikosch and Starica (1999) show that when we generate two independent GARCH processes and juxtapose them, the resulting process may exhibit some long memory behaviour in the volatility dynamics. This is in fact an extreme case of the results of Diebold and Inoue (1999) applied to the variance (where there is only one break, this amounts to considering an absorbent state). This leads to the question of how to deal simultaneously with long memory and structural change.

6.4.2 The Model

Let us now focus on structural change through a Markov switching (MS) process. Although this approach is not the only one allowing for structural change, MS processes have been specifically investigated by some of the above mentioned theoretical contributions. One obvious advantage of this framework is that in detecting structural change, we let "the data speak for themselves". The new model to be estimated becomes an MS-FIGARCH model in which the mean and variance parameters are made dependent on the latent state variable s_t ($s_t = 1, 2$):

$$r_t = \mu_{s_t} + \varepsilon_t, \varepsilon_t | \Omega_t \sim N(0, \sigma_{s_t}^2) \tag{6.3}$$

$$\sigma_{s_t}^2 = \omega_{s_t} + \beta_{1.s_t}\tilde{\sigma}_{t-1}^2 + [1 - \beta_{1.s_t} - (1 - \varphi_{1.s_t})(1 - L)^{d_{s_t}}]\tilde{\varepsilon}_t^2 \tag{6.4}$$

This model is a natural extension of the regime switching GARCH model introduced by Gray (1996), in which d is set to 0 for both regimes.[6] It is worth noticing that here all the parameters are allowed to switch, in contrast to Hamilton and Susmel's (1994) switching ARCH model and Hsieh et al. (1999) (in which the Markov process only governs a scale parameter). To solve the problem of path dependence[7] induced by the GARCH process, Gray (1996) proposes to express the conditional volatility in each regime ($\sigma_{s_t}^2$) in terms of past unconditional volatility ($\tilde{\sigma}_{t-1}^2$) and unconditional squared residuals $\tilde{\varepsilon}_{t-1}^2$ where:[8]

$$\tilde{\varepsilon}_{t-1}^2 = \{r_t - [p_{1,t-1}\mu_1 + (1 - p_{1,t-1})\mu_2]\}^2 \tag{6.5}$$

---

[6] The MS-GARCH(1,1) model is written as: $\sigma_{s_t}^2 = \omega_{s_t} + \beta_{1, s_t}\tilde{\sigma}_{t-1}^2 + \varphi_{1, s_t}\tilde{\varepsilon}_t^2$. For convenience, we use the same notation for the GARCH and the FIGARCH models.

[7] A regular extension of the SWARCH model introduced by Hamilton and Susmel (1994) to the GARCH and FIGARCH framework is not possible due to the time dependence of the conditional variance (because the GARCH model is an ARCH of infinite order). See Gray (1996, p. 34) for further details.

[8] The extension of this model to a three-states Markov process is straightforward but is not investigated in this paper.

$$\tilde{\sigma}_{t-1}^2 = p_{1,t-1}(\mu_1^2 + \sigma_{1,t-1}^2) + (1 - p_{1,t-1})(\mu_2^2 + \sigma_{2,t-1}^2)$$

$$- [p_{1,t-1}\mu_1^2 + (1 - p_{1,t-1})\mu_2^2]^2 \tag{6.6}$$

$$p_{1,t} = \Pr(s_t = 1|\Omega_{t-1}) \tag{6.7}$$

(6.7) defines what is known as the filtered probabilities, *i.e.* the probability of being in a particular regime at time t on the basis of past information. As the results will suggest, s_t, the latent regime variable, will basically capture volatility regimes (high and low volatility); its dynamics are driven by a first-order MS process with (constant) transition probabilities p_{ij}:

$$p_{ij} = \Pr(s_t = j|s_{t-1} = i) \tag{6.8}$$

These transition probabilities are constant in the sense that they depend only on the previous state of the economy and can thus be collected in a transition matrix of type P as previously defined.[9]

6.4.3 Estimation Procedure

This MS model is estimated by the so-called Expected Maximum Likelihood (EML) procedure. As the name of this procedure suggests, it involves two main steps: the computation of the probabilities of being in each regime (the "expectation" part) and the maximisation of the sum of log-likelihoods conditional on each regime (the "maximum likelihood" part). It should be emphasised that because of the path-dependence problem previously evoked, each state of the world involves a joint combination of s_t and s_{t-1}. Basically, the estimation procedure may be described in four steps.

Step 1: Initialisation of the filter at time $t = 0$. At time t and for given values of P, one has to compute the steady-state probabilities (ergodic probabilities) $\pi_j = \Pr(s_0 = j)$ in order to initialise the filter. In the two-states case that we adopt here, this can be computed in a straightforward way:

$$\pi_1 = \frac{1 - p_{22}}{2 - p_{22} - p_{11}} \tag{6.9}$$

$$\pi_2 = \frac{1 - p_{11}}{2 - p_{22} - p_{11}} \tag{6.10}$$

Step 2: Computation of the log-likelihood for given joint probabilities of s_t and s_{t-1}, conditional on past information Ω_{t-1}. The log-likelihood function is written as:

$$\mathrm{Ln}(L) = \sum_{t=1}^{T} \ln f(r_t|s_t, s_{t-1}, \Omega_{t-1}) \tag{6.11}$$

where f is the density of the errors. Notice that for the choice of f, we rely in this paper on the normal distribution. Starting with the conditional joint density of r_t, s_t and s_{t-1},

---

[9] The extension of this model to time-varying probabilities has been proposed by Diebold *et al.* (1994) but is not explored in this paper.

one can write:

$$f(r_t, s_t, s_{t-1}|\Omega_{t-1}) = f(r_t|s_t, s_{t-1}, \Omega_{t-1}) \Pr(s_t, s_{t-1}|\Omega_{t-1}) \qquad (6.12)$$

The idea is to get $f(r_t|\Omega_{t-1})$ by summing this joint density over all possible values of s_t and s_{t-1}:

$$f(r_t|\Omega_{t-1}) = \sum_{s_t=1}^{2} \sum_{s_{t-1}=1}^{2} f(r_t|s_t, s_{t-1}, \Omega_{t-1}) \Pr(s_t, s_{t-1}|\Omega_{t-1}) \qquad (6.13)$$

Using (6.11), the log-likelihood may then be computed for given values of $\Pr(s_t, s_{t-1}|\Omega_{t-1})$.

Step 3: Filtering step; calculate $\Pr(s_t, s_{t-1}|\Omega_t)$. For $t > 1$, update $\Pr(s_t, s_{t-1}|\Omega_{t-1})$, using information up to time t:

$$\Pr(s_t, s_{t-1}|\Omega_t) = \frac{f(r_t, s_t, s_{t-1}|\Omega_{t-1})}{f(r_t|\Omega_{t-1})} \qquad (6.14)$$

This updated joint probability at time t is then used to apply step 2 again to the next observation, *i.e.* observation at time $t + 1$. From (6.14), it is also possible to compute the (2×1) vector of filtered probabilities (see (6.7)):

$$\Pr(s_t|\Omega_t) = \sum_{s_{t-1}=1}^{2} \Pr(s_t, s_{t-1}|\Omega_{t-1}) \qquad (6.15)$$

Step 4: Computation of the smoothed probabilities. Given the parameters of the models and the filtered probabilities computed for the whole sample, one can make inferences on s_t using all the information of this sample. Several algorithms to compute these smoothed probabilities $[\Pr(s_t|\Omega_T)]$ have been proposed (see Hamilton, 1994; Kim, 1994; Gray, 1996). Here we rely on Gray (1996) and do not go through all the details in order to save space.

6.4.4   Estimation Results

The estimation results are gathered in columns 2 to 5 of Table 6.1. The estimation results of the most general model in which we introduce a FIGARCH(1,d,0) process in both regimes are reported in column 4. Column 3 reports the results of the MS-GARCH(1,1) while the last column is related to the MS-FIGARCH(1,d,0). These two preferred models are restricted models in the sense that in the first regime, we impose a constant variance, *i.e.* no (FI)GARCH process. It may be seen that for this model, the FIGARCH parameters in the first regime are highly insignificant and that the log-likelihood value is not significantly different from the one associated with the restricted MS-FIGARCH model.[10]

Some comments are in order. First, our regimes are found to refer to volatility levels: the first regime ($s_t = 1$) turns out to be the high volatility regime while the second one ($s_t = 2$) refers to low volatility.[11] Notice that several specifications of the MS models have

---

[10] The same kind of restriction holds for a model in which a GARCH process (rather than a FIGARCH one) is introduced in the first regime. The results are available upon request.

[11] Indeed, both mean parameters turn out to be insignificant at usual confidence levels.

been estimated. Our retained specifications are a GARCH(1,1) and a FIGARCH($1, d, 0$) for the low volatility regime while a constant variance model turns out to capture the dynamics of the high volatility regime. Ljung–Box statistics on the squared residuals [$Q^2(20)$ and $Q^2(50)$] clearly reject any remaining heteroskedasticity up to 50 lags.

Second, compared to the single-regime FIGARCH model, the MS models involve an important increase in the likelihood value. Of course, as reported by several authors (Hansen, 1992; Garcia, 1998), the usual χ^2-based critical values cannot be formally used because of the nonidentification of some parameters under the null hypothesis of no switching.[12] Another problem for comparing these models is that they are not fully nested due to the presence of $\tilde{\sigma}^2_{t-1}$ and $\tilde{\varepsilon}^2_{t-1}$ in the MS specification. Nevertheless, given the very high values obtained for LR tests (LRT comparing the single-regime FIGARCH and MS-FIGARCH amounts to 147.02 for three additional parameters), we suspect some strong evidence in favour of MS processes. More importantly, the information criteria (AIC and SBIC) clearly favour the MS model.

Finally, the MS-FIGARCH seems to perform better than the MS-GARCH, which is also confirmed by the usual LRT test and the information criteria.[13]

It is also important to compare the relative properties of the competing models in terms of fit. As an illustration, one can compare the conditional variances implied respectively by the FIGARCH($1,d,0$) model and by the MS-FIGARCH($1,d,0$) model. First, Figure 6.3 suggests that these conditional variances can significantly differ during some subperiods, especially during episodes of high volatility. It seems that the FIGARCH($1,d,0$) model implies a conditional variance higher than the one provided by the MS-FIGARCH model.

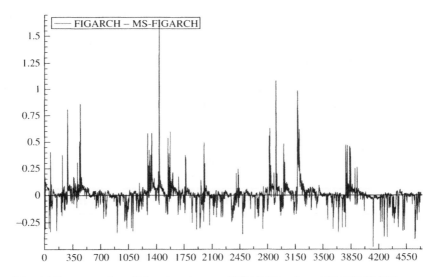

Figure 6.3 Differences of conditional variances: FIGARCH minus MS-FIGARCH

---

[12] Garcia (1998) derived the distributions of critical values for some relatively simple models.

[13] Bollerslev and Mikkelsen (1996) show the usefulness of the AIC and SBIC to discriminate between the GARCH(1,1) and the FIGARCH($1,d,0$).

Second, and more importantly, it may be shown that the latter yields consistent estimates of the volatility while the former provides biased estimates. To see that, we have run regressions of the observed volatility [captured by $(y_t - \mu)^2$] on a constant (denoted α) and on the conditional variances (whose coefficient is denoted by β) produced by the two models. As recalled by Klaassen (1998), the unbiasedness of the variance forecasts of these models implies that $\alpha = 0$ and $\beta = 1$. These restrictions can be tested both individually and simultaneously using OLS estimates for α and β. Table 6.2 shows that the FIGARCH $(1,d,0)$ model yields biased forecasts, both for the constant and the slope coefficient β. The F-test confirms that, as a whole, the restriction $\alpha = 0$ and $\beta = 1$ is rejected. By contrast, the estimates of the conditional variance implied by the MS-FIGARCH appear unbiased, both on an individual and a simultaneous basis. As usual in this kind of exercise (see among others Jiang and van der Sluis, 1998), the R^2 are quite low but consistent with the results of other studies.

Comparing the point estimate of d, our results show that accounting for structural change drastically reduces the estimated persistence of volatility shocks. In this sense, they illustrate the relevance of the theoretical results of Diebold and Inoue (1999) and Granger and Hyung (1999) to the modelling of daily exchange rates. Also, such a result is quite intuitive given the fact that the MS model accounts for the shocks' persistence through the transition probabilities p_{11} and p_{22} that are found to be relatively high. Nevertheless, our estimation results suggest that as far as volatility is concerned, structural change and long memory are *imperfect substitutes*: under the low volatility regime, d remains significant at the usual confidence levels and a FIGARCH$(1,d,0)$ model is required to describe the process. This is consistent with the empirical evidence on stock return volatility provided by Granger and Hyung (1999) and with Diebold and Inoue's (1999) warnings about "*the temptation to jump to conclusions of structural change producing spurious inferences on long memory*".[14] In other terms, both features are necessary to capture the short run dynamics of exchange rate volatility.

Finally, as a joint product of the estimation, one can get the filtered and smoothed probabilities for s_t. These are plotted in Figures 6.4 and 6.5. These confirm that structural changes in the variances captured by regime switches occur quite frequently. Of course, using the whole sample to compute these probabilities rather than information up to time t, *i.e.* using smoothed rather than filtered probabilities, results in less frequent switches. From Figure 6.4, it may be seen that the prevalence of the second regime (the low volatility

Table 6.2 Fit properties of the FIGARCH and MS-(FI) GARCH models. OLS regressions: dependent variable, observed volatility; explanatory variable, conditional variance

	FIGARCH$(1,d,0)$	MS-GARCH$(1,1)$
α	0.079*	0.015
	(0.029)	(0.033)
β	0.828*	0.971
	(0.054)	(0.064)
$F(2,4737)$	4.99*	0.11
R^2	0.046	0.046

* Denotes significance at the 1% level

---

[14] See Diebold and Inoue (1999, p. 25).

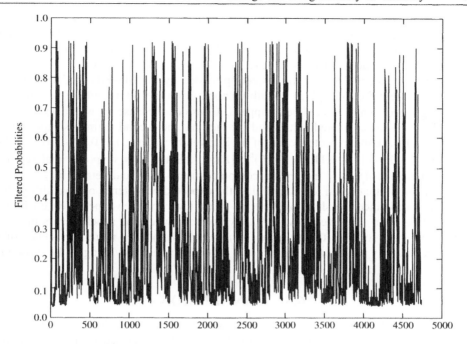

Figure 6.4   Filtered probabilities: $\Pr(s_t = 1|\Omega_t)$

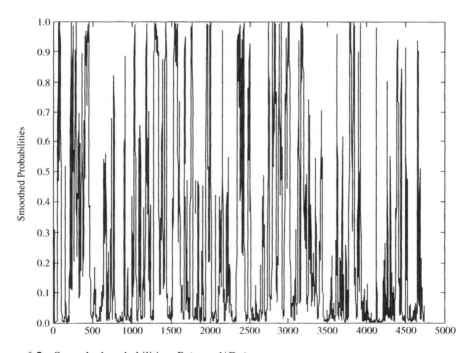

Figure 6.5   Smoothed probabilities: $\Pr(s_t = 1|\Omega_T)$

regime) is higher than that of the first regime, which is in line with the estimates of p_{11} and p_{22}. As a corollary, the second regime is more persistent and opens the door for a long memory process to capture its dynamics. Once more, our estimation results confirm the need for using such a process, at least in a two-regimes framework.

In order to better understand the insights provided by the MS-FIGARCH model, one may analyse the effect of a given volatility shock $\tilde{\varepsilon}_t^2$ on the future volatility, conditional on the regime in which this shock happens. Consider the case in which $\tilde{\varepsilon}_t^2$ occurs in regime 1. Using the estimated values and the fact that the second regime is captured by a FIGARCH $(1,d,0)$, the expected value of σ_t^2 is given by: $E(\sigma_{t+1}^2) = 0.92 * 1.01 + 0.08 * \{0.08 + 0.11 * \tilde{\sigma}_t^2 + [1 - 0.11 - (1 - L)^{0.09}]E(\tilde{\varepsilon}_t^2)\}$. Since it is supposed that regime 1 prevails at time t, $\tilde{\sigma}_t^2$ may in turn be computed using (6.6) and setting $p_{1,t} = 1$. This expression shows that when regime 1 holds, the expected persistence of a volatility shock is quite reduced since the share of the term that allows for such a persistence (the term comprised between {}) is very low (8%). By contrast, when the shock occurs in regime 2, this share rises to 0.97 (the estimate for p_{22}), which induces more persistence of the effect of a volatility shock on the conditional second moment prevailing in the subsequent periods.

6.5 CONCLUSION

In this paper, we have focused on the dynamics of the volatility of the daily exchange rate (DEM/USD) over quite a long period (1980–1998). As suggested by previous studies, the dynamics seems to both exhibit a long memory behaviour and be subject to structural changes. The novelty of this analysis is to study the interaction of these features through a new model, the MS-FIGARCH model that simultaneously integrates these elements. It is first shown that this model outperforms either pure long memory models of the volatility (single-regime FIGARCH model) or a classical MS model that assumes an exponential rate of decay within the low volatility regime (MS-GARCH model).

The estimation results of our MS-FIGARCH model unambiguously show that the long memory documented in the volatility of exchange rates is drastically reduced when we account for the possible structural changes. However, unlike Hsieh et al.'s (1999) investigation for stock returns, we find clear evidence of remaining long memory in the conditional second moment. It turns out that the exchange rate volatility dynamics are quite different from the stock return volatility patterns.

ACKNOWLEDGEMENTS

We would like to thank S. Gray for making available on the web useful codes to estimate unconditional regime switching Models. Comments from L. Broze, F. Jouneau, C. Lecourt, A. Timmermann, J.-P. Urbain, J.-M. Zakoian, the participants of the economic seminar in Lille 3 and the participants of the FFM2000 in London are gratefully acknowledged.

REFERENCES

Andersen, T.G., T. Bollerslev, F.X. Diebold and P. Labys (1999). "The Distribution of Exchange Rate Volatility", NBER working paper no. 6961.
Baillie, R., T. Bollerslev and H.-O. Mikkelsen (1996). "Fractionally Integrated Generalized Autoregressive Conditional Heteroskedasticity", *Journal of Econometrics* **74**, 3–30.

Beine, M. and S. Laurent (2000). "La persistance des chocs de volatilité sur le marché des changes s'est-elle modifiée depuis le début des années quatre-vingts?", *Revue Economique* **51**(3), 703–712.

Beine, M., S. Laurent and C. Lecourt (2000). "Accounting for Conditional Leptokurtosis and Closing Days Effects in FIGARCH Models of Daily Exchange Rates", *Applied Financial Economics*, in press.

Bollen, P.B., S.F. Gray and R.E. Whaley (2000). "Regime-switching in Foreign Exchange Rates: Evidence From Currency Option Prices", *Journal of Econometrics* **94**, 239–276.

Bollerslev, T. and H.-O. Mikkelsen (1996). "Modeling on Pricing Long Memory in Stock Market Volatility", *Journal of Econometrics* **73**, 151–184.

Chung, C.-F. (1999). "Estimating the Fractionally Integrated GARCH Model", working paper, National Taiwan University.

Diebold, F.X. and A. Inoue (1999). "Long Memory and Structural Change", manuscript, Department of Finance, Stern School, NYU, May.

Diebold, F.X., J.H. Lee and G.C. Weinbach (1994). "Regime-switching with Time-varying Transition Probabilities", In C. Hargreaves (ed.), Non-stationary Time Series Analysis and Cointegration. Oxford: Oxford University Press; 283–302.

Garcia, R. (1998). "Asymptotic Null Distribution of the Likelihood Ratio Test in Markov-switching Models", *International Economic Review* **39**(3), 763–788.

Granger, C.W.J. and N. Hyung (1999). "Occasional Structural Breaks and Long Memory", UCSD Discussion Paper 99-14, June.

Gray, S.F. (1996). "Modeling the Conditional Distribution of Interest Rates as a Regime-switching Process", *Journal of Financial Economics* **42**, 27–62.

Hamilton, J.D. (1994). Time Series Analysis, Princeton, NJ: Princeton University Press.

Hamilton, J.D. and R. Susmel (1994). "Autoregressive Conditional Heteroskedasticity and Changes in Regime", *Journal of Econometrics* **64**, 307–333.

Hansen, B.E. (1992). "The Likelihood Ratio Test under Nonstandard Conditions: Testing the Markov Switching Model of GNP", *Journal of Applied Econometrics* **7**, S61–S82.

Hsieh, C.-K., C.-F. Chung and C.-F.J. Lin (1999). "Long-Memory or Regime Changes: the Markov-switching FIGARCH Model", paper presented at the 1999 NBER/NSF Time Series Conference.

Jiang, G.J. and P.J. van der Sluis (1998). "Forecasting Volatility under Multivariate Stochastic Volatility Model via Reprojection", mimeo, University of Groningen.

Kim, C.-J. (1994). "Dynamic Linear Models with Markov-switching", *Journal of Econometrics* **60**, 1–22.

Kim, D. and S.J. Kon (1999). "Structural Change and Time Dependence in Models of Stock Returns", *Journal of Empirical Finance* **6**, 283–308.

Klaassen, F. (1998). "Improving GARCH Volatility Forecasts", Department of Econometrics, Tilburg University.

Mikosch, T. and C. Starica (1999). "Change of Structure in Financial Time Series, Long Range Dependence and the GARCH Model", manuscript, Department of Statistics, University of Pennsylvania.

Timmermann, A. (2000). "Moments of Markov Switching Models", *Journal of Econometrics* **96**(1), 75–111.

Tse, Y.K. (1998). "The Conditional Heteroskedasticity of the Yen–Dollar Exchange Rates", *Journal of Applied Econometrics* **13**(1), 49–56.

7

Long-run Volatility Dependencies in Intraday Data and Mixture of Normal Distributions

AURÉLIE BOUBEL AND SÉBASTIEN LAURENT

ABSTRACT

In this paper, we study the behaviour of the long memory in the return volatility using high-frequency data on the Deutsche Mark–US Dollar. In particular, we provide evidence of the overestimation of the long memory when we do not take into account the presence of jumps (outliers) in the series. After filtering the series from its seasonal pattern, and by using a mixture of normal distributions, the long memory parameter is found to be constant across different sampling frequencies, reduced (compared to the normal distribution) but still significant.

7.1 INTRODUCTION

Temporal dependence in volatility is one of the most striking features of financial series recorded at various frequencies. Quite recently, a huge empirical econometric literature (see Granger and Hyung, 1999 and Mikosch and Starica, 1999 among others) has been devoted to explaining the long memory behaviour of such a series as the result of neglecting structural change. On the contrary, according to Andersen and Bollerslev (1997a, 1998) and Andersen *et al.* (1999), the long memory characteristic appears inherent to the intradaily return series and not due to infrequent structural shifts (see Lamoureux and Lastrapes, 1990). Diebold and Inoue (1999) provide, in the case of various simple models, an analytical proof that long memory and structural change are easily confused but argue that *"even if the truth is structural change, long memory may be a convenient shorthand description, which may remain useful for tasks such as prediction"*. In particular, they show that stochastic regime switching (for instance, mixture model, STOPBREAK, Engle and Smith, 1999 and Markov-switching model, Hamilton, 1989) is observationally equivalent to long memory, so long as only a small amount of regime switching occurs. The above mentioned stochastic regime switching models resemble a standard probability distribution that is called a *mixture of normal distributions* (see Jorion, 1988; Vlaar and Palm, 1993). In this respect, Beine and Laurent (1999) show that the long memory parameter may be reduced (by one half) when modelling four daily exchange rate returns vis-à-vis the USD being generated from a mixture of normal distributions (a Bernoulli–normal distribution).

Developments in Forecast Combination and Portfolio Choice. Edited by C. Dunis, A. Timmermann and J. Moody.
© 2001 John Wiley & Sons Ltd

In this paper, we study the behaviour of the long memory in the return volatility using high-frequency data on the Deutsche Mark–US Dollar spot exchange rate (DM/USD).[1] The aim of the paper is both to provide evidence of the overestimation of the long memory when we do not take into account the presence of jumps (outliers) in the series and to reinforce the argument that long memory may be an intrinsic property of the exchange rate returns.

It is well known that the degree of fractional integration should be identical across different sampling frequencies under quite general distribution assumptions (see Andersen and Bollerslev, 1997a; Bollerslev and Wright, 1998, 1999; Parke, 1999). From frequency-domain methods, Andersen *et al.* (1999) estimate the degree of fractional integration for the 5-, 10-, 15- and 30-minute absolute Nikkei 225 returns (from 2nd January, 1994 to 31st December, 1997). The *d* parameters are respectively 0.429, 0.404, 0.482 and 0.485, which are indistinguishable, and they conclude that '*the long memory feature is an inherent property of the Nikkei 225 volatility*'.[2]

In this respect, we estimate the FIGARCH model for several observation frequencies (5, 10, 15, 20, and 30 minutes). Instead of first filtering the data and then changing the frequency, as proposed by Andersen and Bollerslev (1997b), we first change the frequency and then filter the series by using the corresponding filter. Our estimation results suggest that allowing for jumps in the series (especially in the variance) reduces the long memory property of the series but reinforces the idea that the long memory is an intrinsic property of the exchange rate returns. This is consistent with the empirical evidence on stock returns volatility provided by Granger and Hyung (1999) and with Diebold and Inoue's (1999) warnings about "*the temptation to jump to conclusions of structural change producing spurious inferences on long memory*".[3] In other terms, both features are necessary to capture the short run dynamics of exchange rate volatility. Moreover, unlike the normal assumption, modelling the series as being generated from a mixture of normal distributions tends to stabilise the *d* parameter across different sampling frequencies.

The remainder of the paper is organised as follows. Section 7.2 and its subsections present Andersen and Bollerslev's method to filter the series from its intraday periodicity. Section 7.3 describes the FIGARCH model, the estimation methods and comments on the results. Finally, Section 7.4 concludes.

7.2 THE INTRADAY VOLATILITY

The volatility dynamics of intraday foreign exchange rate returns are complicated. New phenomena become visible as one proceeds from daily returns to intraday returns. Andersen and Bollerslev (1997a,b, 1998), Andersen *et al.* (1999) and Guillaume *et al.* (1995) interpret the overall volatility process as the simultaneous interaction of numerous independent volatility components: periodic volatility components (associated with calendar effects), short-run volatility components (associated with economic news) and longer-run volatility components (associated with persistent unobserved factors). As pointed out by Andersen and Bollerslev (1997b), it is necessary to pre-filter the data for its periodicity before estimating a (Fractionally Integrated) GARCH model.

---

[1] A more detailed description and analysis of the data is contained in Appendix 7.1.

[2] Notice that they also find $d = 0.476$ on a longer time series of daily Nikkei 225 absolute returns.

[3] See Diebold and Inoue (1999, p. 25).

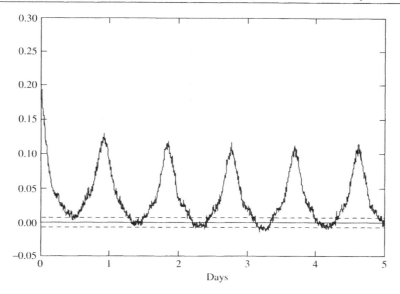

Note: The figure plots the lag 5 through 1440 sample autocorrelations for the 5-minute absolute returns on the DM/USD from 1st October 1992 through 30th September 1993. The 95% Bartlett confidence bands for no serial dependence are also reported in the figure.

Figure 7.1   Five days correlogram of 5 minute absolute returns

In order to motivate the empirical relevance of these ideas, Figure 7.1 plots the lag 5 through 1440 sample autocorrelations for the 5 minute absolute returns $|R_{t,n}|$.[4]

The daily periodicity phenomenon is apparent. Andersen and Bollerslev (1997b, 1998) propose an attractive methodology based on the Flexible Fourier Form (FFF) that allows a direct interaction between the level of the daily volatility and the shape of the intradaily pattern. Their model is a good starting point for high-frequency volatility modelling in a coherent framework. We apply their general framework with some differences: we take into account explicitly the Daylight Saving Time (DST), only the US macroeconomic announcements are studied and the daily volatility component is calculated from a FIGARCH model. Given the estimates of the determinist periodicity effects, we filter the 5-minute absolute returns to obtain an innovation process $|R_{t,n}|/\hat{s}_t$ that should be rid of periodicity effects. Details on this filtering procedure are proposed below.

7.2.1   A Study of the Different Volatility Components

We assume that the volatility process is driven by the simultaneous interaction of numerous components, which are described below. There are intraday volatility patterns, reflecting the daily activity cycle of the regional centres as well as weekend and DST effects, the macroeconomic announcement effects (immediately following the release) and standard volatility clustering at the daily level.

---

[4] Absolute returns are often used as a proxy of the volatility, see Ding *et al.* (1993).

Periodic Volatility Components

As Dacorogna *et al.* (1993) wrote: "*The behaviour of a time series is called seasonal if it shows a periodic structure in addition to less regular movements*". The foreign exchange (FX) market shows strong seasonal effects caused by the presence of the traders in the three major markets according to the hour of the day, the day of the week and the DST. The major movements of intradaily return volatility can be attributed to the passage of market activity around the globe. The global FX market consists of three major markets: the Far East, Europe and North America. Figure 7.2 depicts the average absolute returns over the (288) 5-minute intervals.

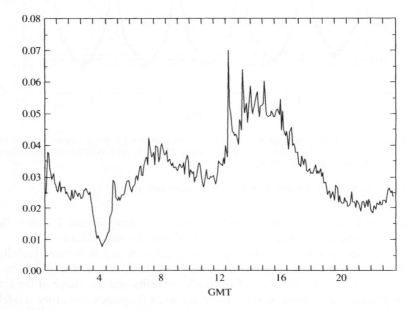

Note: The figure graphs the average absolute 5-minute return for each 5-minute interval, starting with the interval 0:00–0:05 GMT and ending at 23:55–0:00 GMT. The returns are calculated from a linear interpolation (for more details, see Appendix 7.1) over the 1st October 1992 to 30th September 1993 sample period. Quotes from Friday 21:00 GMT through Sunday 21:00 GMT are excluded, resulting in a total of 75,167 return observations. All 261 weekdays are employed in calculating the averages.

Figure 7.2 Intraday average absolute returns for the DM/USD

This intraday pattern is quite similar across all days of the week with discrete changes in quoting activity marking the opening and closing of business hours in the three major regional centres, all of which have their own activity pattern. The following hours can be used as indicative: the Far East is open from 21:00 GMT to 6:00 GMT, Europe trades between 7:00 GMT and 16:00 GMT and trading in North America occurs from 12:00 GMT to 21:00 GMT. Using the discussion of market opening and closures presented above, we explain the intraday seasonal volatility as follows. At 0:00 GMT, the Far Eastern market has already been trading for around three hours and market activity is high. From 0:00 GMT until about 3:00 GMT, activity levels and volatility remain high. Lunchtime in Tokyo (3:00 GMT–4:45 GMT) is the point of the day corresponding to the most prominent feature of the series. Volatility drops sharply and regains its former value at about 5:00 GMT. Generally, Europe begins to contribute to activity at around 7:00 GMT as the Far Eastern market begins to wane: there is a small peak in volatility. During European lunch hours (11:30 GMT), both activity and volatility show a slight lull. The most active period of the day is clearly when both the European and North American markets are open (between 12:00 GMT and 16:00 GMT). Volatility starts to decline as first the European and then the US markets wind down. At around 21:00 GMT, the Pacific market begins to trade again and the daily cycle is repeated after midnight. This intraday pattern is consistent with previous evidence reported by Müller et al. (1990), Dacorogna et al. (1993), Guillaume et al. (1994) and Andersen and Bollerslev (1997b, 1998).

Another intraday pattern often recognised in high-frequency returns is day-of-the-week dependencies. Andersen and Bollerslev (1998), with the same data set, find that Monday appears the least volatile, while Thursday and Friday are the most volatile. Evidence has shown these effects to be the result of macroeconomic news announcements, which are released mainly on these two days (Harvey and Huang, 1991).

DST also have an effect on the seasonal pattern. Indeed, DST changes will influence the local time relative to GMT and thus the intraday volatility pattern in reference to GMT. Both North America and Europe lose one hour relative to GMT in summer months. The Far Eastern local time remains unchanged. Andersen and Bollerslev (1998) and Payne (1997) studied the DST problem. Andersen and Bollerslev show that the volatility pattern appears translated leftward by exactly one hour between 6:00 GMT and 21:00 GMT during the US Summer Time regime.

The seasonal pattern, presented above, seems fully explainable. Failure to take account of those intradaily seasonal patterns is likely to result in misleading statistical analyses. The first authors who have reported intraday analysis (Wasserfallen and Zimmermann, 1985; Feinstone, 1987; Ito and Roley, 1987; Wasserfallen, 1989; Goodhart and Figliuoli, 1991) limited themselves to certain periods of the day, generally the most active ones for a particular market centre, so the problem of daily and weekly seasonality was avoided.

The seasonal phenomena in the volatility of FX markets can be modelled in a variety of ways. Baillie and Bollerslev (1990) use a GARCH specification with seasonal dummy variables for modelling the conditional volatility on hourly FOREX returns on data from the first six months of 1986. For the current study, this would require estimating 288 time-of-day parameters, if one dummy variable were created for each 5-minute interval. The number of variables required is very large and it is unlikely to be effective in capturing the complexity of the seasonal patterns. Another possibility to accommodate seasonality is to modify the traditional GARCH-type models (Bollerslev and Ghysels, 1996). Alternatively, the market volatility can be tied to the intensity of trading via a subordinate stochastic process representation, as suggested by Clark (1973). This approach has been adopted in some recent work by researchers from Olsen and Associates (see, for example, Dacorogna et al., 1993; Müller et al., 1990). Instead of modelling asset price behaviour in calendar time, price movements can be represented as being driven by an information arrival process which itself evolves randomly with certain predictable patterns through time. In Dacorogna et al., especially, the seasonal volatility patterns are modelled by a new timescale, named $v - time$, under the assumption of three main geographical areas where most of the world-wide trading activity is centred: East Asia, Europe and America. Their timescale conversion expands periods with high average volatility and contracts those with low volatility. Their method smooths the seasonal pattern. Another strategy, the one used in this paper, is to seasonally adjust the data. We define the filtered return series $|R_{t,n}|/\hat{s}_{t,n}$ where $\hat{s}_{t,n}$ refers to the periodic intraday volatility component which may be modelled in different ways (see, for instance, Taylor and Xu, 1997; Chang and Taylor, 1996; Andersen and Bollerslev, 1997b). The method, used in this paper, is the FFF adopted by Andersen and Bollerslev (1997b): intraday seasonality was modelled using several sinusoidal and quadratic parameters.[5] The general formulation of the FFF is the following:

$$f(t, n) = \mu_0 + \mu_1 \frac{n}{N_1} + \mu_2 \frac{n^2}{N_2} + \sum_{i=1}^{P}(\gamma_i \cos\alpha_i + \delta_i \sin\alpha_i)$$

$$+ \sum_{j=1}^{2} \omega_j DST_j + \sum_{k=1}^{D} \lambda_k I_k(t, n) \qquad (7.1)$$

where we consider the nth interval[6] in the tth day, N is the number of intervals per day, $N_1 = (N+1)/2$ and $N_2 = (N+1)(N+2)/6$ are normalising constants and $\alpha_i = 2\pi in/N$. As mentioned earlier, the DST alters the form of the seasonal. Therefore, we estimate two seasonal regimes: Summer Time[7] and Transition Period.[8] Hence, there are two different dummy variables according to the time of the year: $j = 1$ is the Transition Time period with $DST_1 = 1$ on this period and 0 otherwise; $j = 2$ is the Summer Time period with $DST_2 = 1$ on this period and 0 otherwise.

The smooth seasonal generated from the Fourier terms is unlikely to cope well with the sharp drop in volatility, for instance, around lunchtime in the Far East and the day of the week dependencies. To fill this gap, we add $\sum_{k=1}^{D} \lambda_k I_k(t, n)$ where $I_k(t, n)$ is an indicator variable for event k during interval n on day t. The events may be calendar and/or announcement effects (see next section). Following Andersen and Bollerslev (1998), we impose a reasonable declining weight structure on the volatility response pattern $\lambda(k, i) = \lambda_k \gamma(i)$, $i = 0, 1, 2, \ldots, N_k$ where the prespecified $\gamma(i)$ coefficients are determined by a specific polynomial and event k impacts volatility over N_k intervals. For the Tokyo open (0:00–0:35 GMT), we choose a linear volatility decay. The volatility decay pattern around the weekends [early Monday morning (21:00–22:30 GMT), late Friday (17:00–21:00 GMT, US Winter Time or 16:00–21:00 GMT, US Summer Time] is restricted to a second-order polynomial.

Short-run Volatility Components: Macroeconomic Announcement Effects

Macroeconomic announcements are relevant for proper modelling of the volatility process. Indeed, Ederington and Lee (1993) showed that the largest returns appear linked to the release of public information (in particular, certain macroeconomic announcements).

---

[5] Payne (1997) uses a similar method in his stochastic variance model of the DM/USD exchange rate. Beattie and Fillion (1999) also use it to assess the effectiveness of Canada's official foreign exchange interventions on intraday volatility of the Can/USD exchange rate.

[6] For 5-minute returns, n equals 144 at 12:00 GMT.

[7] DST changes occurred in Germany and other European countries in the last weekend of March and September. In the US, changes occurred in the first weekend of April and the last week of October. Japan did not have DST changes.

[8] Between the last weekends of September and October, the US is still in Summer Time, but Europe is already in Winter Time. This period lasts four weeks. In the week before the first weekend in April, the US is still in Winter Time but Europe is already in Summer Time.

Studies that examine the impact of scheduled news announcements on high-frequency volatility are various (for instance, Andersen and Bollerslev, 1998; Ederington and Lee, 1993, 1995; Goodhart *et al.*, 1993; Harvey and Huang, 1991; Ito and Roley, 1987; DeGennaro and Shrieves, 1997; Payne, 1997; Boubel *et al.*, 2001). The findings of these studies are consistent, indicating that the releases induce quite dramatic price adjustments but the associated volatility shocks appear short-lived.[9]

We can get a precise economic impact by using the forecast errors associated with announcements (Almeida *et al.*, 1996; Payne, 1997). The forecast errors are created as the difference between the actual announced figure and a median survey expectation. We can also get the general impact of announcements by using a simple dummy specification for announcements. Our analysis focuses on a set of monthly, US, macroeconomic announcements. These announcements are all related to the real economy. It consists of the Employment Report, the Merchandise Trade Deficit, the Producer Price Index, Durable Goods Orders, Retail Sales, Housing Starts, Leading Indicators, Industrial Production and Capacity Utilisation,[10] Consumer Price Index, Consumer Confidence Index, NAPM Survey and Gross Domestic Product (GDP). The category of news is extracted from the Reuters news items[11] using various keyword combinations.

In (7.1), the $I_k(t, n)$ indicators allow for the inclusion of either regular dummy variables or a prespecified volatility response pattern associated with a calendar-related characteristic or news macroeconomic announcements effects. The effect of news on volatility before announcement is not studied here. However, if announcements affect volatility for an hour, there are 13 separate event-specific coefficients to estimate. Given the limited number of occurrences of each type of news announcement, it is not possible to simultaneously estimate separate coefficients for each event and time interval following the news releases. Instead, following Andersen and Bollerslev (1998), we impose a reasonable declining weight structure on the volatility response pattern. The response pattern following each of the announcements is approximated by a third-order polynomial restricted to reach zero at the end of the 1-hour response horizon. The dynamic response pattern is $\lambda(k, i) = \lambda_k \gamma(i)$, $i = 0, 1, 2, \ldots, 12$, where the prespecified $\gamma(i)$ coefficients are determined by a third-order polynomial and λ_k is the announcement-specific loading coefficient.

Daily Volatility Components

Numerous studies suggest that daily and monthly foreign exchange returns exhibit significant volatility clustering. Thus, these ARCH effects at lower frequencies cannot exist exclusively at these frequencies as the aggregation of intraday returns would not be able to accommodate the persistent volatility processes present at the daily level. It is necessary that the low-frequency volatility embodied in high-frequency data have to be modelled. Moreover, Andersen and Bollerslev (1998) demonstrated that daily GARCH volatility predictions are strongly related to the sum of the absolute intraday changes in the foreign exchange for the following day. Indeed, they noted that the correlation between the two

---

[9] There are signs of higher volatility for several hours following the announcement.

[10] The Industrial Production and the Capacity Utilisation are announced together.

[11] The O&A data also include all the news headlines that appeared on the Reuters money news-alerts screens. As with the quotations, these are time stamped to the second in GMT and constitute the basis for our analysis of announcement effects. Comparison of the time stamps for scheduled news releases with the known release schedules indicates that Reuters is timely with respect to scheduled news. During the sample period, a total of 105,065 such headlines appeared.

series is 0.672, or an R-squared of $(0.672)^2 = 45.2\%$. So, to take into account the daily component of foreign exchange volatility, we used a daily volatility forecast $(\hat{h}_t)$.[12]

As Andersen and Bollerslev (1998) write: "*Unfortunately, most empirical work has studied each of the above phenomena—the intraday and intraweekly patterns (calendar effects), the announcements (public information effect), and the interday volatility persistence (ARCH effects)—in isolation. This is ultimately not satisfactory*". Indeed, earlier studies tend to emphasise one of the following three components. Recent findings suggest that the three factors should be accounted for simultaneously to capture the overall intraday pattern.

7.2.2 Modelling Simultaneously the Systematic Components of Volatility

Andersen and Bollerslev (1997b) adopt a method based on the FFF to model the intraday volatility periodicity, the effects of macroeconomic news announcements and the persistent daily volatility dependencies found in foreign exchange data. We apply their framework which consists in decomposing the 5-minute returns $(R_{t,n})$ as:

$$R_{t,n} - \overline{R}_{t,n} = h_{t,n} s_{t,n} Z_{t,n} \qquad (7.2)$$

where $R_{t,n}$ is the expected 5-minute return, $h_{t,n}$ is a daily volatility factor, $s_{t,n}$ represents both the calendar features and the macroeconomic announcement effects and $Z_{t,n}$ is an i.i.d. mean zero and unit variance innovation term. In order to obtain an operational regression equation, Andersen and Bollerslev propose to impose some restrictions and some additional structure (see Andersen and Bollerslev, 1997b for more details). We estimate the following operational regression:[13]

$$2 \ln \frac{|R_{t,n} - \overline{R}|}{\hat{\sigma}_t / N^{1/2}} = c + \mu_0 + \mu_1 \frac{n}{N_1} + \mu_2 \frac{n^2}{N_2} + \sum_{i=1}^{P} (\gamma_i \cos \alpha_i + \delta_i \sin \alpha_i)$$

$$+ \sum_{j=1}^{2} \omega_j DST_j + \sum_{k=1}^{D} \lambda_k I_k(t, n) + \hat{u}_{t,n} \qquad (7.3)$$

where $\overline{R}$ denotes the sample mean of the 5-minute returns, $c = E(\log Z_{t,n}^2) + E(\log h_{t,n}^2 - \log \hat{h}_{t,n}^2)$ and $\hat{u}_{t,n}$ is the error term which is stationary. $\hat{h}_t$ is an estimate of the daily volatility component. The daily volatility component is $\hat{h}_{t,n} = \hat{h}_t / N^{1/2}$ where $\hat{h}_t$ is derived from a daily AR(1)-FIGARCH(1,d,1) model. All coefficients are estimated simultaneously (absolute t-statistics are robust for heteroskedasticity). The estimation results relative to the 5-minute returns are reported in Table 7.1.

After some experimentation, we found that $P = 6$ is sufficient to capture the basic shape of the series. This FFF provides an estimated seasonal pattern that fits reasonably well the intraday periodicity. All coefficients associated with the simple Fourier form are significant, except for the second and last cosine terms. The Tokyo market opening effect is captured by a single coefficient (it allows for a linear decay in the associated volatility

---

[12] This daily volatility is obtained by estimating an AR(1)-FIGARCH(1,d,1) over the period January 1980 to September 1993.

[13] The FFF estimation involves a two-step procedure (Andersen and Bollerslev, 1997b).

Table 7.1   Results of the FFF estimation on 5-minute returns

$\mu_0 + C$	−10.0708	6.151
μ_1	13.6421	2.890
μ_2	−4.3987	2.864
γ_1	1.9814	2.131
γ_2	0.2966	1.556
γ_3	0.4883	6.601
γ_4	0.2621	3.737
γ_5	0.2407	3.799
γ_6	−0.0304	1.229
δ_1	0.4203	2.630
δ_2	0.5181	5.801
δ_3	−0.1062	2.402
δ_4	0.1032	3.255
δ_5	0.2156	5.897
δ_6	0.1607	3.426
ω_1	−0.1961	0.810
ω_2	0.0243	0.192
Tokyo opening	1.4236	4.303
Tokyo lunch 1	−1.3415	9.551
Tokyo lunch 2	−0.1036	3.127
Monday 1	0.2985	1.185
Monday 2	0.0471	0.776
Friday late 1	−0.0009	0.004
Friday late 2	−0.0355	1.804
Tuesday	0.2471	2.697
Wednesday	0.2606	2.505
Thursday	0.2681	2.378
Friday	0.0994	0.549
Consumer Confidence	0.4722	1.374
Consumer Price Index	1.1652	4.356
Capacity Utilisation industrial Production	0.0391	0.167
Durable Goods Orders	1.5073	4.788
Index of Leading Indicators	0.2691	1.524
US NAPM Survey	−0.1448	0.337
Housing Starts	0.6387	1.972
Producer Price Index	0.4658	1.099
Advance Retail Sales	0.5657	1.337
Merchandise Trade Balance	1.2874	3.232
GDP	1.3731	5.501
Jobless Rate	2.7441	8.218

Note: Robust absolute t-statistics are reported in the third column

burst). We note a strong market opening effect. Indeed, it has an immediate response coefficient of 1.42, implying that volatility jumps by 142% at 9 a.m. Tokyo time. The assessment of the remaining calendar and announcement effects is more complicated because the regressors are not simple indicators, but imply prespecified dynamic response patterns. For instance, the Tokyo lunchtime and the Friday late effects are accommodated by a second-order polynomial over the corresponding intervals, resulting in two regression coefficients (Tokyo lunch 1, Tokyo lunch 2, Friday late 1, Friday late 2, see Table 7.1) for each period. Besides, we note that the Tokyo lunchtime exerts a considerable effect. For the announcements, we use a third-order polynomial to capture their impact on the volatility. The actual estimates for this polynomial are given by $\gamma(i) = 1.9228[1 - (i/13)^3] - 0.7205[1 - (i/13)^2]i + 0.0988[1 - (i/13)]i^2$. Hence, the instantaneous jump in the volatility equals $\exp[\lambda_k \gamma(0)/2] - 1$. In particular, the instantaneous jump for the Jobless Rate equals $\exp[2.7441(1.9238/2)] - 1 = 1.63$ or 163%. By the way, the response at the ith lags equals $\exp[\lambda_k \gamma(i)/2]$. Table 7.1 reports estimates of separate λ_k coefficients for each type of announcement. The Jobless Rate clearly has the greatest effect on volatility, the coefficient $\lambda_{jobless}$ being the highest. The next most important announcements are the GDP, the Merchandise Trade Balance, the Durable Goods Orders and the Consumer Price Index. The Consumer Confidence, the Housing Starts, the Producer Price Index and the Advance Retail Sales figures form a medium impact subgroup. Finally, there is a group of low impact announcements, which comprises the Capacity Utilisation/Industrial Production, the Index of Leading Indicators and the US NAPM Survey. In the regression, we incorporated day-of-the-week dummies for all weekdays except Monday. There is a clear distinction between midweek days and Mondays and Fridays. However, both the Monday morning and the Friday afternoon effects are insignificant.

Following Andersen and Bollerslev (1997b), the link between $\hat{s}_{t,n}$ and $\hat{f}_{t,n}$ is as follows:

$$\hat{s}_{t,n} = \frac{T \exp[\hat{f}(t,n)/2]}{\sum_{t=1}^{T} \sum_{n=1}^{N} \exp[\hat{f}(t,n)/2]}$$

where $\hat{s}_{t,n}$ is the estimator of the intraday periodic component for interval n on day t. Figure 7.3 shows the average 1-day estimated seasonality ($\hat{s}_{t,n}$) of the 5-minute returns.

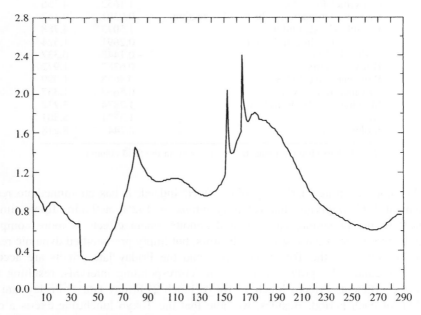

Figure 7.3 Average FFF functional of intraday 5-minute returns for the DM/USD

7.3 LONG MEMORY FROM INTRADAY RETURNS

Quite recently, Andersen and Bollerslev (1997b) stressed the danger of estimating GARCH models on high-frequency data without removing its intraday pattern. After applying the FFF on the raw data (Section 7.2), Figures 7.4 and 7.5 clearly suggest the presence of long memory in the volatility of the filtered DM/USD, which has become a stylised fact in the empirical literature. Figure 7.4 depicts the 50 days correlogram of filtered 5-minute absolute returns, $|\tilde{R}_{t,n}|$.

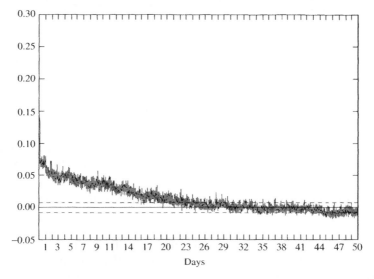

Note: The figure plots the lag 5 through 14,400 sample autocorrelations for the filtered 5-minute absolute returns on the DM/USD from 1st October 1992 through 30th September 1993. The 95% Bartlett confidence bands for no serial dependence are also reported in the figure. We define the filtered 5-minute return series as $\tilde{R}_{t,n} \equiv R_{t,n}/\hat{s}_{t,n}$ where $\hat{s}_{t,n}$ is the estimator of the intraday periodic component for interval n on day t. We use FFF to pre-filter the data for seasonality.

Figure 7.4 Fifty days correlogram of filtered (intraday periodic components and announcement effects) 5-minute absolute returns

This figure shows a strictly positive and slowly declining correlogram. Spikes are apparent at the daily frequencies but they are minor and do not distort the overall pattern.[14] The most striking feature is the initial rapid decay in the autocorrelations followed by an extremely slow rate of decay. This is confirmed by the high value of the Ljung–Box statistic (258,450) at lag 1440 (five days). This correlation structure is not compatible with the standard GARCH process introduced by Bollerslev (1986). Instead, Figure 7.4 clearly suggests the presence of a long memory process in the absolute returns which is consistent with the fractionally integrated long memory volatility model proposed by Baillie *et al.* (1996). When applying the fractional differencing operator $(1 - L)^{0.4}$ to the filtered 5-minute absolute returns, we observe that the autocorrelations display much

---

[14] The regularity of the correlogram in Figure 7.4 can be compared to those of similarly filtered absolute returns presented in Payne (1997) and Andersen and Bollerslev (1997b, 1998).

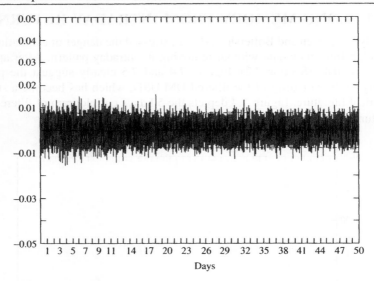

Note: The figure graphs the lag 5 through 14,400 sample autocorrelations for the fractionally differenced filtered, 5-minute absolute returns, $(1 - L)^{0.4}|\tilde{R}_{t,n}|$ where $t = 1, 2, \ldots, 261$, $n = 1, 2, \ldots, 288$. The 95% Bartlett confidence bands for no serial dependence are also reported in the figure.

Figure 7.5   Fifty days correlogram of the fractionally differenced filtered 5-minute absolute returns ($d = 0.4$)

less long-term dependence (see Figure 7.5). The Ljung–Box statistic is reduced to 4307, which is lower than in the previous case and for first differenced data (16,580).

By applying semiparametric tools on the same dataset, Andersen and Bollerslev (1998) find evidence of long memory in the volatility and conclude that the long memory characteristic appears *inherent* to the absolute return series.

The aim of this section is to provide a parametric estimation of the long memory property. The FIGARCH(1,d,1) model proposed by Baillie *et al.* (1996) is given by the two following equations:

$$\tilde{R}_{t,n} = \mu + \rho \tilde{R}_{t,n-1} + \varepsilon_{t,n} \quad \varepsilon_{t,n}|\Omega_{t,n} \sim D(0, h_{t,n}^2) \tag{7.4}$$

$$h_{t,n}^2 = \omega + [1 - (1 - \beta_1 L)^{-1}(1 - \phi_1 L)(1 - L)^d]\varepsilon_{t,n}^2 \tag{7.5}$$

where an AR(1) process is allowed for $\tilde{R}_{t,n}$, μ is the mean of the process and $\Omega_{t,n}$ is the information set at time t and interval n. ρ, μ, ω, β_1, ϕ_1 and d are parameters to be estimated with d being the fractional integration parameter and finally L is the lag operator.[15] For a FIGARCH(1,d,1), sufficient conditions for the conditional variance to be strictly positive are given in Baillie *et al.* (1996).[16] For higher orders, these

---

[15] We follow Baillie *et al.* (1996) and truncate the infinite Taylor approximation of $(1 - L)^d$ at a number of lags equal to 1000. Chung (1999) proposes an alternative specification of the FIGARCH due to the strong relationship between ω and the truncation order. We do not tackle this issue in this paper because the parameter of interest is d, which is not affected by this choice, as shown by Chung (1999).

[16] Some of these sufficient conditions are nevertheless not necessary. For instance, they specify $\omega > 0$. By contrast, our estimation procedure allows ω to be negative but checks the positiveness of the conditional variance on a case-by-case basis (see Nelson and Cao, 1992).

conditions are cumbersome to derive, which obviously hampers the generalisation of the FIGARCH specification to higher orders. Interestingly, the FIGARCH(1,d,1) model nests the GARCH(1,1) model (Bollerslev, 1986) for $d = 0$ and the IGARCH model (Engle and Bollerslev, 1986) for $d = 1$. As advocated by Baillie *et al.* (1996), the IGARCH process may be seen as too restrictive as it implies infinite persistence of a volatility shock. Such dynamics are contrary to the observed behaviour of agents and do not match the persistence observed after important events (see Baillie *et al.*, 1996; Bollerslev and Engle, 1993). By contrast, for $0 < d < 1$, the FIGARCH model implies long memory behaviour, *i.e.* a slow decay of the impact of a volatility shock.

The first candidate distribution (D) for the estimation of this model is the normal one. In the Gaussian case, the log-likelihood of the model takes the following form:

$$\text{Ln}(L_{\text{Norm}}) = \sum_{t=1}^{T} \sum_{n=1}^{N} [-0.5 \ln(2\pi h_{t,n}^2) + (\varepsilon_{t,n}^2 / h_{t,n}^2)] \tag{7.6}$$

where T and N are respectively the number of days and the number of intervals per day.

Recent developments in time series econometrics have been concerned with the interaction between structural change and long memory. Diebold and Inoue (1999) show that stochastic regime switching may be observationally equivalent to long-range dependence. The key idea developed by these authors is that regardless of the sample size, long memory can be detected if realisations tend to have just a few breaks. Granger and Hyung (1999) underline the fact that correcting for outliers may significantly decrease the long memory parameter. To cope with this issue, we use a mixture of normal distributions (Bernoulli–normal) that allows for the possibility of endogenously determined jumps. Mixtures have been introduced in econometrics by Jorion (1988) and more recently adapted to the GARCH framework (with weekly data) by Vlaar and Palm (1993), Neely (1999) and to the FIGARCH (with daily data) by Beine and Laurent (1999). The major findings of these papers are that the volatility persistence significantly decreases when accounting for jumps in the series. This invalidates the IGARCH model, which is a common result in the empirical literature.

Considering this distribution, (7.4) can be rewritten as follows:

$$\tilde{R}_{t,n} = \mu + \lambda\tau + \rho\tilde{R}_{t,n} + \varepsilon_t \tag{7.7}$$

where λ is the probability of a jump and τ is the size of the jump, while (7.5) remains unchanged. The log-likelihood then takes the following form:

$$\text{Ln}(L_{\text{Bern–Norm}}) = -\frac{T}{2}\ln(2\pi) + \sum_{t=1}^{T}\ln\left\{\frac{(1-\lambda)}{h_{t,n}^2}\exp\left[\frac{-(\varepsilon_{t,n}^2 + \lambda\tau)^2}{2h_{t,n}^2}\right]\right\}$$
$$+ \sum_{t=1}^{T}\ln\left\{\frac{\lambda}{\sqrt{h_{t,n}^2 + \delta^2}}\exp\left[\frac{-(\varepsilon_{t,n}^2 - (1-\lambda)\tau)^2}{2(h_{t,n}^2 + \delta^2)}\right]\right\} \tag{7.8}$$

where δ^2 is the variance of the jump size.

As shown by Vlaar (1994), the distribution of the error term of the Bernoulli jump model with $N(\tau, \delta^2)$ distributed jump size and heteroskedastic normal innovations can be expressed in the following way:

$$\varepsilon_{t,n} = (1-\lambda)N(-\lambda\tau, h_{t,n}) + \lambda N((1-\lambda)\tau, h_{t,n} + \delta^2)$$

Vlaar and Palm (1993) and Beine and Laurent (1999), among others, make the jump probability dependent on explanatory variables. Even if this extension is straightforward, it is beyond the scope of the paper. Notice moreover that there is no dynamic on the τ and δ^2 parameters, which means basically that they capture outliers. Both the ARCH-type specification and the jump process can explain the leptokurtosis behaviour of the series (see Vlaar and Palm, 1993).

Approximate quasi-maximum likelihood estimations have been conducted for five frequencies, 5-, 10-, 15-, 20- and 30-minute returns for the normal and the Bernoulli–normal distributions.[17] Andersen and Bollerslev (1997b) first filter the 5-minute returns $(R_{t,n})$ and then estimate the GARCH models on this filtered series $(\tilde{R}_{t,n})$. The method used to change the frequency from 5 to $5k$ minutes $(k = 1, 2, \ldots)$ is straightforward: $R_{t,n}^{(k)} = \sum_{i=(n-1)k+1,nk} R_{t,i}$, where $t = 1, 2, \ldots, T$, $n = 1, 2, \ldots, N$ and $N = 288/k$. In the same way, they calculate the filtered $5k$-minute returns as $R_{t,n}^{(k)} = \sum_{i=(n-1)k+1,nk} \tilde{R}_{t,i}$. In order to avoid an aggregation problem, we propose to change the frequency and then filter the series (finding the FFF relative to the frequency of interest). Details concerning this choice are reported in Appendix 7.2.

Results of the estimations are given in Tables 7.2 and 7.3:

Table 7.2   AR(1)-FIGARCH(1.d,1) with the normal distribution

	5-minute	10-minute	15-minute	20-minute	30-minute
μ	−0.6231	−1.5974	−0.1238	−1.7981	1.1771
	[0.532]	[0.678]	[0.035]	[0.372]	[0.161]
ρ	−0.0981	−0.0983	−0.1035	−0.0886	−0.0729
	[26.084]	[17.675]	[15.423]	[11.155]	[7.218]
$\omega \times 10^{-4}$	1.9519	4.0851	7.4404	10.5540	18.2861
	[46.928]	[33.743]	[33.016]	[27.074]	[23.662]
d	0.4252	0.4009	0.3332	0.2879	0.2607
	[60.604]	[43.411]	[37.232]	[29.970]	[26.090]
β_1	0.7109	0.6634	0.5811	0.3582	0.2265
	[157.351]	[98.022]	[46.916]	[8.156]	[5.044]
ϕ_1	0.5401	0.4653	0.4227	0.2237	0.1236
	[78.490]	[43.719]	[29.995]	[5.516]	[2.833]
b_3	0.3470*	0.0988*	0.0634*	−0.0322**	0.1767*
b_4	22.1597*	9.8128*	8.2316*	4.0885*	6.0243*
AIC	14.9607	15.5806	15.9550	16.1788	16.5811
SBIC	14.9615	15.5819	15.9570	16.1813	16.5846
S(1)	0.0056	0.1152	4.2131	1.6411	0.3304
Log/$L \times 10^{-4}$	− 56.2272	− 29.2777	− 19.9871	− 15.2002	− 10.3849

Note: Absolute t-statistics of maximum likelihood estimates are in brackets. Statistics are computed on normalised residuals. b_3 and b_4 are excess skewness and kurtosis. AIC and SBIC are Akaike and Schwarz Bayesian information criteria. The data have been multiplied by 10^5.
*.**Indicate that the statistic is significant at 1% and 5%, respectively.

---

[17] Intraday returns are very small values. For instance, the mean of the filtered 5-minute returns equals 1.6×10^3. To avoid convergence problems, we multiplied the returns by 10^5. All the computations have been done in Gauss 3.2 and Maxlik 4.0. A Gauss procedure to compute (7.5) is available at http://www.egss.ulg.ac.be/econometrie/FIGARCH.SRC. An OX package with a friendly interface is available upon request (contact the second author).

Table 7.3   AR(1)-FIGARCH(1.d,1) with the Bernoulli–normal distribution

	5-minute	10-minute	15-minute	20-minute	30-minute
μ	3.1289	3.1848	3.9089	7.8521	1.1855
	[2.531]	[1.257]	[1.062]	[1.559]	[0.161]
ρ	−0.1078	−0.1018	−0.1081	−0.0984	−0.0846
	[27.351]	[18.335]	[15.965]	[12.521]	[8.743]
ω	−3.2143	−4.4563	−1.7655	0.4062	4.5819
	[0.006]	[0.002]	[0.000]	[0.000]	[0.000]
d	0.1159	0.1272	0.1204	0.1270	0.1460
	[27.371]	[19.940]	[18.250]	[16.214]	[12.002]
β_1	0.8560	0.8884	0.9702	0.9748	0.8319
	[164.243]	[66.507]	[166.127]	[115.803]	[11.226]
ϕ_1	0.9131	0.9099	0.9770	0.9796	0.8176
	[232.678]	[80.593]	[216.450]	[141.426]	[10.463]
λ	0.1061	0.1231	0.1061	0.1235	0.1261
	[37.840]	[27.068]	[20.4697]	[16.102]	[15.265]
τ	−32.4123	−23.9715	−29.8268	−68.9173	13.1748
	[2.641]	[1.130]	[0.854]	[1.710]	[0.220]
$\delta^2 \times 10^{-5}$	5.8670	10.0062	16.6840	17.1796	29.1330
	[130.685]	[63.925]	[41.3787]	[25.878]	[25.781]
b_3	−0.0338*	−0.0200	−0.0107	−0.0132	0.0276
b_4	0.4658*	0.5226*	0.5878*	0.3588	0.3895*
AIC	14.8607	15.4903	15.8560	16.0977	16.4781
SBIC	14.8618	15.4923	15.8589	16.1015	16.4834
S(1)	2.1986	0.8726	1.4177	0.2187	0.0001
Log/$L \times 10^{-4}$	−55.8509	−29.1076	−19.8627	−15.1237	−10.3201

Note: See Table 7.2

Several comments are in order. First, the Bernoulli–normal distribution seems appropriate to describe the series. Likelihood Ratio Tests (LRT) are not reported here and the information criteria clearly favour the Bernoulli–normal distribution for each sampling frequency. Looking at the Bernoulli parameters reveals that the probability of a jump is about 10%. Interestingly, as in Beine and Laurent (1999, 2000), we can distinguish two *states*: a low volatility state and a high volatility state (τ and δ^2 being respectively highly nonsignificant and significant).

Second, relying on the normalised residuals (see Vlaar and Palm, 1993), all excess kurtosis (b_4) is found to be significant at the 5% level while there is no excess skewness (b_3). Nevertheless, b_4 turns out to be much lower than those obtained for the normal distribution, which confirms that accounting for a non uniform flow of information reduces excess kurtosis. To test for possible remaining ARCH effects, we use the rank test proposed by Wright (1998) that is more powerful than alternative tests when the residuals are highly non-normal (something we suspect here).[18] According to this statistic, the models correctly account for the cluster of volatility phenomena for both distributions.

---

[18] The nonparametric rank test introduced by Wright (1998) can be used as a misspecification test suitable for GARCH and FIGARCH models. For fixed l, the test statistic $S(l)$ is given by $S(l) = T \sum_{i=1}^{l} \rho(s_{1t}, s_{1t-i})^2$ where $\rho(.,.)$ denotes the sample autocorrelation function and is given by $s_{1t} = \left[r(e_t^2) - \dfrac{T+1}{2} \right] \Big/ \sqrt{\dfrac{(T-1)(T+1)}{12}}$ where e_t are the standardised (here, normalised) residuals and $r(e_t)$ is the rank of e_t among $e_1, e_2, \ldots, e_T$. Under the null of a correct specification in the conditional variance,

Third, concerning the constancy of the d parameter, the normal and the Bernoulli–normal distributions lead to different results. While d highly decreases when the sampling frequency decreases in the normal case (from 0.42 to 0.26), d equals about 0.12 in the latter case.[19] Quite interestingly, with the normal distribution, ω evolves in the opposite way to the d parameter (and is always significant). Similarly, δ^2 increases when the sampling frequency decreases in the Bernoulli–normal case (and is always significant) but ω is not significant for the five frequencies.[20] So, there is a strong relation between the long memory parameter and the variance of the jump size δ^2 and neglecting the presence of outliers may lead to an overestimation of the long memory behaviour.

7.4   CONCLUSION

As pointed out by Andersen *et al.* (1999), '*it remains an open issue to identify the specific economic forces that may generate the long-run persistence patterns. At an abstract level, one possibility is that it may arise from the interaction of a large number of heterogeneous information arrival processes*'.

According to Andersen and Bollerslev[21] (1997a, 1998) and Andersen *et al.* (1999), the long memory characteristic appears inherent to the return series because it manifests itself, even over shorter time spans. They concluded that the source of fractional integration in the volatility is related to the data-generating process itself rather than being tied to infrequent structural shifts as suggested by Lamoureux and Lastrapes (1990). By using parametric estimations, we also find evidence of long memory in the DM/USD. However, after allowing for jumps in the series (especially in the variance), we conclude in favour of less long memory than Andersen and Bollerslev (1997a), even if we reinforce their argument that long memory is an intrinsic property of the exchange rate returns.

From our results, we can argue that the volatility of the DM/USD describes the same long memory behaviour across different sampling frequencies. However, accounting for jumps in the series (or for the presence of outliers) highly reduces this long memory, which remains relevant at any significance levels. While d ranges from 0.26 to 0.42 in the normal case, d ranges from 0.11 to 0.14 in the Bernoulli–normal one. This result is in line with the work of Beine and Laurent (2000), who find a large decrease of the d

Wright (1998) proposes to use a $\chi^2(l)$ distribution (the test is not perfectly exact). Results are only reported for $l = 1$ but are consistent with other values of l (5, 10 and 20 for instance).

[19] By estimating a Markov-switching FIGARCH(1,d,0), Beine and Laurent (2000) find $d = 0.09$ on a longer sample of daily DM/USD exchange rate returns (while the standard FIGARCH(1,d,0) leads to $d = 0.27$).

[20] Chung (1999) proposes a different specification of the FIGARCH model, more in line with the ARFIMA model. Equivalence between the two specifications requires that $\omega = 0$. Our results suggest that the normal distribution fails to accept this restriction. Chung (1999) interprets this positiveness of ω (whose theoretical value is zero) as an artefact of the subjective choices of the truncation order of $(1 - L)^d$. However, the Bernoulli–normal distribution leads to a different conclusion, ω being always nonsignificant. By the way, we argue that finding $\omega > 0$ may also be due to the choice of the distribution and using a more appropriate distribution (that takes into account the presence of outliers) may overcome this problem.

[21] Andersen and Bollerslev (1997a) developed a theoretical framework which is built on the idea that the aggregate market volatility represents the manifestation of numerous heterogeneous information arrival processes (some with short-run volatility dependencies and others possessing more highly persistent patterns). When time passes, the short-run processes decay significantly while the more persistent processes remain influential.

parameter (but still significant) when modelling daily DM/USD by a Markov-switching FIGARCH to account for the possible structural change.[22]

ACKNOWLEDGEMENTS

The authors would like to thank M. Boutillier, J. Cai, C. Lecourt and A. Timmermann for helpful comments. Of course, the usual disclaimer applies. The Olsen and Associates dataset (HFDF93) was provided by the OFCE to R. Topol who kindly lent it.

REFERENCES

Almeida, A., C. Goodhart and R. Payne (1996). "The Effects of Macroeconomic 'News' on High Frequency Exchange Rate Behaviour", Financial Markets Group, London School of Economics, October.

Andersen, T. and T. Bollerslev (1997a). "Heterogeneous Information Arrivals and Return Volatility Dynamics: Uncovering the Long-run in High Frequency Returns", *The Journal of Finance* **52**, 975–1005.

Andersen, T. and T. Bollerslev (1997b). "Intraday Periodicity and Volatility Persistence in Financial Markets", *Journal of Empirical Finance* **4**, 115–158.

Andersen, T. and T. Bollerslev (1998). "DM–Dollar Volatility: Intraday Activity Patterns, Macroeconomic Announcements and Longer Run Dependencies", *The Journal of Finance* **53**(1) 219–265.

Andersen, T., T. Bollerslev and J. Cai (1999). "Intraday and Interday Volatility in the Japanese Stock Market", working paper, Department of Finance, Kellogg Graduate School of Management, Northwestern University, 257pp.

Baillie, R. and T. Bollerslev (1990). "Intra-day and Inter-market Volatility in Foreign Exchange Rates", *Review of Economic Studies* **58**, 565–585.

Baillie, R., T. Bollerslev and H. Mikkelsen (1996). "Fractionally Integrated Generalized Autoregressive Conditional Heteroskedasticity", *Journal of Econometrics* **74**, 3–30.

Beattie, N. and J.F. Fillion (1999). "An Intraday Analysis of the Effectiveness of Foreign Exchange Intervention", working paper, 99-4, Bank of Canada, February.

Beine, M. and S. Laurent (1999). "Central Bank Interventions and Jumps in Double Long Memory Models of Daily Exchange Rates", manuscript, University of Liege, FEGSS.

Beine, M. and S. Laurent (2000). "Structural Change and Long Memory in Volatility: New Evidence from Daily Exchange Rates" this volume.

Bollerslev, T. (1986). "Generalized Autoregressive Conditional Heteroskedasticity", *Journal of Econometrics* **31**, 307–327.

Bollerslev, T. and R.F. Engle (1993). "Common Persistence in Conditional Variances", *Econometrica* **61**, 167–186.

Bollerslev, T. and E. Ghysels (1996). "Periodic Autoregressive Conditional Heteroskedasticity", *Journal of Business and Economic Statistics* **14**(2), 139–152.

Bollerslev, T. and J.H. Wright (1998). "Estimating Long Memory Volatility Dependencies: The Role of High-frequency Data", working paper, Departments of Economics, Duke University.

Bollerslev, T. and J.H. Wright (1999). "Semiparametric Estimation of Long Memory Volatility Dependencies: The Role Of High Frequency Data", *Journal of Econometrics*, in press.

Boubel, A., S. Laurent and C. Lecourt (2001). "Impact des signaux de politique monétaire sur la volatilité", *Intra-journaliene du taux de change Deutsche Mark–dollar Revue Economique* **52**(2), Mar 5.

Chang, Y. and S. Taylor (1996). "Information Arrivals and Intraday Exchange Rate Volatility", Department of Accounting and Finance, The Management School, Lancaster, October.

Chung, C.F. (1999). "Estimating the Fractionally Integrated GARCH Model", working paper, National Taiwan University.

Clark, P.K. (1973). "A Subordinated Stochastic Process Model with Finite Variance for Speculative Prices", *Econometrica* **41**, 135–155.

Dacorogna, M., U. Müller, R. Nagler and O. Pictet (1993). "A Geographical Model for the Daily and Weekly Seasonal Volatility in the foreign Exchange Market", *Journal of International Money and Finance* **12**, 413–438.

DeGennaro, R. and R. Shrieves (1997). "Public Information Releases, Private Information Arrival and Volatility in the Foreign Exchange Market", *Journal of Empirical Finance* **4**, 295–315.

---

[22] Unlike the Bernoulli–normal distribution, Markov-switching models can be viewed as time-varying mixtures. They are more flexible but also more computationally demanding, which makes their use unattractive with large database (remember that we have more than 75,000 observations for 5-minute returns).

Diebold, F.X. and A. Inoue (1999). "Long Memory and Structural Change", manuscript, Department of Finance, Stern School, NYU, May.

Ding, Z., C. Granger and R.F. Engle (1993). "A Long Memory Property of Stock Market Returns and a New Model", *Journal of Empirical Finance* **1**, 83–105.

Ederington, L. and J. Lee (1993). "How Markets Process Information: News Releases and Volatility", *The Journal of Finance* **48**(4), 1161–1191.

Ederington, L. and J. Lee (1995). "The Short-run Dynamics of the Price Adjustment to New Information", *Journal of Financial and Quantitative Analysis* **30**(1), 117–134.

Engle, R.F. and T. Bollerslev (1986). "Modeling the Persistence of Conditional Variances", *Econometric Reviews* **5**, 1–50.

Engle, R.F. and A.D. Smith (1999). "Stochastic Permanent Break", *Review of Economics and Statistics* **81**, in press.

Feinstone, L. (1987). "Minute by Minute: Efficiency, Normality and Randomness in Intra-daily Asset Prices", *Journal of Applied Econometrics* **2**, 193–214.

Goodhart, C. and L. Figliuoli (1991). "Every Minute Counts in Financial Markets", *Journal of International Money and Finance* **10**, 23–52.

Goodhart, C., S. Hall, S. Henry and B. Pesaran (1993). "News Effects in High Frequency Model of Sterling–Dollar Exchange Rate", *Journal of Applied Econometrics* **8**, 1–13.

Granger, C.W.J. and N. Hyung (1999). "Occasional Structural Breaks and Long Memory", UCSD discussion paper 99-14, June.

Guillaume, D., M. Dacorogna, R. Davé, U. Müller, R. Olsen and O. Pictet (1994). "From the Bird's Eye to the Microscope: A Survey of New Stylized Facts of the Intradaily Foreign Exchange Markets", International Economics Research Paper, 107.

Guillaume, D., O. Pictet and M. Dacorogna (1995). "On the Intradaily Performance of GARCH Processes", working paper, Olsen & Associates, August.

Hamilton, J.D. (1989). "A New Approach to the Economic Analysis of Nonstationary Time Series and the Business Cycle", *Econometrica* **57**, 357–384.

Harvey, C. and R. Huang (1991). "Volatility in the Currency Futures Market", *Review of Financial Studies* **4**(3), 543–569.

Ito, T. and V. Roley (1987). "News from the US and Japan: Which Moves the Yen/Dollar Exchange Rate?", *Journal of Monetary Economics* **19**, 255–277.

Jorion, P. (1988). "On Jump Processes in the Foreign Exchange and Stock Markets", *The Review of Financial Studies* **1**, 427–445.

Lamoureux, C. and W. Lastrapes (1990). "Persistence in Variance, Structural Change and the GARCH Model', *Journal of Business and Economic Statistics* **8**, 225–234.

Mikosch, T. and C. Starica (1999). "Change of Structure in Financial Time Series, Long Range Dependence and the GARCH Model", manuscript, Department of Statistics, University of Pennsylvania.

Müller, U., M. Dacorogna, R. Olsen, O. Pictet, M. Schwarz and C. Morgenegg (1990). "Statistical Study of Foreign Exchange Rates, Empirical Evidence of a Price Change Scaling Law, and Intraday Analysis", *Journal of Banking and Finance* **14**, 1189–1208.

Neely, C.J. (1999). "Target Zones and Conditional Volatility: The Role of Realignments", *Journal of Empirical Finance* **6**(2), 177–192.

Nelson, D.B. and C.Q. Cao (1992). "Inequality Constraints in the Univariate GARCH Model", *Journal of Business and Economic Statistics* **10**, 229–235.

Parke, W.R. (1999). "What is Fractional Integration", manuscript, University of North Carolina.

Payne, R. (1997). "Announcement Effects and Seasonality in the Intra-day Foreign Exchange Market", London School of Economics working paper, Financial Markets Group Discussion Paper 238.

Taylor, S. and X. Xu (1997). "The Incremental Volatility Information in One Million Foreign Exchange Quotations", *Journal of Empirical Finance* **4**, 317–340.

Vlaar, P.J.G. (1994). "Exchange Rates and Risk Premia within the European Monetary System", Ph.D. thesis, Rijksuniversiteit Limburg, Maastricht, Netherlands.

Vlaar, P.J.G. and F.C. Palm (1993). "The Message in Weekly Exchange Rates in the European Monetary System: Mean Reversion, Conditional Heteroskedasticity and Jumps", *Journal of Business and Economic Statistics* **11**(3), 351–360.

Wasserfallen, W. and H. Zimmermann (1985). "The Behavior of Intradaily Exchange Rates", *Journal of Banking and Finance* **9**, 55–72.

Wasserfallen, W. (1989). "Flexible Exchange Rates: A Closer Look", *Journal of Monetary Economics* **23**, 511–521.

Wright, J.H. (1998). "Rank Tests in GARCH Models", mimeo, November.

Zhou, B. (1996). "High Frequency Data and Volatility In Foreign Exchange Rates", *Journal of Business and Economic Statistics* **14**(1), 45–52.

APPENDIX 7.1: DATA CONSTRUCTION

The exchange rate data are tick-by-tick observations on the German mark price of the US dollar (DM/USD) as displayed on the Reuters FXFX screen from 1st October 1992 through 30th September 1993. There were 1,472,241 quotations in this year. Each quote contains a bid price and an ask price along with the time to the nearest even second. Moreover, we utilise use a daily time series of 3586 spot DM/USD exchange rates from 3rd January 1980 through 30th September 1993. In this paper, only the bid prices are used because Reuters quote the bid price in its entirety. As noted by Dacorogna et al. (1993) and Zhou (1996), only the last two or three digits of the ask price are quoted. Note that the recording events j (for which the times are marked by t_j) is unequally spaced. As we are investigating the time series using equally spaced time intervals, we have to find a mapping procedure to fixed time steps, which are denoted by t_j. Our time steps are defined by using time intervals of $\Delta t = 5$ minute's length.[23] We applied a linear interpolation[24] as an appropriate method for interpolating the prices between the previous t_{j-1} and the next t_j data record surrounding the time step t_i with $t_{j-1} < t_i < t_j$. In general, a trader is not interested in the price; rather they are interested in the return that they will gain from that investment. Statistically speaking, looking at the raw prices is not very constructive, as the prices can be highly correlated and in general are not stationary. The nth return within day t, $R_{t,n}$, can be defined as the change in the logarithms of prices: $R_{t,n} = 100[\log(P_{t,n}) - \log(P_{t,n-1})]$, $t = 1, 2, \ldots, T$, $n = 1, 2, \ldots, N$. All $N = 288$ intervals during the 24-hour cycle and $T = 261$ weekdays in the sample are used. To reduce the influence of the slow-trading pattern over the weekend, we follow the adjustment process of Andersen and Bollerslev (1997b) by excluding returns from Friday 21:00 GMT through Sunday 21:00 GMT. There are 75,167 returns[25] for 5-minute intervals after the adjustment for the weekend periods.

APPENDIX 7.2: DATA TRANSFORMATION

Consider the following extreme case. Let $R_{t,n}$ be 12-hours data ($k = 1$). The two first returns are $R_{1,1}$ and $R_{1,2}$, while the corresponding filters are $\hat{s}_{1,1}$ and $(1 - L)^d$. Following Andersen and Bollerslev (1997b), the first filtered 24-hours (1 day, $k = 2$) return is:

$$\tilde{R}_{1,1}^{(2)} = \frac{R_{1,1}}{\hat{s}_{1,1}} + \frac{R_{1,2}}{\hat{s}_{1,2}} = \frac{R_{1,1}\hat{s}_{1,2} + R_{1,2}\hat{s}_{1,1}}{\hat{s}_{1,1}\hat{s}_{1,2}}$$

Recall that if we only include FFF variables that are related to a 1-day horizon (excluding for instance daily effects) then $\frac{1}{N}\sum_{i=1}^{N}\hat{s}_{i,t} = 1$, which means that $\tilde{R}_{1,1}^{(2)}$ should be equal to $R_{1,1}^{(2)}$. However, following Andersen and Bollerslev (1997b):

$$\tilde{R}_{1,1}^{(2)} = \frac{R_{1,1}\hat{s}_{1,2} + R_{1,2}\hat{s}_{1,1}}{\hat{s}_{1,1}\hat{s}_{1,2}} \neq R_{1,1} + R_{1,2}$$

---

[23] Papers by Ito and Roley (1987) and Ederington and Lee (1993) suggest that sampling frequencies as short as one hour may be too long to assess the impact of macroeconomic announcement on volatility accurately. So, we compute paces at 5-minute intervals because we study announcements.

[24] It is an interpolation between the preceding and immediately following quotes weighted linearly by their inverse relative distance to the desired point in time.

[25] To preserve the number of returns associated with one week we make no corrections for any world-wide or country-specific holidays that occurred during the sample period.

8

Comparison of Parameter Estimation Methods in Cyclical Long Memory Time Series

LAURENT FERRARA AND DOMINIQUE GUEGAN

ABSTRACT

In this paper, we are interested in the study of cyclical time series with long-range dependence. To analyse such time series, a useful tool is the generalised long memory process introduced in the statistical literature by Gray *et al.* (1989). Because of the presence of a singularity in its spectral density, this process possesses the ability to take into account in modelling the phenomenon of persistence, as well as a periodic cyclical behaviour. However, the issue of parameter estimation is not obvious. We discuss the estimation of the spectral density singularity location and present in detail two types of long memory parameter estimation methods: a semiparametric method, based on the expression of the log-periodogram, and a pseudo-maximum likelihood method, based on the Whittle likelihood. Moreover, we give the asymptotic properties of each estimate. Lastly, we compare these two types of estimation methods in order to model the error correction term of a fractional cointegration analysis carried out on the Nikkei spot index data.

8.1 INTRODUCTION

When dealing with financial time series, we are often confronted with the phenomenon of long memory or long-range dependence. For instance, evidence of long memory has been shown in time series of inflation rates (Baillie *et al.*, 1996b), stock market prices (Willinger *et al.*, 1999) or exchange rates (Ferrara and Guégan, 2000a). Moreover, many researchers have shown the empirical evidence of persistence in the conditional variance of diverse time series of asset returns. This slow decay of the sample Autocorrelation Function (ACF) of the squared (or absolute) returns has been pointed out by, for instance, Granger and Ding (1996) or Baillie *et al.* (1996a). However, some time series exhibit a periodic cyclical pattern as well as long-range dependence. Instead of removing this cyclical pattern before the time series long memory analysis, it seems more efficient to take into account both these components in modelling, and the generalised long memory process appears to be a useful parametric model to tackle this issue. In this paper, we recall some properties of this kind of process, consider specifically the parameter estimation issue and we give an application on Nikkei spot index data.

Developments in Forecast Combination and Portfolio Choice. Edited by C. Dunis, A. Timmermann and J. Moody.

A covariance stationary process $(X_t)_{t \in Z}$ is said to be long memory if the infinite sum $\Sigma |\gamma(k)|$ diverges, where γ denotes the autocovariance function of the process. When working with long memory processes, it is often useful to embed in the spectral domain. We recall that the spectral density f_X of a covariance stationary process is the Fourier transform of the autocovariance function, *i.e.* for $\lambda \in [0, 2\pi]$:

$$f_X(\lambda) = (1/2\pi) \sum \gamma(k) \exp(-i\lambda k) \qquad (8.1)$$

In the remainder of this paper, we consider the following very useful definition of the long memory property, established in the spectral domain: a stationary process is said to be long memory if for some frequency $\lambda_G \in [0, \pi]$ its spectral density f_X becomes unbounded. A standard semiparametric model for local behaviour of the spectral density in the neighbourhood of the frequency λ_G is:

$$f_X(\lambda) \sim C|\lambda - \lambda_G|^{-2d} \qquad (8.2)$$

where C is a finite positive constant and where d lies on the open interval $]-1/2, 1/2[$. The parameter d controls the memory component in the neighbourhood of λ_G. Indeed, if $d = 0$, the process is said to have short memory, if $d > 0$, the process is said to have long memory and if $d < 0$, the process is said to be antipersistent. Moreover, $d < 1/2$ and $d > -1/2$ ensure respectively the stationarity and the inversibility of the process. Note that another interesting semiparametric asymmetric model for f_X has recently been proposed by Arteche and Robinson (2000).

Different authors proposed a parametric model for the spectral density verifying (8.2). If $\lambda_G = 0$ or π, the most popular parametric model is the Autoregressive Fractionally Integrated Moving Average (ARFIMA) process, introduced by Granger and Joyeux (1980) and Hosking (1981). If $\lambda_G \in]0, \pi[$, the most general parametric model is the k-factor GARMA process, introduced by Gray et al. (1989, 1994) and discussed in the papers of Robinson (1994b), Giraitis and Leipus (1995), Chung (1996a,b), Yajima (1996), Hosoya (1997), Woodward et al. (1998) and Ferrara and Guégan (2000a,b). In the statistical literature, this process is also known as the *generalised long memory process*, because it includes as special cases the ARFIMA process and the diverse seasonal long memory processes studied by Porter-Hudak (1990), Ray (1993), Hassler (1994) or Sutcliffe (1994).

Let the process $(X_t)_{t \in Z}$ be defined by the following equation:

$$\prod_{i=1}^{k}(I - 2v_i B + B^2)^{d_i}(X_t - \mu) = \varepsilon_t \qquad (8.3)$$

where k is a finite integer, with $|v_i| \leqslant 1$ for $i = 1, \ldots, k$, d_i is a fractional number for $i = 1, \ldots, k$, μ is the mean of the process, B is an operator defined on $(X_t)_{t \in Z}$ such that $BX_t = X_{t-1}$ and $B^b X_t = X_{t-b}$ for $b > 0$, I is the identity operator defined on $(X_t)_{t \in Z}$ such that $IX_t = X_t$ and $(\varepsilon_t)_{t \in Z}$ is a covariance stationary process with finite variance σ_ε^2.

Under the assumption of inversibility, a solution of (8.3) is given by:

$$X_t = \mu + \sum_{j \geqslant 0} \psi_j(d, v)\varepsilon_{t-j} \qquad (8.4)$$

where

$$\psi_j(d, v) = \sum_{\substack{0 \leqslant l_1, \dots, l_k \leqslant j \\ l_1 + \dots + l_k = j}} C_{l_1}(d_1, v_1) \dots C_{l_k}(d_k, v_k)$$ (8.5)

where $[C_j(d, v)]_{j \in Z}$ are the Gegenbauer polynomials defined by the following recursion formula, for $j \geqslant 2$:

$$C_j(d, v) = 2v[(d - 1)/j + 1]C_{j-1}(d, v) - [2(d - 1)/j + 1]C_{j-2}(d, v)$$ (8.6)

where $C_0(d, v) = 1$ and $C_1(d, v) = 2\,dv$. See, for instance, Rainville (1960) for further theoretical aspects on Gegenbauer polynomials. If d_i is a fractional number, for $i = 1, \dots, k$, the process $(X_t)_{t \in Z}$ defined by (8.4) is called a k-factor Gegenbauer process, where $(\varepsilon_t)_{t \in Z}$ is a white noise process, a k-factor GARMA process or a covariance stationary short memory ARMA-type process. Note that it is common to define a k-factor GARMA process by (8.3), however, in that case we mean the solution given in (8.4). In the remainder of the paper, we assume $\mu = 0$ and a k-factor GARMA process, defined in (8.4), will be denoted $\text{GARMA}_k(p, d, v, q)$ [or $\text{GG}_k(d, v)$ if $p = q = 0$] where d is the k-vector $(d_1, \dots, d_k)^t$, v is the k-vector $(v_1, \dots, v_k)^t$ and p and q are respectively the orders of the AR and MA parts of the process.

A description of the main statistical properties of a generalised long memory process can be found in the papers of Gray *et al.* (1989), Robinson (1994b), Giraitis and Leipus (1995), Chung (1996a,b), Woodward *et al.* (1998) and Ferrara and Guégan (2000a,b). Especially for $i = 1, \dots, k$, whether $0 < d_i < 1/2$, with $|v_i| < 1$ or whether $0 < d_i < 1/4$, with $|v_i| = 1$ the k-factor Gegenbauer process $(X_t)_{t \in Z}$ defined by (8.4) is a stationary, causal and invertible long memory process. Moreover, recall that the spectral density of a k-factor GARMA process is given by the following equation:

$$f_X(\lambda) = f_\varepsilon(\lambda) \prod_{i=1}^{k} \left| 4 \sin\left(\frac{\lambda + \lambda_i}{2}\right) \sin\left(\frac{\lambda - \lambda_i}{2}\right) \right|^{-2d_i}$$ (8.7)

where $0 \leqslant \lambda \leqslant \pi$, f_ε is the spectral density of the covariance stationary process $(\varepsilon_t)_{t \in Z}$ and, for $i = 1, \dots, k$, $\lambda_i = \cos^{-1}(v_i)$ are called the Gegenbauer frequencies (G-frequencies). Thus, the spectral density of a k-factor GARMA process clearly exhibits k peaks on the interval $[0, \pi]$ (see, for instance, Ferrara, 2000 for simulations). Note also that forecasting performances of generalised long memory processes are discussed in Ferrara and Guégan (2000a,b).

In this paper, we focus our attention on parameter estimation in k-factor Gegenbauer processes. It seems that parameter estimation of the autoregressive and moving average parts, in the case of a k-factor GARMA process, does not represent a specific issue. In the second section, we present the semiparametric estimation method based on the expression of the log-periodogram. We derive the analytic expression of the log-periodogram estimate of the long memory parameter, in the case of a general process with a single singularity on the interval, and give its limiting distribution. Then, we describe how to use this estimate in order to estimate the long memory parameter of a $\text{GARMA}_k(p, d, v, q)$ process. In the third section, we present some results relevant to the pseudo-maximum likelihood parameter estimation method of a $\text{GARMA}_k(p, d, v, q)$ process. Especially, we consider the Whittle estimation method, often used in the case of an ARFIMA process, and show

how to use this method in practice. The last section contains an application of generalised long memory processes to a fractional cointegration analysis carried out on the Nikkei spot index data.

8.2 SEMIPARAMETRIC ESTIMATION

In this section we consider semiparametric (SP) estimation of the long memory parameter in generalised long memory processes. Especially, we focus on the log-periodogram method introduced by Geweke and Porter-Hudak (1983) and improved by Robinson (1995), and adapt it to the case of generalised long memory processes. Let $(X_t)_{t \in Z}$ be a second-order covariance stationary process, with spectral density having a singularity somewhere on the interval $[0,\pi]$. We assume that this singularity is known and is located at the frequency λ_G, denoted the Gegenbauer frequency (G-frequency). We discuss at the end of this section the case of an unknown frequency. Thus, the spectral density f_X of the process is given by (8.2), as λ tends to λ_G. By evaluating (8.2) at the Fourier frequencies $\lambda_j = 2\pi(j-1)/T$, for $j = 1, \ldots, T$, and by taking logarithms, we get the following relationship, in the neighbourhood of the G-frequency taken among the Fourier frequencies $\lambda_{jG} = 2\pi j_G/T$:

$$\log[I_T(\lambda_j)] \sim K - 2\log|\lambda_j - \lambda_{jG}| + \log[I_T(\lambda_j)/f_X(\lambda_j)] \qquad (8.8)$$

where K is a finite constant and where $I_T(\lambda_j)$ is the periodogram evaluated at the Fourier frequency λ_j, defined by:

$$I_T(\lambda_j) = \frac{1}{2\pi T} \left| \sum_{t=1}^{T} e^{i\lambda_j t} X_t \right|^2 \qquad (8.9)$$

Now, we consider a generalisation of the Robinson (1995) estimate, obtained from the asymptotic regression (8.8). This generalised Robinson estimate is explicitly given by the following equality, for $T > m > l \geqslant 0$:

$$\hat{d}_R(l, m) = \frac{\sum_{j=j_G+l+1}^{j_G+m} (Y_j - \overline{Y}) \log[I_t(\lambda_j)]}{\sum_{j=j_G+l+1}^{j_G+m} (Y_j - \overline{Y})^2} \qquad (8.10)$$

where, for $j \in [j_G + l + 1, j_G + m]$, $Y_j = -2\log|\lambda_j - \lambda_{jG}|$ and $\overline{Y}$ is the empirical mean, l is the number of frequencies trimmed from the regression (8.8), and m is the bandwidth.

Now, we are interested in exhibiting the asymptotic properties of $\hat{d}_R(l, m)$. We specify some assumptions on the process $(X_t)_{t \in Z}$.

Assumption 8.1
As $\lambda \to \lambda_G$ (λ_{G^+}, if $\lambda_G \in [0, \pi/2]$ or λ_{G^-}, if $\lambda_G \in [\pi/2, \pi]$), there exists a strictly positive real C and a real d lying on the interval $]-1/2,1/2[$, such that:

$$f_X(\lambda) = C|\lambda - \lambda_G|^{-2d} + O(|\lambda - \lambda_G|^{2-2d})$$

Assumption 8.2

In the neighbourhood of λ_G, the spectral density f_X can be differentiated with respect to λ and as $\lambda \to \lambda_G$:

$$|df_X(\lambda)/d\lambda| = O(|\lambda - \lambda_G|^{1-2d})$$

Assumption 8.3

The process is Gaussian.

Assumption 8.4

Let the bandwidth m and the trimming number l be such that, as $T \to \infty$:

$$m \longrightarrow \infty, \; l \longrightarrow \infty$$

$$m^5/T^4 \longrightarrow 0, \; \log^2(T)/m \longrightarrow 0$$

and

$$l/m \longrightarrow 0, m^{1/2} \log(m)/l \longrightarrow 0$$

Assumptions 8.1 to 8.4 have been made by Robinson (1995) to get the limiting distribution of his estimate in the case of a spectral density with singularity located at zero. Assumptions 8.1 and 8.2 are technical assumptions, concerning the smooth behaviour of the spectral density in the neighbourhood of the singularity λ_G on the interval $[0,\pi]$. Assumption 8.3 is the strongest assumption and implies that we have to work with Gaussian processes. In practice, note that this assumption is sometimes doubtful, especially when one studies financial time series, which are often leptokurtic. Assumption 8.4 is a technical assumption which means that m tends to infinity with T, but slower, and l tends to infinity with m, but slower.

In order to adapt Robinson's estimate, we add the following fifth assumption.

Assumption 8.5

Let j be the integer related to the Fourier frequency λ_j such that, as T tends to infinity:

$$j \longrightarrow \infty$$

and

$$j/T \longrightarrow 0$$

This assumption means that the integer j tends to infinity with T, but slower, and thus it allows us to reach the G-frequency. This assumption represents the main change in comparison with the classical assumptions of Geweke and Porter-Hudak (1983) or Robinson (1995), for which the integer j is fixed. Thus, we get the following proposition.

Proposition 8.1

Assume we have a covariance stationary process, with spectral density defined by (8.2). Under Assumptions 8.1 to 8.5, as $T \to \infty$ we have:

$$2\sqrt{m}[\hat{d}_R(l, m) - d] \longrightarrow N(0, \pi^2/6) \qquad (8.11)$$

Proof. The proof of Proposition 8.1 consists in proving that the result of Robinson (1995, theorem 3) applies. Without loss of generality, we assume that the known G-frequency lies on the interval $[0, \pi/2]$. We are dealing with the Fourier frequencies $\lambda_j = 2\pi(j - 1)/T$, for $j = 1, \ldots, T$. As T tends to infinity, according to Assumption 8.5, j also tends to infinity, but slower. Therefore, there always exist m and l such that $m > l \geqslant 0$ and

$$\lambda_j \in V_{jG}(l, m) = [j_G + l + 1, j_G + m]$$

For all Fourier frequencies λ_j lying on the interval $V_{jG}(l, m)$, $|\lambda_j - \lambda_{jG}| \to 0^+$ as $T \to \infty$. Thus, we show that the assumptions of Robinson (1995, p. 1055) are proved, and therefore the asymptotic result (theorem 3 of Robinson, 1995) applies.   □

Now, we consider the parametric case of a stationary invertible long memory k-factor Gegenbauer process, denoted $(X_t)_{t \in Z}$, for which the k G-frequencies $(\lambda_1, \ldots, \lambda_k)^t$ are known. We are interested in the estimation of the vectorial parameter $(d_1, \ldots, d_k)^t$. According to the spectral density definition of a $GG_k(d, \nu)$ process (8.7), we clearly see that, as $\lambda \to \lambda_i$, for $i = 1, \ldots, k$, the spectral density $f_X(\lambda)$ becomes unbounded (when $0 < d_i < 1/2$). Moreover, it can be shown (see for instance Giraitis and Leipus, 1995) that the spectral density $f_X(\lambda)$ of a $GG_k(d, \nu)$ process can be approximated as follows, as $\lambda \to \lambda_i$, for $i = 1, \ldots, k$:

$$f_X(\lambda) \sim C|\lambda - \lambda_i|^{-2d_i} \qquad (8.12)$$

Moreover, under the technical assumptions 8.4 and 8.5, the spectral density of a Gaussian $GG_k(d, \nu)$ process verifies all the other assumptions (8.1–8.3). Therefore, by using the local approximation of the spectral density (8.12) for each G-frequency, we get an estimate of each long memory parameter d_i, for $i = 1, \ldots, k$, and by applying Proposition 8.1, we get the limiting distribution of each estimate.

Although this estimation method provides the limiting distribution of each long memory parameter, we have to point out that the asymptotic joint distribution is still unknown under general conditions. However, assuming the independence of the long memory parameter estimates, one could get the Gaussian limiting distribution.

As noted previously, this semiparametric method of estimation requires knowledge of the G-frequency. However, in practice, the G-frequency parameter has to be estimated, excepted in the case of the seasonal long memory processes for which the G-frequencies correspond to the seasonal harmonics. Generally, the estimated G-frequency is taken as the argument that maximises the raw periodogram. Yajima (1996) proves, under smooth conditions on the spectral density, that the argument maximising the periodogram converges in probability towards the true G-frequency. Moreover, it can be shown (see Ferrara, 2000), under the assumption of G-frequency estimate independence, that the frequencies corresponding to the k periodogram local maxima converge in probability towards G-frequencies of a k-factor GARMA process.

From a practical point of view, one of the most difficult problems of this semiparametric method is the choice of the trimming number l and the choice of the bandwidth m. As in many other semiparametric statistical methods, the choice of the interval where the parametric method applies is not very clear. Some theoretical efforts have been made recently on this topic in the case of a G-frequency equal to zero, see for instance Hurvich *et al.* (1998) and Hurvich and Deo (1999). An empirical choice, often used in practice, is $l = 0$ and $m = [T^\alpha]$, with $\alpha \in [0.5, 0.8]$.

Now, we consider the estimation of the scale parameter and short memory parameters of a k-factor GARMA process. Usually, this estimation can be carried out after the long memory parameter SP estimation. Indeed, if we denote by $(Y_t)_{t \in Z}$ the prefiltered series such that:

$$Y_t = \prod_{i=1}^{k} (I - 2\nu B + B^2)^{\hat{d}_{R,i}} X_t \qquad (8.13)$$

where $(X_t)_{t \in Z}$ is a k-factor GARMA process defined by (8.4), thus we have:

$$\phi(B)Y_t = \theta(B)\varepsilon_t \qquad (8.14)$$

where $\phi(B) = 1 - \phi_1 B - \phi_2 B^2 - \cdots - \phi_p B^p$, $\theta(B) = 1 + \theta_1 B + \theta_2 B^2 + \cdots + \theta_q B^q$, and the roots of $\phi(B)$ and $\theta(B)$ lie outside the unit circle. Therefore, the $(p + q)$ short memory parameters and the scale parameter can be estimated using classical methods inherent in the Box and Jenkins (1976) methodology. Note that, in order to compute the prefiltered series $(Y_t)_{t \in Z}$, this estimation method involves a truncation of the infinite sum in (8.13). However, it is important to highlight that, in this case, no theoretical results on the estimates are available. In the case of ARFIMA processes, many authors have shown that SP estimation methods of the long memory parameter are not robust to the presence of AR and MA parts. Thus, this parameter estimation method has to be carried out very carefully.

It is well known in the statistical spectral theory (see for instance Priestley, 1981) that the periodogram I_T, used in the regression (8.8), is a nonconsistent estimate of the spectral density of a covariance stationary process, although asymptotically unbiased. Two classical statistical techniques are available in order to try to improve the performances of the periodogram as a spectral density estimate, namely tapering and smoothing. We quickly introduce both these techniques, but we refer to Priestley (1981) for further details.

Tapering allows us to improve the periodogram precision through a data transformation prior to the analysis. Actually, the sample $X_1, \ldots, X_T$ is replaced by the tapered sample $h_1 X_1, \ldots, h_T X_T$, where $(h_t)_{t=1,\ldots,T}$ is a suitable sequence of constants. As an example of such a sequence, we often use in practice a cosine bell sequence, given for $t = 1, \ldots, T$ by:

$$h_t = 0.5\{1 - \cos(2\pi t/T)\} \qquad (8.15)$$

Sometimes a trapezoidal sequence is used, which is equal to one for the central part of the series and decreases linearly towards zero for the t_0 first and last values of the series. The practitioner chooses the value of t_0, but usually t_0 is such that $t_0 = 0.1 \times T$.

The smoothed periodogram, denoted f_S, is given by the following expression:

$$f_s(\lambda) = \frac{1}{2\pi} \sum_{h=-r}^{r} \omega(h/r)\hat{\gamma}_T(h)e^{-ih\lambda} \qquad (8.16)$$

where $\hat{\gamma}_T(h)$ is the empirical autocovariance function, the real positive parameter r is a function of T such that if $T \to \infty$, $r \to \infty$ and $r/T \to 0$, and $\omega(.)$ is the lag window and is an even piecewise continuous function satisfying the conditions $\omega(0) = 1$; $|\omega(x)| \leqslant 1$ for all x; $\omega(x) = 0$ for $|x| > 1$. Note that if $\omega \equiv 1$ and $r = T$, we get $2\pi f_S(\lambda) = I_T(\lambda)$ for all Fourier frequencies $\lambda = \lambda_j \neq 0$. Several types of lag window are available in the statistical literature, proposed by famous statisticians (Bartlett, Parzen, Blackman–Tukey, Daniell, etc.). However, in practice, two special types of lag window are often used.

1.   The rectangular or truncated window, defined by:

$$\omega(x) = 1 \text{ if } |x| \leqslant 1 \text{ and } 0 \text{ otherwise}$$

2.   The Bartlett or triangular window, defined by:

$$\omega(x) = 1 - |x| \text{ if } |x| \leqslant 1 \text{ and } 0 \text{ otherwise}$$

These two types of lag window are used in the last section, in order to compute the generalised Robinson estimate given by (8.10).

8.3   PSEUDO-MAXIMUM LIKELIHOOD ESTIMATION

We are now interested in parameter estimation of a $GG_k(d, \nu)$ process defined by (8.4), with mean μ equal to zero, using the Pseudo-Maximum Likelihood (PML) estimation method, developed by Whittle (1951). If the process is not centred, the mean can be estimated by the empirical mean. Indeed, Chung (1996b) proved that the convergence rate of the empirical mean of a GARMA process, with $|\nu| < 1$, is the usual rate $O(T^{-1/2})$, when the convergence rate of the empirical mean of an ARFIMA process is $O(T^{-1/2+d})$ (see for instance Adenstedt, 1974). In the remainder of this paper, we assume that the number k of factors is known, and moreover, for sake of simplicity, we assume that $k = 1$.

Let $X_1, \ldots, X_T$ be an observed finite sequence generated by a Gaussian linear causal stationary invertible $GG_1(d, \nu)$ process $(X_t)_{t \in Z}$. The Whittle estimate of $\xi = (d, \nu, \sigma_\varepsilon^2)'$ is obtained by minimising the following approximation of the log-likelihood function:

$$L_w(X, \xi) = \frac{1}{2\pi} \int_{-\pi}^{\pi} \log[f_x(\lambda, \xi)] + \frac{I_T(\lambda)}{f_x(\lambda, \xi)} \, d\lambda \tag{8.17}$$

where $f_X(\lambda, \xi)$ is the spectral density of the process $(X_t)_{t \in Z}$ and $I_T(\lambda)$ is the periodogram defined by (8.9). To get the Whittle estimate $\hat{\xi}_t = (\hat{d}_T, \hat{\nu}_T, \hat{\sigma}_{\varepsilon,T})'$, we have to minimise $L_W(X, \xi)$. After a reparameterisation (see for instance Beran, 1994), we proceed in two stages.

(1)   We obtain $\hat{\theta}_T = (\hat{d}_T, \hat{\nu}_T)'$ by minimising, with respect to θ, the function:

$$U_T(\theta) = T \int_{-\pi}^{\pi} \frac{I_T(\lambda)}{f_x(\lambda, \theta)} \, d\lambda \tag{8.18}$$

where

$$f_X(\lambda, \theta) = \prod_{i=1}^{k} \left| 4 \sin\left(\frac{\lambda - \lambda_i}{2}\right) \sin\left(\frac{\lambda + \lambda_i}{2}\right) \right| \tag{8.19}$$

(2)   Then, we get $\hat{\sigma}_{\varepsilon,T}^2$ such that:

$$\hat{\sigma}_{\varepsilon,T}^2 = \frac{U_T(\hat{\theta}_T)}{T} \tag{8.20}$$

We now specify the range to which parameters belong.

Assumption 8.6

Let θ and $\hat{\sigma}^2_{\varepsilon,T}$ be such that $0 < \hat{\sigma}^2_{\varepsilon,T} < \infty$ and $\theta \in \Theta = D \times (]-1, \cos(\lambda_G) - \varepsilon[\cup]\cos(\lambda_G) + \varepsilon, 1[)$, where λ_G is the G-frequency and $D = [\delta, 1/2 - \delta]$, with δ such that $0 < \delta < 1/4$ for some $\varepsilon > 0$.

We denote by $\theta_0 = (d_0, \nu_0)'$ and $\sigma^2_{\varepsilon,0}$ the true values of θ and σ^2_{ε} respectively. First, we show the strong consistency of $\hat{\xi}_T = (\hat{d}_T, \hat{\nu}_T, \hat{\sigma}_{\varepsilon,T})'$.

Proposition 8.2

If $(X_t)_{t \in \mathbb{Z}}$ is a Gegenbauer process defined by (8.4) with $k = 1$, and if $\theta = (d, \nu)'$, then under Assumption 8.6:

$$\lim_{T \to \infty} \hat{\theta}_T = \theta_0 \text{ a.s. and } \lim_{T \to \infty} \hat{\sigma}^2_{\varepsilon,T} = \sigma^2_{\varepsilon,0} \text{ a.s.}$$

Proof. The result is obtained in the same way as theorem 1 of Hannan (1973). Giraitis and Leipus (1995) have already given this result in the case of a k-factor Gegenbauer process. □

We now get the limiting distribution of $\hat{d}_T$ and $\hat{\sigma}_{\varepsilon,T}$.

Proposition 8.3

If $(X_t)_{t \in \mathbb{Z}}$ is a Gegenbauer process defined by (8.4) with $k = 1$, $\theta = (d, \nu)'$, and $0 < d < 1/4$, then under Assumption 8.6, as $T \to \infty$:

$$T^{1/2}(\hat{d}_T - d_0) \longrightarrow N(0, \Lambda_d)$$
$$T^{1/2}(\hat{\sigma}^2_{\varepsilon,T} - \sigma^2_{\varepsilon,0}) \longrightarrow N(0, 2\sigma^4_{\varepsilon,0})$$

Proof. To prove Proposition 8.3, we extend the proof of Yajima (1985), obtained in the case of an ARFIMA process. We refer to Ferrara (2000) for the details of the proof. □

It is worthwhile to note that the convergence rate of this PML estimate is greater than the convergence rate of the semiparametric estimate presented in the previous section. In many statistical problems for which a singularity is observed, it seems that the discontinuity localisation parameter possesses a rate of convergence greater than the rates of convergence of the other parameters. In the case of the Gegenbauer process, this phenomenon has been highlighted by Chung (1996a,b), who notes that the convergence rate of the Conditional Sum of Squares (CSS) estimate of the G-frequency is $O(T^{-1})$. Thus, we make the following conjecture.

Conjecture 8.1

If $(X_t)_{t \in \mathbb{Z}}$ is a Gegenbauer process defined by (8.4) with $k = 1$, and if $\theta = (d, \nu)'$, then under the Assumption 8.6:

$$(\hat{\nu}_T - \nu_0) = O(T^{-1})$$

The limiting distribution of the Whittle estimate $\hat{\nu}_T$ is a difficult issue and, to our knowledge, the limiting distribution has not been exhibited. This is mainly due to the unboundness of the spectral density, which therefore does not fulfil some regularity assumptions often used in classical Central Limit Theorems.

From a practical point of view, we get the Whittle estimate by using a discrete approximation of U_T, given in (8.18). This expression is replaced by a sum across the Fourier frequencies λ_j, for $j = 1, \ldots, n^*$, where n^* is the integer part of $T/2 + 1$. Thus, as the continuous Whittle estimate, the discrete Whittle estimate is computed in two steps.

(1)   We obtain $\hat{\theta}_T = (\hat{d}_T, \hat{v}_T)'$ by minimising, with respect to θ, the function:

$$Q_T(\theta) = \sum_{j=1}^{n^*} \frac{I_T(\lambda_j)}{f_X(\lambda_j, \theta)} \tag{8.21}$$

where

$$f_X(\lambda_j, \theta) = \prod_{i_G=1}^{k} \left| 4 \sin \left(\frac{\lambda_j - \lambda_{i_G}}{2} \right) \sin \left(\frac{\lambda_j + \lambda_{i_G}}{2} \right) \right| \tag{8.22}$$

where the λ_{i_G} are the G-frequencies among the Fourier frequencies.
(2)   Then we get $\hat{\sigma}^2_{\varepsilon,T}$ such that:

$$\hat{\sigma}^2_{\varepsilon,T} = \frac{4\pi}{T} Q_T(\hat{\theta}_T) \tag{8.23}$$

In practice, parameter estimation in statistical long memory models having spectral density with singularities is done in two steps (Gray et al., 1989; Chung, 1996a,b; Woodward et al., 1998). The first step consists of a grid-search procedure to estimate the frequencies for which the spectral density is unbounded (parameter v) and in a second step the memory parameter d is estimated using a classical parametric method. In the case of a Gegenbauer process, Yajima (1996) proposes to estimate first the frequency of unbounded spectral density by maximising the periodogram. This method can be generalised to the case of a spectral density with several singularities (see Ferrara, 2000). Other authors consider a simultaneous global estimation of the whole of the parameters (Giraitis and Leipus, 1995; Ferrara, 2000). The two-step method of Yajima (1996) and the simultaneous method have the great advantage of avoiding a grid-search procedure, which is a very time-consuming method. Moreover, it has been shown, through Monte Carlo simulations, that the two-step procedure of Chung (1996a) and the simultaneous procedure provide quasi-similar results (see Ferrara, 2000).

8.4 APPLICATION

In this section, we provide an application of the long memory Gegenbauer process, which points out the interest of such a model to analyse time series with long-range dependence. This application is motivated by the observed persistent sinusoidal decay of the ACF of the error correction term in cointegration analysis carried out on financial data. We refer especially to the paper of Barkoulas et al. (1997), dealing with interest rates of industrialised countries, and also to the paper of Lien and Tse (1999), dealing with the Nikkei spot index data. In both applications, fractional cointegration is considered by using a long memory ARFIMA process in order to model the long-range dependence of the error correction term, without taking into account the persistent cyclical behaviour. We propose here to reconsider the analysis of the error correction term by using a Gegenbauer process.

Our dataset stems from the one used in the paper of Lien and Tse (1999) and consists of $T = 1064$ daily observations of the spot index and futures prices of the Nikkei Stock Average 225 (NSA), covering the period from May 1992 through August 1996. Daily closing values of the spot index and the settlement price of the futures contracts are used. The regular futures contracts mature in March, June, September and December. The contracts expire on the third Wednesday of the contract month. For further details on the futures price series, we refer to the paper of Lien and Tse (1999).

Let $(S_t)_t$ denote the logarithm of the spot prices and $(F_t)_t$ the logarithm of the futures prices. Lien and Tse (1999) assume that $(S_t)_t$ and $(F_t)_t$ are both integrated of order one and they model the relationship between $(S_t)_t$ and $(F_t)_t$ with the following Error Correction Model (ECM) proposed by Engle and Granger (1987):

$$\Delta S_t = \phi_0 + \sum_{i=1}^{p} \phi_i \Delta S_{t-i} + \sum_{j=1}^{q} \psi_j \Delta F_{t-j} + \gamma Z_{t-1} + \varepsilon_{S_t} \qquad (8.24)$$

where $(Z_t)_t$ may be approximated by the basis defined as $Z_t = F_t - S_t$, for $t = 1, \ldots, T$. Note that the error correction term $(Z_t)_t$ is simply the difference between the log futures and log stock prices. Our aim in this section is to model the error correction term $(Z_t)_t$ presented in Figure 8.1. To reach our goal, we consider two different approaches to modelling and compare competitively diverse long memory models and diverse estimation methods, according to their goodness of fit. To assess the goodness of fit, we use the three following information criteria:

$$AICC = T \log(\hat{\sigma}_{\varepsilon,T}^2) + \frac{2T(p+q+\delta)}{T-1-(p+q+\delta)}$$

$$BIC = T \log(\hat{\sigma}_{\varepsilon,T}^2) + (p+q+\delta) \log(T)$$

$$HIC = T \log(\hat{\sigma}_{\varepsilon,T}^2) + 2(p+q+\delta)c \log[\log(T)]$$

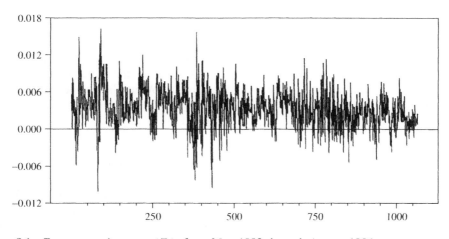

Figure 8.1   Error correction term $(Z_t)_t$ from May 1992 through August 1996

where $c = 1.0001$, p and q are respectively the degrees of the AR and MA parts and δ is equal to the sum of long memory parameters to estimate. Thus, $\delta = k$ if the G-frequencies are known and $\delta = 2k$ if the G-frequencies have to be estimated. Note that we propose these generalisations of information criteria by extending the definitions given in the long memory domain (see Gray *et al.*, 1989 or Bisaglia, 1998).

In the first approach, we model the long-range dependence of $(Z_t)_t$ with a classical ARFIMA model (model (M1)), this case is well known in the statistical literature and is referred to as "fractional cointegration" (Granger, 1986). In the second approach, we model both the persistence and the cyclical patterns in the ACF of $(Z_t)_t$ (see Figures 8.2 and 8.3) with a Gegenbauer process. Parameter estimation will be done using either the simultaneous PML method introduced in previous sections (model (M2)) or a "two-step" PML method (model (M3) and model (M4)). Moreover, SP estimations of the long memory parameter are carried out using diverse spectral density estimation.

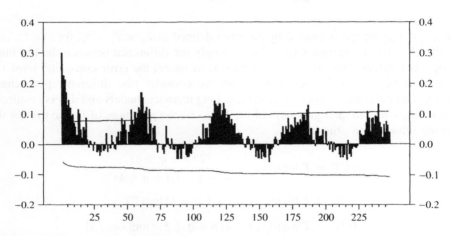

Figure 8.2   ACF empirical estimation of the error correction term $(Z_t)_t$

8.4.1   ARFIMA Modelling

In order to take into account the long-range dependence of the error correction term $(Z_t)_t$, we consider first an ARFIMA$(1, d, 0)$ model, as in the paper of Lien and Tse (1999). Parameter estimation is done using the classical Whittle's method. We obtain the following results:

$$(I + 0.0705B)(I - B)^{0.2756}(Z_t - m_Z) = \varepsilon_t \qquad \text{(M1)}$$

where m_Z is the empirical mean of the time series $(Z_t)_t$, equal to 3.261×10^{-3}.

When considering the ACF of the error correction term $(Z_t)_t$ (Figure 8.2), there is evidence of a persistent cyclical pattern, which cannot be caught by an ARFIMA model. Moreover, the spectral density of $(Z_t)_t$ (Figure 8.3) clearly possesses a peak for a frequency located very close, but not equal, to zero. Thus, both these observations of the ACF and the spectral density suggest fitting a Gegenbauer process to this series $(Z_t)_t$.

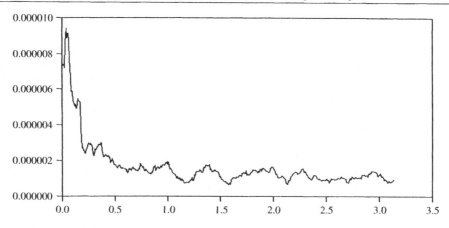

Figure 8.3 Spectral density empirical estimation of the error correction term $(Z_t)_t$

8.4.2 Gegenbauer Modelling

In a first step, we estimate the degree of persistence, by using the semiparametric log-periodogram estimation method. The G-frequency estimate is taken such that the corresponding periodogram value is maximum. Thus, $\hat{\lambda}_G^M = 0.10039$, *i.e.* $\cos(\hat{\lambda}_G^M) = 0.9950$. Long memory parameter estimation is carried out using the log-periodogram method introduced previously and considering diverse spectral density estimation, based on the expression of the periodogram. We use nine various estimation techniques provided by the combinations of the two smoothing methods and the two tapering methods presented in Section 8.2. The bandwidth m is chosen such that $m = T^{0.6}$, and the trimming number l is supposed to be zero, according to the results on finite sample properties (see for instance Ferrara, 2000). The results are contained in Table 8.1.

We note that the results are quite similar, except for the raw periodogram combined with the tapering method, for which the estimate is lower. We also note that the two tapering techniques do not imply a significant difference in the estimate value. However, smoothing with the triangular window implies a greater estimate than smoothing with the rectangular window. It is also clear that smoothing tends to increase the estimate value. From our practical experience, it seems that smoothing improves greatly the quality of

Table 8.1 Semiparametric log-periodogram estimation of the memory parameter d

Estimation method	$\hat{d}_R(l, m)$
Raw	0.15608
Raw + Cosine Taper	0.12754
Raw + Trapezoidal Taper	0.12161
Smooth Rectangular	0.14864
Smooth Triangular	0.16659
Smooth Rectangular + Cosine Taper	0.15230
Smooth Rectangular + Trapezoidal Taper	0.15442
Smooth Triangular + Cosine Taper	0.16685
Smooth Triangular + Trapezoidal Taper	0.16906

the log-periodogram estimate if the sample size is small (less than 100 data points) and generally improves the robustness of the method.

In a second step, we fit a Gegenbauer process to the series $(Z_t)_t$, and estimate the parameter of the process by using the PML method. However, we compare three various methods of parameter estimation. First, parameter estimation is done using the simultaneous Whittle's method. The choice of initial values in the estimation algorithm is crucial, and we take as initial values $d^{(0)} = 0.135$ and $\lambda_G^{(0)} = 0.10$. The value of 0.10 is chosen because the length of the period in Figure 8.2 seems to be around 60, which corresponds to a Gegenbauer frequency approximately equal to 0.10. Regarding the value of $d^{(0)}$, as the G-frequency tends to zero, the Gegenbauer process $GG(d, \nu)$ tends to an ARFIMA$(0, 2d, 0)$ and therefore we take $d^{(0)}$ equal to half of the estimated long memory parameter in model (M1). Thus, we obtain the following model for the series $(Z_t)_t$:

$$[1 - (2 \times 0.99491)B + B^2]^{0.12739}(Z_t - m_Z) = \varepsilon_t \qquad (M2)$$

with $\hat{\lambda}_G = 0.10096$.

Finally, following the idea of Chung (1996a), parameter estimation is done using a "two-step" method. Two different methods are considered. First, we assume the G-frequency is estimated by the frequency corresponding to the periodogram maximum ($\hat{\lambda}_G = 0.10039$), and estimate the long memory parameter d using the classical Whittle's method. Thus, we get the following model:

$$[1 - (2 \times 0.99497)B + B^2]^{0.10996}(Z_t - m_Z) = \varepsilon_t \qquad (M3)$$

Secondly, we consider a grid-search procedure, and for each λ_G belonging to the interval [0.0401,0.1400], we estimate the long memory parameter d by using the classical Whittle's method. The pair of parameters for which the residual variance $\hat{\sigma}_{\varepsilon,T}^2$ is minimum is retained. Thus, we obtain the following model for the series $(Z_t)_t$:

$$[1 - (2 \times 0.99496)B + B^2]^{0.11480}(Z_t - m_Z) = \varepsilon_t \qquad (M4)$$

with $\hat{\lambda}_G = 0.1004$. It is worthwhile to note that the G-frequency estimate obtained by the grid-search procedure is very close to the frequency for which the periodogram is maximum.

The information criteria of each long memory model are presented in Table 8.2. From Table 8.2, it is clear that Gegenbauer processes (model (M2), model (M3) and model (M4)) provide a better fit than the ARFIMA process (model (M1)). We point out here the flexibility of the Gegenbauer process, which allows unboundness for the spectral density anywhere on the interval $[0,\pi]$. Thus, even when the G-frequency is very close to zero, a Gegenbauer process seems to be more efficient in fitting than an ARFIMA process.

Regarding the comparative performances of parameter estimation methods in Gegenbauer processes, there is no strong difference in values of criteria. However, it turns out that the "two-step" procedure, with the G-frequency estimated by the value maximising the periodogram (model (M3)), provides a better goodness of fit than the two other methods. In practice, the major drawback of the grid-search procedure (model (M4)) is the call on CPU time, which increases with the estimate precision. Therefore, from a practical point of view, we advise the successive use of the simultaneous Whittle's procedure and the "two-step" procedure with the G-frequency estimated by the value maximising the

Table 8.2 Goodness of fit results on the error correction term $(Z_t)_t$

Model	$\hat{\sigma}^2_{\varepsilon,T}$	AICC	BIC	HIC
ARFIMA (M1)	1.751×10^{-5}	-11650	-11640	-11646
Gegenbauer (M2) 1-step estimation	0.908×10^{-5}	-12349	-12339	-12345
Gegenbauer (M3) 2-step estimation (1)	0.903×10^{-5}	-12356	-12344	-12351
Gegenbauer (M4) 2-step estimation (2)	0.905×10^{-5}	-12352	-12342	-12348

periodogram. However, when using the simultaneous Whittle's method of estimation, it is worthwhile to note that a careful choice of initial values in the estimation algorithm is needed.

If we compare the estimation results on the long memory parameter provided by the SP method and the ones provided by the PML method, this latter method gives lower estimate values. However, the parameter values of the PML method are very close to the ones of the SP method using the tapered periodogram, without smoothing. It turns out that tapering can be a very helpful statistical technique for this estimation issue. As the convergence rate of the PML memory parameter estimate is greater than the convergence rate of the SP method, we believe that the PML estimates are more reliable, especially in the case of small sample sizes. Moreover, in the case of small sample sizes it has been empirically shown (see for instance Ferrara, 2000) that the simultaneous use of smoothing and tapering clearly improves the quality of the estimate.

8.5 CONCLUSION

We show in an application to financial data how we can improve the goodness of fit, by taking into account in modelling the persistent periodic cyclical behaviour of a time series, through generalised long memory processes. We point out here the interest of such processes in comparison with the classical long memory ARFIMA process, even when the G-frequency is close to zero, which often happens in practice. The distinctive feature of generalised long memory processes is to possess a spectral density with k singularities lying on the interval $[0,\pi]$, referred to as the G-frequencies. Therefore, the location of these G-frequencies is a parameter to estimate, except in the case of seasonal processes, for which the location of the G-frequencies is known.

In this paper, we are especially interested in the issue of long memory parameter estimation. We compare two types of estimation methods: a semiparametric method, based on the log-periodogram and a pseudo-maximum likelihood method, based on the Whittle likelihood. The semiparametric method requires first the estimation of the G-frequencies, and we use as estimates the values for which the periodogram is maximum. Moreover, we give the asymptotic behaviour of each estimate.

The semiparametric estimate has the great advantage of being easily computed, but possesses nevertheless a slow convergence rate. Thus, this estimate must be carefully used in the case of small sample sizes, although statistical techniques, such as smoothing and tapering, can greatly improve the semiparametric estimate performances in such cases.

Moreover, as in the case of ARFIMA processes, the presence of a short memory component may damage the estimate quality. The pseudo-maximum likelihood estimate seems to be generally more reliable, under the assumption that the process is well specified.

As future research, the development of nonparametric estimates, such as variance type estimates (see Giraitis *et al.*, 1998) and other semiparametric estimates, especially based on summing the periodogram across the discrete Fourier frequencies (see Robinson, 1994a), are of potential interest. Moreover, the estimates presented in this paper should be reconsidered in the case of cyclical long memory process with heteroskedasticity (see Guégan, 1999, 2000).

ACKNOWLEDGEMENTS

The authors wish to thank Yiu Kuen Tse for providing the data and Allan Timmermann for helpful comments.

REFERENCES

Adenstedt, R.K. (1974). "On Large-sample Estimation for the Mean of a Stationary Random Sequence", *Annals of Statistics* **6**, 1095–1107.

Arteche, J. and P.M. Robinson (2000). "Semiparametric Inference in Seasonal and Cyclical Long Memory Processes", *Journal of Time Series Analysis* **21**(1), 1–25.

Baillie, R.T, T. Bollerslev and H.-O. Mikkelsen (1996a). "Fractionally Integrated Generalised Autoregressive Conditional Heteroskesdasticity", *Journal of Econometrics* **74**, 3–30.

Baillie, R.T., C.-F. Chung and M.A. Tieslau (1996b). "Analysing Inflation by the Fractionally Integrated ARFIMA–GARCH Model", *Journal of Applied Econometrics* **11**, 23–40.

Barkoulas, J., C.F. Baum and G.S. Oguz (1997). "Fractional Cointegration Analysis of Long Term Interest Rates", *International Journal of Finance* **9**(2), 586–606.

Beran, J. (1994). *Statistics for Long-Memory Processes*. London: Chapman & Hall.

Bisaglia, L. (1998). "Processi a memoria lunga: problemi di stima, identificazione e previsione", Dottora di Ricerca in Statistica, Ciclo X, Universita degli Studi di Padova.

Box, G.E.P. and G.M. Jenkins (1976). *Time Series Analysis: Forecasting and Control*, 2nd ed. San Francisco: Holden-Day.

Chung, C.-F. (1996a). "Estimating a Generalised Long Memory Process", *Journal of Econometrics* **73**, 237–59.

Chung, C.-F. (1996b). "A Generalised Fractionally Integrated ARMA Process", *Journal of Time Series Analysis* **17**(2), 111–140.

Engle, R.F. and C.W.J. Granger (1987). "Co-integration and Error Correction: Representation, Estimation And Testing", *Econometrica* **55**, 251–276.

Ferrara, L. (2000), "Processus Longue Mémoire Généralisés: Estimation, Prévision et Applications", Thèse de Doctorat, Université Paris 13-RATP.

Ferrara, L. and D. Guégan (2000a). "Forecasting Financial Time Series with Generalised Long Memory Processes", C.L. Dunis (ed.), *Advances in Quantitative Asset Management*. Boston: Kluwer; 319–342.

Ferrara, L. and D. Guégan (2000b). "Forecasting with *k*-Factor Gegenbauer Processes", *Journal of Forecasting*, in press.

Geweke, J. and S. Porter-Hudak (1983). "The Estimation and Application of Long-memory Time Series Models", *Journal of Time Series Analysis* **4**, 221–238.

Giraitis, L. and R. Leipus (1995). "A Generalised Fractionally Differencing Approach in Long Memory Modeling", *Lithuanian Mathematical Journal* **35**, 65–81.

Giraitis, L., P.M. Robinson and D. Surgailis (1998). "Variance-type Estimation of Long-memory", Preprint, London School of Economics.

Granger, C.W.J. (1986). "Developments in the Study of Cointegrated Economic Variables", *Oxford Bulletin of Economics and Statistics* **48**, 213–228.

Granger, C.W.J. and R. Joyeux (1980). "An Introduction to Long-memory Time Series Models and Fractional Differencing", *Journal of Time Series Analysis* **1**, 15–29.

Granger, C.W.J. and Z. Ding (1996). "Varieties of Long Memory Models", *Journal of Econometrics* **73**, 61–77.

Gray, H.L., N.-F. Zhang and W.A. Woodward (1989). "On Generalised Fractional Processes", *Journal of Time Series Analysis* **10**, 233–257.

Gray, H.L., N.-F. Zhang and W.A. Woodward (1994). "Correction to On Generalised Fractional Processes", *Journal of Time Series Analysis* **15**, 561–562.

Guégan, D. (1999), "Note on Long Memory Processes with Cyclical Behavior and Heteroscedasticity", working paper 99-08, University of Reims, France, 1–21.

Guégan, D. (2000). "A New Model: The k-Factor GIGARCH Process", *Journal of Signal Processing* **4**(3), 265–71.

Hannan, E.J. (1973). "The Asymptotic Theory of Linear Time-series Models", *Journal of Applied Probabilities* **10**, 130–145.

Hassler, U. (1994). "(Mis)specification of Long Memory in Seasonal Time Series", *Journal of Time Series Analysis* **15**(1), 19–30.

Hosking, J.R.M. (1981). "Fractional Differencing", *Biometrika* **68**(1), 165–176.

Hosoya, Y. (1997). "A Limit Theory of Long-range Dependence and Statistical Inference in Related Model", *Annals of Statistics* **25**, 105–137.

Hurvich, C.M., R. Deo and J. Brodsky (1998). "The Mean-squared Error of Geweke and Porter-Hudak's Estimates of the Memory Parameter of a Long Memory Time Series", *Journal of Time Series Analysis* **19**(1), 19–46.

Hurvich, C.M. and R. Deo (1999). "Plug-in Selection of the Number of Frequencies in Regression Estimates of the Memory Parameter of a Long Memory Time Series", *Journal of Time Series Analysis* **20**(3), 331–341.

Lien, D. and Y.K. Tse (1999). "Forecasting the Nikkei Spot Index with Fractional Cointegration", *Journal of Forecasting* **18**, 259–273.

Porter-Hudak, S. (1990). "An Application to the Seasonal Fractionally Differenced Model to the Monetary Aggregates", *Journal of the American Statistical Association* **85**(410), 338–344.

Priestley, M.B. (1981). *Spectral Analysis of Time Series*. New York: Academic Press.

Rainville, E.D. (1960). *Special Functions*, New York: Mac Millan.

Ray, B.K. (1993). "Long-range Forecasting of IBM Product Revenues Using a Seasonal Fractionally Differenced ARMAc Model", *International Journal of Forecasting* **9**, 255–269.

Robinson, P.M. (1994a). "Semiparametric Analysis of Long Memory Time Series", *Annals of Statistics* **22**, 515–539.

Robinson, P.M. (1994b). "Efficient Tests of Nonstationary Hypotheses", *Journal of the American Statistical Association* **89**, 1420–1437.

Robinson, P.M. (1995). "Log-periodogram Regression of Time Series with Long Range Dependence", *Annals of Statistics* **23**, 1048–1072.

Sutcliffe, A. (1994). "Time-series Forecasting Using Fractional Differencing", *Journal of Forecasting* **13**, 383–393.

Whittle, P. (1951). *Hypothesis Testing in Time Series Analysis*. New York: Hafner.

Willinger, W., M.S. Taqqu and V. Teverovsky (1999). "Stock Market Prices and Long Range Dependence", *Finance and Stochastics* **3**, 1–13.

Woodward, W.A., Q.C. Cheng and H.L. Gray (1998). "A k-Factor Garma Long-memory Model", *Journal of Time Series Analysis* **19**(5), 485–504.

Yajima, Y. (1985). "On Estimation of Long-memory Time Series Models", *Australian Journal of Statistics* **27**(3), 303–320.

Yajima, Y. (1996), "Estimation of the Frequency of Unbounded Spectral Densities", discussion paper, Faculty of Economics, University of Tokyo.

Theme III
Controlling Downside Risk and Investment Strategies

—————— 9 ——————

Building a Mean Downside Risk Portfolio Frontier[1]

GUSTAVO M. DE ATHAYDE

ABSTRACT

In contrast to the classical Markowitz portfolio frontier, downside risk optimisation deals with a positive definite matrix that is endogenous to portfolio weights. This aspect makes the problem far more difficult to handle. For this purpose, a simple algorithm that ensures the convergence to the solution is presented in this work. Based on that, a mean downside risk-efficient set is constructed, and its properties carefully analysed. Bawa and Lindenberg (1977) have derived the Lower Partial Moment CAPM for the continuous case. In this paper, once the mean downside risk portfolio frontier is built, a new approach for the Lower Partial Moment CAPM is presented in a more general framework, which allows for discrete-time observations and the absence of a riskless asset.

9.1 INTRODUCTION

The dissatisfaction with the traditional notion of variance as a measure of risk is becoming a common feature of financial markets all over the world. The main argument against the use of variance is that it makes no distinction between gains and losses. In fact, in Markowitz's original work (1952) he argues for other measures of risk. Two ways were suggested. The first would be to include higher moments. This has been approached by a few authors like Ingersoll (1975), Kraus and Litzenberger (1976), among others. However, the complete formal characterisation of the portfolio frontier with higher moments has not been done since Athayde (2001). In that paper the portfolio set with higher moments and all of its features were presented.

The second way that Markowitz proposed was to use what he called semivariance. That is the sum of the squares of negative deviations from the mean, divided by the total number of observations:

$$\frac{1}{n} \sum_{i=1}^{n} [\min(r_i - \mu, 0)]^2 \tag{9.1}$$

The great advantage of the use of semivariance over variance is that it does not include positive gains, so what is considered as risk takes into account only negative deviations.

---

[1] The opinions expressed here are not necessarily those of Banco Itaú.

Developments in Forecast Combination and Portfolio Choice. Edited by C. Dunis, A. Timmermann and J. Moody.
© 2001 John Wiley & Sons Ltd

However, one may be led to the wrong conclusion that minimising semivariance necessarily means minimising only negative deviations. This common mistake becomes even clearer if the distributions we are dealing with are symmetric, like the normal curve. In this case minimising variance and semivariance will lead to the same problem. The only case that justifies the use of semivariance is when the presence of skewness is observed. That would lead us back to the problem of adding moments. The presence of non-normality aspects in asset returns that would justify the use of semivariance, especially in emerging markets, can be found in Eftekhari and Satchell (1996).

Although the approach to use higher moments is far more complete than the use of semivariance, the popularity of the latter is larger, maybe because it measures risk in one number, while the use of variance, skewness and possibly kurtosis would give us three different values to capture risk. In terms of portfolio frontier, we will be dealing only with two dimensions, rather than three or four, and make the analysis simpler (although not so efficient if compared to the multidimensioned three or four moment portfolio frontier).

Finding the portfolios with minimum semivariance is not an easy task. This is due to the fact that we do not have a fixed number to represent the downside risk of an asset. For instance, if we have acquired a single asset, its semivariance will be given by negative deviations, while if we short sell this asset, we have to deal with positive deviations (because now the risk is for the asset to go up). Thus what will be used to construct its semivariance depends on whether we are short or long.

The problem becomes even more complex when we are dealing with more than one asset. Suppose we have a given portfolio P_0. To compute the semivariance of this portfolio we have to take into consideration only the observations that were negative deviations. If we change a little the weights of this portfolio, creating a new portfolio P_1, some observations in which the former portfolio was negative might become positive, and viceversa. Thus they will have to be included or excluded from the semivariance of portfolio P_1. Therefore the set of observations that will be taken into account when building the semivariance of this portfolio will be a function of the portfolio weights, making the problem more difficult to handle than in the case of minimising variance *per se*.

For instance, suppose we have two assets, with zero mean. On a particular day one has a return of 1%, and the other a return of −1%. If the weight of the first asset is more (less) than 1/2, the portfolio's return will be positive (negative), and therefore excluded (included) in the semivariance of the portfolio.

The definition of semivariance becomes even more complicated in terms of the cross-product. By semicovariance, which of the following terms are we referring to?:

$$\frac{1}{n}\sum_{i=1}^{n}[\min(r_a^i - \mu_a,0)][\min(r_b^i - \mu_b,0)]$$

$$\frac{1}{n}\sum_{i=1}^{n}[\min(r_a^i - \mu_a,0)](r_b^i - \mu_b)$$

$$\frac{1}{n}\sum_{i=1}^{n}(r_a^i - \mu_a)[\min(r_b^i - \mu_b,0)]$$

$$\frac{1}{n}\sum_{i=1}^{n}\min[(r_a^i - \mu_a)(r_b^i - \mu_b),0]$$

Even if we pick any of the definitions above, it should be clear that there is no such thing as a well-behaved positive definite semivariance matrix, that we can pre- and postmultiply by the vector of weights of any portfolio and get its respective semivariance. Therefore the minimisation problem becomes much more complicated, because the set of observations that will be taken into account is endogenous to the weights of the portfolio in question.

Nevertheless, one common approach used in the market is to approximate what would be a semivariance matrix by:

$$
\begin{bmatrix}
\frac{\sigma_{11}^*}{\sigma_{11}} & 0 & \cdots & 0 \\
0 & \frac{\sigma_{22}^*}{\sigma_{22}} & \ddots & \vdots \\
\vdots & \ddots & \ddots & 0 \\
0 & \cdots & 0 & \frac{\sigma_{kk}^*}{\sigma_{kk}}
\end{bmatrix}^{1/2}
\begin{bmatrix}
\sigma_{11} & \sigma_{12} & \cdots & \sigma_{1k} \\
\sigma_{21} & \sigma_{22} & \cdots & \sigma_{2k} \\
\vdots & \vdots & \ddots & \vdots \\
\sigma_{k1} & \sigma_{k2} & \cdots & \sigma_{kk}
\end{bmatrix}
\begin{bmatrix}
\frac{\sigma_{11}^*}{\sigma_{11}} & 0 & \cdots & 0 \\
0 & \frac{\sigma_{22}^*}{\sigma_{22}} & \ddots & \vdots \\
\vdots & \ddots & \ddots & 0 \\
0 & \cdots & 0 & \frac{\sigma_{kk}*}{\sigma_{kk}}
\end{bmatrix}^{1/2}
$$

$$
=
\begin{bmatrix}
\sigma_{11}^* & \rho_{12}\sqrt{\sigma_{11}^* \sigma_{22}^*} & \cdots & \rho_{1k}\sqrt{\sigma_{11}^* \sigma_{kk}^*} \\
\rho_{21}\sqrt{\sigma_{22}^* \sigma_{11}^*} & \sigma_{22}^* & \cdots & \rho_{2k}\sqrt{\sigma_{22}^* \sigma_{kk}^*} \\
\vdots & \vdots & \ddots & \vdots \\
\rho_{k1}\sqrt{\sigma_{kk}^* \sigma_{11}^*} & \rho_{k2}\sqrt{\sigma_{kk}^* \sigma_{22}^*} & \cdots & \sigma_{kk}^*
\end{bmatrix}
$$

Here, σ_{jj}^* is the semivariance of asset j.

This formula gives us a symmetric positive definite matrix. The semivariances will be on this matrix diagonal. It is feasible to find a portfolio to pre- and postmultiply this matrix that gives us the minimum value of this function, which is not the minimum semivariance. Depending on the correlations and other characteristics of the assets in question, these minima can differ by an enormous amount.

Before we go on, we must define Downside Risk (DSR). The latter is a generalisation of semivariance:

$$
DSR \implies \frac{1}{n}\sum_{i=1}^{n}[\min(r_i - \mu, 0)]^k \tag{9.2}
$$

where k is any power you can choose (when $k = 1$, it should be considered the absolute value of the term in brackets), and μ is a chosen benchmark (not necessarily the mean).

9.2 THE MEAN DSR PORTFOLIO FRONTIER: THE BIVARIATE CASE

Let us assume that we have two risky assets a and b. The return of a portfolio p that has w units of a and $(1 - w)$ units of b at time i can be expressed as:

$$
r_p^i(w) = wr_a^i + (1 - w)r_b^i
$$

where r_j^i denotes the return of asset j at time i.

Suppose we want to find the optimal combination w of these assets that gives us the minimum downside risk of portfolio p. To start, let us consider the case where $k = 2$ (if the benchmark is the mean of the portfolio, then we will be dealing with semivariance). Thus we must find w that minimises the DSR below:

$$DSR = \frac{1}{n+1} \sum_{i=0}^{n} [\min(r_p^i(w) - \mu, 0)]^2$$

The portfolio's return at time 0 will be given by:

$$r_p^0(w) = wr_a^0 + (1-w)r_b^0$$

The value of w at time 0 that makes the portfolio's return equal to the benchmark μ is given by:

$$w_0 = \frac{\mu - r_b^0}{r_a^0 - r_b^0} \qquad (9.3)$$

If we had only this observation, assuming that $r_a^0 > r_b^0$, the DSR of this portfolio will be given by:

$$DSR(w) = [w(r_a^0 - r_b^0) - (\mu - r_b^0)]^2 \quad \text{if } w < w_0 \text{ and } 0 \text{ otherwise}$$

$$DSR'(w) = 2[w(r_a^0 - r_b^0) - (\mu - r_b^0)](r_a^0 - r_b^0) < 0 \quad \text{if } w < w_0 \text{ and } 0 \text{ otherwise}$$

$$DSR''(w) = 2(r_a^0 - r_b^0)^2 > 0 \quad \text{if } w < w_0 \text{ and } 0 \text{ otherwise}$$

The function is illustrated in Figure 9.1.

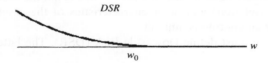

Figure 9.1   DSR at time 0

Consider now the returns at time 1. Suppose that $r_a^1 > r_b^1$ and that $w_1 < w_0$. If we take only this observation into consideration, its DSR will be given by the graph in Figure 9.2, just like in the former case.

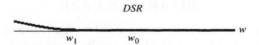

Figure 9.2   DSR at time 1

When we be compute the DSR of our portfolio with these two observations, we will be adding these two piecewise quadratic functions, so that the new curve will be as in Figure 9.3.

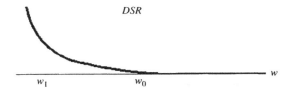

Figure 9.3 Adding the two previous curves

Since we have only two observations ($n = 2$), the new DSR will be given by:

$$DSR(w) = \frac{1}{2} \sum_{i=0}^{1} [w(r_a^i - r_b^i) - (\mu - r_b^i)]^2 \quad \text{if } w < w_1$$

$$DSR(w) = \frac{1}{2}[w(r_a^0 - r_b^0) - (\mu - r_b^0)]^2 \quad \text{if } w_1 < w < w_0$$

$$DSR(w) = 0 \quad \text{otherwise}$$

The first derivative is given by:

$$DSR'(w) = \sum_{i=0}^{1} [w(r_a^i - r_b^i) - (\mu - r_b^i)](r_a^i - r_b^i) < 0 \quad \text{if } w < w_1$$

$$DSR'(w) = [w(r_a^0 - r_b^0) - (\mu - r_b^0)](r_a^0 - r_b^0) < 0 \quad \text{if } w_1 < w < w_0$$

$$DSR'(w) = 0 \quad \text{otherwise}$$

The convexity is given by:

$$DSR''(w) = \sum_{i=0}^{1} (r_a^i - r_b^i)^2 > 0 \quad \text{if } w < w_1$$

$$DSR''(w) = (r_a^0 - r_b^0)^2 > 0 \quad \text{if } w_1 < w < w_0$$

$$DSR''(w) = 0 \quad \text{otherwise}$$

As can be seen, the function is monotonically decreasing with respect to w. The most important aspect however is that once we cross the point w_1 the convexity changes, and we start to deal with a new quadratic function. The convexity is therefore nonincreasing with w. For some specific regions the convexity is fixed, until a new quadratic function is formed as we cross one of the critical points w_0 or w_1. If we keep adding more and more observations in which $r_a > r_b$, the curve will become steeper and steeper as we decrease w.

Consider now the situation in which we only have observations in which $r_a < r_b$. The curve will look exactly like the former, but it will be increasing with w, becoming steeper and steeper, as we will be adding more and more piecewise quadratic functions. This is illustrated in Figure 9.4.

When we include all observations (those in which $r_a > r_b$ and $r_a < r_b$), the whole DSR will be a curve as in Figure 9.5.

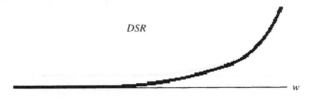

Figure 9.4   DSR when $r_a < r_b$

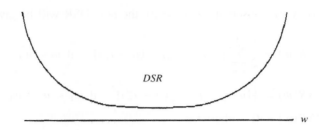

Figure 9.5   The whole DSR

The expected return of the portfolio will be given by:

$$E(r_p) = wE(r_a) + (1 - w)E(r_b) \Longleftrightarrow w = \frac{E(r_p) - E(r_b)}{E(r_a) - E(r_b)}$$

Thus, since we have a linear relation between w and $E(r_p)$, we may conclude that the shape of the set $DSR \times E(r_p)$ will be as in Figure 9.6.

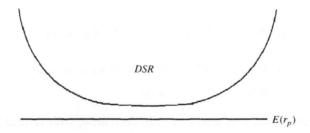

Figure 9.6   The portfolio set

As has been shown, this curve is made of segments of quadratic functions, each one becoming steeper and steeper as we move toward the extremes, in either direction. The more observations we have, the more quadratic functions will appear and the smaller the segment of each will become. The changes in the convexity, when we move from one quadratic function to another, will become more frequent and smoother. In the limit case, where we have an infinite number of observations, each of these quadratic functions will degenerate to a single point, creating a continuous smooth change in the convexity of the curve. Thus, we may conclude that, in the bivariate case, the portfolio set, and consequently the portfolio frontier, will have a convex shape.

9.3   THE ALGORITHM

Suppose we have n observations of returns of assets a and b, and we want to find the portfolio weights that give us the minimum DSR (the vertex of the curve above). The algorithm is explained below.

We start with some portfolio $w^{(0)}$, and calculate its downside risk. We select only the set of observations S_0 that contains negative deviations of this portfolio $w^{(0)}$.

$$S_0 = \{i \mid 1 < i < n \ \& \ r_i(w^{(0)}) < \mu\}$$

Consider the following curve given by:

$$\sigma_0^2(w) = \frac{1}{n} \sum_{i \in S_0} (r_p^i(w) - \mu)^2 \quad \text{where } r_p^i(w) = w r_a^i + (1 - w) r_b^i \tag{9.4}$$

It should be clear from the last section that for a small neighbourhood of w_0, the set of days with negative deviations remains the same as S_0, without adding or excluding any observation, remaining on the same quadratic function. When w becomes very different from w_0, some days will enter and some will go away when we compute the downside risk of w (because we have moved to another segment of a different quadratic function in the DSR curve). In this case the curve that describes the downside risk and $\sigma_0^2(w)$ will become more and more different. However, for small changes on w, if the set of negative deviations is still given by S_0, the two curves will coincide.

The second step is to find a portfolio $w^{(1)}$ that minimises $\sigma_0^2(w)$. Note that this problem is analogous to minimising variance, implying that this curve is a convex well-behaved function whose minimum is easily obtained. This optimal portfolio will be given by:

$$w^{(1)} = \frac{\sum_{i \in S_0} (r_a^i - r_b^i)(\mu - r_b^i)}{\sum_{i \in S_0} (r_a^i - r_b^i)^2}$$

Once we find $w^{(1)}$, we compute its DSR, creating a new set of observations S_1, which has only negative deviations of $w^{(1)}$ with respect to the benchmark μ:

$$S_1 = \{i \mid 1 < i < n \ \& \ r_i(w^{(1)}) < \mu\}$$

In the neighbourhood of $w^{(1)}$, the DSR will coincide with the following quadratic function:

$$\sigma_1^2(w) = \frac{1}{n} \sum_{i \in S_1} (r_p^i(w) - \mu)^2 \quad \text{where } r_p^i(w) = w r_a^i + (1 - w) r_b^i \tag{9.5}$$

We then minimise (9.5) with respect to w. The solution is given by:

$$w^{(2)} = \frac{\sum_{i \in S_1} (r_a^i - r_b^i)(\mu - r_b^i)}{\sum_{i \in S_1} (r_a^i - r_b^i)^2} \tag{9.6}$$

From $w^{(2)}$ we separate the new set of observations with negative deviations S_2, construct a new quadratic function that takes into consideration only the observations in S_2, minimise it with respect to w, finding $w^{(3)}$ that will give us a new set S_3, and so on. The algorithm will stop when $S_t = S_{t+1}$, which will be the unique minimum DSR. Once we found the minimum for that specific set of observations, it will not be necessary to change the set of observations. We will have achieved our objective.

In other words, the algorithm can be expressed by:

$$S_t = \{i | 1 < i < n \ \& \ r_i(w^{(t)}) < \mu\}$$

$$w^{(t+1)} \text{ minimises } \sigma_t^2(w) = \frac{1}{n} \sum_{i \in S_t} (r_p^i(w) - \mu)^2 \quad \text{where } r_p^i(w) = wr_a^i + (1 - w)r_b^i$$

Consider the example in Figure 9.3. We have three possible situations, depending on where our initial portfolio w might start.

1. If we had started with $w \geqslant w_0$, the DSR would be null, so we would stop right there.
2. If we had started with $w_1 \geqslant w > w_0$, we would have the quadratic function given by $\frac{1}{2}[w(r_a^0 - r_b^0) - (\mu - r_b^0)]^2$. The minimum point would be given by w_0. The DSR on this point is zero. The next step would be given by the case above.
3. If we had started with $w < w_1$, we would have the quadratic function given by $\frac{1}{2}\sum_{i=0}^{1}[w(r_a^i - r_b^i) - (\mu - r_b^i)]^2$. The minimum point would be somewhere between w_1 and w_0. The next step would be given by the case above.

In order to extend the last example—which was very trivial—consider Figure 9.7 in which we have three quadratic functions, each one representing a segment of the DSR, which is given by the thick black line. It is easy to see that no matter which quadratic function we pick from the start, if we follow the proposed algorithm, we end up in P_3. The minimum of this quadratic function is also the minimum of DSR, guaranteeing the convergence.

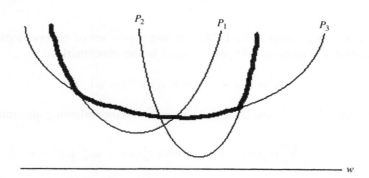

Figure 9.7 How the algorithm works

For instance, if our initial guess of w is very low, we select the observations in such a way that we start at P_1. Once we find w that minimises this quadratic function, we select a new set of observations that are negative, ending up with a new quadratic function P_3.

Again, we find the portfolio w that minimises this quadratic function. However, after this portfolio is found, the new set of observations whose deviations are negative is the same as before, so we remain at P_3, and the minimum DSR (which coincides with the minimum of P_3) is achieved.

The same goes for the case in which our initial guess of w is high. In this situation, we would have started at P_2 and, on the next iteration, be driven back to P_3.

In case we have started at P_3, only one iteration would be necessary to achieve the minimum.

The procedure can be extended to the case where there are several observations, and consequently several quadratic functions.

9.4   THE MULTIVARIATE CASE

The procedure for the multivariate case is analogous to the former. Let us say we have m assets. we will start with a given portfolio w_0. Then we select the set S_0 of observations in which this portfolio w_0 had negative deviations. We construct the following positive semidefinite matrix:

$$M^{(0)} = \sum_{i \in S_0} \begin{bmatrix} R_1^i \\ R_2^i \\ \vdots \\ R_m^i \end{bmatrix} [R_1^i \quad R_2^i \quad \cdots \quad R_m^i]$$

where R_j^i means the excess return (actual return minus the benchmark) of asset j on date i.

The next step is to find the portfolio w_1 that solves the following problem:

$$\min_w w' M^{(0)} w \text{ s.t. } w'1 = 1 \quad \text{where 1 is a vector of 1's}$$

The solution to the problem will be given by:

$$w^{(1)} = \frac{M^{(0)-1}1}{1'M^{(0)-1}1}$$

If $M^{(0)}$ is noninvertible, this means that we have few observations, and it will be possible to find a portfolio that will give us a null DSR. This is not an interesting case, it does not mean there is no DSR, it only means that the sample in question is poor, leaving us with few degrees of freedom.

With the new portfolio $w^{(1)}$ we collect the set of observations S_1 that contains only negative excess returns of portfolio $w^{(1)}$. we now form a new positive semidefinite matrix $M^{(1)}$:

$$M^{(1)} = \sum_{i \in S_1} \begin{bmatrix} R_1^i \\ R_2^i \\ \vdots \\ R_m^i \end{bmatrix} [R_1^i \quad R_2^i \quad \cdots \quad R_m^i]$$

The next step is to find the portfolio $w^{(2)}$ that solves the following problem:

$$\min_{w} w' M^{(1)} w \text{ s.t. } w' 1 = 1$$

The solution to the problem will be given by:

$$w^{(2)} = \frac{M^{(1)^{-1}} 1}{1' M^{(1)^{-1}} 1}$$

From then on, we form a new matrix $M^{(2)}$ collecting only the negative observations of portfolio $w^{(2)}$, and so on. The iterations will stop when the matrix $M^{(T)}$ is the same as $M^{(T+1)}$. The solution will be given by:

$$w^{(T)} = \frac{M^{(T)^{-1}} 1}{1' M^{(T)^{-1}} 1} \tag{9.7}$$

This portfolio will give us the minimum DSR. In terms of the portfolio frontier, this will represent the vertex of the curve. In order to build the portfolio frontier, we have to find some other points on the efficient set. Since we are interested in points with a higher expected return than the vertex, we fix an expected return a bit higher than the minimum downside risk portfolio above. So the new recursive minimisation procedure will take the following form:

$$\min_{w} w' M w \text{ s.t. } w' 1 = 1 \text{ and } w' e = E(R_p)$$

where e is the vector of expected returns.

Like in the former case, we start with a given portfolio, select only its negative deviations, construct a new matrix $M^{(0)}$ with these observations, make the minimisation above, and find a new portfolio. Again, select its negative observations, construct a matrix $M^{(1)}$, repeat the minimisation with $M^{(1)}$, find a new portfolio, select its negative deviations, and so on. After we have achieved the convergence, after T iterations, the minimum downside risk portfolio with expected excess return given by $E(R_p)$ will be given by:

$$w = \frac{\alpha E(R_p) - \gamma}{\alpha \theta - \gamma^2} M^{(T)^{-1}} e + \frac{\theta - \gamma E(R_p)}{\alpha \theta - \gamma^2} M^{(T)^{-1}} 1 \tag{9.8}$$

where $\alpha = 1' M^{(T)^{-1}} 1$, $\gamma = e' M^{(T)^{-1}} 1$, $\theta = e' M^{(T)^{-1}} e$.

It should be noted that for small changes in the expected return, the matrix we end up with remains unchanged. Premultiplying (9.8) by $w' M^{(T)}$:

$$\sigma^2(w) = \frac{\alpha [E(R_p)]^2 - 2\gamma E(R_p) + \theta}{\alpha \theta - \gamma^2}$$

The equation above shows us that while the final matrix $M^{(T)}$ does not change, downside risk will be a quadratic function on the expected return, just like in the bivariate case. However, if we change considerably the expected return, we end up with a new matrix, and therefore a new quadratic function. Thus, like in the bivariate case, the portfolio frontier will be described as a sequence of segments of different quadratic functions.

This result is expected because the portfolio frontier is a convex combination of several bivariate cases, each one like Figure 9.6. One interesting aspect is that the more assets are used, the smoother will be the portfolio frontier in question, creating a similar effect as if we were adding more observations.

Since this algorithm is a series of standard minimisation procedures, adding linear constraints, like not exceeding a given amount of a given asset, or not allowing short sales, is still valid. Minimising quadratic functions with linear constraints are defined as Quadratic Programming (QP) problems, and efficient algorithms have been developed for solving such problems. The only inconvenience is that we do not have an explicit closed form solution, as in the case above.

To construct the portfolio frontier then, we start with the simplest problem: minimise downside risk. From that point, we get the vertex of the curve, and the other points of the portfolio frontier will be constructed using the procedure above, each time with a higher expected return. The only recommendation is that we should use the minimum downside risk portfolio as a warm start for the next point (the one with a higher expected return). After this point is achieved, after all the iterations suggested above, this portfolio should be used as a warm start for the next point, with an even higher expected return, and so on.

Since the matrix $M^{(T)}$ will differ for frontier portfolios with very different expected returns, we will not have the traditional two-fund separation property. Looking at (9.8), it would only happen if we had a fixed matrix $M^{(T)}$, like in the variance case. However, since it will change as we move along for higher expected returns, this property will be violated. We will have only a local two-fund separation (while the matrix does not change). As we add more assets, or more observations, this matrix will be changing more frequently, until in the limit case we have a given matrix (and a "collapsed" quadratic function) for every point in the frontier.

9.5   ASSET PRICING

In this section, we provide a new version of the mean–variance CAPM. The latter was derived by Sharpe (1964), Lintner (1965) and Mossin (1969). Like in the portfolio frontier case, the first way to extend the CAPM was to include higher moments. This has been done in Ingersoll (1975), Krauss and Litzenberger (1976), Athayde and Flôres (1997, 2000) and Athayde (2001). The second way was to make use of DSR. This can be found in Hogan and Warren (1974), Bawa and Lindenberg (1977), Price et al. (1982), Harlow and Rao (1989) and Pedersen (1999).

The main difference between this section and those works above is not in the formula per se (it is the same), but in the approach used to derive it. In contrast to the previous works, we make use of the properties of the frontier shown in the last sections to construct the formula.

Consider a portfolio z that has the following zero cross-DSR with a frontier portfolio p:

$$\frac{1}{n}\sum_{i=1}^{n}[\min(R_p^i - \mu,0)](R_z^i - \mu) = 0$$

If we premultiply (9.8) by $z'M^{(T)}$, we have:

$$0 = \frac{\alpha E(R_p) - \gamma}{\alpha\theta - \gamma^2}E(R_z) + \frac{\theta - \gamma E(R_p)}{\alpha\theta - \gamma^2}$$

Substituting in (9.8) it becomes:

$$p = \frac{\alpha E(R_p) - \gamma}{\alpha\theta - \gamma^2} M^{(T)^{-1}} [e - E(R_z)1] \tag{9.9}$$

If we premultiply the equation above by $p' M^{(T)}$, we have:

$$\sigma_{pp}^* = \frac{\alpha E(R_p) - \gamma}{\alpha\theta - \gamma^2} [(E(R_p) - E(R_z)]$$

Consider now a given portfolio k. If we premultiply (9.9) by $k' M^{(T)}$, we have:

$$\sigma_{kp}^* = \frac{\alpha E(r_p) - \gamma}{\alpha\theta - \gamma^2} [E(R_k) - E(R_z)] \quad \text{where } \sigma_{kp}^* = \sum_{i \in S_T} (r_k^i - \mu)(r_p^i - \mu)$$

Comparing the two equations above, we see that:

$$E(R_k) - E(R_z) = \beta_k^* [E(R_p) - E(R_z)] \quad \text{where } \beta_k^* = \frac{\sigma_{kp}^*}{\sigma_{pp}^*} \tag{9.10}$$

This means that any asset or portfolio k can be expressed as this version of the CAPM for any portfolio p of the portfolio frontier. The only difficulty in transforming it into a CAPM is that we do not have the two-fund separation property to guarantee that the market portfolio is an efficient portfolio.

Let us consider now the case where we also have a riskless asset, with a given fixed return r_f. Our problem now becomes:

$$\min w' M w \text{ s.t. } E(R_p) - [w'e + (1 - w'1)r_f]$$

Let us call this optimal portfolio p. After all the iterations, p will be given by:

$$p = \frac{[M^{(T)}]^{-1} d}{d'[M^{(T)}]^{-1} d} [E(R_p) - r_f] \quad \text{where } d = e - r_f 1 \tag{9.11}$$

If we premultiply the equation above by $p' M^{(T)}$, we have:

$$\sigma_{pp}^* = \frac{[E(R_p) - r_f]^2}{d'[M^{(T)}]^{-1} d}$$

Consider now a given portfolio k. If we premultiply (9.11) by $k' M^{(T)}$, we have:

$$\sigma_{kp}^* = \frac{[E(R_k) - r_f][(E(R_p) - r_f]}{d'[M^{(T)}]^{-1} d}$$

Comparing these two equations above, we see that:

$$E(R_k) - r_f = \beta_k^* [E(R_p) - r_f] \tag{9.12}$$

(9.12) is called the Lower Partial Moment CAPM, and it was first derived by Bawa and Lindenberg (1977) for the continuous case. It should be emphasised again that, in the present situation, we would not have a fixed coefficient because the final matrix is endogenous to the expected return desired. This will make the so-called Capital Market Line (CML) convex in our case. Bawa and Lindenberg (1977) have also shown that when the benchmark is in fact the risk-free return r_f, then two-fund separation will be obtained.

9.6 CONCLUSION

Downside risk requires a positive definite matrix that is endogenous to the weights of the respective portfolio. As a consequence, achieving its minimal value is a complex task. In this paper an algorithm to solve this problem was presented in which the convergence to the minimum was guaranteed. Some properties of the portfolio frontier, like convexity discontinuity (even when short sales are allowed) and the absence of two-fund separation were also analysed. Asset pricing relations, like the well-known Lower Partial Moment CAPM, were also derived, but under a more general approach.

ACKNOWLEDGEMENTS

The author thanks David Basterfield for helpful comments.

REFERENCES

Athayde, G. (2001). "A Few More Moments to Finance Theory: Introducing Higher Moments in Investment Theory and Econometrics". Ph.D. thesis, EPGE/FGV, Rio de Janeiro, Brazil.

Athayde, G. and R. Flôres (2000). "Introducing Higher Moments in the CAPM: Some Basic Ideas". Advances in Quantitative Asset Management. Boston: Kluwer Academic.

Athayde, G. and R. Flôres (1997). "A CAPM with Higher Moments: Theory and Econometrics". Ensaios Econômicos 317, EPGE/FGV, Rio de Janeiro, Brazil.

Bawa, V. and E. Lindenberg (1977). "Capital Market Equilibrium in a Mean-Lower Partial Moment Framework", Journal of Financial Economics 5, 189–200.

Eftekhari, B. and S. Satchell (1996). "Non-Normality of Returns in Emerging Markets". Research in International Business and Finance Supplement 1, 267–277.

Harlow, W. and R. Rao (1989). "Asset Pricing in a Generalised Mean-Lower Partial Moment Framework: Theory and Evidence", Journal of Financial and Quantitative Analysis 24(3), 285–311.

Hogan, W. and J. Warren (1974). "Toward the Development of an Equilibrium Capital Market Model Based on Semivariance". Journal of Financial and Quantitative Analysis 9, 1–12.

Ingersoll, J. (1975). "Multidimensional Security Pricing", Journal of Financial and Quantitative Analysis 10, 785–798.

Kraus, A. and R.H. Litzenberger (1976). "Skewness Preference and the Valuation of Risky Assets", Journal of Finance 31, 1085–1100.

Lintner, J. (1965). "The Valuation of Risk Assets and The Selection of Risky Investments in Stock Portfolios and Capital Budgets", Review of Economics and Statistics 47, 13–37.

Markowitz, H. (1952). "Portfolio Selection", Journal of Finance 7, 77–91.

Mossin, J. (1969). "Security Pricing and Investment Criteria in Competitive Markets", American Economic Review 59, 749–756.

Pedersen, C. (1999). "Four Essays on Risk in Finance". Ph.D. thesis, Cambridge University.

Price, K., B. Price and T. Nantell (1982). "Variance and Lower Partial Moment Measures of Systematic Risk: Some Analytical and Empirical Results", Journal of Finance 37, 843–855.

Sharpe, W. (1964), "Capital Asset Prices: A Theory of Market Equilibrium under Conditions of Risk", Journal of Finance 19, 425–442.

10

Implementing Discrete-time Dynamic Investment Strategies with Downside Risk: A Comparison of Returns and Investment Policies

MATTIAS PERSSON

ABSTRACT

This paper compares a downside risk approximation for calculating optimal portfolios in the discrete-time dynamic investment model to the exact power function formulation that springs from the dynamic reinvestment model. Future returns are estimated via the empirical probability assessment approach. The results show that the downside risk model approximates the dynamic model surprisingly well under both quarterly and annual revision. However, the approximation seems to be correlated with the target rate of return in the downside risk formulation. The results suggest that the approximation performs best when the target rate of return is set high compared to the mean returns of the basic assets.

10.1 INTRODUCTION

In several studies discrete-time dynamic portfolio theory (see Mossin, 1968; Hakansson, 1971, 1974; Leland, 1972; Ross, 1974; Huberman and Ross, 1983) was applied to the asset allocation problem in conjunction with the Empirical Probability Assessment Approach (EPAA) to implement a set of "active" investment strategies. Grauer and Hakansson (1982, 1985, 1986) employed the model to construct and rebalance portfolios composed of US stocks, corporate bonds, government bonds and a risk-free asset. In the first article borrowing was excluded, while margin purchases were permitted in the other two. Grauer and Hakansson (1987) also used the model in a global setting; they explored the performance of the model by including US asset categories and non-US equity and bond categories in the asset universe. The EPAA was also refined in Grauer and Hakansson (1998) by including an inflation adapter and applying it to the problem of timing the market, that is, the problem of choosing between a stock portfolio and cash or borrowing. Furthermore, in a number of cases Grauer and Hakansson find that the model earns both economically and statistically significant abnormal returns.

Developments in Forecast Combination and Portfolio Choice. Edited by C. Dunis, A. Timmermann and J. Moody.
© 2001 John Wiley & Sons Ltd

The purpose of this paper is to compare the performance of a downside risk approximation, the Lower Partial Moment (LPM) framework, to the exact power function formulation that springs from the dynamic reinvestment model. The attractiveness of downside risk measures for decision-making purposes has been noted in the financial economics literature for almost half a century. For early research on the topic, see Roy (1952) and Markowitz (1991).[1] In addition, a growing number of academics and practitioners are claiming that standard deviation and beta are no longer relevant measures of risk for many investment situations and that these risk measures do not capture how the investors perceive risk. This view is also supported by Unser (2000), who, in an experiment of investors' risk perception, finds that symmetrical risk measures like variance are dismissed in favour of shortfall measures like LPM.

The approximation in the downside risk approach to the dynamic reinvestment model is chosen so that for each power function the downside risk investor has similar levels of risk aversion. Furthermore, there is a close link between the LPM framework and stochastic dominance, which, at least theoretically, suggests that the LPM and power function framework should produce similar strategies. Mean–variance (MV) and quadratic approximations to the power formulation were examined in Grauer and Hakansson (1998), and their results showed that the MV approximation worked well for quarterly portfolio revision over the whole spectrum of risk aversions. However, when annual portfolio revisions were used they found a clear difference between the models.

The remainder of this paper is organised as follows: Section 10.2 gives a review of the investment models used in the study, in Section 10.3 the data is presented, results are presented in Section 10.4 and a summary and concluding remarks are provided in Section 10.5.

10.2   INVESTMENT MODELS

10.2.1   The Dynamic Investment Model

The basic model used is the same as that employed in (for example) Grauer and Hakansson (1986). The reader is referred to that paper for details. Let $U_n(W_n)$ be the induced utility of wealth W of the investment horizon n. As shown by Hakansson (1974), the following convergence result:

$$U_n(W_n) \longrightarrow \frac{1}{\gamma} W^\gamma \quad \text{for some } \gamma < 1 \tag{10.1}$$

holds for a very broad class of terminal utility functions $U_0(W_0)$ when returns are independent, but possibly nonstationary, from period to period. The important convergence result implies that the use of the myopic decision rule:

$$\max E\left[\frac{1}{\gamma}(1+r)^\gamma\right] \quad \text{where } \gamma < 1 \tag{10.2}$$

in each period of time is the optimal solution. The formulation in (10.2) also allows us to incorporate the full range of risk attitudes, since the relative risk aversion for (10.2) is $1 - \gamma$.

[1] See Nawrocki (1999) for a brief history and survey of downside risk.

At the beginning of each period t, the investor chooses a portfolio x_t on the basis of some member γ of the family of utility functions for returns r by solving the following problem in each t:

$$\max_{x_t} E\left[\frac{1}{\gamma}(1 + r_t(x_t))^\gamma\right] = \sum_s \pi_s \frac{1}{\gamma}(1 + r_{ts}(x_t))^\gamma \tag{10.3}$$

subject to

$$x_{it} \geqslant 0, x_{Lt} \geqslant 0, x_{Bt} \leqslant 0 \quad \text{all } i \tag{10.4}$$

$$\sum_i x_{it} + x_{Lt} + x_{Bt} = 1 \tag{10.5}$$

$$\sum_i M_{it}x_{it} \leqslant 1 \tag{10.6}$$

$$\Pr(1 + r_t(x_t) \geqslant 0) = 1 \tag{10.7}$$

where $r_{ts} = \Sigma_i x_{it}r_{its} + x_{Lt}r_{Lt} + x_{Bt}r_{Bt}$ is the *ex ante* return on the portfolio in period t if state s occurs, $\gamma \leqslant 1$ is the risk aversion parameter and remains fixed over time, x_{it} is the fraction of own capital invested in risky asset i in period t, x_{Lt} is the fraction of own capital that is lent in period t, x_{Bt} is the fraction of own capital borrowed in period t, r_{it} is the anticipated total return on asset i in period t, r_{Lt} is the return of the risk-free asset in period t, r_{Bt} is the interest rate on borrowing at the time of the decision at the beginning of t, M_{it} is the initial margin requirement for asset i in period t expressed as a fraction, π_{it} is the probability of state s at the end of period t, in which the random variable r_{it} will assume the value r_{its}.

Constraint (10.4) rules out short sales and ensures that lending (borrowing) is a positive (negative) fraction of capital. Constraint (10.5) is the budget constraint. Constraint (10.6) serves to limit borrowing, when desired, to the maximum under the given marginal requirements that apply to that asset class. Constraint (10.7) rules out the *ex ante* probability of bankruptcy.

In the optimisations, the model is based on the empirical probability assessment approach. If quarterly revision is used, then at the beginning of quarter t, the portfolio optimisations (10.3)–(10.7) for that quarter use the following inputs: the observable risk-free return, the observable call money rate at the beginning of quarter $t + 1\%$ and the realised returns for the risky assets for the previous n periods.[2] That is, the estimates are updated each quarter on a moving basis, and the realised returns are used in raw format without any form of adjustment. It should, however, be noted that the whole joint distribution is specified and used in the optimisations, and no information loss occurs since all moments are implicitly taken into account. This strategy of using the empirical distribution of the past n quarters is in fact the optimal strategy if the investor has no information of the form and parameters of the true, but unknown, distribution, but believes that this distribution went into effect n periods ago (Bawa and Klein, 1979).[3]

---

[2] A service charge which is usually added by the broker to the call money rate.

[3] Persson (2000) compares different methods to improve portfolio optimisations in the LPM model, while Grauer and Shen (2000) study whether constraints improve portfolio performance.

The optimal weights and the proportion of assets borrowed are obtained by solving (10.3)–(10.7).[4] The realised returns for the assets and the borrowing rate are observed at the end of the period of time t, and with the weights selected through (10.3)–(10.7) in the beginning of period t the realised return of the portfolio is calculated. This cycle is then repeated in all subsequent periods.

10.2.2   The Lower Partial Moment Model

Bawa (1975, 1976), Bawa and Lindenberg (1977) and Fishburn (1977) have shown that the LPM provides a more general alternative to the traditional MV model. Consider an investor who is averse to downside risk with target rate of return τ. Let X denote the investor's portfolio allocation across k assets with $X' = (X_1, X_2, \ldots, X_k)$ and let R represent the vector of security returns $R' = (R_1, R_2, \ldots, R_k)$. Let F and F_X denote the joint distribution of security returns and the probability distribution of returns on the portfolio, respectively. The nth order LPM of the distribution of returns under the allocation X about τ, $LPM_n(\tau;X)$ is then:

$$LPM_n(\tau;X) = \int_{-\infty}^{\tau} (\tau - R_X)^n dF_X(R_X) = \int_{-\infty}^{\tau} (\tau - X'R)^n dF(R) \qquad (10.8)$$

The investor's optimisation problem is then to minimise (10.8) subject to:

$$\sum_{i=1}^{k} X_i E(R_i) = \mu$$

$$\sum_{i=1}^{k} X_i = 1 \text{ or } \sum_{i=1}^{k} X_i = 1, X_i > 0 \qquad (10.9)$$

Bawa (1976) has shown that the $LPM_n(\tau;X)$ is a convex function of X. Furthermore, the optimal value of $LPM_n(\tau;X)$, as a function of μ, is increasing and convex for all μ greater than the mean of the portfolio that yields the minimum LPM over the feasible set. This is the same property exhibited by the admissible boundary in the MV model. The target rate of return τ can be fixed, variable but deterministic and stochastic. For example, when the downside risk is measured against some benchmark portfolio, we have a stochastic target rate of return.[5]

The Mean Lower Partial Moment (MLPM) model was proposed as an approximation for arbitrary distributions by Bawa (1975) and Bawa and Lindenberg (1977), and is a way of reducing the dimensionality of stochastic dominance to a two-parameter framework. In fact, the admissible set obtained in the MLPM model for a fixed τ is a subset of the admissible set under second-order stochastic dominance when n is equal to zero or one, and third-order stochastic dominance when n is equal to two. The analysis in the MLPM model holds exactly if the distribution of stock returns belongs to the two-parameter location scale family, which includes normal distributions, Student t-distributions with the

---

[4] The optimisation routine e04ucf, from the NAG Foundation toolbox for Matlab, was used to solve the optimisation problem.

[5] In terms of equilibrium valuation, a target rate of return equal to the risk-free rate of return and normality are both required for the MLPM-CAPM to be reduced to the standard CAPM, see Bawa and Lindenberg (1977).

same degree of freedom, and stable distributions with the same characteristic exponent (between one and two) and skewness parameter (not necessarily zero). Many popular notations of risk are special cases of the MLPM model. For example, with $n = 0$ and the target rate of return equal to zero, LPM_0 is the probability of a loss.[6] For $n = 2$ and a target rate of return equal to the mean of the distribution, LPM_2 becomes the traditional semivariance measure. Moreover, for a normal distribution LPM_2 is proportional to the variance, and would result in the same ordering of the risky assets as the MV model.

The MLPM model is justified for a general set of utility functions. The order n of the LPM_n measure determines the type of utility functions consistent with that risk measure. LPM_0 is consistent with all utility functions that prefer more to less ($u' > 0$) and LPM_1 with all risk averse utility functions ($u' > 0$ and $u'' < 0$), LPM_2 is valid for all risk averse functions displaying skewness preference ($u' > 0$, $u'' < 0$ and $u''' > 0$). That is, LPM_1 is consistent with the familiar HARA class of utility functions, while LPM_2 is consistent with the DARA class of utility functions.[7] In general, downside risk averse investors are equivalently expected utility maximisers with utility functions of the form $u(y; n, \tau)$ where y is the random variable (Fishburn, 1977). Let:

$$u(y; n, \tau) = \begin{cases} a + by - (\tau - y)^n & \text{if } y \leqslant \tau \\ a + by & \text{if } y > \tau \end{cases} \tag{10.10}$$

where a, b and c are constants. When $n = 2$, this utility function is quadratic below the target rate of return and linear above the target; this provides a correction for the standard quadratic utility. The formulation used to derive the optimal portfolios is based on the classical parametric formulation (Markowitz et al., 1992). Let μ_{it} be the expected return on security i at time t, and $LPM_n(\tau; X)_t$ be the risk of the portfolio in time t. Then the LPM investment problem is

$$\max_X \lambda(1 + m_t) - \tfrac{1}{2} LPM(\tau; X)_t \tag{10.11}$$

subject to the constraints (10.4)–(10.7), where the mean and risk of the portfolio are:

$$m_t = \sum_i x_{it} \mu_{it} + x_{Lt} r_{Lt} + x_{Bt} r_{Bt}$$

$$LPM(\tau; X) = \frac{1}{T - 1} \sum_{i=1}^{T} \min(r_{it} x_{it} - \tau, 0)^2$$

respectively, and λ may be interpreted either as a parametric programming parameter or an investor's "risk tolerance". The optimisation problem in (10.11) can be solved efficiently by the critical-line algorithm in Markowitz et al. (1992, 1993). λ is used in the study as an approximation in the LPM framework for the relative risk aversions in (10.2):

$$\lambda = \frac{1}{1 - \gamma}$$

---

[6] Kataoka (1963) has, among others, studied the probability of loss as a measure of risk.
[7] HARA-hyperbolic absolute risk aversion. DARA-decreasing absolute risk aversion.

Under certain conditions this approximation holds exactly in continuous time (see Merton, 1973, 1980), since the LPM framework results in the same ordering of the uncertain prospects and the MV model and the risk, *i.e.* the LPM, is proportional to the variance.

In order to study what impact the target rate of return has on the portfolio strategies, three different target rates of return are used. The first target rate of return is set equal to zero, which is a strategy that penalises loss. Unser (2000), who finds that risk is perceived relative to the initial price, also supports this target. The second target rate of return is set equal to the risk-free lending rate in time t. While the target rate of return is identical for all assets in the cases above, the third target rate is asset-dependent and is set equal to the mean return of the assets.

10.3 DATA

The data used to estimate the probabilities of next period's returns on risky assets, and to calculate each period's realised returns comes from Globalfindata. We have monthly total return series for US categories (common stock, long-term government bonds), and monthly total return series for eight non-US equity returns (Australia, Canada, France, Germany, Japan, Italy, Sweden and UK). The data covers the period 1950–1997. All returns are expressed in US dollars and represent total returns since both dividends (net of foreign taxes withheld) and capital appreciation or depreciation are taken into account.

The risk-free asset is assumed to be the 90-day US Treasury bill maturing at the end of the quarter, and the borrowing rate is assumed to be the brokers–dealers call money rate +1%. When annual revision is used, the risk-free return was obtained from the one-year constant maturity US Treasury bills, as of the beginning of that year. Finally, margin requirements for stocks were obtained from the *Federal Reserve Bulletin* and these requirements were assumed to apply to non-US equities as well.

Initial margins are set at 10% for government bonds. This is a conservative assumption, which is designed to compensate for the absence of maintenance requirements.[8] For comparison with the active investment strategies, the asset categories, the passive portfolios and their symbols are presented in Table 10.1. The passive portfolios are used as a comparison with the active strategies, the compositions of these portfolios are reported

Table 10.1 Assets and passive portfolios

Assets		Passive portfolios	
RL	Risk-free lending	E	Equally weighted portfolio
GB	Long-term US government bonds	E2	20% in E and 80% in RL
CS	US common stocks	E5	50% in E and 50% in RL
B	Borrowing	E8	80% in E and 20% in RL
AU	Australian equities	W	MSCI World Index
CA	Canadian equities	W2	20% in W and 80% in RL
FR	French equities	W5	50% in W and 50% in RL
GE	German equities	W8	80% in W and 20% in RL
IT	Italian equities		
JA	Japanese equities		
SW	Swedish equities		
UK	British equities		

---

[8] I am grateful to Robert Grauer who supplied me with the datafile of the margin requirements.

in Table 10.1. The passive portfolio E is the equally weighted portfolio of the 10 risky assets, that is the equities and the long-term government bonds. In the portfolio E2, 20% is invested in the equally weighted portfolio and 80% is invested in the risk-free asset.

10.4 RESULTS

10.4.1 Quarterly Portfolio Revision

We first examine the results when quarterly revision strategies were used to optimise the portfolios for the power utility functions and the LPM framework. Table 10.2 shows, and

Table 10.2 Comparison of geometric means and standard deviations of annual portfolio returns for power function and LPM decision makers, 1960–1997 (Quarterly portfolio revisions, 40-quarter estimating period, no borrowing)

Portfolio	Power function		LPM, $\tau = 0$		LPM, $\tau = rf$		LPM, $\tau = m_t$	
	Geometric mean	Standard deviation	Geometric mean	Standard deviation	Geometric mean	Standard deviation	Geometric mean	Standard deviation
CS	6.20	16.14						
GB	6.97	9.24						
RL	6.16	1.30						
AU	−1.00	32.81						
CA	3.76	17.02						
FR	8.48	22.74						
GE	7.93	18.15						
IT	2.37	25.03						
JA	10.18	23.35						
SW	11.53	18.79						
UK	9.73	20.70						
−75	6.75	2.80	6.24	1.31	6.43	5.89	6.90	3.60
−50	6.97	3.38	6.27	1.35	6.98	6.33	7.36	4.73
−30	7.39	4.40	7.81	10.86	6.57	6.82	8.12	6.36
−20	7.94	5.52	9.93	12.34	6.92	8.71	9.15	8.13
−15	8.48	6.60	10.07	14.15	6.89	9.59	9.82	9.85
−7	10.12	10.47	11.12	17.20	8.18	13.25	10.93	14.81
−5	10.74	12.45	11.47	18.47	8.45	15.57	11.02	16.84
−3	11.09	15.26	12.54	18.65	10.38	17.33	11.84	18.45
−2	11.28	17.19	13.00	20.48	10.96	18.13	12.25	19.19
−1	12.16	18.55	13.46	20.42	11.77	19.09	12.76	19.88
−0.5	12.58	19.18	14.05	20.45	12.80	20.15	13.62	20.49
0	13.72	20.03	14.01	20.52	13.19	20.42	13.91	20.55
0.25	13.98	20.33	13.67	20.37	13.74	20.51	14.02	20.51
0.5	14.43	20.52	14.57	20.50	14.92	19.24	14.37	20.45
0.75	14.43	20.52	14.57	20.50	14.92	19.24	14.37	20.45
E10	7.94	12.73						
E2	6.66	2.64						
E5	7.27	6.27						
E8	7.73	10.11						
W	6.97	9.24						
W2	6.40	2.20						
W5	6.68	4.73						
W8	6.88	7.42						

Note: Standard deviation is for $\ln(1 + r_t)$.

Figure 10.1 plots, the geometric means and standard deviations of the realised returns of the basic asset categories. Of the 15 active power function strategies, x corresponding to values of γ in (10.2) range from -75, extremely risk averse, to 0.75. Of the 15 LPM approximations to the power strategies, plus signs denote the case when $\tau = 0$ and diamonds the cases when $\tau = rf_t$ and the mean returns of the assets are used as target rates; that is, when τ is equal to m_t, for the 38-year period 1960–1997. The estimating period is 40 quarters and no borrowing is allowed.

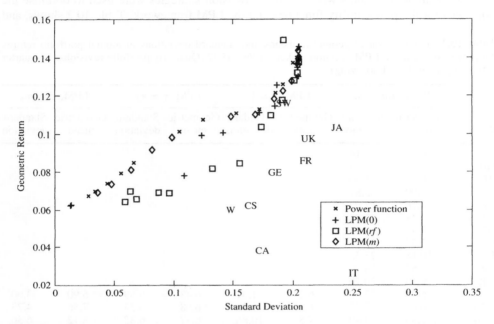

Figure 10.1 Comparison of geometric means and standard deviations of annual portfolio returns for power function and LPM decision makers, 1960–1997 (Quarterly portfolio revisions, 40-quarter estimating period, no borrowing)

Over the period, the geometric mean returns of the international stock markets were quite similar, with the exception of Australia which performed poorly and had a negative geometric mean return for a US investor over the period. Overall the geometric mean returns range from -1% to 11.53% per annum. Treasury bills earned 6.16% with a standard deviation of 1.30%. During this period, the international arena provided a generous environment for the US investor; most international markets earned higher geometric returns than the US stock and bond markets. Sweden was the winner with an annual geometric mean return of 11.53%, with Japan as the runner up with a geometric mean return of 10.18%.

Turning to the power function policies, we observe that the geometric mean returns were not spectacular, ranging from 6.75% for the -75 power to 14.43% for the 0.75 power. On the other hand, the standard deviations of the power strategies are lower than the basic assets, for example, the power -75 earned a higher geometric mean return than common stock with a more than five times smaller standard deviation. The power strategies result in general in somewhat higher geometric mean returns and lower standard deviation than the basic assets, which indicates that frequent updating of the portfolios is adding value, *i.e.* higher mean returns and lower standard deviations, to the portfolios. This is especially true if we compare the power strategies with the passive portfolios in Table 10.1; this can also be seen in Figure 10.1. The passive portfolios are clearly dominated by the active strategies. However, for the purpose of this study, the most important observation to be drawn from Figure 10.1 and Table 10.2 is that for each power γ the returns of the exact policy and of the LPM approximation appear to be quite similar, at least when $\tau = rf_t$ and $\tau = m_t$. In the case when the target rate of return was set equal to zero there are larger differences between the LPM approximation and the power strategies. The LPM strategy is in general more risky but also has higher geometric returns. However, the approximation seems to be better for the other two LPM approximations.

It can be seen in Figure 10.1 that especially the case when $\tau = m_t$, lies very close to the power strategies. The results for the case when borrowing is allowed are presented in Figure 10.2 and Table 10.3. It can be seen in Table 10.3 that the introduction of borrowing does not affect the more risk averse strategies; the geometric mean returns and standard deviation are unaffected by the possibility of borrowing for the power strategies with γ equal to -75, -50 and -30. In fact, the introduction of borrowing has only increased the power strategies' geometric mean returns marginally, whereas the risk in the portfolios is much higher. If we compare the geometric mean returns and risk of the power strategies with the LPM approximations we find, as in the case with no borrowing allowed, that

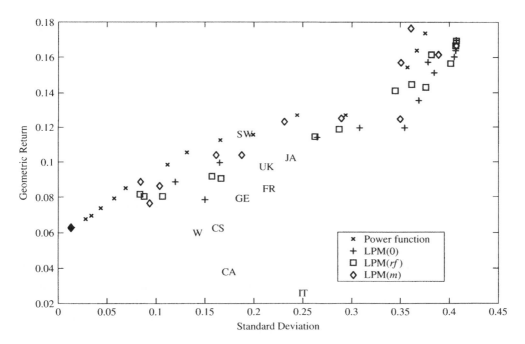

Figure 10.2 Comparison of geometric means and standard deviations of annual portfolio returns for power function and LPM decision makers, 1960–1997 (Quarterly portfolio revisions, 40-quarter estimating period, borrowing)

Table 10.3 Comparison of geometric means and standard deviations of annual portfolio returns for power function and LPM decision makers, 1960–1997 (Quarterly portfolio revisions, 40-quarter estimating period, borrowing)

Portfolio	Power function		LPM, $\tau = 0$		LPM, $\tau = rf$		LPM, $\tau = m_t$	
	Geometric mean	Standard deviation	Geometric mean	Standard deviation	Geometric mean	Standard deviation	Geometric mean	Standard deviation
CS	6.20	16.14						
GB	6.97	9.24						
RL	6.16	1.30						
AU	−1.00	32.81						
CA	3.76	17.02						
FR	8.48	22.74						
GE	7.93	18.15						
IT	2.37	25.03						
JA	10.18	23.35						
SW	11.53	18.79						
UK	9.73	20.70						
−75	6.75	2.80	6.24	1.31	8.18	8.39	6.24	1.31
−50	6.97	3.38	6.28	1.37	8.04	8.79	6.28	1.34
−30	7.38	4.39	8.89	12.00	8.05	10.71	8.85	8.41
−20	7.94	5.77	7.86	14.98	9.20	15.72	7.68	9.35
−15	8.52	6.90	9.97	16.51	9.05	16.68	8.62	10.36
−7	9.85	11.20	11.40	26.49	11.43	26.25	10.41	16.10
−5	10.56	13.18	11.95	30.81	11.89	28.72	10.41	18.75
−3	11.26	16.57	11.96	35.44	14.10	34.45	12.31	23.12
−2	11.56	19.92	13.54	36.85	14.45	36.16	12.51	28.92
−1	12.67	24.44	15.73	37.80	14.31	37.60	12.47	34.94
−0.5	12.70	29.38	15.13	38.44	16.15	38.15	15.68	35.06
0	15.43	35.69	16.06	40.48	15.66	40.15	16.18	38.90
0.25	16.40	36.62	16.39	40.66	16.67	40.63	17.66	36.08
0.5	17.38	37.53	16.98	40.68	16.96	40.67	16.68	40.69
0.75	17.38	37.53	16.98	40.68	16.96	40.67	16.68	40.69
E10	7.94	12.73						
E2	6.66	2.64						
E5	7.27	6.27						
E8	7.73	10.11						
W	6.97	9.24						
W2	6.40	2.20						
W5	6.68	4.73						
W8	6.88	7.42						

Note: Standard deviation is for $\ln(1 + r_t)$.

the LPM approximation with $\tau = m_t$ appears to be the one that closest approximates the power strategies. The most striking factor in Figure 10.2 is that the portfolios in the LPM approximation seem to be worse when borrowing is allowed than not allowed. Turning to the question of whether or not the differences between the strategies and the LPM approximations are significant, paired t-tests are calculated on the quarterly observations of the different strategies. Thus the following statistic is calculated:

$$t = \frac{\bar{d}}{\sigma(d)/\sqrt{n}}$$

where $\bar{d}$ is the average difference in return between the power strategies and the LPM approximations respectively, that is $\bar{d}$ is calculated as:

$$\bar{d} = \sum_{t=1}^{n} \frac{\ln(1 + r_t^p) - \ln(1 + r_t^{LPM})}{n}$$

where $\sigma(d)$ is the standard deviation of the differences in return between the strategies, r_t^p is the realised return on the power function portfolio in period t, and r_t^{LPM} is the realised return on the LPM portfolio. The results for the paired t-tests are presented in Table 10.4. The results from the case with borrowing not allowed are presented in Panel A, and it can be seen that the LPM approximations generally have higher quarterly portfolio returns. However, in most cases we are not able to distinguish between the power portfolios and the portfolios resulting from the LPM approximations even though there seem to be, in

Table 10.4 Return comparison of portfolio returns for power function and LPM decision makers, 1960–1997

Portfolio	LPM, $\tau = 0$		LPM, $\tau = rf$		LPM, $\tau = m_t$	
	$\bar{d}$	P-value	$\bar{d}$	P-value	$\bar{d}$	P-value
	Panel A					
−75	0.0024	0.02	−0.0042	0.06	−0.0031	0.00
−50	0.0031	0.02	−0.0028	0.15	−0.0035	0.00
−30	−0.0056	0.13	−0.0020	0.24	−0.0045	0.00
−20	−0.0099	0.00	−0.0032	0.17	−0.0061	0.00
−15	−0.0094	0.03	−0.0029	0.25	−0.0068	0.00
−7	−0.0081	0.08	−0.0025	0.33	−0.0070	0.01
−5	−0.0064	0.16	−0.0025	0.36	−0.0056	0.05
−3	−0.0069	0.06	−0.0019	0.37	−0.0051	0.03
−2	−0.0047	0.15	−0.0016	0.39	−0.0039	0.05
−1	−0.0048	0.08	0.0001	0.93	−0.0025	0.18
−0.5	−0.0051	0.06	0.0011	0.51	−0.0036	0.12
0.25	−0.0013	0.58	−0.0005	0.62	−0.0016	0.24
0.5	−0.0014	0.28	−0.0011	0.19	−0.0012	0.26
0.75	−0.0018	0.37	−0.0005	0.27	−0.0010	0.11
	Panel B					
−75	0.0013	0.21	−0.0042	0.13	0.0013	0.21
−50	0.0017	0.17	−0.0034	0.21	0.0018	0.16
−30	−0.0051	0.17	−0.0028	0.38	−0.0041	0.06
−20	−0.0021	0.62	−0.0056	0.22	0.0000	0.98
−15	−0.0062	0.18	−0.0041	0.36	−0.0010	0.68
−7	−0.0105	0.12	−0.0105	0.11	−0.0030	0.33
−5	−0.0122	0.09	−0.0107	0.11	−0.0018	0.54
−3	−0.0129	0.10	−0.0170	0.02	−0.0057	0.13
−2	−0.0153	0.03	−0.0169	0.02	−0.0073	0.10
−1	−0.0161	0.01	−0.0127	0.04	−0.0063	0.19
−0.5	−0.0122	0.01	−0.0142	0.00	−0.0110	0.00
0.25	−0.0051	0.18	−0.0039	0.30	−0.0042	0.13
0.5	−0.0031	0.33	−0.0037	0.25	−0.0028	0.42
0.75	−0.0015	0.56	−0.0014	0.57	−0.0008	0.74

Note: Panel A, no borrowing. Panel B, borrowing allowed. $\bar{d}$ is the average difference between the quarterly returns for the power function and the LPM approximations, respectively.

some cases, large differences between the portfolios in Table 10.3 and Table 10.4. There are only significant differences between the portfolios in Table 10.4 in eight cases on a 5% significance level. Thus, the LPM formulation appears to provide a good approximation to the power policies, for the full range of risk levels γ, even in the case when borrowing is allowed, Panel B.

10.4.2   Annual Portfolio Revision

Let us turn to the results when annual revision, no borrowing, strategies were used in the portfolio optimisations. In the annual revision case, the estimating period was 10 years. The returns for the basic assets, passive portfolios and the investment strategies are reported in Figure 10.3 and Table 10.5 for the 38-year period 1960–1997.

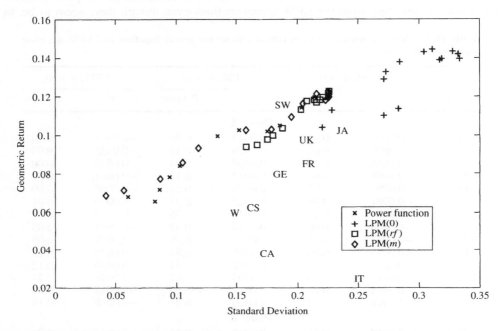

Figure 10.3   Comparison of geometric means and standard deviations of annual portfolio returns for power function and LPM decision makers, 1960–1997. (Annual portfolio revisions, 10-year estimating period, no borrowing)

Again, it is apparent that the international arena provided a quite generous environment for the US investor, although not as generous as when quarterly revisions were used. The exception in the international arena is again Australia, which over the period of time resulted in a negative geometric return of 0.20%. Italy also performed poorly over the period, with a geometric mean return of 2.21%, almost 65% lower than the US stock market of 6.20%, but with standard deviation almost twice as high. Sweden was again the winner with an annual geometric return of 10.92%, and Japan was the runner up with 9.31%.

It is also notable that the US government bonds performed more or less as a riskless asset over the period of time. The geometric returns for the power function policies were

Table 10.5 Comparison of geometric means and standard deviations of annual portfolio returns for power function and LPM decision makers, 1960–1997 (Annual portfolio revisions, 10-year estimating period, no borrowing)

Portfolio	Power function		LPM, $\tau = 0$		LPM, $\tau = rf$		LPM, $\tau = m_t$	
	Geometric mean	Standard deviation	Geometric mean	Standard deviation	Geometric mean	Standard deviation	Geometric mean	Standard deviation
CS	6.22	14.98						
GB	6.86	8.29						
RL	6.00	2.43						
AU	−0.19	29.03						
CA	4.08	14.96						
FR	8.33	19.39						
GE	7.77	17.31						
IT	2.21	25.28						
JA	9.31	24.92						
SW	10.92	19.16						
UK	8.06	28.48						
−75	6.80	6.01	9.94	17.66	9.41	15.79	6.84	4.21
−50	6.55	8.22	9.41	18.87	9.53	16.66	7.13	5.67
−30	7.15	8.59	9.89	19.04	9.79	17.52	7.73	8.64
−20	7.83	9.43	10.48	19.80	9.99	17.97	8.60	10.51
−15	8.43	10.26	11.12	20.42	10.36	18.79	9.35	11.84
−7	9.97	13.41	11.65	21.24	11.31	20.32	10.25	15.80
−5	10.26	15.24	11.75	21.56	11.78	20.80	10.28	17.89
−3	10.20	17.52	11.86	21.78	11.83	21.41	10.94	19.52
−2	10.50	18.54	11.93	21.93	11.70	21.57	11.64	20.44
−1	11.43	20.34	12.14	22.23	11.84	21.88	12.14	21.61
−0.5	11.96	21.41	12.21	22.41	11.96	22.13	11.79	22.35
0	11.91	22.49	12.16	22.56	12.15	22.56	11.93	22.56
0.25	12.04	22.74	12.19	22.57	12.18	22.57	12.02	22.57
0.5	12.24	22.67	12.28	22.59	12.27	22.60	12.23	22.55
0.75	12.24	22.67	12.29	22.60	12.27	22.60	12.23	22.55
E10	7.68	12.73						
E2	6.48	3.17						
E5	7.36	6.64						
E8	7.60	10.24						
W	5.94	14.35						
W2	6.66	3.44						
W5	6.55	7.03						
W8	6.26	11.29						

Note: Standard deviation is for $\ln(1 + r_t)$.

not spectacular over the period, the geometric returns ranging from 6.55% to 12.24%. If we look at the standard deviations, we observe that the power strategies generally resulted in portfolios with lower risk than the basic assets. The active portfolios also have higher mean returns and lower standard deviations than the passive portfolios, see Figure 10.3. Turning to the comparison between the power strategies and the LPM approximations, we see that the LPM(m) approximation is very close to the portfolios of the power function. In fact, the LPM(m) portfolios actually dominate the power function portfolios for higher levels on the risk aversion. The LPM(rf) approximation, plus signs, results in portfolios that, compared to the power portfolios, have geometric mean returns and standard deviations that are too high. This is even more evident for the portfolios when the target rate of return is equal to zero, it seems that the LPM approximations result in portfolios that are too risky compared to the amount of risk in the power function portfolios.

In Table 10.6 the results from annual portfolio revisions and with borrowing allowed are presented. It can be seen that there are large differences between the LPM(0) and the LPM(rf) on the one side and the power function portfolios on the other side. The LPM approximations have much higher standard deviations and geometric mean returns for portfolios with high levels of risk aversion, $i.e.$ low γ. The LPM(m) approximation

Table 10.6 Comparison of geometric means and standard deviations of annual portfolio returns for power function and LPM decision makers, 1960–1997 (Yearly portfolio revisions, 10-years estimating period, borrowing)

Portfolio	Power Function		LPM, $\tau = 0$		LPM, $\tau = rf$		LPM, $\tau = m_t$	
	Geometric mean	Standard deviation	Geometric mean	Standard deviation	Geometric mean	Standard deviation	Geometric mean	Standard deviation
CS	6.22	14.98						
GB	6.86	8.29						
RL	6.00	2.43						
AU	−0.19	29.03						
CA	4.08	14.96						
FR	8.33	19.39						
GE	7.77	17.31						
IT	2.21	25.28						
JA	9.31	24.92						
SW	10.92	19.16						
UK	8.06	28.48						
−75	6.85	5.28	10.40	22.04	9.64	22.48	6.59	4.60
−50	7.17	6.75	11.28	22.86	10.48	25.51	7.05	5.65
−30	5.90	13.88	11.35	28.32	10.86	26.78	7.42	8.65
−20	6.94	15.13	11.00	27.11	11.11	25.76	7.92	11.35
−15	7.48	16.02	12.88	27.17	12.10	25.24	8.11	15.45
−7	9.54	17.82	13.28	27.30	11.50	27.15	9.94	20.93
−5	10.39	19.28	13.78	28.46	12.46	27.47	10.79	22.31
−3	10.91	21.44	14.28	30.40	13.68	29.29	10.86	24.58
−2	11.34	22.69	14.44	31.12	13.99	29.91	11.08	26.17
−1	12.04	25.06	13.89	31.71	14.53	30.74	11.93	28.03
−0.5	12.40	26.79	13.95	31.89	13.13	32.09	12.87	29.53
0	13.62	30.22	14.32	32.80	14.27	32.58	13.92	31.77
0.25	13.79	31.28	13.96	33.34	13.83	32.96	13.96	32.72
0.5	14.05	33.02	14.18	33.27	14.02	33.33	14.08	33.19
0.75	14.05	33.02	14.18	33.27	14.02	33.33	14.08	33.19
E10	7.68	12.73						
E2	6.48	3.17						
E5	7.36	6.64						
E8	7.60	10.24						
W	5.94	14.35						
W2	6.66	3.44						
W5	6.55	7.03						
W8	6.26	11.29						

Note: Standard deviation is for $\ln(1 + r_t)$.

is again very close to the power function strategies; the two strategies have similar levels of geometric mean returns and standard deviations. When comparing portfolios with borrowing allowed to portfolios with borrowing not allowed we find that there are only small increases in the portfolio geometric mean returns, while the increase in the portfolio standard deviations is much higher.

The results from the paired t-test between the power function portfolios and the LPM approximations are reported in Table 10.7. From Table 10.7 it can be seen that even though there seem to be differences between the portfolios in Figure 10.3, the paired t-test cannot distinguish between the power function portfolio returns and the returns of the portfolios generated from the LPM approximations. Thus, we conclude that the LPM approximation works very well as a downside risk approximation to the power function also on an annual portfolio revision basis.

Table 10.7 Return comparison of portfolio returns for power function and LPM decision makers, 1960–1997

Portfolio	LPM, $\tau = 0$		LPM, $\tau = rf$		LPM, $\tau = m_t$	
	$\bar{d}$	P-value	$\bar{d}$	P-value	$\bar{d}$	P-value
			Panel A			
−75	−0.3163	0.10	−0.0371	0.12	0.0006	0.94
−50	−0.0568	0.04	−0.0407	0.06	−0.0041	0.53
−30	−0.1198	0.13	−0.0384	0.08	−0.0059	0.15
−20	−0.0429	0.09	−0.0337	0.11	−0.0089	0.07
−15	−0.0433	0.09	−0.0323	0.13	−0.0111	0.05
−7	−0.0314	0.18	−0.0257	0.20	−0.0065	0.35
−5	−0.0275	0.21	−0.0260	0.18	−0.0047	0.56
−3	−0.0260	0.16	−0.0248	0.17	−0.0116	0.23
−2	−0.0220	0.16	−0.0188	0.22	−0.0156	0.07
−1	−0.0117	0.28	−0.0077	0.44	−0.0101	0.15
−0.5	−0.0049	0.53	−0.0017	0.81	−0.0004	0.95
0.25	−0.0028	0.54	−0.0027	0.54	−0.0004	0.88
0.5	−0.0011	0.76	−0.0011	0.77	0.0006	0.79
0.75	−0.0003	0.92	−0.0001	0.97	0.0003	0.84
			Panel B			
−75	−0.0600	0.09	−0.0532	0.15	0.0030	0.70
−50	−0.0668	0.06	−0.0650	0.10	0.0019	0.82
−30	−0.0879	0.04	−0.0788	0.05	−0.0099	0.40
−20	−0.0684	0.07	−0.0659	0.07	−0.0053	0.62
−15	−0.0812	0.04	−0.0679	0.05	−0.0055	0.54
−7	−0.0612	0.06	−0.0431	0.20	−0.0102	0.26
−5	−0.0584	0.08	−0.0425	0.20	−0.0107	0.25
−3	−0.0601	0.09	−0.0509	0.13	−0.0073	0.54
−2	−0.0568	0.10	−0.0482	0.13	−0.0066	0.60
−1	−0.0397	0.18	−0.0433	0.12	−0.0073	0.52
−0.5	−0.0321	0.19	−0.0245	0.31	−0.0127	0.29
0.25	−0.0164	0.32	−0.0153	0.34	−0.0085	0.48
0.5	−0.0086	0.38	−0.0063	0.52	−0.0068	0.43
0.75	−0.0021	0.55	−0.0007	0.87	−0.0007	0.87

Note: Panel A, no borrowing. Panel B, borrowing allowed. $\bar{d}$ is the average difference between the quarterly returns for the power function and the LPM approximations, respectively.

10.5 SUMMARY AND CONCLUDING REMARKS

The purpose of this study was to compare the performance of a downside risk, the LPM, approximation to the exact power function formulation that springs from the dynamic reinvestment model. In the LPM framework, the approximation was chosen so that, for each power function the downside risk investor had similar levels of risk aversion. The data used for this exercise was monthly total return series for US categories (common stock, long-term government bonds), and monthly total return series for eight non-US equity returns (Australia, Canada, France, Germany, Japan, Italy, Sweden and UK). The data covers the period 1950–1997, and all returns were expressed in US dollars. In order to see if the number of portfolio revisions affected the LPM approximations, both quarterly and annual portfolio revisions were analysed.

During the time period studied, the international arena provided a generous environment for the US investor, and most international markets earned higher geometric returns than the US stock and bond markets. The geometric mean returns of the LPM strategies were found to be very close to the geometric mean returns of the power formulation when quarterly revisions were used. The power function portfolios and the portfolios generated from the LPM approximations also had higher geometric mean returns and lower standard deviations than the basic assets and the passive portfolio, thus it seems like there was some gain in the active strategies. The geometric returns in the LPM approximations were particularly close to the corresponding geometric mean returns of the power function, when the target rate of return in the LPM model was equal to the mean return on the portfolio, *i.e.* the asset mean returns. For the case when the target rate of return was equal to the riskless rate of return or equal to zero, there were some, but no significant, differences between the models for the highly risk averse strategies. The two models also generated similar portfolios when borrowing was allowed. Thus, the results show that the LPM model approximates the strategies of the power function very well when quarterly portfolio revisions were used.

When annual portfolio revisions were used the international arena again provided a quite generous environment for the US investor, although not as generous as when quarterly revisions was used. When annual portfolio revision were used in the power function framework and LPM approximations, the geometric mean returns and standard deviations of the portfolios changed marginally. But still, the LPM(m) approximation was very close to the power function strategies; the two strategies had similar levels of geometric mean returns and standard deviations. In a comparison between the portfolios with borrowing allowed on the one side and borrowing not allowed on the other side, there were only small increases in the portfolio geometric mean returns, while the increase in the portfolio standard deviations is much higher. Over this period of time the possibility to borrow did not add value to the portfolios.

We therefore conclude that the LPM approximation seems to work very well as a downside risk approximation to the power function both under quarterly and annual portfolio revision and with borrowing allowed and not allowed. The approximation seems, however, to perform best when the target rate of return used is set high compared to the basic assets.

REFERENCES

Bawa, V.S. (1975). "Optimal Rules for Ordering Uncertain Prospects", *Journal of Financial Economics* **2**, 95–121.

Bawa, V.S. (1976). "Admissible Portfolios for All Individuals", *Journal of Finance* **31**(4), 1169–1183.

Bawa, V.S. and R.W. Klein (1979). "The Effect of Estimation Risk on Optimal Portfolio Choice". *Estimation Risk and Optimal Portfolio Choice*. Amsterdam: North-Holland.

Bawa, V.S. and E.B. Lindenberg (1977). "Capital Market Equilibium in a Mean-Lower Partial Moment Framework", *Journal of Financial Economics* **5**, 189–200.

Fishburn, C.P. (1977). "Mean-Risk Analysis with Risk Associated with Below-Target Returns", *American Economic Review* **67**(5), 116–126.

Grauer, R. and N. Hakansson (1982). "Higher Return, Lower Risk: Historical Returns on Long-Run, Actively Managed Portfolios of Stocks, Bonds and Bills, 1936–1978", *Financial Analysts Journal* **38**, 39–53.

Grauer, R. and N. Hakansson (1985). "Returns on Levered, Actively Managed Long-Run Portfolios of Stocks, Bonds and Bills, 1934–1984", *Financial Analysts Journal* **41**, 24–43.

Grauer, R. and N. Hakansson (1986). "A Half-Century of Returns on Levered and Unlevered Portfolios of Stocks, Bonds and Bills, With and Without Small Stocks", *Journal of Business* **59**, 287–318.

Grauer, R. and N. Hakansson (1987). "Gains from International Diversification: 1968–85 Returns on Portfolios of Stocks and Bonds", *Journal of Finance* **42**, 721–739.

Grauer, R. and N. Hakansson (1998). "On Timing the Market: The Empirical Probability Assessment Approach With an Inflation Adapter". In W. Ziemba and J.M. Mulvey (eds.), *Worldwide Asset and Liability Modeling*. Cambridge: Cambridge University Press.

Grauer, R. and F.C. Shen (2000). "Do Constraints Improve Portfolio Performance", *Journal of Banking and Finance* **24**, 1253–1274.

Hakansson, N. (1971). "On Optimal Myopic Portfolio Policies, With and Without Serial Correlation of Yields", *Journal of Financial Economics* **1**, 201–224.

Hakansson, N. (1974). "Convergence to Isoelastic Utility and Policy in Multi-period Portfolio Choice", *Journal of Business* **44**, 324–334.

Huberman, G. and S. Ross (1983). "Portfolio Turnpike Theorems, Risk Aversion and Regularly Varying Utility Functions", *Econometrica* **51**, 1104–1119.

Kataoka, S. (1963). "A Stochastic Programming Model", *Econometrica* **31**, 181–196.

Leland, H. (1972). "On Turnpike Portfolios". In K. Shell and G.P. Szegö (eds.), *Mathematical Methods in Investment and Finance*. Amsterdam: North-Holland.

Markowitz, H. (1991). "Portfolio Selection—Efficient Diversification of Investments". Oxford: Blackwell (first published 1959).

Markowitz, H., P. Todd, G. Xu and Y. Yamane (1992). "Fast Computation of Mean–Variance Efficient Sets Using Historical Covariances", *Journal of Financial Engineering* **1**(2), 117–132.

Markowitz, H., P. Todd, G. Xu and Y. Yamane (1993). "Computation of Mean–Semivariance Efficient Sets by the Critical Line Algorithm", *Annals of Operations Research: Financial Engineering* **45** (special issue), 307–317.

Merton, R.C. (1973). "An Intertemporal Capital Asset Pricing Model", *Econometrica* **41**, 867–887.

Merton, R.C. (1980). "On Estimating the Expected Return on the Market: An Exploratory Investigation", *Journal of Financial Economics* **8**, 323–361.

Mossin, J. (1968). "Optimal Multi-period Portfolio Policies", *Journal of Business* **41**, 215–229.

Nawrocki, D.N. (1999). "A Brief History of Downside Risk Measures", *Journal of Investing*, **Fall**, 9–25.

Persson, M. (2000), "Estimation Risk and Portfolio Selection in the Lower Partial Moment", working paper, Department of Economics, Lund University.

Ross, S. (1974). "Portfolio Turnpike Theorems for Constant Policies", *Journal of Financial Economics* **1**, 171–198.

Roy, A.D. (1952). "Safety-first and the Holding of Assets", *Econometrics* **20**, 431–449.

Unser, M. (2000). "Lower Partial Moments as Measures of Perceived Risk: An Experimental Study", *Journal of Economic Psychology* **21**, 253–280.

—————— 11 ——————

Portfolio Optimisation in a Downside Risk Framework[1]

RICCARDO BRAMANTE AND BARBARA CAZZANIGA

ABSTRACT

In modern portfolio theory, the goal is to maximise the expected return subjected to some risk constraint. There is no standard definition of risk. In our approach, we develop an asset allocation model in which the optimal portfolio satisfies a shortfall constraint defined as a Value at Risk limit relative to a specified benchmark, which reflects the potential downside risk of the portfolio.

11.1 INTRODUCTION

In modern portfolio theory the goal is to maximise the expected return of a portfolio subjected to some risk constraint. There are no risk measures universally adopted in financial applications.

Over the last decade, mean–variance analysis has been widely applied to asset allocation. In this framework, risk is defined in terms of the standard deviation of each asset, which implies that the probability of negative returns, as the probability of positive returns, is weighted in the same way by the investor.

In order to measure only the downside risk of a portfolio, it is possible to think of risk as the failure to achieve a target or as a below-target outcome. In this case, the statistical measure of risk that can be used was introduced by Markowitz (1959) and is called semivariance.

Our approach is to define an asset allocation model in which the optimal portfolio satisfies a shortfall constraint defined as a Value at Risk (VaR) limit relative to a specified benchmark, which reflects the potential downside risk of the portfolio. VaR is an estimate, with a predefined confidence interval, of how much one can lose from holding a position over a chosen time horizon. VaR has become a useful tool for monitoring risk, and the Bank for International Settlements is encouraging its use.

The aim of this paper is to introduce into the asset allocation process VaR as a limit that determines the maximum allowed loss with a given probability. The following section provides a description of the model.

---

[1] Sections 11.1, 11.2 and 11.4 are attributed to Riccardo Bramante; Section 11.3 to Barbara Cazzaniga.

Developments in Forecast Combination and Portfolio Choice. Edited by C. Dunis, A. Timmermann and J. Moody.
© 2001 John Wiley & Sons Ltd

11.2 METHODOLOGY

Before we make an investment, we do not know exactly its rate of return. We assume that, to cope with this degree of uncertainty, the portfolio manager must meet a VaR limit relative to an amount C_0, to which can eventually be added an amount B representing borrowing, to be invested for a planning period of t days. The budget constraint can be defined as follows:

$$C_0 + B = \sum_{i=1}^{k} w_i P_{i,0} \tag{11.1}$$

where the w_i are the weights invested in the k assets and $P_{i,0}$ is the price of asset i at time 0. To introduce VaR into our model, we consider a shortfall constraint defined such that the probability of the portfolio falling down the benchmark over the holding period is bounded by a specified probability:

$$\Pr\{C_{t,b} - C_{t,P} \geqslant \text{Var}_{0,t}\} \leqslant (1 - \alpha) \tag{11.2}$$

where $\text{Var}_{0,t}$ is the VaR limit, α the desired confidence level, whereas $C_{t,b}$ and $C_{t,P}$ are defined below.

There are, of course, many types of asset allocation strategies following different rules and there is no reason to believe that any particular type of strategy is the best for every investor. We assume that the portfolio manager is attempting to beat a passive market mix, the portfolio benchmark. In this case, there will be a logical justification for active management if the expected excess returns are able to compensate for additional risk. In this case, the expected value of the "active" portfolio and of the benchmark at time t can be written as follows:

$$C_{t,P} = C_0(1 + r_f) + (r_P - r_f)\left[\sum_{i=1}^{k} w_i P_{i,0}\right] \tag{11.3}$$

$$C_{t,b} = (C_0 + B)(1 + r_b) - B(1 + r_f) \tag{11.4}$$

where r_f is the risk-free rate and r_P and r_b are respectively the expected return on the portfolio P and on the benchmark b in the planning period.

But within the Capital Asset Pricing Model (CAPM) framework, we can relate the expected return on the portfolio to the return on the benchmark portfolio by:[2]

$$r_P = r_f + (r_b - r_f)\,\beta_P \tag{11.5}$$

where β_P is the beta of portfolio P.

Substituting (11.5) back for r_b in (11.4) we have:

$$C_{t,b} = C_0(1 + r_f) + (C_0 + B)\frac{r_P - r_f}{\beta_P} \tag{11.6}$$

---

[2] The CAPM framework does not require returns on the portfolio to be normally distributed.

In order to determine the optimal portfolio, we have to define more precisely the downside risk constraint in (11.2). In particular, substituting (11.6) into (11.2) we have:

$$\Pr\left\{(C_0 + B)\frac{r_P - r_f}{\beta_P} - (r_P - r_f)\left[\sum_{i=1}^{k} w_i P_{i,0}\right] \geq \text{Var}_{0,t}\right\} \leq (1 - \alpha)$$

and so

$$\Pr\left\{(r_P - r_f) \leq -\frac{\text{Var}_{0,t}}{\displaystyle\sum_{i=1}^{k} w_i P_{i,0}}\left(\frac{\beta_P}{\beta_P - 1}\right)\right\} \leq (1 - \alpha) \tag{11.7}$$

On the basis of (11.7) we have all the elements to determine, from the returns distribution of the portfolio P, the quantile $v_{\alpha, P, b}$ that corresponds to the specified probability $(1 - \alpha)$:

$$v_{\alpha, P, b} = r_f - \frac{\text{Var}_{0,t}}{\displaystyle\sum_{i=1}^{k} w_i P_{i,0}}\left(\frac{\beta_P}{\beta_P - 1}\right) \tag{11.8}$$

and so

$$\left[\sum_{i=1}^{k} w_i P_{i,0}\right] = \frac{\text{Var}_{0,t}}{r_f - v_{\alpha, P, b}}\left(\frac{\beta_P - 1}{\beta_P}\right) \tag{11.9}$$

Substituting (11.9) back into (11.3) we can determine the expected return on the initial investment C_0 for the portfolio P:

$$\frac{C_{t,P} - C_0}{C_0} = r_f + \frac{r_P - r_f}{\beta_P}\frac{\text{Var}_{0,t}/C_0}{r_f - v_{\alpha, P, b}}(\beta_P - 1) \tag{11.10}$$

$$\frac{C_{t,P} - C_0}{C_0} = r_f + \frac{r_P - r_f}{\beta_P}\frac{\text{Var}\%_{0,t}}{r_f - v_{\alpha, P, b}}(\beta_P - 1) \tag{11.11}$$

where $\text{Var}\%_{0,t}$ is the specified VaR limit expressed in terms of the initial investment.

(11.11) defines the expected return on the portfolio P as the risk-free rate plus a term which is a function of the Treynor index T_P of the portfolio:

$$T_P = \frac{r_P - r_f}{\beta_P} \tag{11.12}$$

corrected by a coefficient D_P which reflects the potential portfolio downside risk:

$$D_P = \frac{\text{Var}\%_{0,t}}{r_f - v_{\alpha, P, b}}(\beta_P - 1) \tag{11.13}$$

Then the maximisation problem becomes:

$$\hat{P} = \max_{P} \frac{T_P}{r_f - v_{\alpha, P, b}}(\beta_P - 1) \tag{11.14}$$

It is now evident that, whilst the quantile $v_{\alpha,P,b}$ depends upon the specified VaR limit, the optimal portfolio is independent of the limit. If the estimated portfolio VaR differs from the specified limit it is possible to determine the amount of borrowing (or lending) necessary to meet the limit. Substituting (11.9) back into the budget constraint we obtain:

$$B = C_0 \left(\frac{D_P}{\beta_P} - 1 \right) \tag{11.15}$$

In order to determine the optimal portfolio, it is necessary to estimate the Beta β_P and to specify the distribution of the returns to which the critical value $v_{\alpha,P,b}$ is related. Many are the solutions to these problems and an example will be presented in the next section.

11.3 EMPIRICAL EVIDENCE

To illustrate the application of our model, we suppose a portfolio manager has to define an optimal asset allocation, meeting a VaR constraint, and choosing between:

- Italian Fixed Rate Bonds (BTP[3] Index)
- Italian Floating Rate Bonds (CCT[4] Index)
- Italian Stocks (MIB30 Index)

The risk-free rate is the BOT[5] rate while the benchmark is established in 50% bonds and 50% stocks. The data are recorded every day over the period 4th January 1994–4th February 2000.

To investigate the statistical properties of the data, we have computed the log returns of each series. For all the cases, the study of some preliminary statistics (Table 11.1) allows us to conclude that the considered time series are characterised by asymmetry and high leptokurtosis.

The normality hypothesis has been refused for every series through the Jarque–Bera test:[6] thus the use of the normal distribution, which is the case in a mean–variance approach, tends to give poor evidence of what is observed in our return series and in general in financial time series. In fact, VaR calculated under the normality assumption underestimates the actual risk since the tails of the empirical distribution are "fatter" than those implied by the normal one. In order to incorporate this evidence into the VaR

Table 11.1 Statistical summary of the data

Class of asset	Mean	Standard deviation	Skewness	Excess kurtosis	Jarque–Bera
BTP	0.0395%	0.3900%	12.9653	327.7686	6,882.338
CCT	0.0335%	0.2692%	24.6311	772.0089	38,076.275
MIB30	0.0898%	1.7175%	−0.0203	2.3201	344.9967
Benchmark	0.0618%	0.7465%	0.4449	8.0381	4,162.6520

[3] Buoni del Tesoro Poliennali.
[4] Certificati di Credito del Tesoro.
[5] Buoni Ordinari del Tesoro.
[6] All the tests are significant at the 1% level.

Table 11.2 Daily VaR of individual classes of assets: 99% confidence level

Class of asset	Empirical VaR
BTP	−0.037%
CCT	−0.024%
MIB30	−5.711%
Benchmark	−1.195%

Table 11.3 Downside and upside volatilities

Class of Asset	% of Downs	% of Ups	Downside volatility	Upside volatility	% Downside
BTP	40.58%	57.02%	0.2824%	0.4613%	37.97%
CCT	27.60%	72.40%	0.1387%	0.3070%	31.12%
MIB30	48.18%	51.82%	1.6884%	1.7486%	49.13%
Benchmark	44.48%	55.52%	0.7429%	0.7541%	49.63%

calculation, we decided to adopt the empirical distribution of past returns for the various portfolios.[7] Results for individual classes of assets are reported in Table 11.2.

In order to have an overall perspective of the data, we examine in Table 11.3 downside and upside volatility of the returns series.[8] It is interesting to note that, perhaps due to the period considered, all the series exhibit less downside than upside volatility. It is also evident that, the more risky the class of assets, the more deviations below the mean occur and so the downside volatility grows higher. In addition, if we consider the benchmark, which represents the risk of placing one half of the funds in bonds and stocks, the dispersion referred to negative returns in stocks is somewhat reduced relative to the same measure associated with this single class of assets.

The use of a benchmark in the asset allocation model calls for an estimate of the beta of the portfolio. Estimates of future betas can be accomplished by calculating beta from past observations. It is well known that the risk associated with a portfolio might change over time, and so its beta. To take this problem into account we decided to estimate betas of each individual class of assets using a time-varying parameter model written in state space form, computing the beta of the portfolio as a weighted average of individual betas:

$$\beta_P = \sum_{i=1}^{3} w_i \beta_i$$

Table 11.4 provides us with the estimates of betas referred to four different time periods, once every 10 days, on which we decided to test our asset allocation model.[9] The strategy consists of allocating wealth among the possible class of assets, assigning a non-negative

---

[7] In calculating the VaR, a 99th percentile, one-tailed confidence interval is used. This is in accordance with the recommendation of the Basle Committee on Bank's capital requirements.

[8] These measures are more precisely the lower and upper partial moment of the distribution of returns using a target return of zero.

[9] All beta estimates are significant at the 1% level.

Table 11.4   Beta estimates

Date	BTP	CCT	MIB30
17/12/1999	0.1692	0.0311	1.6810
30/12/1999	0.1317	0.0301	2.0553
14/01/2000	0.1130	0.0208	2.2172
28/01/2000	0.0926	0.0197	2.4538

Table 11.5   Optimal portfolios: 99% confidence level

Date	Weights			Beta
	BTP	CCT	MIB30	
17/12/1999	0.00%	79.74%	20.26%	0.3654
30/12/1999	0.00%	84.92%	15.08%	0.3335
14/01/2000	0.00%	80.12%	19.88%	0.4574
28/01/2000	0.00%	74.65%	25.65%	0.6367

weight to each asset, holding the portfolio over the entire period and then redefining the asset allocation weights for the next 10 days.

Now, let us turn to our optimisation problem, which requires us to maximise (11.14) under the budget constraint. In Table 11.5, one can examine the weights for the three different classes of assets in all the periods considered.[10]

The efficient portfolio is at every time a mix of a floating rate note and stocks.[11] Rebalancing is required at each time to take into consideration changes in return expectations and risk expressed by the betas of each asset class.

11.4   SUMMARY AND CONCLUDING REMARKS

The results we reported in this paper suggest that the introduction of VaR into an asset allocation model allows the portfolio manager to focus attention on downside risk. In particular, the model developed allows us to determine the assets that have to enter the optimal portfolio in order to meet a shortfall constraint defined as a VaR limit.

Further research is continuing, within the Laboratory of Applied Statistics in Milan Catholic University, on the evaluation of this approach. Our work is primarily focused on the analysis of different distributional assumptions for the returns, parametric and nonparametric, and option-based portfolio strategies.

REFERENCES AND BIBLIOGRAPHY

Arzac, E.R. and V.S. Bawa (1977). "Portfolio Choice and Equilibrium in Capital Markets with Safety-first Investors", *Journal of Financial Economics* **4**(3), 277–288.
Beckers, S. (1996). "A Survey of Risk Measurement Theory and Practice". In C. Alexander (ed.), *The Handbook of Risk Management and Analysis*. New York: Wiley; 171–192.

---

[10] Optimisation computations were carried out using SAS[TM].

[11] This is due to the expectations of a rise in interest rates in Italy during the periods considered.

Bentz Y. and J.T. Connor (1998). "Time Varying Factor Sensitivities in Equity Investment Management". In A.-P.N. Refenes, A.N. Burgess and J.E. Moody (eds.), *Decision Technologies for Computational Management Science*. Boston:Kluwer Academic; 291–308.

Bond, S. (1998). "An Econometric Model of Downside Risk". In J. Knight and S. Satchell (eds.), *Forecasting Volatility in the Financial Markets*. Oxford: Butterworth-Heinemann; 251–286.

Bramante, R., R. Colombo and G. Gabbi (1998). "Are Neural Network and Econometric Forecasts Good for Trading? Stochastic Variance Model as a Filter Rule". In A.-P.N. Refenes, A.N. Burgess and J.E. Moody (eds.), *Decision Technologies for Computational Management Science*. Boston: Kluwer Academic; 417–424.

French, K., G. Schwert and R. Stambaugh (1987). "Expected Stock Returns and Volatility", *Journal of Financial Economics* **19**, 3–30.

Huisman, R., C.G. Koedijk and R.A. Pownall (1998). "Var-x: Fat Tails in Financial Risk Management", *Journal of Risk* **1**, 47–61.

Hull, J. and A. White (1998). "Value at Risk When Daily Changes in Market Variables are not Normally Distributed", *Journal of Derivatives* **5**(3), 09–19.

Kupiec, P. (1995). "Techniques for Verifying the Accuracy of Risk Measurement Models", *Journal of Derivatives* **Winter**(2), 73–84.

Leibowitz, M.L. and S. Kogelman (1991). "Asset Allocation under Shortfall Constraint", *Journal of Portfolio Management* **Winter**, 18–23.

Markowitz, H.M. (1959). Portfolio Selection: Efficient Diversification of Investments. New York: Wiley.

Nantell, T.J. and B. Price (1979). "An Analytical Comparison of Variance and Semivariance Capital Market Theories", *Journal of Financial and Quantitative Analysis* **14**, 221–242.

Roy A.D. (1952). "Safety First and the Holding of Assets", *Econometrica* **20**, 431–49.

Sharpe W. (1970). *Portfolio Theory and Capital Markets*. New York: McGraw Hill.

Sharpe, W. (1994). "The Sharpe Ratio", *Journal of Portfolio Management* **21**, 49–58.

Sortino, F.A. and H.J. Forsey (1996). "On the Use and Misuse of Downside Risk", *Journal of Portfolio Management* **22**(2), 35–42.

West, K. (1988). "Bubbles, Fads and Stock Market Volatility Tests: A Partial Evaluation", *Journal of Finance* **43**, 636–661.

Zangari, P. (1996). "An Improved Methodology for Measuring VaR". *Risk Metrics Monitor*, Vol. 2. JP Morgan.

12

The Three-moment CAPM: Theoretical Foundations and an Asset Pricing Model Comparison in a Unified Framework

EMMANUEL JURCZENKO AND BERTRAND MAILLET

ABSTRACT

The purpose of this paper is to present the three-moment Capital Asset Pricing Model (CAPM) and some recent extensions. The traditional CAPM is based on several restrictive hypotheses. In particular, the normality of the return distribution and "small" risk are supposed to be valid.

These hypotheses are subject to two traditional criticisms: one tied to their theoretical foundations; the other related to their inadequacy with the stylised facts highlighted in empirical studies. Following the seminal work of Krauss and Litzenberger (1976) and more recently those of Simaan (1993), Gamba and Rossi (1998a,b) and Harvey and Siddique (2000a,b), we extend the Sharpe–Lintner–Mossin framework to incorporate the effect of skewness on asset valuation. Using a two–fund monetary separation theorem, we develop an exact three-moment capital asset pricing relation. We then present a three-mutual fund theorem, allowing us to extend the three-moment CAPM in a market without a riskless asset. Finally, we put into perspective the link between some multifactor models and this revisited three-moment CAPM.

Keywords: CAPM; Asset Pricing Models; Return Densities

12.1 INTRODUCTION

The validity of the Sharpe–Lintner–Mossin Capital Asset Pricing Model (CAPM[1]) has been questioned by several empirical tests. This model remains, nevertheless, one of the most important contributions of modern finance theory, as emphasised by Black (1993) or Jagannathan and Wang (1996) for instance.

This model of the financial market equilibrium is based on several restrictive hypotheses; two of them concern the normality of the return distribution and the

---

[1] See Sharpe (1964), Lintner (1965) and Mossin (1966).

Developments in Forecast Combination and Portfolio Choice. Edited by C. Dunis, A. Timmermann and J. Moody.

characteristics of the agent preferences. The latter is necessary to legitimise this formalisation of the investors' optimisation in a risky situation while, in the former, the expected utility function can be expressed as an exact function of the mean and the variance of the return distribution.

These hypotheses are subject to two traditional criticisms: the first one tied to the theoretical foundations of the approach; the second based on their inadequacy with the stylised facts highlighted in empirical studies. The return normality hypothesis implies indeed that the investor can lose more than his initial wealth and the quadratic utility function does not correspond to the rational agent behavioural characteristics. In particular, it is hardly possible to accept that a financial asset is generally an inferior good (see Pratt, 1964; Arrow, 1964) and to explain that risk averse agents would participate in a risky lottery (see Friedman and Savage, 1948; Kahneman and Tversky, 1979; Golec and Tamarkin, 1998). Moreover, the quadratic approximation is usually justified economically by the existence of a "small" absolute risk in the sense of Samuelson (1970) or by a "small" relative risk in the sense of Tsiang (1972).

These hypotheses do not correspond to all asset characteristics because of leverage effects. The hypothesis of normality of returns densities[2] is clearly rejected according to the results of many empirical studies (see for instance Engle, 1982; Bollerslev, 1986; Mandelbrot, 1997). In particular, asymmetry and leptokurticity have been found as characteristics of empirical return distributions.

The inadequacy of these traditional hypotheses, as well as many empirical difficulties, have led several authors to reject the existence of a linear relation between the systematic risk and the return of an asset. These relative failures of the traditional CAPM led to alternative approaches to improve theoretical consistency and empirical performance of the model. Among the main possibilities investigated, the following extensions can be distinguished (without pretence to exhaustiveness). Different probability densities have been substituted for the Gaussian distribution to estimate the CAPM parameters (see Harvey and Zhou, 1993). A time-varying version of the CAPM has also been proposed to deal with the autoregressive character of the conditional variance (see Bollerslev et al., 1988; Jagannathan and Wang, 1996) or, more generally with the parameter variability. Financial risk measures, different from variance,[3] have allowed others to develop asset pricing models such as Gini-CAPM (see Okunev, 1990), lower-moment CAPM (see Nantel et al., 1982; Pedersen and Satchell, 2001) and VaR-CAPM (see Alexander and Baptista, 2000). Multifactor models, based on an arbitrage argument or on heuristic considerations, permit authors to improve explanatory power compared to the original model (see Fama and French, 1992). Finally, the last stream of the literature to be highlighted concerns the use of moments higher than the variance in a pricing relation using more general laws (see Simaan, 1993; Adcock and Shutes, 1999a,b) and utility functions (see Kraus and Litzenberger, 1976; Hwang and Satchell, 1998; Fang and Lai, 1997).

In this last approach, the skewness of return distribution is valued by economic agents.[4] The worldwide success of derivatives markets, active portfolio management and hedge

---

[2] Which can be encompassed by the lognormality hypothesis. Nevertheless, this one has some other drawbacks (see for instance Feller, 1971).

[3] For an extended survey of financial risk measures, see Pedersen and Satchell (1998).

[4] Much literature has already been dedicated to the relevance of skewness in asset pricing: see, among others, Aggarwal et al. (1989), Aggarwal (1990), Aggarwal et al. (1993), Beckaert et al. (1998), Beedles and Simkowitz (1978, 1980), Harvey (1995) and Peiro (1999).

fund strategies lead to convex payoff functions. Departures from normality have been proven to be powerful factors in pricing options (see Jarrow and Rudd, 1982; Madan and Milne, 1994; Corrado and Su, 1996a,b). The skewness could also be very important for a lottery (see Prakash *et al.*, 1996; Golec and Tamarkin, 1998) because it can reconcile a risk averse agent with risky bets. Moreover, the presence of limited liability and agency problems may induce an option like asymmetry in portfolio return (see Christie and Andrew, 1982; Brennan, 1993). As underlined by Harvey and Siddique (2000a), the skewness can also capture the variation of some variables used in extended CAPM, such as industry, book-to-market value, size or momentum effects. Finally, two further factors may induce asymmetry: the correlation between prices and volatilities, highlighted by Black (1976) and Christie and Andrew (1982), and compound return in a multiperiod framework (see Fama, 1996). All these stylised facts clearly indicate that investors care for higher moments than the second one. To take account of the effect of asymmetry of return distribution on asset valuation, Rubinstein (1973) and Krauss and Litzenberger (1976) first proposed an extension of the classical CAPM. The main characteristic of the model is based on a link between the expected return and a systematic skewness *premium*. This is proved via a third-order Taylor series expansion of a von Neumann–Morgenstern utility function and a two-fund monetary separation theorem. Using, this time, a three-fund separation property of the set of *optimal* portfolios, Simaan (1993) and Gamba and Rossi (1998a,b) also obtain a linear relation describing the expected return on any traded asset as a function of expected returns of particular portfolios: the market portfolio, the riskless asset and a portfolio that spans skewness. However, due to particular distributional hypotheses, Simaan (1993) was unable to give on *a priori* grounds the sign of the preference for skewness and, in Gamba and Rossi (1998a,b), the sign of the second risk factor is always positive whatever the sign of the portfolio market skewness.

The aim of this paper is to propose a unified theory in a three-moment Capital Asset Pricing framework, conjugating some of the results of the Expected Utility Theory, the Portfolio Choice Theory and the Asset Pricing Theory. Indeed, a unified framework is required in order to obtain a generalisation of the CAPM in a skewed world. When focusing on the theoretical foundations of rational choices, it is possible to justify a mean–variance–skewness *criterion* (see Arditti, 1967; Prakash *et al.*, 1996; Kane, 1982) and to explain a risky behaviour by a risk averse agent (see Prakash *et al.*, 1996; Golec and Tamarkin, 1998). But, to our knowledge, no conclusion had yet been applied to portfolio choice and asset pricing relations. When focusing on portfolio choice, some authors obtain an asset pricing relation, with or without a risk-free asset (see Simaan, 1993; Adcock and Shutes, 1999a,b; Gamba and Rossi, 1998a,b). It is then possible to define a mean–variance–skewness efficient frontier (see Simaan, 1993; Gamba and Rossi, 1998a,b; Athayde and Flôres, 1999). Nevertheless, shortcomings can be found in the unrealistic characterisation of return densities that lead to identification problems of moment preferences and, consequently, to identification problems of risk *premia* (see Simaan, 1993). When focusing on pricing asset relations, those problems can be encompassed, but a two-fund separation theorem is required, entailing restrictive linear preference characterisation and supposing the existence of a risk-free asset (see Kraus and Litzenberger, 1976). Assuming that agents are endowed with a cubic utility function, our work benefits from the advantages of all of these approaches with very slight distributional hypotheses,[5]

---

[5] As pointed out by the referee, the approach adopted here required explicitly the existence of the first moments. A more general approach would consist in not imposing such a constraint (in an asymmetric stable

in a very tractable presentation (proposed by Diacogiannis, 1994), with or without a risk-free asset. In fact, it leads to the generalisation of a security market line into a market plane, the identification of *premia* and signs of *premia*. We then deduce a linear relation describing the expected return on any traded asset as a function of expected returns of three particular portfolios: the market portfolio, the riskless asset and a portfolio that spans skewness. We also present the general properties of the *minimum* variance frontier in a free distributional assumption framework. It is then possible to make the link between the three-moment CAPM, Black's CAPM (1972), Treynor–Mazuy's quadratic market model (1966) and the APT model of Ross (1976).

This paper is organised as follows. In Section 12.2, we review the main hypotheses relative to a multimoment partial equilibrium pricing model. Next, in Section 12.3, we describe the equilibrium relation in a uniperiod framework. Using a two-fund monetary separation, we develop an exact three-moment capital asset pricing relation. We also obtain a three-mutual fund theorem. This theorem leads to a three-moment CAPM extension when there is no risk-free asset in the market. Results given in the previous section lead to the quadratic market model and allow a comparison of this model with some other asset pricing models such as the Sharpe–Lintner–Mossin CAPM, Black's CAPM (1972) and the APT of Ross (1976). Section 12.4 is devoted to our conclusions.

12.2 INVESTOR'S PREFERENCES AND THE THREE-MOMENT CAPM

The definition of a decision's *criterion* under uncertainty constitutes a prerequisite for the derivation of any equilibrium asset pricing relation. Based on a mean–variance–skewness portfolio selection *criterion*, the three-moment CAPM assumes that any rational investor chooses his portfolio using only the first three moments of the securities return distribution. The theoretical justification of such a *criterion* is however far from simple (see Brockett and Kahane, 1992; Lhabitant, 1997; Brockett and Garven, 1998). The agents, maximising their expected utility function,[6] do not, in general, have preferences that can be expressed as a simple comparison between the first moments of their investment's return density. The expected utility function uses all the information concerning the probability density function of the asset returns.

Under certain conditions, however, the expected utility function can be linked to all the centred moments of the asset returns. Expected utility can then be expressed as an increasing function of mean and skewness, and a decreasing function of variance. In this case, the solution of the agent's expected utility maximisation problem is identical to that obtained using a mean–variance–skewness portfolio selection *criterion*.

Traditionally, the necessary restrictions are essentially of two types: the first is related to the nature of the agent's preferences and the second refers to the risky asset characteristics.

12.2.1 Expected Utility and Moments

We consider a one-period single exchange economy with one single consumption good serving as *numeraire*. Each agent has an initial endowment W_0, arbitrarily fixed to one

---

Paretian framework for instance—see Rachev and Mittnik, 2000, for a review of the latest developments in this strand of literature).

[6] The expected utility *criterion* remains the traditional one for rational individual decisions in a risky environment.

without any loss of generality, and a von Neumann–Morgenstern utility function $U(\cdot)$, defined over its final wealth denoted W_F. The function is defined from $\mathbb{R}$ to $\mathbb{R}$ and is assumed to belong to the Nonincreasing Absolute Risk Aversion (NIARA) utility class,[7] characterised by the following properties:

$$U^{(1)}(\cdot) \geqslant 0; \quad U^{(2)}(\cdot) \leqslant 0; \quad U^{(3)}(\cdot) \geqslant 0 \tag{12.1}$$

where $U^{(1)}(\cdot)$, $U^{(2)}(\cdot)$ and $U^{(3)}(\cdot)$ are the three first partial derivatives of $U(\cdot)$.

At the beginning of the period, each agent maximises the expected utility of the return of his investment denoted R and defined such that $R = W_F/W_0$.

If the utility function is differentiable up to the nth order, it is possible to express the investor's utility function as a Taylor series expansion of order n around the expected value of the random variable:

$$U(R) = \sum_{n=0}^{+\infty} U^{(n)}[E(R)][R - E(R)]^n + R_n \tag{12.2}$$

where $E(R)$ is the expected return, $U^{(n)}(\cdot)$ is the nth derivative of the utility function and R_n is the Taylor remainder.

If, moreover, we assume that the Taylor series is convergent and that the return distribution is uniquely determined by its moments, taking the expected value of the previous equation, we obtain:[8]

$$E[U(R)] = U[E(R)] + \frac{1}{2}U^{(2)}[E(R)]\sigma^2(R) + \frac{1}{3!}U^{(3)}[E(R)]m^3(R)$$

$$+ \sum_{n=0}^{+\infty} \frac{1}{n!}U^{(n)}[E(R)] \times E[R - E(R)]^n \tag{12.3}$$

where $\sigma^2(R)$, $m^3(R)$ and $E[R - E(R)]^n$ are respectively the second, third and nth centred moment of the return probability distribution.

---

[7] Arrow (1964) and Pratt (1964) showed that nonincreasing absolute risk aversion is an essential property for risk-averse agents.

[8] The first condition implies that the realisations of the random variable must stay in the interval of convergence of the utility function specified. In particular, concerning the logarithmic and the power utility functions, it implies that (see Tsiang, 1972; Loistl, 1976; Lhabitant, 1997):

$$0 \leqslant R \leqslant 2E(R)$$

On the contrary, concerning the exponential function, the interval of convergence imposes no restrictions on the Taylor series expansion.

The second condition implies, for distributions which are not concentrated on some finite interval, that (see Feller, 1971, p. 228):

$$\sum_{n=1}^{+\infty} \{E[R - E(R)]^{2n}\}^{-\frac{1}{2n}} = +\infty$$

The lognormal distribution does not satisfy this restriction. It is indeed easy to show that the distribution:

$$f(R) = \frac{1}{\sqrt{2\pi}}R^{-1} \exp\left\{-\frac{1}{2}\ln(R)^2\right\}\{1 + a\sin[2\pi \ln(R)]\}$$

for $|a| < 1$ possesses exactly the same sequence of moments as the lognormal one, which corresponds to $a = 1$.

12.2.2 Expected Utility as an Exact Function of the First Three Moments

As the preceding relation shows, any investor who has a utility function belonging to the class of (NIARA) utility functions must have a preference for mean, an aversion to variance and a preference for (positive) skewness.[9] However, the expected utility of such an investor depends generally on all the other centred moments of the probability distribution of the investment return, so that the mean–variance–skewness approach is restrictive.[10]

A first theoretical justification for transforming the expected maximisation principle into a moment preference ordering is to specify a particular density function for asset returns. In that case, several hypotheses had been proposed since the seminal Gaussian one from Markowitz (1952). Without caring about exhaustiveness, we can underline the choice of a nonspherical distribution (see Simaan, 1993), a mixture of a spherical and a negative exponential density with an exponential utility function (see Gamba and Rossi, 1998a,b), the multivariate skew–normal (Adcock and Shutes, 1999a), a Levy-stable density (see Rachev and Mittnik, 2000) and the multivariate Student density (see Adcock and Shutes, 1999b).[11] But, if the normal density is perfectly defined by its two first moments, this might not be the case when other density functions are considered. This last point leads in fact to real difficulties. For instance, as shown by Brockett and Kahane (1992), by Simaan (1993), and more recently by Brockett and Garven (1998), it is unlikely to find, on *a priori* grounds, the sign of sensitivities of the expected utility function to skewness and higher moments. Indeed, when moments are not orthogonal one to the others, the effect of increasing one of them might not be clear. Moreover, even if the density function considered could be in accordance to some of the stylised facts highlighted in the literature (such as leptokurticity, asymmetry, leverage effect and clustering in the volatility, aggregation properties of the process, etc.), additional utility assessments are required to obtain a consistent preference ordering in the sense of Scott and Horvath (1980).

A second justification for transforming the expected maximisation principle into a moment preference ordering is to consider some specific utility functions. For instance, a cubic utility function can be considered since it depends upon the three first moments of the return distribution. It is defined as follows (see Levy, 1969; Rossi and Tibiletti, 1996; Gamba and Rossi, 1998a,b):[12]

$$U(R) = a_0 + a_1 R + a_2 R^2 + a_3 R^3 \tag{12.4}$$

with $a_i \in \mathbb{R}$, $i = [0, \ldots, 3]$.

---

[9] When differentiating (12.3) with respect to $E(R)$, $\sigma^2(R)$ and $m^3(R)$, we have:

$$\begin{cases} \dfrac{\partial E[U(R)]}{\partial E(R)} = \displaystyle\sum_{n=0}^{+\infty} \dfrac{U^{(n+1)}[E(R)]E[R - E(R)]^n}{n!} = U^{(1)}[E(R)] > 0 \\[2mm] \dfrac{\partial E[U(R)]}{\partial \sigma^2(R)} = U^{(2)}[E(R)] < 0 \\[2mm] \dfrac{\partial E[U(R)]}{\partial m^3(R)} = U^{(3)}[E(R)] > 0 \end{cases}$$

[10] The mean–variance *criterion* suffers from the same flaw.

[11] Furthermore, one can think about the Burr III and Pearson type III density functions for future developments.

[12] Since a von Neumann–Morgenstern utility function is uniquely defined up to an increasing affine transformation, it is always possible to give a simpler and equivalent expression for the cubic utility function.

In this case, all the partial derivatives of higher order than three vanish and the last term in (12.3) disappears. Consequently:

$$E[U(R)] = a_0 + a_1 E(R) + a_2 E(R^2) + a_3 E(R^3)$$
$$= a_0 + a_1 E(R) + a_2 E(R)^2 + a_3 E(R)^3 + [a_2 + 3a_3 E(R)]\sigma^2(R) + a_3 m^3(R)$$

(12.5)

Since the mean, variance and skewness are supposed to be finite, it is possible to express the preferences for all investors as a function depending only on the three moments of returns. We verify that for each cubic utility function[13] that possesses the following properties:

$$\begin{cases} a_1 > a_2^2/(3a_3) & \text{(nondecreasing)} \\ -a_2/(3a_3) > R & \text{(concave)} \\ a_3 > 0 & \text{(convex marginal utility)} \end{cases}$$

(12.6)

agents exhibit a preference for mean, an aversion to variance and a preference for (positive) skewness:

$$\begin{cases} \dfrac{\partial E[U(R)]}{\partial E(R)} = a_1 + 2a_2 E(R) + 3a_3 E(R)^2 > 0 \\ \dfrac{\partial E[U(R)]}{\partial \sigma^2(R)} = a_2 + 3a_3 E(R) < 0 \\ \dfrac{\partial E[U(R)]}{\partial m^3(R)} = a_3 > 0 \end{cases}$$

(12.7)

Nevertheless, the presupposed concavity of the cubic utility function in (12.6) leads to certain restrictions on asset return realisations. Indeed, when restricting an investor's preferences to a third-degree polynomial utility function in order to ensure concavity, we have to make sure that the range of asset return realisations is in the interval where these functions are concave. In other words, the *ex post* return must respect the following inequality:

$$R < -a_2/(3a_3)$$

(12.8)

Moreover, since absolute risk aversion decreases with the return only if the discriminant Δ is negative, where:

$$\Delta = \left[-\frac{\partial U(R)}{\partial R} \frac{\partial^3 U(R)}{\partial R^3} + \left(\frac{\partial^2 U(R)}{\partial R^2} \right)^2 \right]$$

Subtracting a_0 from (12.4) and dividing by a_1 gives:

$$U(R) = R + bR^2 + cR^3$$

where $b = a_2/a_1$ and $c = a_3/a_1$.

[13] For a complete study of the properties of the cubic utility function in the DARA and in the IRRA cases, see Rossi and Tibiletti (1996). For an extension of the analysis to fourth-order polynomial utility function, see Benishay (1987, 1992).

the *ex post* return has to respect the following second inequality:

$$\frac{-a_2 - \sqrt{3a_1 a_3 - a_2^2}}{3a_3} < R < \frac{-a_2 + \sqrt{3a_1 a_3 - a_2^2}}{3a_3} \tag{12.9}$$

These are well-known limits of using a third-order polynomial function to represent an agent's preferences. We can note however that, contrary to the quadratic utility function, the cubic utility function can always, by a judicious choice of its coefficients and of the support of the return distribution, mimic any risk attitude (*i.e.* prudence in the sense of Kimball, 1990 and nonincreasing absolute risk aversion).

12.2.3   Expected Utility as an Approximating Function of the First Three Moments

An alternative approach is to explore the conditions under which the mean–variance–skewness analysis can provide a good approximation of the expected utility decision *criterion*. Initially developed by Samuelson (1970) and Tsiang (1972) to justify economically the mean–variance analysis, these conditions are twofold.

The first one consists in admitting that the absolute risk borne by investors is "small" (in other words, return distributions are compact) and that the length of the trading interval is arbitrarily small and finite. Under these assumptions, Samuelson (1970) has shown that the mean–variance–skewness analysis produces an asymptotically valid approximation to expected utility and a better one than the quadratic approximation.

The second approach is to consider that the relative risk, that is the ratio of standard deviation by mean return, is so large that we cannot neglect it. In this case, Tsiang (1972) has shown that for most of the usual utility functions used in the financial field, it is always possible to find an interval on which the relative risk is defined, such that taking into account the first three centred moments provides a good local approximation of expected utility. This approach is however less satisfactory than the first one, since it cannot give on *a priori* grounds the limits of validity of the mean–variance–skewness analysis. However, whatever the theoretical justification chosen, the accuracy of an approximation restricted to considering several centred moments still has to be determined.

Several authors, such as Levy and Markowitz (1979), Kroll *et al.* (1984), Markowitz (1991) and Simaan (1997), show that the mean–variance approach performs well and that mean–variance efficient portfolios are close to those obtained by maximisation of utility functions such as the logarithmic one. Nevertheless, Ederington (1986) shows that the third-order Taylor series expansion of expected utility provides little improvement, whereas fourth-order expansion improves the approximation considerably and never worsens it whatever the utility function. Whether the introduction of higher moments than the first two improves the quality of the approximation of the expected utility function is still an open question.

Thus, the introduction of the third centred moment in a decision *criterion* is theoretically justifiable when the investor's utility function is cubic and the support of the return probability distribution is restricted to the domain (see Rossi and Tibiletti, 1996; Gamba and Rossi, 1998a,b):

$$\frac{(-a_2 - \sqrt{3a_1 a_3 - a_2^2})}{3a_3} < R < -\frac{a_2}{3a_3} \tag{12.10}$$

or when the return probability function is compact and the time interval between actions and their consequences is small but finite (see Samuelson, 1970). Under these conditions, it is possible to obtain exact equilibrium relations explaining the securities return process. Considering the first three moments rather than the first two, as in the traditional CAPM case, leads to generalising the mean–variance approach in the three-moment CAPM framework. This model is developed in the following sections.

12.3   THE THREE-MOMENT CAPM

Initially proposed by Rubinstein (1973) and Krauss and Litzenberger (1976), the three-moment CAPM implies that asset equilibrium prices are, in the presence of skewed return distributions, an exact linear function of two parameters.

The first one, denoted β, characterises the asset return sensitivity to market portfolio variations, and the second one, γ, depends on the relative coskewness of asset returns with the market portfolio returns.

We present two versions of this model in the following subsections. One corresponds to the traditional version of Krauss–Litzenberger (1976), the second relies heavily on Markowitz's portfolio selection theory (1952).

In the case of the first approach (Section 12.3.1), the individual's asset demand is obtained by the maximisation of an indirect utility function. Once the equilibrium is reached, and using a two-fund monetary separation theorem, we can establish a financial market equilibrium relation, called here the three-moment CAPM fundamental relation. It requires however the existence of a risk-free asset.

In the second approach (Section 12.3.2), the properties of the mean–variance–skewness efficient frontier are exploited. Under certain conditions, we can generalise the fundamental three-moment CAPM relation without a risk-free asset.

The link with other multifactor models—such as Black's model (1972), the APT[14] model of Ross (1976) or the quadratic model of Treynor and Mazuy (1966)—is then possible (Section 12.3.3).

12.3.1   Aggregation of the Individual Asset Demands and a Two-fund Monetary Separation Theorem

After recalling the main hypotheses of the model, we present the equilibrium relation, following Krauss and Litzenberger (1976). This equilibrium relation is the three-moment CAPM fundamental relation.

Notation and Hypotheses

The following hypotheses are assumed. There are N risky assets (with $N \geqslant 3$) and one risk-free asset. Let **R** be the $(N \times 1)$ vector of returns of risky assets, R_f the return of the riskless asset, **E** the $(N \times 1)$ vector of the expected returns of risky assets and Ω the nonsingular $(N \times N)$ variance–covariance matrix of the risky asset returns. The capital market is supposed to be perfect and competitive with no taxes. All investors have a NIARA utility function and hold homogeneous probability beliefs about returns. Strict consistency with our previous results implies that each investor maximises his expected

---

[14] For Arbitrage Pricing Theory model.

utility, which can be represented by an (indirect) utility function, denoted $V(\cdot)$, concave and increasing with expected portfolio return, concave and decreasing with variance, and concave and increasing with skewness.[15]

The expected utility function can be written as:

$$E[U(R_p)] = V[E(R_p), \sigma^2(R_p), m^3(R_p)] \qquad (12.11)$$

with

$$V_1 = \frac{\partial V(\cdot)}{\partial E(R_p)} \geqslant 0, \; V_2 = \frac{\partial V(\cdot)}{\partial \sigma^2(R_p)} \leqslant 0 \text{ and } V_3 = \frac{\partial V(\cdot)}{\partial m^3(R_p)} \geqslant 0$$

where $R_p = W_F/W_0$ is the expected return of the portfolio held by the investor, and W_F and W_0 are his initial and final wealth.

Consider an agent investing w_{p_i} of his wealth in the ith risky asset, $i = [1, \ldots, N]$, and w_{p_0} in the risk-free asset. The mean, variance and skewness of his portfolio return are respectively[16]:

$$\begin{cases} E(R_p) = w_{p_0} R_f + \mathbf{w}'_p \mathbf{E} \\ \sigma^2(R_p) = \mathbf{w}'_p \mathbf{\Omega} \mathbf{w}_p \\ m^3(R_p) = \mathbf{w}'_p \Sigma_p \end{cases} \qquad (12.12)$$

where $\mathbf{w}_p$ is the $(N \times 1)$ vector of the investor's holdings of risky assets, $\mathbf{\Omega}$ is the $(N \times N)$ variance–covariance of the N asset returns and Σ_p is the $(N \times 1)$ vector of coskewness between securities and portfolio p returns. Each component of the coskewness vector is defined as:

$$\text{Cos}(R_i, R_p) = E\{[R_i - E(R_i)][R_p - E(R_p)]^2\} \qquad (12.13)$$

An intuitive interpretation of the components of Σ_p is to view them as a "weighted" covariance between random variables R_i and R_p^2. Moreover, if we write:

$$\text{Cos}(R_i, R_p) = E\{[R_i - E(R_i)][R_p - E(R_p)]^2 - \sigma^2(R_p)\} \qquad (12.14)$$

we can see that it is the covariance between the instantaneous volatility and the return on security i. If the coskewness of the asset's return with the portfolio's return is high, then the security return will be more amplified when the movements of the portfolio returns are important than when they concern small variations.[17]

It is also assumed that the distribution of the market portfolio return is skewed and that the vector of expected returns cannot be expressed as an exact linear combination of the unit vector and the coskewness vector between the returns on N risky assets and the return on that portfolio p.

---

[15] Whilst, in general, skewness is understood to be the standardised third centred moment, it is used here as the third centred moment.

[16] See Diacogiannis (1994) and Appendix 12.1 for the matrix notation of the skewness of a portfolio p.

[17] Following Racine (1998), the coskewness of an asset's returns with the returns of a portfolio corresponds to the asset's ability to hedge shocks on portfolio returns variance (*i.e.* the unexpected movements of volatility).

Financial Market's Equilibrium

In such a framework, the agent's portfolio problem can be stated as:

$$\max_{\mathbf{w}_p'}\{E[U(R_p)]\} = \max_{\mathbf{w}_p'}\{V[E(R_p), \sigma^2(R_p), m^3(R_p)]\} \tag{12.15}$$

$$\text{s.t.: } \mathbf{w}_p'\ \mathbf{1} = 1 - w_{p0}$$

where $\mathbf{1}$ is the $(N \times 1)$ unit vector.

The first-order conditions for a *maximum* are:[18]

$$\frac{\partial V(\cdot)}{\partial \mathbf{w}_p'} = (V_1)(\mathbf{E} - R_f\mathbf{1}) + (2V_2)\mathbf{\Omega}\mathbf{w}_p + (3V_3)\mathbf{\Sigma}_p \tag{12.16}$$

In order to move from the equilibrium conditions for individual investors to the market equilibrium, it is necessary to introduce a portfolio separation theorem. If agents' probability beliefs are identical, a necessary and sufficient condition for a two-fund monetary separation is that all agents have a hyperbolic absolute risk aversion utility (HARA) with the same "cautiousness" parameter (see Cass and Stiglitz, 1970, pp. 145–147). In this case, the investor's *optimum* risky portfolio weights are the same as those of the market portfolio.

Summing demands across all individuals and invoking a two-fund monetary separation theorem, we obtain the following equilibrium relation:

$$\mathbf{E} - R_f\ \mathbf{1} = \theta_2\sigma^2(R_m)\boldsymbol{\beta} + \theta_3 m^3(R_m)\boldsymbol{\gamma} \tag{12.17}$$

where $\theta_2 = -2V_2/V_1$ and $\theta_3 = -3V_3/V_1$ are respectively a measure of the agent's aversion to variance and a measure of his preference for skewness; $\sigma^2(R_m)$, $m^3(R_m)$ and $\mathbf{w}_m$ are respectively the variance, skewness and the $(N \times 1)$ vector of the weights of the market portfolio; $\boldsymbol{\beta} = (1/\sigma^2(R_m))\mathbf{\Omega}\mathbf{w}_m$ and $\boldsymbol{\gamma} = (1/m^3(R_m))\mathbf{\Sigma}_m$ are the $(N \times 1)$ relative covariance vector and the $(N \times 1)$ relative coskewness vector of specific returns with the market portfolio returns.

Rearranging terms yields the following theorem.

Theorem 12.1   *The three-moment CAPM relation can be written as:*

$$\mathbf{E} - R_f\mathbf{1} = b_1\boldsymbol{\beta} + b_2\boldsymbol{\gamma} \tag{12.18}$$

where $b_1 = \theta_2\sigma^2(R_m)$ and $b_2 = \theta_3 m^3(R_m)$.

Proof. See previous discussion.   □

Thus, for all securities i, $i = [1, \ldots, N]$:

$$E(R_i) - R_f = b_1\beta_i + b_2\gamma_i \tag{12.19}$$

where $\beta_i = \text{Cov}(R_i, R_m)/\sigma^2(R_m)$ and $\gamma_i = \text{Cos}(R_i, R_m)/m^3(R_m)$ are respectively the ith entry, with $i = [1, \ldots, N]$, of the $(N \times 1)$ vectors $\boldsymbol{\beta}$ and $\boldsymbol{\gamma}$.

---

[18] The first derivatives of the expected utility function with respect to $\mathbf{w}_p$ constitute necessary and sufficient conditions for a *maximum* since the hessian matrix of the objective function of the investor is negative definite (see for instance Athayde and Flôres, 1999 and Appendix 12.12). We can notice also that the first partial derivative of the skewness with respect to $\mathbf{w}_p$ is equal to $3\mathbf{\Sigma}_p$ (see for instance Diacogiannis, 1994 and Appendix 12.3).

This relation is similar[19] to the three-moment pricing relation developed[20] by Krauss and Litzenberger (1976). The expected excess return on a security is a linear function[21] of the parameters β_i and γ_i in the presence of a skewed return distribution. The parameters yield measures of the marginal contribution of an asset to the variance for the first one and the skewness of the market portfolio return for the second one. The coefficients b_1 and b_2 are interpreted as market risk *premia*. Investors are assumed to be risk averse and coherent in their preferences in the sense of Scott and Horvath (1980), implying that b_1 is positive because $\theta_2 \geqslant 0$ and that b_2 has the opposite sign to $m^3(R_m)$ because $\theta_3 \leqslant 0$. Investors are compensated in terms of expected excess return for bearing relative risks, measured by the coefficients β_i and γ_i corresponding to the asset i. When the utility function of the agent is independent of the skewness (*i.e.* $b_2 = 0$), the (12.18) collapses to the traditional CAPM relation:

$$\mathbf{E} - R_f \mathbf{1} = b_1 \boldsymbol{\beta} \tag{12.20}$$

Following Sears and Wei (1985, 1988), it is possible to give a theoretical implication for the three-moment CAPM leading to another interpretation of the coefficients b_1 and b_2. Since the three-moment CAPM relation is valid for all securities' returns, it is naturally verified by the market portfolio return. That is:

$$E(R_m) - R_f = b_1 + b_2 \tag{12.21}$$

Dividing this 12.1 by (12.18) yields the following corollary.

Corollary 12.1   *The three-moment CAPM relation can also be written as:*

$$\mathbf{E} - R_f \mathbf{1} = (\alpha_1 \boldsymbol{\beta} + \alpha_2 \boldsymbol{\gamma})[E(R_m) - R_f] \tag{12.22}$$

with

$$\begin{cases} \alpha_1 = \dfrac{2}{2 + 3\eta} \\[2mm] \alpha_2 = \dfrac{3\eta}{2 + 3\eta} \\[2mm] \eta = \dfrac{b_2}{b_1} = \dfrac{3}{2} \times \dfrac{\partial E(R_m)}{\partial m^3(R_m)} \times \left[\dfrac{\partial E(R_m)}{\partial \sigma^2(R_m)} \right]^{-1} \times \dfrac{m^3(R_m)}{\sigma^2(R_m)} \end{cases}$$

---

[19] The only difference lies in the definition of the coefficients b_1 and b_2. Krauss and Litzenberger (1976) have considered an indirect utility function that does not depend on the first three centred moments but on the mean, standard deviation and cubic root of the skewness. This has no consequence for the following developments.

[20] This equation is equally similar to the relation developed by Gamba and Rossi (1998a,b). The only difference is in the definition of the market portfolio, which includes this time the risk-free asset holdings.

[21] If the market portfolio return distribution is not skewed, the three-moment CAPM relation becomes:

$$\mathbf{E} - R_f \mathbf{1} = \theta_2 \boldsymbol{\Omega} \mathbf{w}_m + \theta_3 \boldsymbol{\Sigma}_m$$

where θ_2 and θ_3 are defined as previously and $\boldsymbol{\Omega} \mathbf{w}_m$ and $\boldsymbol{\Sigma}_m$ are the $(N \times 1)$ covariance vector and the $(N \times 1)$ coskewness vector of specific returns with the market portfolio return.

Thus, for all security i, $i = [1, \ldots, N]$:

$$E(R_i) - R_f = \theta_2 \operatorname{Cov}(R_i, R_m) + \theta_3 \operatorname{Cos}(R_i, R_m)$$

Proof. See previous discussion.   □

Thus, for all securities i, $i = [1, \ldots, N]$:

$$E(R_i) - R_f = (\alpha_1\beta + \alpha_2\gamma)[E(R_m) - R_f] \qquad (12.23)$$

This equation is equivalent to the previous equilibrium relation (12.18), if we recall that, for $j = [1, 2]$:

$$b_j = \alpha_j[E(R_m) - R_f] \qquad (12.24)$$

Rearranging terms, the three-moment CAPM relation depends only on the unique parameter η. Formally, we have:

$$\mathbf{E} - R_f\mathbf{1} = \left(\frac{\eta}{2+3\eta}\right)\left(\frac{2}{\eta}\beta + 3\gamma\right)[E(R_m) - R_f] \qquad (12.25)$$

where η is defined as previously.

The coefficients b_1 and b_2 depend on two elements: the market risk *premium* $[E(R_m) - R_f]$ and a parameter η. The latter is an elasticity of substitution between the skewness and the variance of the market portfolio return. Since rational investors prefer positive skewness and dislike variance, the sign of the parameter η, measuring the ratio of b_2 by b_1, must be the opposite of the sign of the market portfolio return's skewness. The two coefficients b_2 and η constitute two complementary measures of the agent's preference for skewness. The coefficient b_2 depends on the sign and size of the market risk *premium*. It represents the marginal rate of substitution between expected return and skewness of the market portfolio (since it depends on θ_2). On the contrary, the second parameter η is independent of market fluctuations. The parameter η highlights the relation between second and third centred moments of the market's portfolio return distribution.

In the traditional CAPM framework, the coefficient b_1 corresponds to the market portfolio risk *premium*, whatever the elementary utility function considered.[22] In the three-moment CAPM case,[23] using a third portfolio in addition to the risk-free asset and the market portfolio becomes necessary for identifying the coefficients b_1 and b_2 independently of the form of the utility function used. The following subsection is devoted to the definition of this third portfolio. With this portfolio, it is possible to establish the canonical three-moment CAPM relation and its representations generalising the capital market and the security market lines in the spaces defined by the triplets[24] $[E(R_i), \sigma(R_i), m(R_i)]$ and $[E(R_i), \beta_i, \gamma_i]$.

The Three-moment CAPM Fundamental Relation and the Security Market Plane

To obtain the three-moment CAPM fundamental relation, we need to introduce, besides the risk-free asset and the market portfolio, a third specific portfolio denoted Z whose return has a zero covariance with the market portfolio return. As in the traditional CAPM

---

[22] As defined by von Neumann and Morgenstern (1947). Amongst these functions, we consider only the utility functions of the hyperbolic absolute risk aversion class (HARA).

[23] Unless using a logarithmic utility function; see for example Krauss and Litzenberger (1976) and Hwang and Satchell (1998).

[24] Where $m(R_m) = \sqrt[3]{m^3(R_m)}$.

framework, we can identify the coefficient b_2 by premultiplying (12.18) by $\mathbf{w}'_Z$, the ($N \times 1$) transpose vector of the portfolio Z weights. We get:

$$b_2 = \left[\frac{E(R_Z) - R_f}{\gamma_Z} \right] \tag{12.26}$$

where $E(R_Z)$ is the return of a portfolio Z uncorrelated with the market portfolio,[25] $\beta_Z = \text{Cov}(R_Z, R_m)/\sigma^2(R_m) = 0$ and $\gamma_Z = \text{Cos}(R_Z, R_m)/m^3(R_m)$.

Combining this result with (12.21), we get the following expression for b_1:

$$b_1 = [E(R_m) - R_f] - b_2 \tag{12.27}$$

The equilibrium equation then becomes:

$$\mathbf{E} - R_f\mathbf{1} = \left\{ [E(R_m) - R_f] - \left[\frac{E(R_Z) - R_f}{\gamma_Z} \right] \right\} \boldsymbol{\beta} + \left[\frac{E(R_Z) - R_f}{\gamma_Z} \right] \boldsymbol{\gamma} \tag{12.28}$$

If, following Simaan (1993), we suppose that it is possible to find—in a large set of feasible portfolios—a portfolio Z whose relative coskewness with the market portfolio is unitary, *i.e.* $\gamma_Z = 1$, the relation can be simplified as follows:

$$\mathbf{E} - R_f\mathbf{1} = [E(R_m) - E(R_Z)]\boldsymbol{\beta} + [E(R_Z) - R_f]\boldsymbol{\gamma} \tag{12.29}$$

These relations lead to the following theorem.

Theorem 12.2   *When a risk-free asset exists, the risk premium of an asset is given by the equation:*

$$\mathbf{E} - R_f\mathbf{1} = [E(R_m) - R_f]\boldsymbol{\beta} + [E(R_Z) - R_f](\boldsymbol{\gamma} - \boldsymbol{\beta}) \tag{12.30}$$

with

$$\boldsymbol{\beta} = \frac{1}{\sigma^2(R_m)}\boldsymbol{\Omega}\mathbf{w}_m \text{ and } \boldsymbol{\gamma} = \frac{1}{m^3(R_m)}\boldsymbol{\Sigma}_m$$

and where $E(R_Z)$ is the return of the portfolio with zero covariance with the market portfolio and unitary relative coskewness.

Proof. See previous discussion.   ☐

The relation is thus, for any security i, $i = [1, \ldots, N]$:

$$E(R_i) - R_f = [E(R_m) - R_f]\beta_i + [E(R_Z) - R_f](\gamma_i - \beta_i) \tag{12.31}$$

where $\beta_i = \text{Cov}(R_i, R_m)/\sigma^2(R_m)$ and $\gamma_i = \text{Cos}(R_i, R_m)/m^3(R_m)$ are respectively the ith entry, with $i = [1, \ldots, N]$, of the ($N \times 1$) vectors $\boldsymbol{\beta}$ and $\boldsymbol{\gamma}$.

Nevertheless, the validity of this relation depends crucially on the existence and uniqueness of the portfolio Z. When it is verified, we could note that, without any assumption about the return distribution as in Ingersoll (1987) or Gamba and Rossi (1998a,b), it is possible to sign the market *premia*:

$$\begin{cases} [E(R_m) - E(R_Z)] \geqslant 0 \\ \text{sign}[E(R_Z) - R_f] = -\text{sign}[m^3(R_m)] \end{cases} \tag{12.32}$$

---

[25] We suppose that there exists at least one portfolio whose returns are uncorrelated with the market portfolio's ones.

and, when $m^3(R_m) \geqslant 0$:

$$E(R_m) - E(R_f) \geqslant 0 \qquad (12.33)$$

Such a result might not be obtainable with other assumptions (see for instance Simaan, 1993).

Under this form, the three-moment CAPM is a direct generalisation of the Sharpe–Lintner–Mossin model.[26] It differs from the mean–variance model by the term $[E(R_Z) - R_f](\gamma_i - \beta_i)$. If this term is positive, the traditional CAPM relation underestimates the risk *premium* and we confirm here Krauss and Litzenberger's intuition[27] that taking into account skewness explains some of the CAPM anomalies.

If, for some equities i, $\gamma_i = 0$ (coskewness is null), then (12.30) differs from the two-moment CAPM, since $[E(R_Z) - R_f]$ could be nonzero. This happens because skewness is valued by economic agents. The three-moment CAPM collapses to the Sharpe–Lintner–Mossin model if and only if (i) $[E(R_Z) - R_F] = 0$ or (ii) $\beta_i = \gamma_i$. The first condition is met when all the agents are indifferent to non-null (positive) return skewness. The second condition is satisfied for securities i whose sensitivities to the variance and skewness of the market portfolio return are equal. Thus, prices for a subset of assets—those for which $\beta_i = \gamma_i$—can possibly be correctly evaluated by the CAPM but this relation does not hold for all assets.

We can represent the three-moment CAPM relation in the space $[E(R_i), \beta_i, \gamma_i]$. When the three-moment CAPM relation is satisfied, all the expected asset returns must theoretically lie on a plane. This plane corresponds to a security market plane[28] (see Figure 12.1) and is defined by the following coordinates: $[E(R_m), 1, 1]$, $[E(R_Z), 0, 1]$ and $[R_f, 0, 0]$.

The *optimal* portfolios set can be equally represented in the space $[E(R_i), \sigma(R_i), m(R_i)]$ by a capital market line, defined by the characteristics of the risk-free asset, the zero-beta unitary-gamma portfolio and those of the market portfolio.

Using the definitions of the covariance and coskewness, the three-moment CAPM relation can be written for any portfolio p as:

$$E(R_p) - R_f = [E(R_m) - E(R_Z)]\frac{\sigma(R_p)}{\sigma(R_m)}\rho_{p,m} + [E(R_Z) - R_f]\frac{m(R_p)}{m(R_m)}\varsigma_{p,m} \qquad (12.34)$$

---

[26] In order to take into account the leptokurticity of the return distribution, some authors (see Rachev and Mittnik, 2000) have proposed a generalisation of the Sharpe–Lintner–Mossin CAPM under the hypothesis of a symmetric joint stable return distribution. Formally, the relation can be written for any asset i, as:

$$E(R_i) - R_f = [E(R_i) - R_f]\beta_i'$$

with

$$\beta_i' = \frac{\langle R_i; R_m \rangle_\alpha}{\|R_m\|_\alpha^\alpha}$$

where α is the characteristic exponent, $1 < \alpha < 2$ and: $\langle R_i; R_m \rangle_\alpha = E\{[R_i - E(R_i)][R_m - E(R_m)]^{\langle p-1 \rangle}\} = \iint_{\mathbb{R}\mathbb{R}} r_i r_m^{(\alpha-1)} f(R_i, R_m) dr_i dr_m$; $r_i = [R_i - E(R_i)]$ with $i = [1, \ldots, N]$; $r_m^{(\alpha)} = |r_m|^\alpha \text{ sign}(r_m)$ and $f(R_i, R_m)$ denotes the joint density of the centred random variables and $\|R_m\|_\alpha^\alpha = \langle R_m; R_m \rangle_\alpha$ (see Samorodnitsky and Taqqu, 1994). A similar approach consistent with the three-moment CAPM would consist to consider skewed joint stable return distributions.

[27] See Krauss and Litzenberger (1976, pp. 1085–1086).

[28] This expression was previously used by Diacogiannis (1999) in a different setting.

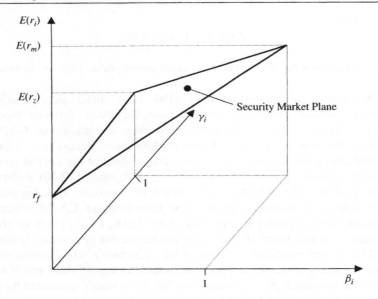

Figure 12.1   The security market plane

where $\sigma(R_p)$ and $m(R_p)$ are respectively the standard deviation and the cubic root of the skewness of the portfolio p return; $\sigma(R_m)$ and $m(R_m)$ are the standard deviation and the cubic root of the skewness of the market portfolio return, and $\rho_{p,m}$ and $\varsigma_{p,m}$ are respectively the coefficient of correlation and the coefficient of coskewness between the portfolio return p and the market portfolio return, that is:

$$\rho_{p,m} = \frac{\text{Cov}(R_p, R_m)}{\sigma(R_p)\sigma(R_m)} \quad \text{and} \quad \varsigma_{p,m} = \frac{\text{Cos}(R_p, R_m)}{m(R_p)m^2(R_m)}$$

Using the two-fund monetary separation theorem, we deduce that the expected return of any *optimal* portfolio p must satisfy the following relation:

$$E(R_p) - R_f = [E(R_m) - E(R_Z)]\frac{\sigma(R_p)}{\sigma(R_m)} + [E(R_Z) - R_f]\frac{m(R_p)}{m(R_m)} \tag{12.35}$$

with

$$\begin{cases} \sigma(R_p) = \alpha_p\sigma(R_m) \\ m(R_p) = \alpha_p m(R_m) \end{cases}$$

where α_p, $0 \leqslant \alpha_p \leqslant 1$, is the proportion of the agent's wealth invested in the market portfolio.

The *optimal* portfolio set can thus be represented in the space $[E(R_i), \sigma(R_i), m(R_i)]$ by a line that we call the capital market line as in the traditional CAPM case.

A linear relation between the market portfolio return and the return on a zero-beta portfolio is highlighted as in Black's (1972) model. But here, we consider a market with a risk-free asset, and the return of the uncorrelated portfolio Z is multiplied by a constant γ_i specific to each asset. (12.29) is equally compatible with a multifactor arbitrage pricing model.[29] The interesting aspect is that the three-moment CAPM allows us to pre-identify factors. All asset pricing relations established previously, as in Krauss and Litzenberger (1976), assume the existence of a risk-free asset. The study of the mean–variance–skewness efficient frontier properties in the space $[E(R_i), \sigma(R_i), m(R_i)]$ generalises the approach in the N risky assets case.

12.3.2 An N Risky Asset Three-moment CAPM Extension

The aggregation of the individual's equilibrium conditions, given by the maximisation of a third-order limited expansion of expected utility, permits us to establish the fundamental three-moment CAPM relation. To achieve this goal, the use of a two-fund monetary separation theorem is necessary, restricting the domain of validity of the three-moment CAPM to the existence of a risk-free asset. In the following subsection, we adopt the approach of the portfolio selection theory, developed by Markowitz (1952) in the mean–variance framework and recently generalised by Simaan (1993) when return disturbances have a spherical component. In this framework, the investor selects the portfolio minimising the variance of his portfolio return for a given mean and skewness.[30] We can derive a characterisation of the mean–variance–skewness frontier (see first subsection below). The hypothesis of a *Pareto-optimal* equilibrium allocation leads to the generalisation of the three-moment CAPM relation in the absence of a risk-free asset (see second subsection below).

General Properties of the Mean–Variance–Skewness Efficient Set

As Simaan (1993) shows in the case of generalised elliptic distributions, the optimisation program of an investor can be reformulated as:[31]

$$\min_{w_p'} \{ \tfrac{1}{2} w_p' \Omega w_p \} \tag{12.36}$$

$$\text{s.t} \begin{cases} w_p' E = \mu \\ w_p' 1 = 1 \\ w_p' \Sigma_p = s \end{cases}$$

where μ and s represent respectively some given levels of expected return and skewness.

The *optimal* portfolios set, corresponding to different couples of coordinates $[\mu, s]$, characterises the mean–variance–skewness efficient set. By definition, it corresponds to the set of portfolios maximising the mean for some given variance and skewness. We illustrate in Figures A12.1 and A12.2 in Appendix 12.10, the set of characteristics

---

[29] In Section 12.3.3, we study the links between the three-moment CAPM and the APT of Ross (1976).

[30] Or, equivalently, the investor selects the portfolio that maximises the skewness of his/her portfolio return for some given variance and mean, or chooses the portfolio that maximises the expected return of his/her portfolio for some given mean and skewness.

[31] The portfolio selection programme of the investor is not unique. For instance, Lai (1991) and Chun-hachinda *et al.* (1997) propose—using a polynomial goal programming approach—to incorporate multiple objectives such as maximising both return and skewness of the portfolio return for a given level of variance.

corresponding to portfolios composed of five world stock indexes (as in Chunhachinda *et al.*, 1997).

We can now state the two following theorems.

Theorem 12.3 *The vector of asset weights of any mean–variance–skewness efficient portfolio* p *is a linear combination of those of three distinct funds defined by:*

$$\mathbf{w}_{a_1} = \frac{\mathbf{\Omega}^{-1}\mathbf{E}}{\mathbf{1}'\mathbf{\Omega}^{-1}\mathbf{E}}, \quad \mathbf{w}_{a_2} = \frac{\mathbf{\Omega}^{-1}\mathbf{1}}{\mathbf{1}'\mathbf{\Omega}^{-1}\mathbf{1}} \quad and \quad \mathbf{w}_{a_3} = \frac{\mathbf{\Omega}^{-1}\Sigma_p}{\mathbf{1}'\mathbf{\Omega}^{-1}\Sigma_p} \tag{12.37}$$

Proof. See Appendix 12.4.   □

Corollary 12.2 *If there exists a risk-free asset, every efficient portfolio vector of weights is a linear combination of those of the risk-free asset and of the two distinct funds defined by:*

$$\mathbf{w}_{a_4} = \frac{\mathbf{\Omega}^{-1}(\mathbf{E} - R_f\mathbf{1})}{\mathbf{1}'\mathbf{\Omega}^{-1}(\mathbf{E} - R_f\mathbf{1})} \quad and \quad \mathbf{w}_{a_5} = \frac{\mathbf{\Omega}^{-1}\Sigma_p}{\mathbf{1}'\mathbf{\Omega}^{-1}\Sigma_p} \tag{12.38}$$

Proof. See Appendix 12.5.   □

Compared to the mean–variance analysis, the introduction of a third centred moment has the effect of changing the structure of the efficient set: it is no longer determined by two but rather by three portfolios.[32] The first two are common to all investors and correspond to the two mutual funds generating a mean–variance efficient frontier. We remark in particular that[33] $\mathbf{w}_{a_2}$ is the global *minimum* variance portfolio. The third portfolio $\mathbf{w}_{a_3}$ (or $\mathbf{w}_{a_5}$ if there is a riskless asset) is specific to each investor. It represents the portfolio that, for a given variance, maximises the skewness. Consequently, the mean–variance–skewness efficient set includes the mean–variance efficient set since it is generated by $\mathbf{w}_{a_1}$ and by $\mathbf{w}_{a_2}$ (or the risk-free asset and $\mathbf{w}_{a_4}$ if there is a riskless asset). Since investors have demands differing from their preferences, it is clear that the standard portfolio separation result is no longer verified when return densities are asymmetric.[34]

---

[32] We can notice here that $\mathbf{w}_{a_3}$ (or $\mathbf{w}_{a_5}$) differs from the third portfolio used by Simaan (1993), in the sense that $\mathbf{w}_{a_3}$ (or $\mathbf{w}_{a_5}$) depends here on the agent preferences.

[33] We verify that the mean and variance of the portfolio defined by the weights vector $\mathbf{w}_{a_2}$ are given by:

$$\begin{cases} E(R_{a_2}) = a/c \\ \sigma^2(R_{a_2}) = 1/c \end{cases}$$

where $a = \mathbf{E}'\mathbf{\Omega}^{-1}\mathbf{1}$ and $c = \mathbf{1}'\mathbf{\Omega}^{-1}\mathbf{1}$.

[34] Considering a particular class of return distribution and using the cubic root of $m^3(R_p)$ as a measure of skewness preference of investors, it is however possible to obtain an exact three-mutual fund theorem (see for instance Ingersoll, 1987; Simaan, 1993; Gamba and Rossi, 1998a,b).

Theorem 12.4 *A necessary condition for a portfolio* p *to belong to a mean–variance–skewness efficient set is—except for portfolios that are variance–skewness efficient*[35]—*that there exist two portfolios* Z_0 *and* Z_1 *uncorrelated with* p, *such that:*

$$\mathbf{E} - E(R_{Z_0})\mathbf{1} = \left[\frac{E(R_p) - E(R_{Z_1})}{\sigma^2(R_p)}\right]\Omega\mathbf{w}_p + \left[\frac{E(R_{Z_1}) - E(R_{Z_0})}{m^3(R_p)}\right]\Sigma_p \qquad (12.39)$$

where $E(R_{Z_0})$ *represents the expected return on a portfolio whose return is zero-correlated and has a zero-coskewness with the return of the portfolio* p, *and* $E(R_{Z_1})$ *represents the expected return on a portfolio whose return is zero-correlated with the portfolio* p *and has a coskewness equal to the skewness of that portfolio return.*

Proof. See Appendix 12.6.   □

For any security i, $i = [1, \ldots, N]$, we can write:

$$E(R_i) - E(R_{Z_0}) = \left[\frac{E(R_p) - E(R_{Z_1})}{\sigma^2(R_p)}\right]\mathrm{Cov}(R_i, R_p) + \left[\frac{E(R_{Z_1}) - E(R_{Z_0})}{m^3(R_p)}\right]\mathrm{Cos}(R_i, R_p)$$

$$(12.40)$$

where $\mathrm{Cov}(R_i, R_p)$ and $\mathrm{Cos}(R_i, R_p)$ are respectively the ith entries, for $i = [1, \ldots, N]$, of the $(N \times 1)$ vectors $\Omega\mathbf{w}_p$ and Σ_p.

This relation states that a portfolio p is mean–variance–skewness efficient if its return is such that every single expected asset return $E(R_i)$, for $i = [1, \ldots, N]$, is a linear combination of the covariance and the coskewness between each return R_i and the efficient portfolio p return. Both terms $\{[E(R_p) - E(R_{Z_1})]/\sigma^2(R_p)\}$ and $\{[E(R_{Z_1}) - E(R_{Z_0})]/m^3(R_p)\}$ can be interpreted as subjective risk *premia*. The fact that investors dislike variance and have a preference for (positive) skewness implies that:

$$\begin{cases} \dfrac{E(R_p) - E(R_{Z_1})}{\sigma^2(R_p)} > 0 \\[2mm] \dfrac{E(R_{Z_1}) - E(R_{Z_0})}{m^3(R_p)} < 0 \end{cases} \qquad (12.41)$$

Once these properties are stated, it is then possible to give a three-moment CAPM relation when there is no risk-free asset. To achieve this goal, it is sufficient to identify a specific mean–variance–skewness efficient portfolio: the market portfolio.

A Zero-beta Zero-gamma Three-moment CAPM

The general hypotheses of the model are those of Krauss and Litzenberger (1976): the agents have mean–variance–skewness preferences and homogenous probability beliefs. We assume moreover that there exists a *Pareto-optimal* equilibrium allocation.[36] Under this last hypothesis, the mean–variance–skewness efficient set is convex (see Ingersoll, 1987, pp. 194–195). Since all the investors choose efficient portfolios, the market portfolio is, at equilibrium, a mean–variance–skewness efficient portfolio. The main result is then that the expected return on a security is, at equilibrium, a linear function of its covariance and of its coskewness with the market portfolio return. We have the following theorem.[37]

---

[36] See for instance Simaan (1993) on this point.

[37] With different hypotheses and notations, Gamba and Rossi (1998a,b) establish the same relation.

Theorem 12.5 *In the absence of a risk-free asset, the asset's risk premium of a Pareto-optimal equilibrium is given by the equation:*

$$\mathbf{E} - E(R_{Z_0})\mathbf{1} = [E(R_m) - E(R_{Z_1})]\boldsymbol{\beta} + [E(R_{Z_1}) - E(R_{Z_0})]\boldsymbol{\gamma} \tag{12.42}$$

with

$$\boldsymbol{\beta} = \frac{1}{\sigma^2(R_m)}\boldsymbol{\Omega}\mathbf{w}_m \ and \ \boldsymbol{\gamma} = \frac{1}{m^3(R_m)}\boldsymbol{\Sigma}_m$$

where $E(R_{Z_0})$ represents the expected return on a zero-beta and a zero-gamma portfolio and $E(R_{Z_1})$ corresponds to the expected return on a zero-beta and unitary-gamma portfolio.

Proof. See Appendix 12.7.   □

Thus for any security i, $i = [1, \ldots, N]$:

$$E(R_i) - E(R_{Z_0}) = [E(R_m) - E(R_{Z_1})]\beta_i + [E(R_{Z_1}) - E(R_{Z_0})]\gamma_i \tag{12.43}$$

where $\beta_i = \mathrm{Cov}(R_i, R_m)/\sigma^2(R_m)$ and $\gamma_i = \mathrm{Cos}(R_i, R_m)/m^3(R_m)$ are respectively the ith entries, for $i = [1, \ldots, N]$, of the $(N \times 1)$ vectors $\boldsymbol{\beta}$ and $\boldsymbol{\gamma}$.

We remark that:

$$[E(R_m) - E(R_{Z_1})] \geqslant 0, \ \mathrm{sign}[E(R_{Z_1}) - E(R_{Z_0})] = -\mathrm{sign}[m^3(R_m)] \tag{12.44}$$

and, when $m^3(R_m) \leqslant 0$:

$$[E(R_m) - E(R_{Z_0})] \geqslant 0 \tag{12.45}$$

This equation is the three-moment CAPM relation with N risky assets.[38] As for the fundamental three-moment CAPM relation derived by Krauss and Litzenberger (1976), it indicates that the risk *premium* on any financial asset must be equal to the sum of two risk *premia*: one market *premium* $[E(R_m) - E(R_{Z_1})]$ proportional to the β of the asset corresponding to the *premium* placed by the market on variance and a *premium* on a zero-beta unitary-gamma portfolio, $[E(R_{Z_1}) - E(R_{Z_0})]$, proportional to the γ of the asset representing the risk *premium* placed by the market on skewness.

Introducing the risk *premium* on the market portfolio $[E(R_m) - E(R_{Z_0})]$ in (12.42), it is then possible to rewrite it as:

$$\mathbf{E} - E(R_{Z_0})\mathbf{1} = [E(R_m) - E(R_{Z_0})]\boldsymbol{\beta} + [E(R_{Z_1}) - E(R_{Z_0})](\boldsymbol{\gamma} - \boldsymbol{\beta}) \tag{12.46}$$

Thus for any security i, $i = [1, \ldots, N]$:

$$E(R_i) - E(R_{Z_0}) = [E(R_m) - E(R_{Z_0})]\beta_i + [E(R_{Z_1}) - E(R_{Z_0})](\gamma_i - \beta_i) \tag{12.47}$$

where $\beta_i = \mathrm{Cov}(R_i, R_m)/\sigma^2(R_m)$ and $\gamma_i = \mathrm{Cos}(R_i, R_m)/m^3(R_m)$ are respectively the ith entries, for $i = [1, \ldots, N]$, of the $(N \times 1)$ vectors $\boldsymbol{\beta}$ and $\boldsymbol{\gamma}$.

Under this presentation, the N risky assets three-moment CAPM version constitutes a direct extension of Black's (1972) zero-beta CAPM. This relation does not however

---

[38] With our general hypotheses, it is possible to give on *a priori* grounds the sign of risk *premia* (see Simaan, 1993 on this point).

collapse to Black's model under the same conditions that make the fundamental relation collapse to the Sharpe–Lintner–Mossin model in the presence of a risk-free asset. Indeed, unless the zero-beta zero-gamma portfolio is identical to the global *minimum* variance portfolio, the intercept of the security market line that we obtain when $[E(R_m) - E(R_{Z_0})] = 0$ or when $\gamma_i = \beta_i$ with $i = [1, \ldots, N]$, does not have any reason to be equal to the intercept of the Black's (1972) model. If a risk-free asset exists, its return replaces $E(R_{Z_0})$ in the equilibrium relation and we are back to the fundamental relation with a risk-free asset derived in Section 12.3.1.

12.3.3 The Three-moment CAPM, the Quadratic Market Model and the Arbitrage Asset Pricing Model

The return process is assumed to be governed, in a skewed world, by two risk factors determining portfolios held by investors. Such risk factors yield *premia* claimed by any rational agent. In that sense, and following Krauss and Litzenberger (1976, 1983), Barone-Adesi (1985) and Brooks and Faff (1998), it is then possible to make the link between some of the main multifactor models and the three-moment CAPM described previously. We focus, in the next subsection, on the quadratic market model and the APT model.

The Quadratic Market Model and the Three-moment CAPM

While the quadratic market model has been primarily proposed to assess the market timing ability of the mutual funds managers (see Treynor and Mazuy, 1966),[39] it is also possible, as shown by Krauss and Litzenberger (1976), to use it as a consistent DGP in a three-moment CAPM framework. The quadratic market model assumes that the excess return on any security is generated by the following factor model:

$$
\begin{cases}
\mathbf{R}_t - R_f \mathbf{1} = \boldsymbol{\alpha}_0 + \boldsymbol{\alpha}_1 (R_{mt} - R_f) + \boldsymbol{\alpha}_2 [R_{mt} - E(R_m)]^2 + \boldsymbol{\varepsilon}_t \\
E(\boldsymbol{\varepsilon}_t) = \mathbf{0} \\
E(\boldsymbol{\varepsilon}_t | R_{mt}) = E(\boldsymbol{\varepsilon}_t | R_{mt}^2) = \mathbf{0}
\end{cases}
\tag{12.48}
$$

where $\mathbf{R}_t$ is the $(N \times 1)$ vector of the returns of risky assets, $\boldsymbol{\alpha}_0$ is the $(N \times 1)$ vector of asset return intercepts, $\boldsymbol{\alpha}_1$ and $\boldsymbol{\alpha}_2$ are the $(N \times 1)$ vectors of asset return sensitivities with, respectively, the market portfolio return and the squared market portfolio return, and $\boldsymbol{\varepsilon}_t$ is the $(N \times 1)$ vector of asset return disturbances.

Under this hypothesis, the coefficients $\boldsymbol{\alpha}_1$ and $\boldsymbol{\alpha}_2$ of this DGP are linked with the parameters $\boldsymbol{\beta}$ and $\boldsymbol{\gamma}$ of the three-moment CAPM. Subtracting the expected value of (12.48) from (12.48), and using the definition of the relative risk measures $\boldsymbol{\beta}$ and $\boldsymbol{\gamma}$, yields the following result (see Appendix 12.8):

$$
\begin{cases}
\beta = \alpha_1 + \alpha_2 \dfrac{m^3(R_m)}{\sigma^2(R_m)} \\[3mm]
\gamma = \alpha_1 + \alpha_2 \dfrac{\kappa^4(R_m) - [\sigma^2(R_m)]^2}{m^3(R_m)}
\end{cases}
\tag{12.49}
$$

where $\sigma^2(R_m)$ and $m^3(R_m)$ are defined as before and $\kappa^4(R_m)$ represents the kurtosis of the market portfolio.

---

[39] See also Lehman and Modest (1987), Cumby and Glen (1990), Lee and Rhaman (1990) and Chen *et al.* (1992).

Thus, for any security i, $i = [1, \ldots, N]$:

$$
\begin{cases}
\beta_i = \alpha_{1i} + \alpha_{2i} \dfrac{m^3(R_m)}{\sigma^2(R_m)} \\[2ex]
\gamma_i = \alpha_{1i} + \alpha_{2i} \dfrac{\kappa^4(R_m) - [\sigma^2(R_m)]^2}{m^3(R_m)}
\end{cases}
\tag{12.50}
$$

where $\beta_i = \text{Cov}(R_i, R_m)/\sigma^2(R_m)$ and $\gamma_i = \text{Cos}(R_i, R_m)/m^3(R_m)$ are respectively the ith entries, for $i = [1, \ldots, N]$, of the $(N \times 1)$ vectors $\boldsymbol{\beta}$ and $\boldsymbol{\gamma}$.

These equations provide some insights into the nature of the relation between the quadratic market model and the three-moment CAPM. For example, if the weights on α_{2i} are equal, then we have $\beta_i = \gamma_i$. If either α_{1i} or α_{2i} is constant, then β_i and γ_i are collinear.

Under certain restrictions on the parameters, the quadratic market model is consistent with the three-moment CAPM and when the market model is linear, the three-moment CAPM collapses to the traditional CAPM.

The Arbitrage Pricing Model and the Three-moment CAPM

In the same way, it is also possible to link the three-moment CAPM with the APT model of Ross (1976).

Consider first the following quadratic market model:

$$
\begin{cases}
\mathbf{R}_t = \boldsymbol{\alpha}_0^* + \boldsymbol{\alpha}_1^* R_{mt} + \boldsymbol{\alpha}_2^* v_{mt}^2 + \boldsymbol{\varepsilon}_t \\
\text{Cov}(R_{mt}, v_{mt}^2) = 0 \\
E(\boldsymbol{\varepsilon}_t) = \mathbf{0} \\
E(\boldsymbol{\varepsilon}_t | R_{mt}) = E(\boldsymbol{\varepsilon}_t | v_{mt}^2) = \mathbf{0} \\
E(\boldsymbol{\varepsilon}_t' \boldsymbol{\varepsilon}_t) = \mathbf{D}
\end{cases}
\tag{12.51}
$$

where $\mathbf{R}_t$, $\boldsymbol{\alpha}_i^*$, with $i = [0, 1, 2]$, and $\boldsymbol{\varepsilon}_t$ are defined as previously when market portfolio return and squared market portfolio return are orthogonal; v_{mt}^2 is the squared market portfolio return component independent of the variation of the market portfolio return and $\mathbf{D}$ is the $(N \times N)$ diagonal variance–covariance matrix of asset return disturbances.

If (12.51) represents the DGP of the asset returns then, under the standard assumptions of APT, the expected returns of all the securities must satisfy asymptotically the following equality:[40]

$$
\mathbf{E} - R_f \mathbf{1} = \boldsymbol{\alpha}_1^* [E(R_1) - R_f] + \boldsymbol{\alpha}_2^* [E(R_2) - R_f]
\tag{12.52}
$$

where $E(R_1)$ and $E(R_2)$ are the expected returns on large well-diversified portfolios,[41] perfectly correlated, respectively, with R_{mt} and with v_{mt}^2.

For the market portfolio $\alpha_{1m}^* = 1$ and $\alpha_{2m}^* = 0$, implying that:

$$
E(R_1) = E(R_m)
\tag{12.53}
$$

---

[40] To write (12.52) as an exact pricing relation in an infinite economy, we suppose here that the conditions of theorem 5 in Ingersoll (1987, p. 184) are met (that is, the market portfolio is well diversified and the factors are pervasive).

[41] A large well-diversified portfolio is one containing a large number of assets with relative weights of order $1/N$.

Concerning the portfolio whose return is denoted R_2, it is hardly possible to give a similar simple definition. It can be shown, however, that R_2 has an upper bound (see Appendix 12.9):

$$E(R_2) < E(v_m^2) \qquad (12.54)$$

Substituting (12.53) in (12.52), we have:

$$\mathbf{E} - R_f \mathbf{1} = \boldsymbol{\alpha}_1^*[E(R_m) - R_f] + \boldsymbol{\alpha}_2^*[E(R_2) - R_f] \qquad (12.55)$$

This equilibrium relation indicates that the expected excess return of a security is a linear function of two risk *premia*: the first one corresponds to the market portfolio excess return, the second relies on the excess return of a portfolio whose return is perfectly correlated with the squared market portfolio return and independent of the market return. Taking the expected value of (12.51) and setting the resulting equation equal to (12.55), yields for any asset i, $i = [1, \dots, N]$:

$$\alpha_{0i}^* + \alpha_{1i}^* E(R_m) + \alpha_{2i}^* E(v_m^2) = R_f + \alpha_{1i}^*[E(R_m) - R_f] + \alpha_{2i}^*[E(R_2) - R_f] \qquad (12.56)$$

Rearranging terms yields, $\forall i$, $i = [1, \dots, N]$:

$$\alpha_{0i}^* = (1 - \alpha_{1i}^*)R_f - \alpha_{2i}^*\phi \qquad (12.57)$$

with $\phi = E(v_m^2) - E(R_2) + R_f$.
That entails:

$$\phi = R_f \left(\frac{1}{\alpha_{2i}^*} - \frac{\alpha_{1i}^*}{\alpha_{2i}^*} \right) - \frac{\alpha_{0i}^*}{\alpha_{2i}^*} \qquad (12.58)$$

The APT leads to a restriction on a unique value ϕ, defined as a nonlinear combination of the coefficients of the quadratic market model.[42]

It is then possible to test, as in the case of the traditional CAPM, the three-moment CAPM with this restriction or, more precisely, the two-factor APT version consistent with the three-moment CAPM. Indeed, rewriting the exact three-moment asset pricing relation for the portfolio whose return is v_{mt}^2, we have:

$$E(v_m^2) - R_f = [E(R_m) - E(R_Z)]\beta_{v_m^2} + [E(R_Z) - R_f]\gamma_{v_m^2} \qquad (12.59)$$

with $\beta_{v_m^2} = \text{Cov}(v_m^2, R_m)/\sigma^2(R_m)$ and $\gamma_{v_m^2} = \text{Cos}(v_m^2, R_m)/m^3(R_m)$.

Since R_2 is also perfectly correlated with v_m^2 and $E(R_2) < E(v_m^2)$, we can write the three-moment CAPM and the quadratic market model restrictions as:

$$[E(R_2) - R_f] < [E(R_m) - E(R_Z)]\beta_{v_m^2} + [E(R_Z) - R_f]\gamma_{v_m^2} \qquad (12.60)$$

Moreover, since, by definition, the portfolio whose return is v_{mt}^2 has a beta equal to zero, we obtain:

$$\pi = [E(R_2) - R_f] - [E(R_m) - E(R_Z)]\beta_{v_m^2} - [E(R_Z) - R_f]\gamma_{v_m^2} < 0 \qquad (12.61)$$

---

[42] For an empirical investigation of this restriction, see for instance Barone-Adesi (1985), Faff (1993) and Faff *et al.* (1998).

The market value of π gives an upper bound to the skewness *premium* on the portfolio generating an expected return of $E(R_2)$. This further restriction is obtained under the hypothesis that the three-moment CAPM is the true model.

12.4 CONCLUSION

In this paper, we recall the main hypotheses necessary for establishing a multifactor valuation relation based on equilibrium arguments. Investors here are supposed to be rational, maximising a utility objective function depending on the three first centred moments of return densities. Using a monetary separation fund theorem, it is then possible to get an equilibrium pricing model for financial assets. In this model, a specific asset return is a function, as in the CAPM framework, of the market portfolio return, but the relation is no longer linear but convex as supposed by Treynor and Mazuy (1966).

Using the portfolio choice theory, and applying it in the case of non-Gaussian returns, we generalise the previous relation when no risk-free asset exists. We illustrate—Figures A12.1 and A12.2 in Appendix 12.10—statistical characteristics of simulated portfolios composed of world stock indexes. We then make the link between different multifactor models of returns such as Black's (1972) model, the quadratic market model or the APT model, and the three-moment CAPM. They appear to be different because of constraints on the implicit parameters. All these differences have now to be verified on real data. One advantage of the last model is the pre-identification of market factors.

We have given the foundations of a three-moment decision criterion and presented some testable restrictions. Empirical evidence concerning different multifactor relations when considering stock assets is now required (see Friend and Westerfield, 1980; Lim, 1989; Nummelin, 1995; Racine, 1998; Faff *et al.*, 1998; Sanchez-Torres and Sentana, 1998; Harvey and Siddique, 2000a,b). It would also be interesting to consider portfolios built using derivatives and mutual funds to check whether the third moment considered in the three-moment CAPM is statistically significant and provides an improvement in the quality of the results of the traditional CAPM. Furthermore, the more recent developments in this field of research have been to consider the kurtosis coefficient as a supplementary variable in the asset relation analysis (see for instance Fang and Lai, 1997; Hwang and Satchell, 1998; Athayde and Flôres, 1999; Adcock and Shutes, 1999b). Tests regarding the information content of higher moments—if they exist—would be a worthy research direction.

ACKNOWLEDGEMENTS

We thank Christian Dunis, Alan Timmermann and John Moody (the editors) and Thomas Bundt (the referee) for relevant remarks as well as Chris Adcock, Simon Benninga, Thierry Chauveau, Renato Flôres, Louis Levy-Garboua, Thierry Michel, François Quittard-Pinon and Jean-Marie Rousseau for helpful comments when preparing this paper. We also gratefully acknowledge comments by participants at the Vth Spring Meeting of Young Economists (Oxford, March 2000), the VIIth International Conference in Forecasting Financial Markets and Computational Finance (London, May 2000), the XVIIth International Meeting of the GDR-CNRS Money and Finance (Lisbon, June 2000) and the

1st International Portuguese Finance Network Conference (Braga, July 2000). Errors and weaknesses of this paper rest under our sole responsibility.

REFERENCES

Adcock, C. and K. Shutes (1999a). "Portfolio Selection Based on the Multivariate Skew Normal Distribution", working paper, University of Bath, **January**, 9 pp.

Adcock, C. and K. Shutes (1999b). "Fat Tails and The Capital Asset Pricing Model", working paper, University of Bath, **February**, 28 pp.

Aggarwal, R. (1990). "Distribution of Spot and Forward Exchange Rates: Empirical Evidence and Investor Valuation of Skewness and Kurtosis", *Decision Sciences*, 588–595.

Aggarwal, R. and R. Aggarwal (1993). "Security Return Distributions and Market Structure: Evidence from the NYSE/AMEX and the NASDAQ Markets", *Journal of Financial Research* **14**, 209–220.

Aggarwal, R., R. Rao and T. Hiraki (1989). "Skewness and Kurtosis in Japanese Equity Returns: Empirical Evidence", *Journal of Financial Research* **12**, 253–261.

Alexander, G. and A. Baptista (2000). "Economic Implications of Using a Mean–VaR Model for Portfolio Selection: A Comparison with Mean–Variance Analysis", working paper, University of Minnesota, 40 pp.

Arditti, F. (1967). "Risk and the Required Return on Equity", *Journal of Finance* **22**, 19–36.

Arrow, K. (1964). *Essays in the Theory of Risk Bearing*, Amsterdam: North-Holland.

Athayde, G. and R. Flôres (1999). "Introducing Higher Moments in the CAPM: Some Basic Ideas", Discussion Paper *EPGE-FGV*, November, 23 pp.

Barone-Adesi, G. (1985). "Arbitrage Equilibrium with Skewed Asset Returns", *Journal of Financial and Quantitative Analysis* **20**, 299–311.

Beckaert, G., C. Erb, C. Harvey and T. Viskanta (1998). "Distributional Characteristics of Emerging Markets Returns and Asset Allocation", *Journal of Portfolio Management* **Winter**, 103–117.

Beedles, W. and M. Simkowitz (1978). "Diversification in a Three-moment World", *Journal of Financial and Quantitative Analysis* **13**, 927–941.

Beedles, W. and M. Simkowitz (1980). "Morphology of Asset Asymmetry", *Journal of Business* **8**, 457–468.

Benishay, H. (1987). "A Fourth-degree Polynomial Utility Function and its Implications for Investor's Responses Toward Fourth Moments of the Wealth Distribution", *Journal of Accounting, Auditing and Finance* **2**, 203–238.

Benishay, H. (1992). "The Pratt–Arrow Requirement in a Fourth Degree Polynomial Utility Function", *Journal of Accounting, Auditing and Finance* **7**, 97–115.

Black, F. (1972). "Capital Market Equilibrium with Restricted Borrowing", *Journal of Business* **7**, 444–454.

Black, F. (1976), "Studies of Stock Price Volatility Changes". In Proceedings of the 1976 Meeting of the Business and Economic Statistics Section. American Statistical Association; 177–181.

Black, F. (1993). "Beta and Return", *Journal of Portfolio Management*, Fall, 8–18.

Brennan, M. (1993). "Agency and Asset Pricing", Unpublished Manuscript, UCLA and London Business School.

Bollerslev, T. (1986). "Generalized Autoregressive Conditional Heteroskedasticity", *Journal of Econometrics* **31**, 307–327.

Bollerslev, T., R. Engle and J. Wooldridge (1988). "A Capital Asset Pricing Model with Time-varying Covariances", *Journal of Political Economy* **96**(1), 116–131.

Brockett, P. and Y. Kahane (1992). "Risk, Return, Skewness and Preference", *Management Science* **38**, 851–866.

Brockett, P. and R. Garven (1998). "A Reexamination of the Relationship Between Preferences and Moments Orderings by Rational Risk Averse Investors", *Geneva Papers on Risk and Insurance Theory* **23**, 127–137.

Brooks, R. and R. Faff (1998). "A Test of a Two-factor APT based on the Quadratic Market Model: International Evidence", *Studies in Economics and Econometrics* **22**, 65–76.

Cass, D. and J. Stiglitz (1970). "The Structure of Investor Preferences and Asset Returns, and Separability in Portfolio Allocation: A Contribution to the Pure Theory of Mutual Funds", *Journal of Economic Theory* **2**, 122–160.

Chen, C., S. Rahman and A. Chan (1992). "Cross-sectional Analysis of Mutual Fund's Market Timing and Security Selection Skill", *Journal of Business and Accounting* **19**, 659–675.

Christie, A. and A. Andrew (1982). "The Stochastic Behavior of Common Stocks Variances: Value, Leverage, and Interest Rate Effects", *Journal of Financial Economics* **23**, 407–432.

Chunhachinda, P., K. Danpani, S. Hamid and A. Prakash (1997). "Portfolio Selection and Skewness: Evidence from International Stocks Markets", *Journal of Banking and Finance* **21**, 143–167.

Corrado, Ch. and T. Su (1996a). "S& P 500 Index Option Tests of Jarrow and Rudd's Approximate Option Valuation Formula", *Journal of Futures Markets* **16**(6), 611–629.

Corrado, Ch. and T. Su (1996b). "Skewness and Kurtosis in S& P 500 Index Returns Implied by Option Prices", *Journal of Future Markets* **19**(2), 175–192.

Cumby, R. and J. Glen (1990). "Evaluating the Performance of International Mutual Funds", *Journal of Finance* **45**, 497–521.

Diacogiannis, G. (1994). "Three-parameter Asset Pricing", *Managerial and Decision Economics* **15**, 149–158.

Diacogiannis, G. (1999). "A Three-dimensional Risk–return Relationship Based upon the Inefficiency of a Portfolio: Derivation and Implications", *The European Journal of Finance* **5**, 225–235.

Ederington, L. (1986). "Mean–variance as an Approximation to Expected Utility Maximisation", working paper 86-5, Washington University.

Engle, R. (1982). "Autoregressive Conditional Heteroskedasticity with Estimates of the Variance of United Kingdom Inflation", *Econometrica* **50**, 987–1007.

Faff, R. (1993). "An Empirical Test of Arbitrage Equilibrium with Skewed Asset Returns: Australian", *Asia Pacific Journal of Management* **10**, 195–211.

Faff, R., Y. Ho and L. Zhang (1998). "A GMM Test of the Three-moment CAPM in the Australian Equity Market", *Asia Pacific Journal of Finance* **1**, 45–60.

Fama, E. (1996). "Discounting under Uncertainty", *Journal of Business* **69**, 415–428.

Fama, E. and K. French (1992). "The Cross-section of Expected Stock Returns", *Journal of Finance* **47**, 427–465.

Fang, H. and T. Lai (1997). "Co-kurtosis and Capital Asset Pricing", *Financial Review* **32**, 293–307.

Feller, W. (1971). *An Introduction to Probability Theory and its Applications*, Vol. II, New York: Wiley.

Friedman, M. and L. Savage (1948). "The Utility Analysis of Choices Involving Risk", *Journal of Political Economy* **56**, 279–304.

Friend, I. and R. Westerfield (1980). "Co-skewness and Capital Asset Pricing", *Journal of Finance* **35**, 897–913.

Gamba, A. and F. Rossi (1998a). "A Three-moment Based Portfolio Selection Model", *Rivista di Matematica per le Scienze Economiche e Sociali* **20**, 25–48.

Gamba, A. and F. Rossi (1998b). "Mean–Variance–Skewness Analysis in Portfolio Choice and Capital Markets", *Ricerca Operativa* **28**, 5–46.

Golec, J. and M. Tamarkin (1998). "Betters Love Skewness, not Risk, at the Horse Track", *Journal of Political Economy* **106**, 205–225.

Harvey, C. (1995). "Predictable Risk and Returns in Emerging Markets", *Review of Financial Studies* **8**, 773–816.

Harvey, C. and G. Zhou (1993). "International Asset Pricing with Alternative Distributional Specifications", *Journal of Empirical Finance* **1**, 107–131.

Harvey, C. and S. Siddique (2000a). "Conditional Skewness in Asset Pricing Tests", *Journal of Finance* **54**, 1263–1296.

Harvey, C. and S. Siddique (2000b). "Time-Varying Conditional Skewness and the Market Risk Premium", *Research in Banking and Finance* **1**, 25–58.

Hwang, S. and S. Satchell (1998), "Modelling Emerging Market Risk Premia Using Higher Moments", *DAE Working Paper 9806*, University of Cambridge, 36 pp.

Ingersoll, J. (1987). Theory of Financial Decision Making. Totowa: Rowman & Littlefield; 474 pp.

Jagannathan, R. and Z. Wang (1996). "The Conditional CAPM and the Cross-section of Expected Returns", *Journal of Finance* **51**, 3–53.

Jarrow, R. and A. Rudd (1982). "Approximate Option Valuation for Arbitrary Stochastic Processes", *Journal of Financial Economics* **10**, 347–369.

Kane, A. (1982). "Skewness Preference and Portfolio Choice", *Journal of Financial and Quantitative Analysis* **17**, 15–25.

Kahneman, D. and A. Tversky (1979). "Prospect Theory: An Analysis of Decision under Risk", *Econometrica* **47**, 263–291.

Kimball, M. (1990). "Precautionary Saving in the Small and in the Large", *Econometrica* **58**, 53–73.

Kraus, A. and R. Litzenberger (1976). "Skewness Preference and the Valuation of Risk Assets", *Journal of Finance* **31**, 1085–1099.

Kraus, A. and R. Litzenberger (1983). "On the Distributional Conditions for a Consumption-oriented Three-moment CAPM", *Journal of Finance* **38**, 1381–1391.

Kroll, Y., H. Levy and H. Markowitz (1984). "Mean Variance versus Direct Utility Maximisation", *Journal of Finance* **39**, 47–61.

Lai, T. (1991). "Portfolio Selection with Skewness: A Multiplicative-objective Approach", *Review of Quantitative Finance and Accounting* **1**, 293–305.

Lhabitant, F. (1997), "On the (Ab)use of Expected Utility Approximations for Portfolio Selection and Portfolio Performance", working paper, University of Lausanne, **April**, 23 pp.

Lee, C. and S. Rhaman (1990). "Market Timing, Selectivity, and Mutual Fund Performance: An Empirical Investigation", *Journal of Business* **42**, 261–278.

Lehman, B. and D. Modest (1987). "Mutual Fund Performance Evaluation: A Comparison of Benchmarks and Benchmark Comparisons", *Journal of Finance* **42**, 233–265.

Levy, H. (1969). "A Utility Function Depending on the First Three Moments", *Journal of Finance* **24**, 715–719.

Levy, H. and H. Markowitz (1979). "Approximating Expected Utility by a Function of Mean and Variance", *American Economic Review* **69**, 308–317.

Lim, K. (1989). "A New Test of the Three-moment Capital Asset Pricing Model", *Journal of Financial and Quantitative Analysis* **24**, 205–216.

Lintner, J. (1965). "The Valuation of Risk Assets and the Selection of Risky Investments in Stock Portfolios and Capital Budgets", *Review of Economic and Statistics* **13**, 13–37.

Loistl, O. (1976). "The Erroneous Approximation of Expected Utility by Means of a Taylor's Series Expansion: Analytic and Computational Results", *American Economic Review* **66**, 905–910.

Madan, D. and F. Milne (1994). "Contingent Claims Valued and Hedged by Pricing and Investing in a Basis", *Mathematical Finance* **4**, 223–245.

Mandelbrot, B. (1997). *Fractals and Scaling in Finance*, New York: Spinger; pgs551 pp.

Markowitz, H. (1952). "Portfolio Selection", *Journal of Finance* **7**, 77–91.

Markowitz, H. (1991). "Foundations of Portfolio Theory", *Journal of Finance* **46**, 469–477.

Mossin, J. (1966). "Equilibrium in a Capital Market", *Econometrica* **34**, 768–783.

Nantell, T., B. Price and K. Price (1982). "Variance and Lower Partial Moments Measures of Systematic Risk: Some Analytical and Empirical Results", *Journal of Finance* **37**, 843–855.

Nummelin, K. (1995). "Global Coskewness and Swedish Stock Returns". *Meddelanden Working Papers 311*. Swedish School of Economics and Business Administration; 20 pp.

Okunev, J. (1990). "An Alternative Measure of Mutual Fund Performance", *Journal of Business, Finance and Accounting* **17**(2), 247–264.

Pedersen, C. and S. Satchell (1998). "An Extended Family of Financial Risk Measures", *Geneva Papers on Risk and Insurance Theory* **23**, 89–117.

Pedersen, C. and S. Satchell (2001). "Asymmetric Equilibrium Risk Measures", *Journal of Empirical Finance*, in press.

Peiro, A. (1999). "Skewness in Financial Returns", *Journal of Banking and Finance* **23**, 847–862

Prakash, A., C. Chang and S. Hamid (1996). "Why a Decision Maker May Prefer a Seemingly Unfair Gamble", *Decision Sciences* **27**, 239–253.

Pratt, J. (1964). "Risk Aversion in the Small and the Large", *Econometrica* **32**, 122–136.

Racine, M. (1998), "Asset Valuation and Coskewness in Canada". *Working Paper Series 9802*. University of Wilfrid Laurier; 34 pp.

Rachev, S. and S. Mittnik (2000). Stable Paretian Models in Finance Series, Financial Economics and Quantitative Analysis Series. New York: Wiley, 855 pp.

Ross, S. (1976). "The Arbitrage Theory of Capital Asset Pricing Theory", *Journal of Economic Theory* **13**, 341–360.

Rossi, G. and L. Tibiletti (1996). "Higher Order Polynomial Utility Functions: Advantages in their Use", *working paper,* Dipartimento Di Statistica e Matematica Applicata Alle Scienze Umane Quaderno 1, Universita Degli Studi Di Torino, 13 pp.

Rubinstein, M. (1973). "The Fundamental Theorem of Parameter-preference Security Valuation", *Journal of Financial and Quantitative Analysis* **8**, 61–69.

Samorodnitsky, G. and M. Taqqu (1994). *Stable Non-Gaussian Random Processes*, NewYork: Chapman & Hall.

Samuelson, P. (1970). "The Fundamental Approximation Theorem of Portfolio Analysis in Terms of Means, Variances and Higher Moments", *Review of Economic Studies* **37**, 537–543.

Sanchez-Torres, P. and E. Sentana (1998). "Mean–Variance–Skewness Analysis: An Application to Risk Premia in the Spanish Stock Market", *Investigaciones Economicas* **22**, 5–17.

Scott, R. and P. Horvath (1980). "On the Direction of Preference for Moments of Higher Order than the Variance", *Journal of Finance* **35**, 915–919.

Sears, R. and K. Wei (1985). "Asset Pricing, Higher Moments, and the Market Risk Premium: A Note", *Journal of Finance* **40**, 1251–1253.

Sears, R. and K. Wei (1988). "The Structure of Skewness Preferences in Asset Pricing Models with Higher Moments: An Empirical Test", *Financial Review* **23**, 25–38.

Sharpe, W. (1964). "Capital Asset Prices: A Theory of Market Equilibrium under Conditions of Risk", *Journal of Finance* **19**, 425–442.

Simaan, Y. (1993). "Portfolio Selection and Asset Pricing Three Parameter Framework", *Management Science* **5**, 568–577.

Simaan, Y. (1997). "What is the Opportunity Cost of mean–variance Investment Strategies", *Management Science* **5**, 578–587.

Treynor, J. and F. Mazuy (1966). "Can Mutual Funds Outguess the Market", *Harvard Business Review* **44**, 131–136.

Tsiang, S. (1972). "The Rationale of the Mean–Standard Deviation Analysis, Skewness Preference, and the Demand for Money", *American Economic Review* **62**, 354–371.

von Neuman, J. and O. Morgenstern (1947). *Theory of Games and Economic Behaviour*. Princeton, NJ: Princeton University Press.

APPENDIX 12.1

Following Diacogiannis (1994), the skewness of the portfolio return can be written as a weighted average of the coskewness of the returns of the N securities present in that portfolio, that is:

$$m^3(R_p) = \sum_{i=1}^{N} w_i \, \text{Cos}(R_i, R_p) \tag{A12.1}$$

Proof. The coskewness between the returns on a security i and a portfolio p is given by:

$$\text{Cos}(R_i, R_p) = E\{[R_i - E(R_i)][R_p - E(R_p)]^2\} \tag{A12.2}$$

Squaring the second term in brackets and rearranging, we have:

$$\text{Cos}(R_i, R_p) = E(R_i R_p^2) - E(R_i)E(R_p^2) - 2E(R_p)[E(R_i R_p) - E(R_i)E(R_p)] \tag{A12.3}$$

Which is equivalent to:

$$\text{Cos}(R_i, R_p) = \text{Cov}(R_i, R_p^2) - 2E(R_p)\,\text{Cov}(R_i, R_p) \tag{A12.4}$$

The skewness of the return of a portfolio p is given by:

$$m^3(R_p) = E(R_p^3) - 3E(R_p^2)E(R_p) + 3[E(R_p)]^3 - [E(R_p)]^3 \tag{A12.5}$$

Using the definition of variance and the bilinear property of the covariance operator, (A12.5) can be simplified to:

$$m^3(R_p) = \text{Cov}(R_p, R_p^2) - 2E(R_p)\sigma^2(R_p) \tag{A12.6}$$

Rearranging (A12.6) and using the previous results, we have:

$$m^3(R_p) = \sum_{i=1}^{N} w_i[\text{Cov}(R_i, R_p^2) - 2E(R_p)\,\text{Cov}(R_i, R_p)] \tag{A12.7}$$

That is:

$$m^3(R_p) = \mathbf{w}_p' \Sigma_p \tag{A12.8}$$

where $\mathbf{w}_p$ is the $(N \times 1)$ vector of portfolio weights on a portfolio p and Σ_p is the $(N \times 1)$ vector of coskewness between the returns of N risky assets and the portfolio p. $\square$

APPENDIX 12.2

The first-order conditions of the agent's portfolio problem are sufficient for a *maximum* since the hessian matrix of the expected utility function, with respect to $\mathbf{w}_p'$, is negative definite.

Proof. The second partial derivative of the investor's expected utility with respect to w_i and w_j yields:

$$\frac{\partial^2 E[U(R_p)]}{\partial w_i \partial w_j} = E[U^{(2)}(R_p)R_i R_j] \tag{A12.9}$$

with $(i, j) = [1, \dots, N]^2$.

The $(N \times N)$ hessian matrix $\mathbf{H}$ of the expected utility function is then given by:

$$\mathbf{H} = E\left[U^{(2)}(R_p) \begin{pmatrix} R_1^2 & R_1 R_2 & \cdots & R_1 R_N \\ R_1 R_2 & R_2^2 & \cdots & R_2 R_N \\ \vdots & \vdots & \ddots & \vdots \\ R_1 R_N & R_1 R_n & \cdots & R_N^2 \end{pmatrix} \right] \qquad \text{(A12.10)}$$

Premutiplying and postmultiplying (A12.10) by $\mathbf{w}_p$ leads to the following quadratic form:

$$Q = \mathbf{w}'_p \mathbf{H} \mathbf{w}_p$$

$$= \sum_{i=1}^{N} \sum_{j=1}^{N} w_i w_j E[U^{(2)}(R_p) R_i R_j]$$

$$= E\left[U^{(2)}(R_p) \left(\sum_{i=1}^{n} w_i R_i \right)^2 \right] \qquad \text{(A12.11)}$$

which is negative since, by definition, investors are risk averse, *i.e.* $U^{(2)}(R_p) < 0$. The hessian matrix is then negative definite and the concavity condition is met. $\qquad \square$

APPENDIX 12.3

The first derivative of the skewness of the return portfolio with respect to $\mathbf{w}'_p$ is equal to three times the coskewness vector, that is:

$$\frac{\partial m^3(R_p)}{\partial \mathbf{w}'_p} = 3\Sigma_p \qquad \text{(A12.12)}$$

Proof. The skewness of the return of a portfolio p is given by:

$$m^3(R_p) = E\{[R_p - E(R_p)]^3\}$$

$$= E\left\{ \left[\sum_{i=1}^{N} w_i (R_i - E(R_i)) \right]^3 \right\} \qquad \text{(A12.13)}$$

Taking the first partial derivative of the portfolio return skewness with respect to w_i, the ith entry of the $(1 \times N)$ vector $\mathbf{w}'_p$ yields:

$$\frac{\partial m^3(R_p)}{\partial w_i} = 3E\{[R_i - E(R_i)][R_p - E(R_p)]^2\} = 3\,\mathrm{Cos}(R_i, R_p) \qquad \text{(A12.14)}$$

Which leads in the vectorial case to:

$$\frac{\partial m^3(R_p)}{\partial \mathbf{w}'_p} = \begin{pmatrix} \dfrac{\partial m^3(R_p)}{\partial w_1} \\ \vdots \\ \dfrac{\partial m^3(R_p)}{\partial w_N} \end{pmatrix} = \begin{pmatrix} 3\,\mathrm{Cos}(R_1, R_p) \\ \vdots \\ 3\,\mathrm{Cos}(R_N, R_p) \end{pmatrix} = 3\Sigma_p \qquad \text{(A12.15)}$$

$\qquad \square$

APPENDIX 12.4

When return densities are skewed, the vector of relative asset weights of any efficient portfolio p is a linear combination of those of the three following distinct funds:

$$\mathbf{w}_{a_1} = \frac{\Omega^{-1}\mathbf{E}}{\mathbf{1}'\Omega^{-1}\mathbf{E}}, \quad \mathbf{w}_{a_2} = \frac{\Omega^{-1}\mathbf{1}}{\mathbf{1}'\Omega^{-1}\mathbf{1}} \text{ and } \mathbf{w}_{a_3} = \frac{\Omega^{-1}\Sigma_p}{\mathbf{1}'\Omega^{-1}\Sigma_p} \quad (A12.16)$$

Proof. The solution of the investor's portfolio selection programme is given by solving the following Lagrangian:

$$L = \frac{1}{2}\mathbf{w}'_p\Omega\mathbf{w}_p + \delta_1[E(R_p) - \mathbf{w}'_p\mathbf{E}] + \delta_2[1 - \mathbf{w}'_p\mathbf{1}] + \frac{1}{3}\delta_3\left[m^3(R_p) - \mathbf{w}'_p\Sigma_p\right] \quad (A12.17)$$

where δ_1, δ_2 and δ_3 are the Lagrange coefficients.

The first-order conditions are:

$$\begin{cases} \dfrac{\partial L}{\partial \mathbf{w}'_p} = \Omega\mathbf{w}_p + \delta_1\mathbf{E} + \delta_2\mathbf{1} + \delta_3\Sigma_p \\[2mm] \dfrac{\partial L}{\partial \delta_1} = E(R_p) - \mathbf{w}'_p\mathbf{E} \\[2mm] \dfrac{\partial L}{\partial \delta_2} = 1 - \mathbf{w}'_p\mathbf{1} \\[2mm] \dfrac{\partial L}{\partial \delta_3} = m^3(R_p) - \mathbf{w}'_p\Sigma_p \end{cases} \quad (A12.18)$$

Premultiplying (A12.17) by the inverse matrix of Ω and rearranging terms yields:

$$\mathbf{w}_p = \delta_1\Omega^{-1}\mathbf{E} + \delta_2\Omega^{-1}\mathbf{1} + \delta_3\Omega^{-1}\Sigma_p \quad (A12.19)$$

that is:

$$\mathbf{w}_p = \lambda_1\frac{\Omega^{-1}\mathbf{E}}{\mathbf{1}'\Omega^{-1}\mathbf{E}} + \lambda_2\frac{\Omega^{-1}\mathbf{1}}{\mathbf{1}'\Omega^{-1}\mathbf{1}} + \lambda_3\frac{\Omega^{-1}\Sigma_p}{\mathbf{1}'\Omega^{-1}\Sigma_p} \quad (A12.20)$$

with:

$$\begin{cases} \lambda_1 = \delta_1\mathbf{1}'\Omega^{-1}\mathbf{E} \\ \lambda_2 = \delta_2\mathbf{1}'\Omega^{-1}\mathbf{1} \\ \lambda_3 = \delta_3\mathbf{1}'\Omega^{-1}\Sigma_p \end{cases}$$

and:

$$\lambda_1 + \lambda_2 + \lambda_3 = 1 \qquad\qquad \square$$

APPENDIX 12.5

When a risk-free asset exists, the vector of asset weights of any efficient portfolio is a linear combination of those of the risk-free asset and of the two following distinct risky funds:

$$w_{a_4} = \frac{\Omega^{-1}(\mathbf{E} - R_f \mathbf{1})}{\mathbf{1}'\Omega^{-1}(\mathbf{E} - R_f \mathbf{1})} \quad \text{and} \quad w_{a_5} = \frac{\Omega^{-1}\Sigma_p}{\mathbf{1}'\Omega^{-1}\Sigma_p} \tag{A12.21}$$

Proof. If we introduce a risk-free asset, the investor's programme becomes:

$$\min_{\mathbf{w}_p}\{\tfrac{1}{2}\mathbf{w}'_p\Omega\mathbf{w}_p\} \tag{A12.22}$$

$$\text{s.t.} \quad \begin{cases} \mathbf{w}'_p\mathbf{E} + (1 - \mathbf{w}'_p\mathbf{1})R_f = E(R_p) \\ \mathbf{w}'_p\Sigma_p = m^3(R_p) \end{cases}$$

Using the same approach as previously, we obtain:

$$\mathbf{w}_p = \delta'_1\Omega^{-1}(\mathbf{E} - R_f\mathbf{1}) + \delta'_2\Omega^{-1}\Sigma_p \tag{A12.23}$$

where δ'_1 and δ'_2 are the Lagrange coefficients.
  That is:

$$\mathbf{w}_p = \lambda_4\frac{\Omega^{-1}(\mathbf{E} - R_f\mathbf{1})}{\mathbf{1}'\Omega^{-1}(\mathbf{E} - R_f\mathbf{1})} + \lambda_5\frac{\Omega^{-1}\Sigma_p}{\mathbf{1}'\Omega^{-1}\Sigma_p} \tag{A12.24}$$

with:

$$\begin{cases} \lambda_4 = \delta'_1\mathbf{1}'\Omega^{-1}(\mathbf{E} - R_f\mathbf{1}) \\ \lambda_5 = \delta'_2\mathbf{1}'\Omega^{-1}\Sigma_p \end{cases}$$

and

$$\mathbf{w}_{a_6} = 1 - \mathbf{w}'_p\mathbf{1} = 1 - \lambda_4 - \lambda_5 \qquad \qquad \square$$

APPENDIX 12.6

In the absence of a risk-free asset, the three-moment CAPM relation is written as:

$$\mathbf{E} - E(R_{Z_0}) = \left[\frac{E(R_p) - E(R_{Z_1})}{\sigma^2(R_p)}\right]\Omega\mathbf{w}_p + \left[\frac{E(R_{Z_1}) - E(R_{Z_0})}{m^3(R_p)}\right]\Sigma_p \tag{A12.25}$$

Proof. The vector $(N \times 1)$ of the covariances between the return of a portfolio p and the returns of the N risky assets is $\Omega\mathbf{w}_p$. Consequently, using the first equation in (A12.18) we obtain:

$$\Omega\mathbf{w}_p = \delta_1\mathbf{E} + \delta_2\mathbf{1} + \delta_3\Sigma_p \tag{A12.26}$$

which can be rewritten, if we assume that $\delta_1 \neq 0$ (*i.e.* the variance constraint is binding), as:

$$\mathbf{E} = \theta_{p_1}\mathbf{\Omega}\mathbf{w}_p + \theta_{p_2}\mathbf{1} + \theta_{p_3}\mathbf{\Sigma}_p \qquad (A12.27)$$

where:

$$\begin{cases} \theta_{p_1} = (\delta_1)^{-1} \\ \theta_{p_2} = -(\delta_2/\delta_1) \\ \theta_{p_3} = -(\delta_3/\delta_1) \end{cases}$$

To determine the values of the parameters θ_{p_1}, θ_{p_2} and θ_{p_3}, we premultiply (A12.26) by the transpose vectors $\mathbf{w}'_p$, $\mathbf{w}'_{Z_0}$ and $\mathbf{w}'_{Z_1}$, denoting respectively the $(N \times 1)$ vector of portfolio weights for the efficient portfolio p, the $(N \times 1)$ vector of portfolio weights for a portfolio Z_0 whose return is uncorrelated with the return of the portfolio p and which possesses a zero-coskewness with it and the $(N \times 1)$ vector of portfolio weights for a portfolio Z_1 whose return is uncorrelated with the return of that portfolio p and which possesses a unitary relative coskewness with it.[43] We thus obtain:

$$\begin{cases} E(R_p) = \theta_{p_1}\sigma^2(R_p) + \theta_{p_2} + \theta_{p_3}m^3(R_p) \\ E(R_{Z_0}) = \theta_{p_2} \\ E(R_{Z_1}) = \theta_{p_2} + \theta_{p_3}m^3(R_p) \end{cases} \qquad (A12.28)$$

The resolution of this system for θ_{p_1}, θ_{p_2} and θ_{p_3} gives:

$$\begin{cases} \theta_{p_1} = \left[\dfrac{E(R_p) - E(R_{Z_1})}{\sigma^2(R_p)} \right] \\ \theta_{p_2} = E(R_{Z_0}) \\ \theta_{p_3} = \left[\dfrac{E(R_{Z_1}) - E(R_{Z_0})}{m^3(R_p)} \right] \end{cases} \qquad (A12.29)$$

Substituting these values in (A12.27) leads to the desired result.   □

APPENDIX 12.7

In the absence of a risk-free asset, the asset's risk *premium* of a *Pareto-optimal* equilibrium is given by the equation:

$$\mathbf{E} - E(R_{Z_0})\mathbf{1} = [E(R_m) - E(R_{Z_1})]\boldsymbol{\beta} + [E(R_{Z_1}) - E(R_{Z_0})]\boldsymbol{\gamma} \qquad (A12.30)$$

Proof. The study of the properties of the mean–variance–skewness frontier showed that any efficient portfolio p—that does not belong to the variance–skewness efficient set—must satisfy the following equality:

$$\mathbf{E} - E(R_{Z_0})\mathbf{1} = \left[\dfrac{E(R_p) - E(R_{Z_1})}{\sigma^2(R_p)} \right]\mathbf{\Omega}\mathbf{w}_p + \left[\dfrac{E(R_{Z_1}) - E(R_{Z_0})}{m^3(R_p)} \right]\mathbf{\Sigma}_p \qquad (A12.31)$$

---

[43] That is:

$$Cos(R_p, R_{Z_1}) = m^3(R_p)$$

with $\{[E(R_p) - E(R_{Z_1})]/\sigma^2(R_p)]\} > 0$ and $\{[E(R_{Z_1}) - E(R_{Z_0})]/m^3(R_p)\} < 0$, where $E(R_p)$ is the expected return on the efficient portfolio p and $E(R_{Z_0})$ and $E(R_{Z_1})$ are the expected returns on portfolios uncorrelated with portfolio p which possess respectively a zero and a unitary relative coskewness with it.

Previously, we have established that when there exists a *Pareto-optimal* equilibrium allocation, the market portfolio must be efficient. Consequently, to obtain the relation (A12.30), it is sufficient to show that the market portfolio does not belong to the variance–skewness efficient frontier. This condition is always satisfied, unless we assume that all the traded assets possess the same expected return, which is in contradiction with our hypotheses of nonredundancy of the securities.   □

APPENDIX 12.8

If the asset returns conform to the quadratic market model, the systematic risk measures of the three-moment CAPM are a linear combination of the coefficients of the quadratic DGP.

Proof. Consider the quadratic market model:

$$\begin{cases} \mathbf{R}_t - R_f \mathbf{1} = \alpha_0 + \alpha_1(R_{mt} - R_f) + \alpha_2[R_{mt} - E(R_m)]^2 + \varepsilon_t \\ E(\varepsilon_t) = \mathbf{0} \\ E(\varepsilon_t|R_{mt}) = E(\varepsilon_t|R_{mt}^2) = \mathbf{0} \end{cases} \quad (A12.32)$$

where $\mathbf{R}_t$ is the $(N \times 1)$ vector of the returns of risky assets, α_0 is the $(N \times 1)$ vector of asset return intercepts, α_1 and α_2 are respectively the $(N \times 1)$ vector of asset return sensitivities with the market portfolio return and with the squared market portfolio return and ε_t is the $(N \times 1)$ vector of asset return disturbances.

Subtracting the expected value of (A12.32) from (A12.32) gives:

$$\mathbf{R}_t - \mathbf{E} = \alpha_1[R_{mt} - E(R_m)] + \alpha_2[R_{mt} - E(R_m)]^2 - \sigma^2(R_m) + \varepsilon_t \quad (A12.33)$$

Using the definition of the relative risk measures β and γ, we obtain the desired result, that is:

$$\begin{cases} \beta = \alpha_1 + \alpha_2 \dfrac{m^3(R_m)}{\sigma^2(R_m)} \\ \gamma = \alpha_1 + \alpha_2 \dfrac{\kappa^4(R_m) - [\sigma^2(R_m)]^2}{m^3(R_m)} \end{cases} \quad (A12.34)$$

□

APPENDIX 12.9

If asset returns conform to the quadratic market model and when standard APT hypotheses are met, the expected return on a large diversified portfolio, denoted $E(R_2)$, perfectly correlated with the squared orthogonolised component of the market return v_{mt}^2, has to verify the following inequality:

$$E(R_2) < E(v_m^2) \quad (A12.35)$$

Proof. Consider a large well-diversified portfolio p, with zero net investment, $\alpha_{1p}^* = 0$ and $\alpha_{2p}^* = 1$. From the APT, we obtain:

$$E(R_p) = E(R_2) \quad (A12.36)$$

Due to the perfect correlation of the well-diversified portfolio p with the factor (v_{mt}^2), it is possible to express the return of this portfolio, conditional on the market return, as:

$$E(R_p|R_{mt}) = \alpha_{0p}^* + v_{mt}^2 \qquad (A12.37)$$

Taking the expected value of this expression yields:

$$E[E(R_p|R_{mt})] = E(R_p) = \alpha_{0p}^* + E(v_m^2) \qquad (A12.38)$$

That is:

$$\alpha_{0p}^* = E(R_2) - E(v_m^2) \qquad (A12.39)$$

Substituting this expression in (A12.37), we obtain:

$$E(R_p|R_{mt}) = E(R_2) - E(v_m^2) + v_{mt}^2 \qquad (A12.40)$$

When $E(R_2) < E(v_m^2)$ does not hold, these returns are always non-negative and then no market equilibrium is possible.   □

APPENDIX 12.10

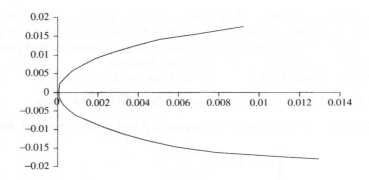

This figure represents the simulated *minimum* variance frontier in the plane mean–variance obtained using bootstrapped random weights relative to five index returns (MSCI USA in EUR, MSCI Europe in EUR, MSCI Asia–Pacific—excluded Japan—in EUR, MSCI Emerging Markets in EUR, MSCI Japan in EUR) observed on a weekly frequency for the period January 1997 to July 2000. Short sales have been forbidden in this example.

Figure A12.1   Simulated *minimum* variance frontier in the plane mean–variance

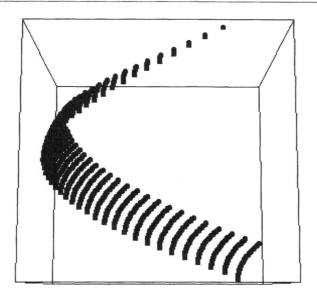

This figure represents the simulated *minimum* variance frontier in the space mean–variance–skewness, obtained using bootstrapped random weights relative to five index returns (MSCI USA in EUR, MSCI Europe in EUR, MSCI Asia–Pacific—excluded Japan—in EUR, MSCI Emerging Markets in EUR, MSCI Japan in EUR) observed on a weekly frequency for the period January 1997 to July 2000. Short sales have been forbidden in this example.

Figure A12.2   Simulated *minimum* variance frontier in the space mean–variance–skewness

This figure represents the simulated minimum variance frontier in the space mean-variance-skewness, computed using bootstrapped quantum weights relative to six index returns (MSCI USA in BLM, MSCI EMU in BLM, MSCI Asia-Pacific excluding Japan in EUR, MSCI Emerging Markets in EUR, MSCI Japan in EUR) observed on a weekly frequency for the period from 1991 to July 2008. Short sales have been forbidden in this example.

Figure 5.2.2. *Simulated minimum variance frontier in the space mean-variance-skewness*

13

Stress-testing Correlations: An Application to Portfolio Risk Management[1]

FRÉDÉRICK BOURGOIN

ABSTRACT

The implication of the Long Term Capital Management crisis in August 1998 made people aware of the potential pitfalls inherent in every risk management system. The financial crisis was not predicted by any system. It is only now that people are trying to come up with solutions in order to take these extreme events into account in their risk systems using extreme value theory or stress testing. The aim of this paper is to focus on the latter method.

We provide evidence of correlation breakdown from the period of August to October 1998 by using weighted-decay and multivariate GARCH models and apply these techniques to Merrill Lynch US Treasuries and the US High Yield Indexes. We present a methodology to stress the general level of correlation within a portfolio by using a method introduced by Finger (1997), the so-called average "implied" correlation. We provide new results for the boundaries of that important number and show the implication for portfolio management using JP Morgan's Government Bond Index as an example. We then generalise further and show two methods to overcome the problems that one encounters when stressing individual correlations within the correlation matrix. This enables us to obtain a consistent correlation matrix needed to calculate the VaR and/or the tracking error of a portfolio under stress scenarios. Finally, we discuss the implications for portfolio risk management.

13.1 THE FALL OF LTCM AND THE CREDIT CRISIS OF AUGUST 1998

This section will present the simplest case of stressing VaR with a two-asset portfolio. During the summer of 1998, the famous hedge fund Long Term Capital Management (LTCM) went bust. As reported in Dunbar (1998) and Jorion (1999), one of the main reasons explaining the fall of LTCM was that they were playing spread narrowing bets in the US:

---

[1] The views expressed herein are those of the author and do not necessarily reflect the views of Barclays Global Investors. The author retains responsibility for any errors.

Developments in Forecast Combination and Portfolio Choice. Edited by C. Dunis, A. Timmermann and J. Moody.
© 2001 John Wiley & Sons Ltd

- Long High Yield Market/Mortgage Backed Securities;
- Short US Treasuries.

In most cases, hedging the interest rate risk of a high yield position with US Treasury futures to end up with only spread risk works **until** there is a correlation breakdown. This means that the assumed strong positive correlation between the two assets is breaking down and going negative. In that case, instead of hedging interest rate risk, it is compounding! For illustration, we take a two-asset (index) portfolio: the Merrill Lynch All High Yield Index and the Merrill Lynch US Treasuries Benchmark. As we can see from Figure 13.1, most of the time the correlation between US Treasury yields and high yields seems positive, until August 1998. In August 1998, both yields go in opposite directions because:

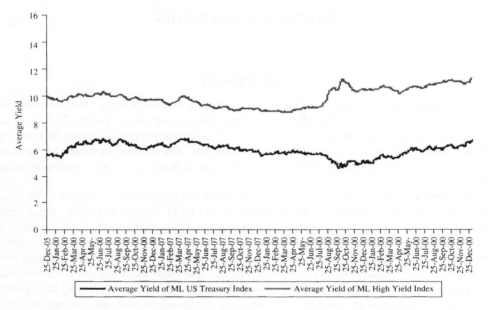

Figure 13.1   Average yield of Merril Lynch High Yield Index and US Treasuries Index

- US Treasuries became the "safest security" to hold during the panic;
- The Credit Market went into a liquidity crisis at the same time because major investors were liquidating their credit positions without any buyers.

To measure the correlation breakdown that occurred during that period, we use a diagonal multivariate GARCH model[2] with the following specification:

$$\text{vech}(H_t)' = \begin{vmatrix} h_{11,t} \\ h_{12,t} \\ h_{22,t} \end{vmatrix} = \begin{vmatrix} \omega_{11} \\ \omega_{12} \\ \omega_{22} \end{vmatrix} + \begin{vmatrix} \alpha_{11} & 0 & 0 \\ 0 & \alpha_{12} & 0 \\ 0 & 0 & \alpha_{22} \end{vmatrix} \cdot \begin{vmatrix} \varepsilon_{1,t-1}^2 \\ \varepsilon_{1,t-1}\varepsilon_{2,t-1} \\ \varepsilon_{2,t-1}^2 \end{vmatrix}$$

$$+ \begin{vmatrix} \beta_{11} & 0 & 0 \\ 0 & \beta_{12} & 0 \\ 0 & 0 & \beta_{22} \end{vmatrix} \cdot \begin{vmatrix} h_{11,t-1} \\ h_{12,t-1} \\ h_{22,t-1} \end{vmatrix}$$

---

[2] See Bollerslev *et al.* (1992).

where $\varepsilon_{1,t}$ is the yield difference of the Merrill Lynch US Treasuries Index and $\varepsilon_{2,t}$ is the yield difference of the Merrill Lynch High Yield Index; vech is the vector-half operator that transforms a triangular matrix into a vector.

In order to calculate the conditional correlation from a GARCH model, we need to apply the correlation formula to the time-varying elements above:

$$\rho_{12,t} = \frac{h_{12,t}}{\sqrt{h_{11,t}}\sqrt{h_{22,t}}}$$

The graph in Figure 13.2 shows the impact of correlation estimation calculated with a one-year rolling estimation period versus the above diagonal GARCH. Figure 13.2 shows the obvious lagging effect of using an unconditional estimator of the correlation between the two assets. This emphasises how important is the methodology used to calculate correlation. This is very well documented in the literature.[3] The rolling window estimator is dropping during the crisis from 0.6 to 0.3 but is still positive and that means that by playing a long and short strategy we are still diversifying risk (respectively long/short position of negatively/positively correlated asset) where in reality we are not because the GARCH correlation is dropping from 0.4 to -0.4!

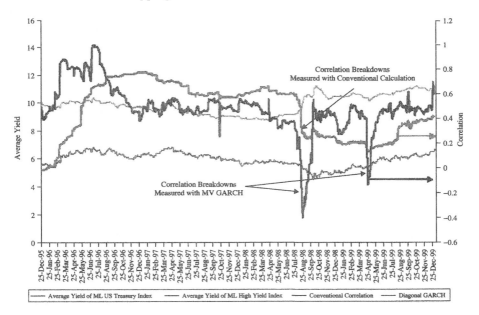

Figure 13.2   Average yield of Merril Lynch High Yield Index and US Treasuries Index with correlation

To show the impact of a correlation breakdown we construct a portfolio consisting of a long position of 1,000,000 USD of High Yield Securities and a short position of 1,000,000 USD in the Treasury Market. A positive correlation between the two-asset classes does not mean reducing the risk going forward (when a short position is held in this asset). In this case, what was done was to hedge the government bond risk inherent in a credit

---

[3] See Alexander (1998).

exposure to be left with only credit spread exposure. This was working fine before the crisis as the VaR of both portfolios was very similar, but when everything went wrong the VaR of the portfolio increased by 50%! (Figure 13.3).

In Figure 13.4, we can see that the VaR of a portfolio can be very different depending on which risk model one uses (conventional rolling, RiskMetrics[4], GARCH).

The impact on the P/L of this portfolio in this case is dramatic and the VaR should be able to reflect it (Figure 13.5). If we look at the returns from the following strategies:

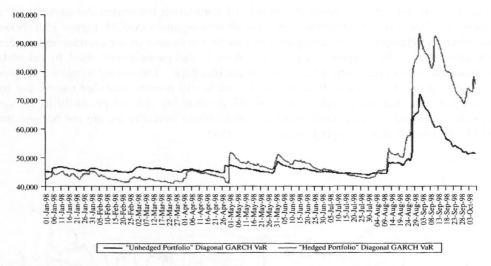

Figure 13.3   Value at Risk (VaR) of two portfolios: Unhedged Credit Exposure and "Interest Rate Hedged" Credit Exposure

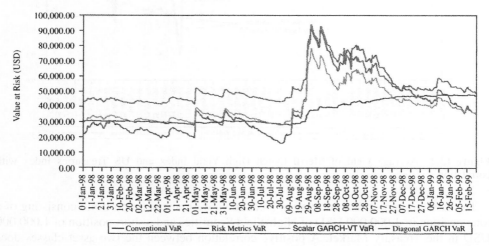

Figure 13.4   VaR in USD with different type of calculation for an "Interest Rate Hedged" Credit Exposure

---

[4] See JP Morgan (1995).

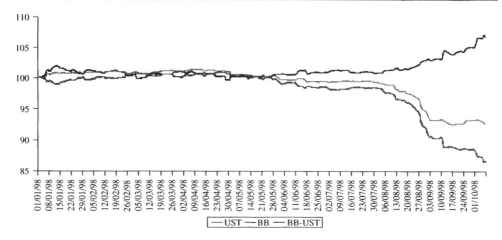

Figure 13.5   Price index of three strategies Long HY, Long UST and Long HY + Short UST

long US Treasuries, long credit and long credit + short US Treasuries, we can see that the impact that we saw on the VaR numbers is reflected in the P/L of each portfolio.

Since we know that it is not possible to forecast events like the August 1998 crisis, it is better to try to gauge what is the absolute maximum level of risk that our portfolio could be faced with by stressing the correlations and volatilities. The aim of this paper is to show this and to focus on the correlation structure because changing the volatilities is straightforward and does not require any special treatment.[5] The credit bet shown earlier is the simplest case, because there is just one correlation number to change, but as we will see the implication for portfolio management or VaR measurement is important.

If one stresses the correlation between US Treasuries and the High Yield market before the crisis, one could see that the risk of the portfolio is increasing in absolute terms, and that the potential risk on the upside is more and more limited because the assets are decorrelating quickly (Figure 13.2).

The graph in Figure 13.6 shows the daily impact on the VaR of the portfolio when the correlation is changed arbitrarily from −1 to 1 (the band defines the effect of the correlation changes). Assuming the volatility stays the same, we can see that the current VaR is moving slowly towards the upper band of the interval before the crisis. From this observation, we can define a "crisis indicator" (or concentration risk indicator) which can be defined as the ratio of the current VaR (or volatility) of the portfolio divided by the maximum VaR (or volatility) if all the correlations are against the portfolio (in that case −1 if short the asset, +1 if long the asset). The graph in Figure 13.7 shows the crisis indicator for the LTCM US credit bet.

In the next section, we will extend the concept of stressing correlation to an n-asset portfolio and show that the average "implied" level of correlation in the portfolio is an elegant tool to assess correlation risk. We will show that the crisis indicator defined earlier is linked to this average "implied" correlation.

---

[5] This will be shown later in the paper.

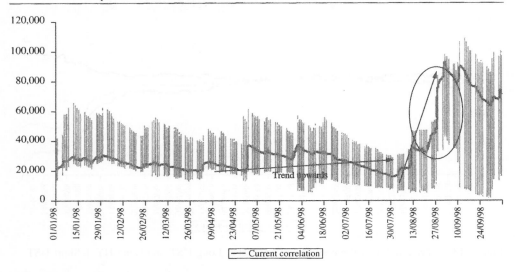

Figure 13.6   Stressing portfolio VaR

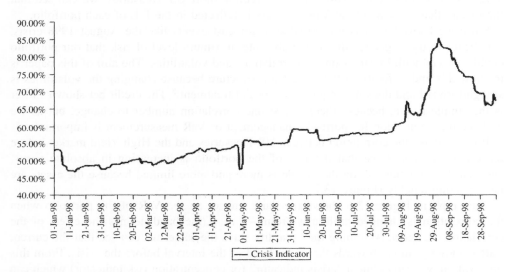

Figure 13.7   Crisis Indicator: VaR/(maximum VaR with correlation breakdown)

13.2   STRESSING THE GENERAL LEVEL OF CORRELATION OF A GIVEN PORTFOLIO

13.2.1   The Average "Implied" Correlation

In the previous section, we saw with the LTCM example that it is useful to stress the correlation assumption in order to provide a more accurate picture of the worst-case diversification scenario. The aim of this section is to provide an easy way to stress the correlation matrix of a portfolio by using the concept introduced by Finger (2000) of an average "implied" correlation coefficient within a given portfolio and use this to stress the relative (tracking error) and absolute Value at Risk of a portfolio. An applied example will be shown using the JP Morgan Government Bond Index.

In the general case, we have the following:

$$x'_B = \text{benchmark weights} = |x_{1,B}, \ldots, x_{N,B}|$$

$$x'_P = \text{portfolio weights} = |x_{1,P}, \ldots, x_{N,P}|$$

$$\Omega = \begin{vmatrix} 1 & \rho_{1,2} & \cdots & & \rho_{1,N} \\ \rho_{2,1} & 1 & \ddots & & \vdots \\ \vdots & \ddots & 1 & & \rho_{N-1,N} \\ \rho_{N,1} & \cdots & & \rho_{N,N-1} & 1 \end{vmatrix}$$

$$\Sigma = |\sigma_1 \quad \cdots \quad \sigma_N|$$

where Ω is the correlation matrix of all the assets in the portfolio (the subscript t is not written for simplification purposes) and Σ is the vector of the volatilities of each of the assets.

So, the variance of the portfolio is given by:

$$\sigma_P^2 = \sum_{i=1}^{N} x_{i,P}^2 \sigma_i^2 + \sum_{i=1}^{N} \sum_{j \neq i} x_{i,P} x_{j,P} \rho_{i,j} \sigma_i \sigma_j$$

or

$$\sigma_P^2 = (x_P)' \Theta (x_P)$$

with $\Theta_{ij} = \Omega_{ij} \sigma_i \sigma_j$. If the correlations in the portfolio are perfect (100%) then:

$$\sigma_{P,\text{perfect correlation}}^2 = \sum_{i=1}^{N} x_{i,P}^2 \sigma_i^2 + \sum_{i=1}^{N} \sum_{j \neq i} x_{i,P} x_{j,P} \sigma_i \sigma_j$$

If all the assets in the portfolio are independent then we have the following:

$$\sigma_{P,\text{zero correlation}}^2 = \sum_{i=1}^{N} x_{i,P}^2 \sigma_i^2$$

Let us assume that instead of having $n(n-1)/2$ correlation coefficients within the correlation matrix we have one number that is constant, hence $\rho_{i,j} = \rho$. Because we know the portfolio weights, the asset volatilities and the overall portfolio volatility we can solve the following equation for ρ:

$$\sigma_P^2 = \sum_{i=1}^{N} x_{i,P}^2 \sigma_i^2 + \rho \sum_{i=1}^{N} \sum_{j \neq i} x_{i,P} x_{j,P} \sigma_i \sigma_j$$

$$\implies \sum_{i=1}^{N} x_{i,P}^2 \sigma_i^2 + \rho \sum_{i=1}^{N} \sum_{j \neq i} x_{i,P} x_{j,P} \sigma_i \sigma_j = \sum_{i=1}^{N} x_{i,P}^2 \sigma_i^2 + \sum_{i=1}^{N} \sum_{j \neq i} x_{i,P} x_{j,P} \rho_{i,j} \sigma_i \sigma_j$$

$$\iff \rho \sum_{i=1}^{N} \sum_{j \neq i} x_{i,P} x_{j,P} \sigma_i \sigma_j = \sum_{i=1}^{N} \sum_{j \neq i} x_{i,P} x_{j,P} \rho_{i,j} \sigma_i \sigma_j$$

$$\iff \rho = \frac{\sum_{i=1}^{N} \sum_{j \neq i} x_{i,P} x_{j,P} \rho_{i,j} \sigma_i \sigma_j}{\sum_{i=1}^{N} \sum_{j \neq i} x_{i,P} x_{j,P} \sigma_i \sigma_j} = \frac{\sigma_P^2 - \sigma_{P,\text{zero correlation}}^2}{\sigma_{P,\text{perfect correlation}}^2 - \sigma_{P,\text{zero correlation}}^2}$$

So the average "implied" correlation within a portfolio is a linear approximation of the variance of the portfolio between the minimum variance portfolio (to be justified later) and the maximum variance portfolio. Which means that the implied correlation within the portfolio cannot be negative, *i.e.* $0 \leqslant \rho \leqslant 1$.

Proof. The problem is the following. Suppose you have a correlation matrix as follows:

$$\Omega_1 = \begin{pmatrix} 1 & \rho & \cdots & \rho \\ \rho & 1 & \ddots & \vdots \\ \vdots & \ddots & 1 & \rho \\ \rho & \cdots & \rho & 1 \end{pmatrix} \quad \text{of size } n$$

With $|\rho| < 1$ obviously the problem is to demonstrate which constraints are required for Ω_1 to be <u>at least</u> semidefinite positive.

If we take the following matrix:

$$\Omega_2 = \begin{pmatrix} 0 & \rho & \cdots & \rho \\ \rho & 0 & \ddots & \vdots \\ \vdots & \ddots & 0 & \rho \\ \rho & \cdots & \rho & 0 \end{pmatrix} = \Omega_1 - I_n$$

we know that:

$$\sum_{i=1}^{n} \lambda_i = \sum_{i=1}^{n} \Omega_{2,ii} = 0$$

It is easy to demonstrate that Ω_2 has an eigenvalue ρ of multiplicity $(n-1)$. It then follows that the last eigenvalue of the matrix is:

$$\lambda_{1,\dots,n-1} = -\rho$$

$$\lambda_n = (n-1)\rho$$

Now we need to find the eigenvalues of the matrix Ω_1.

Recall $Ax = \lambda x \Rightarrow |A - \lambda I| = 0$, then:

$$|A - \lambda I|x = |A - kI - (\lambda - k)I|x$$
$$\Longrightarrow (A - kI)x = (\lambda - k)x$$

If the vector λ is the set of eigenvalues of A, then $\lambda - k$ is the set of eigenvalues of $A - kI$, $\lambda_i(A - kI) = \lambda_i(A) - k$.

We know that $\Omega_1 = \Omega_2 + kI$ with $k = 1$, so the eigenvalues of Ω_1 are the following:

$$\lambda_{1,\dots,n-1} = 1 - \rho$$
$$\lambda_n = \lambda_{min} = 1 + (n - 1)\rho$$

Since we must ensure that the correlation matrix is <u>at least</u> semidefinite positive ($\lambda_i \geqslant 0 \ \forall i$), we need the following constraints:

$$\rho \leqslant 1 \text{ and } \rho \geqslant \frac{-1}{n - 1}$$

If we assume that there is a single implied correlation coefficient within the portfolio, stressing the correlation must be within these boundaries:

$$\frac{-1}{n - 1} < \rho_{stress} < 1 \Longrightarrow \rho_{min} < \rho < 1$$

That is why the implied average correlation of a portfolio is always between zero and one when the number of assets tends to be large, mathematically:

$$\lim_{n \to +\infty} \rho_{min} \longrightarrow 0$$

$\square$

13.2.2 Average "Implied" Correlation and the Crisis Indicator

In Section 13.1, we saw that the Crisis Indicator (CI) defined as the current VaR divided by the maximum VaR of the portfolio is a good indicator of adverse correlation risk embedded in the portfolio. We can show how the average "implied" correlation and the CI link with each other:

$$CI = \frac{\sigma_P^2}{\sigma_{perfect \ correlation}^2}$$

We know now that we can define the variance of the portfolio with ρ, the average "implied" correlation in the portfolio.[6] The rest follows easily:

$$CI = \frac{\sum_{i=1}^{N} x_{i,P}^2 \sigma_i^2 + \rho \sum_{i=1}^{N} \sum_{j \neq i} x_{i,P} x_{j,P} \sigma_i \sigma_j}{\sigma_{perfect \ correlation}^2}$$

---

[6] The implied correlation for a two-asset problem equals the correlation between the two assets.

$$= \frac{\sum_{i=1}^{N} x_{i,P}^2 \sigma_i^2 + \rho(\sigma_{\text{perfect correlation}}^2 - \sigma_{\text{zero correlation}}^2)}{\sigma_{\text{perfect correlation}}^2}$$

$$= \frac{\sigma_{\text{zero correlation}}^2 + \rho(\sigma_{\text{perfect correlation}}^2 - \sigma_{\text{zero correlation}}^2)}{\sigma_{\text{perfect correlation}}^2}$$

$$= \rho + \frac{\sigma_{\text{zero correlation}}^2 - \rho\sigma_{\text{zero correlation}}^2}{\sigma_{\text{perfect correlation}}^2}$$

$$= \rho + (1-\rho)\frac{\sigma_{\text{zero correlation}}^2}{\sigma_{\text{perfect correlation}}^2} = \rho(1) + (1-\rho)\left(\frac{\sigma_{\text{zero correlation}}^2}{\sigma_{\text{perfect correlation}}^2}\right)$$

We can see that the crisis indicator is a weighted average of one (perfect correlation) and the ratio of the variance of the portfolio with zero correlation and the variance of the portfolio with perfect correlation. The weighting scheme is the average "implied" correlation in the portfolio. This indicator is then quite easy to calculate. Using the LTCM example we can see clearly the relationship between the crisis indicator and the average "implied" correlation (Figure 13.8).

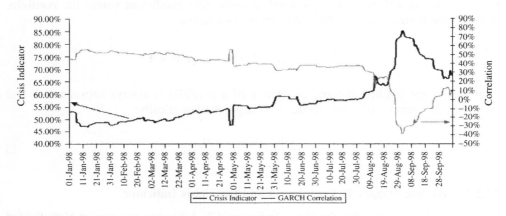

Figure 13.8   Crisis Indicator: VaR/(maximum VaR with correlation breakdown)

13.2.3   Average "Implied" Correlation and Portfolio Risk Management Implications

The tracking error of a portfolio given a benchmark is the relative risk of the portfolio versus the benchmark portfolio; the analogy with the VaR is straightforward. The Value at Risk of a portfolio is the expected loss of the portfolio at a specified probability percentage given the market conditions (market volatilities and correlations), and the annualised tracking error multiplied by 1.65 is the expected relative underperformance that the portfolio can suffer versus the benchmark over a year horizon with 5% probability (assuming normality). One is in absolute space (VaR) and the other is in relative space (benchmark space, the tracking error). We will show how the correlation affects the tracking error of a two-asset portfolio (for simplification purposes) and present the sensitivity analysis. We will use the JP Morgan Government Bond Index (13 countries) hedged and unhedged in USD in order to show what are the implications of being short the Japanese bond market in the global index. This trade has been the consensus view among a lot of investors benchmarked against global government bonds.

For a two-asset portfolio we have the following:

$$TE^2 = (x_{1,P} - x_{1,B})^2\sigma_1^2 + (x_{2,P} - x_{2,B})^2\sigma_2^2 + 2\rho\sigma_1\sigma_2(x_{1,P} - x_{1,B})(x_{2,P} - x_{2,B})$$

If we assume that the volatilities are not too different from each other, we have the following:

$$TE^2 \approx (x_{1,P} - x_{1,B})^2\sigma^2 + (x_{2,P} - x_{2,B})^2\sigma^2 + 2\rho\sigma^2(x_{1,P} - x_{1,B})(x_{2,P} - x_{2,B})$$

$$\approx [(x_{1,P} - x_{1,B})^2 + (x_{2,P} - x_{2,B})^2 + +2\rho(x_{1,P} - x_{1,B})(x_{2,P} - x_{2,B})]\sigma^2$$

We know that because we are working in active space (relative to the benchmark), the following relationship holds:

$$(x_{1,P} - x_{1,B}) + (x_{2,P} - x_{2,B}) = 0$$

$$\Longleftrightarrow [(x_{1,P} - x_{1,B}) + (x_{2,P} - x_{2,B})]^2 = 0$$

$$\Longleftrightarrow (x_{1,P} - x_{1,B})^2 + (x_{2,P} - x_{2,B})^2 = -2(x_{1,P} - x_{1,B})(x_{2,P} - x_{2,B})$$

Substituting this into the tracking error equation:

$$TE^2 \approx [-2(x_{1,P} - x_{1,B})(x_{2,P} - x_{2,B}) + 2\rho(x_{1,P} - x_{1,B})(x_{2,P} - x_{2,B})]\sigma^2$$

$$\approx -2[1 - \rho](x_{1,P} - x_{1,B})(x_{2,P} - x_{2,B})\sigma^2 > 0$$

If we are underweight one asset, we are automatically overweight the other by the same amount, this means that the cross-product of the active weights is always negative in order to have a meaningful tracking error, hence:

$$-2(x_{1,P} - x_{1,B})(x_{2,P} - x_{2,B}) = 2(x_{1,P} - x_{1,B})^2$$

So the square of the tracking error is:

$$TE^2 \approx 2[1 - \rho](x_{1,P} - x_{1,B})^2\sigma^2 > 0$$

when $\rho < 1$. Otherwise all assets within the portfolio are identical and any bet of one asset against another asset is completely offsetting in risk terms, i.e. $TE = 0$.

Several remarks can be made.

• $\partial TE^2/\partial\rho = -2(x_{1,P} - x_{1,B})^2\sigma^2 < 0$: when the average implied correlation in the portfolio increases, the square of the tracking error (and the tracking error) decreases. This is due to the fact that the bets are increasingly identical. So if all correlations in the portfolio are perfectly positive $(+1)$ then the tracking error of the portfolio is equal to zero (the eigenvalue spectra of the correlation matrix has $n - 1$ eigenvalues equal to 0 and the first eigenvalue equal to the size of the matrix, i.e. n, because the trace of the matrix is n).

- $\partial TE^2/\partial\sigma = 4[1-\rho](x_{1,P}-x_{1,B})^2\sigma > 0$: when the average implied volatility within the portfolio increases, so does the tracking error (with square root scaling).
- $\partial TE^2/\partial(x_{1,P}-x_{1,B}) = 4[1-\rho](x_{1,P}-x_{1,B})\sigma^2 > 0$: if we increase the active bet in the portfolio, we will increase the tracking error by the same amount.

We will now apply this concept to the JP Morgan Government Bond Index. We present two cases (see Figure 13.9):

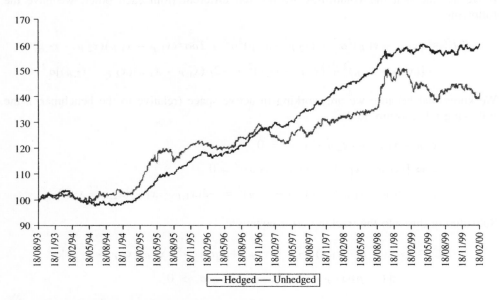

Figure 13.9 Total return index from JP Morgan Government Bond Index in USD

- the hedged benchmark (no currency risk);
- the unhedged benchmark (including currency risk).

On the one hand, it is obvious that the unhedged benchmark is a lot more volatile than the hedged benchmark. It is more risky to track the currency "exposed" benchmark than the hedged index because the currency volatilities are very high relative to the bond component of the benchmark. On the other hand, as we can see from Figure 13.10, the average "implied" correlation within the unhedged benchmark is lower than the hedged benchmark.

The RiskMetrics methodology is used to calculate the correlation matrix that is used to compute the average "implied" correlation in each index. At first sight we may think that the lower average implied correlation of the unhedged benchmark is better for the portfolio manager (everything else being equal) because there is more diversification, but in fact it is the opposite. Each relative bet versus the benchmark is magnified compared to the hedged benchmark. We demonstrated earlier that when assuming the relative bets are the same, decreases in the correlation increase the tracking error of the portfolio.

Figures 13.11 and 13.12 show the behaviour of the tracking error of a portfolio in which we take a short Japanese and a long world ex-Japan position. We then analyse the tracking error of this portfolio under different scenarios.

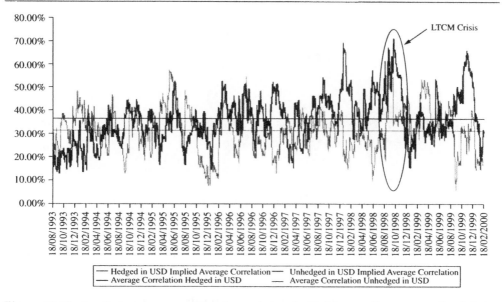

Figure 13.10 Implied average conditional correlation in JP Morgan Government Bond Index hedged and unhedged in USD and their long-term average

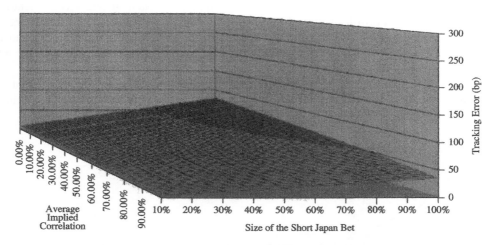

Figure 13.11 Tracking error as a function of the average "implied" correlation and the size of the Japan bet with a hedged benchmark

- By stressing the average "implied" correlation of the benchmark, we can assess the impact of a massive move of capital flow in the market like the flight to quality that happened during the LTCM crisis (see Figure 13.10).
- By increasing the size of the asset allocation bet out of Japan into world ex-Japan we can calculate the impact on the tracking error of the portfolio.

We can see that the remarks made above concerning the tracking error are still valid on an n-asset portfolio:

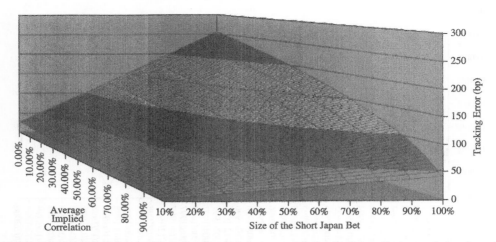

Figure 13.12 Tracking error as a function of the average "implied" correlation and the size of the Japan bet with an unhedged benchmark

- when the implied correlation decreases it increases the tracking error;
- the bigger the size of the bet the bigger the tracking error.

The implications for portfolio management are quite important: if one sets a tracking error target for the portfolio versus the benchmark, it is a fixed (not time-varying) target and in order to achieve an average level of tracking error equal to the target, one must dynamically adjust the bets within the portfolio in order to keep the tracking error as stable as possible.

Figures 13.13 and 13.14 stress the average "implied" correlation and the average volatility of each asset in the portfolio; the size of the bet out of Japanese bonds being equal to 10% and 50% respectively.

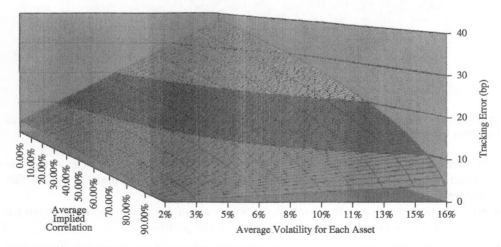

Figure 13.13 Tracking error as a function of the average "implied" correlation and the average volatility of each asset with a short Japanese bond position of 10% of the benchmark

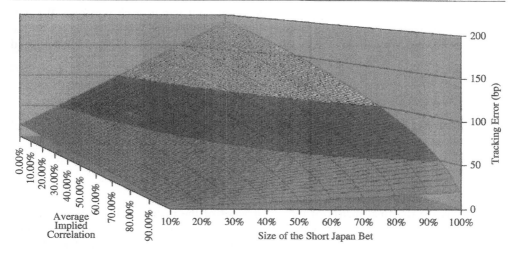

Figure 13.14   Tracking error as a function of the average "implied" correlation and the average volatility of each asset with a short Japanese bond position of 50% of the benchmark

13.3   STRESS-TESTING CORRELATION MATRICES

In the first section of this paper, we saw that being able to stress a correlation matrix could provide insight into what can happen if things go wrong. In Section 13.2, we provided the framework to stress the general level of correlation embedded in a portfolio. This section provides the framework in order to stress correlation matrices. For a two-asset portfolio, stressing the correlation matrix is straightforward, but for an n-asset portfolio with n greater than two (the only case worthwhile!) a major problem arises: the correlation matrix very quickly becomes inconsistent, $i.e.$ all the off-diagonal elements in a correlation matrix are bound together and changing a number is hardly possible without changing all the others too. A very good example is provided by Finger (1997). We will review the methods available and try to provide a framework to enhance them in the context of risk management.

The aim is to provide a correlation matrix that is <u>at least</u> semidefinite positive (SDP), which mean that regardless of the combination of assets in the portfolio, the variance of the portfolio will be guaranteed to be at least equal or greater than zero by construction, $i.e.$:

$$\sigma_P^2 = (x_P)'\Theta(x_P) \geqslant 0 \quad \forall x_P \neq 0 \quad \text{where} \quad \Theta_{ij} = \Omega_{ij}\sigma_i\sigma_j$$

Here, Σ is the vector of volatility and Ω is the correlation matrix of all assets in the portfolio. With a little bit of algebra we can show that in order to satisfy the condition above we need to have all the eigenvalues of the correlation matrix equal to or above zero, $i.e.$ $\lambda_i \geqslant 0 \quad \forall i = 1, \ldots, n$. This is the principle of the two methods we are going to show. They transform a nonpositive definite correlation matrix (most likely obtained after stressing individual correlations) into a positive definite one.

First, we will present two methods using this property (SDP) in order to obtain a self-consistent correlation matrix when we stress individual correlation coefficients inside a matrix. Second, we will provide a somewhat easier framework to stress correlation by using the concept of average "implied" correlation built within each portfolio. We will show that the average "implied" correlation has a suitable range that is dependent on the size of the matrix. We will then apply these methodologies to the JP Morgan Global Bond Index.

13.3.1 Spectral Decomposition

This method has been widely used in industry. See Best (1998) and Rebonato and Jackel (2000) for an earlier explanation of the method.

Let Ω be a correlation matrix. We can decompose Ω as:

$$\Omega = P\Lambda P^{-1} = P\Lambda P'$$

where Λ is the diagonal matrix of the eigenvalues of the matrix and P is the matrix of the associated eigenvectors. If Ω is well behaved, *i.e.* at least semidefinite positive, then if we use this matrix in a risk management framework, any combination of assets will yield a positive or null portfolio variance (and volatility). This is a necessary condition for a risk manager. To make sure that this is always the case, we must check that all the eigenvalues of Ω are at least positive or null.

If we stress the correlation structure within the matrix, we will most likely end up with a not semidefinite positive matrix, which can produce negative variance for particular portfolios.

The common procedure is as follows.

- Calculate the correlation matrix (flat weights, weighted-decay, multivariate GARCH, etc.).
- Calculate the associated eigenvalues and eigenvectors.
- If some eigenvalues are not positive, set them to zero, $\Lambda \Rightarrow \Lambda^*$.
- Calculate the "new" correlation matrix $\Omega^* = P\Lambda^*P'$.
- Rescale the new correlation matrix in order to have a diagonal of one:

$$\Omega^{**} = \Omega_{ij} \frac{1}{\sqrt{\Omega_{ii}^*}} \frac{1}{\sqrt{\Omega_{jj}^*}}$$

- The result is a semidefinite positive correlation matrix.

Let us take the JP Morgan Global Government Bond Index hedged in USD; there are 13 countries in the benchmark.

- Dollar Bloc:
  — Australia, Canada, United States
- Euro Bloc:
  — Belgium, France, Germany, Netherlands, Spain, Italy
- Non-Euro Bloc:
  — United Kingdom, Denmark, Sweden
- Japan

The correlation matrix calculated using a weighted-decay of 0.94 (RiskMetrics Daily Data parameter) at the end of February 2000 is:

	AUD	BEF	CAD	DKK	FRF	ITL	JPY	NLG	ESP	SEK	GBP	USD	DEM
AUD	1.00												
BEF	0.36	1.00											
CAD	0.50	0.46	1.00										
DKK	0.54	0.75	0.49	1.00									
FRF	0.50	0.85	0.48	0.76	1.00								
ITL	0.24	0.48	0.48	0.41	0.49	1.00							
JPY	0.06	−0.01	0.05	0.02	0.02	−0.09	1.00						
NLG	0.45	0.89	0.53	0.75	0.81	0.51	0.01	1.00					
ESP	0.34	0.51	0.26	0.56	0.59	0.45	−0.01	0.60	1.00				
SEK	0.32	0.41	0.40	0.52	0.31	0.45	0.01	0.48	0.40	1.00			
GBP	0.36	0.61	0.45	0.63	0.65	0.42	0.01	0.66	0.50	0.27	1.00		
USD	0.55	0.50	0.82	0.52	0.56	0.27	0.11	0.53	0.25	0.23	0.44	1.00	
DEM	0.41	0.84	0.42	0.75	**0.84**	0.47	−0.02	0.84	0.61	0.34	0.72	0.47	1.00

The correlation matrix is positive definite, *i.e.* self-consistent, or mathematically speaking all the eigenvalues of the matrix are strictly above zero. Let us assume the risk manager wants to change the correlation between France and Germany because he thinks a correlation of 84% is too low and instead uses 100%. This single change in the correlation structure renders the matrix unusable for risk management because the matrix is indefinite (not definite positive or negative, *i.e.* $\lambda_{min} < 0$ and $\lambda_{max} > 0$). If we filter the correlation matrix using the spectral decomposition proposed above, we will generate the well-behaved correlation matrix below (semidefinite positive):

	AUD	BEF	CAD	DKK	FRF	ITL	JPY	NLG	ESP	SEK	GBP	USD	DEM
AUD	1.00												
BEF	0.36	1.00											
CAD	0.50	0.46	1.00										
DKK	0.54	0.75	0.49	1.00									
FRF	0.49	0.84	0.48	0.76	1.00								
ITL	0.24	0.48	0.48	0.41	0.49	1.00							
JPY	0.06	−0.01	0.05	0.02	0.02	−0.09	1.00						
NLG	0.45	0.89	0.53	0.75	0.80	0.51	0.01	1.00					
ESP	0.34	0.51	0.26	0.56	0.59	0.45	−0.01	0.60	1.00				
SEK	0.32	0.41	0.40	0.52	0.31	0.45	0.01	0.48	0.40	1.00			
GBP	0.36	0.61	0.44	0.63	0.65	0.42	0.01	0.66	0.50	0.27	1.00		
USD	0.55	0.50	0.81	0.52	0.55	0.27	0.11	0.53	0.25	0.23	0.44	1.00	
DEM	0.41	0.83	0.42	0.75	**0.98**	0.47	−0.01	0.83	0.61	0.34	0.72	0.47	1.00

We can see that the correlation most affected by the algorithm is one that we just changed (Figure 13.15).

The main advantage is that we now have a correlation matrix that has changed according to our view of the market and that is self-consistent, which is crucial for portfolio optimisation or risk management purposes.

The main disadvantage of the standard methodology is that there is a linear combination of risky assets in the portfolio that yield a zero risk portfolio (cash)! This means that if the expected returns from this combination of assets differ from the cash return, there will be risk arbitrage opportunities![7]

The consequence is that we should avoid a correlation matrix that is semidefinite positive, and prefer a strictly positive definite correlation matrix! Effectively we need to

---

[7] See Ledoit (1998) for more details on risk arbitrage.

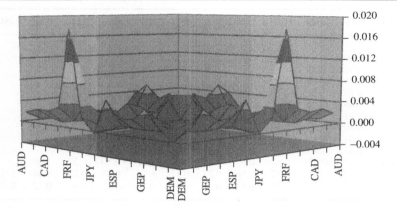

Figure 13.15   Changes implied by the algorithm

replace the negative eigenvalue not by zero but by a small positive number. How can we do this without disturbing the correlation matrix too much?

We know that the sum of eigenvalues of a correlation matrix is equal to the trace of the matrix and equal to n, so we have the following relationship:

$$\sum_{i=1}^{n} \lambda_i = \sum_{i=1}^{n} \Omega_{ii} = n$$

The first eigenvalue of the correlation matrix is equal to 6.88, which explains 63% of the total variance and can be interpreted as the world ex-Japan.[8]

We propose the following rule: we replace the zero in the common spectral filtration by a new number that is derived from the normal correlation matrix (before stressing the correlation matrix). Since the sum of the eigenvalues needs to equal n, the size of the matrix, we will subtract the residual from the largest eigenvalue. This is important because the smallest eigenvalue of the correlation matrix carries a lot of information regarding the risks of the market. Figure 13.16 shows the minimum eigenvalue calculated from a weighted-decay correlation matrix on a daily basis for the unhedged and hedged JPM GBI.

Several remarks can be made.

- When a crisis happens in the bond market it is reflected in the value of the minimum eigenvalue, *i.e.* the large positive changes in this value indicate a crisis or increased overall volatility in the market (of the less risky combination of assets).
- The crisis detected from the large changes of the minimum eigenvalue are synchronised with the increases in percentage of variance explained associated with this eigenvalue (see Figure 13.17).
- The trend of EURO convergence is very clear from the graph in Figure 13.16.
- Since we are replacing the minimum eigenvalue (negative) of the stressed correlation matrix by the minimum eigenvalue before stressing the correlations, we are in effect eliminating the risk of a riskless portfolio and false risk arbitrage opportunities created by altering the correlation matrix structure.

---

[8] This is due to the fact that Japanese bonds are uncorrelated with every other market.

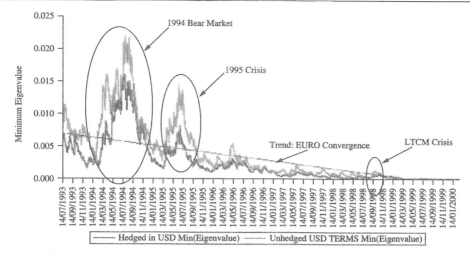

Figure 13.16 Conditional minimum eigenvalue for JP Morgan GBI unhedged hedged in USD from 14/07/1993 to 22/03/2000

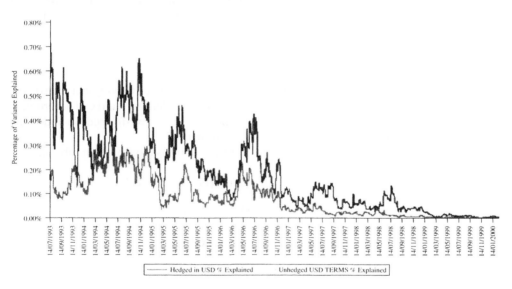

Figure 13.17 Percentage of variance explained by the minimum eigenvalue for JP Morgan GBI unhedged/hedged in USD from 14/07/1993 to 22/03/2000

13.3.2 Shrinkage Correction: The Rayleigh–Ritz Transform

Following in the footsteps of Kim and *et al.* (1999), let us define the following correlation matrices:

- Ω_0 is the correlation matrix before any correlation scenarios are applied;
- Ω is the inconsistent correlation matrix after the correlation scenarios are applied;
- Ω^* is the consistent correlation matrix after the correlation scenarios are applied.

Let us look at the properties of a correlation matrix Ω. We know that the matrix is real, symmetric and that all the eigenvalues are real. So Ω is hermitian and unitarily diagonisable, and we can rank the eigenvalues as:

$$\lambda_{\min} = \lambda_1 \leqslant \lambda_2 \leqslant \cdots \leqslant \lambda_N = \lambda_{\max}$$

From the Rayleigh–Ritz theorem, we know that the minimum and maximum eigenvalues of a hermitian matrix are the solution of the optimisation problem:

$$\lambda_{\max}(\Omega) = \max_{x \neq 0} \frac{x'\Omega x}{x'x} = \max_{x'x=1} x'\Omega x$$

$$\lambda_{\min}(\Omega) = \min_{x \neq 0} \frac{x'\Omega x}{x'x} = \min_{x'x=1} x'\Omega x$$

Let I be the identity matrix of the same dimension as Ω. We know that I is hermitian with all its eigenvalues identical and equal to 1. So I is a definite positive matrix. So what we need is to "shrink" the ill-conditioned correlation matrix to a correlation matrix that has the right properties (symmetric, real, positive definite). The literature of Bayesian shrinkage estimators is huge. Ledoit, Frost and Savarino to name a few in the context of portfolio management propose the following:

$$\Omega^* = (1 - \alpha)\Omega + \alpha I$$

where $\alpha \in [0, 1]$, so when α equals 0, there is no transformation of the original matrix and when α equals 1, the transformed matrix "shrinks" to the identity matrix. The problem that arises is the following: how do we know that we have transformed an indefinite correlation matrix into a positive definite correlation matrix?

Let us recall the fact that $\lambda_{\min}$ is the solution of the optimisation problem above:

$$\lambda_{\min}(\Omega^*) = \min_{x'x=1} x'\Omega^* x = \min_{x'x=1} x'[(1 - \alpha)\Omega + \alpha I]x$$

$$= \min_{x'x=1} [(1 - \alpha)x'\Omega x + \alpha x'I x]$$

$$= \min_{x'x=1} [(1 - \alpha)x'\Omega x + \alpha x'I x]$$

$$= (1 - \alpha) \min_{x'x=1} x'\Omega x + \alpha$$

$$= (1 - \alpha)\lambda_{\min}(\Omega) + \alpha$$

Now we can find the value of α that will make Ω^* at least semi positive definite:

$$\lambda_{\min}(\Omega^*) = (1 - \alpha)\lambda_{\min}(\Omega) + \alpha \geqslant 0$$

$$\Longleftrightarrow \alpha \geqslant \frac{-\lambda_{\min}(\Omega)}{1 - \lambda_{\min}(\Omega)}$$

As we stated in the previous paragraph, having α set to the value above is the limiting case (semidefinite positive correlation matrix). What we really need is to have the minimum

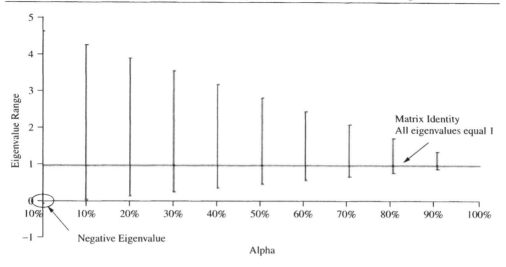

Figure 13.18   Eigenvalue shrinkage under Rayleigh–Ritz transform

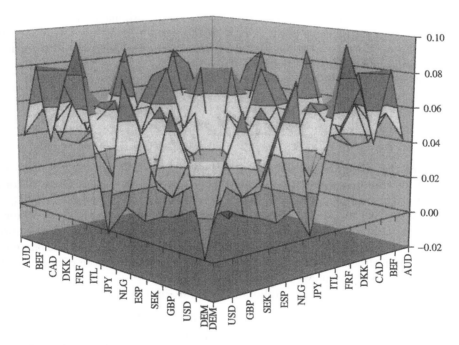

Figure 13.19   Changed implied by the Rayleigh–Ritz transform

eigenvalue set to the minimum eigenvalue of the correlation matrix before we applied any stress scenario to it:

$$\lambda_{min}(\Omega^*) = (1 - \alpha)\lambda_{min}(\Omega) + \alpha = \lambda_{min}(\Omega_0)$$

where Ω_0 is the original correlation matrix. We then have:

$$\alpha = \frac{\lambda_{\min}(\Omega_0) - \lambda_{\min}(\Omega)}{1 - \lambda_{\min}(\Omega)}$$

So we have the following consistent correlation matrix:

$$\Omega^* = \left(\frac{1 - \lambda_{\min}(\Omega_0)}{1 - \lambda_{\min}(\Omega)}\right)\Omega + \frac{\lambda_{\min}(\Omega_0) - \lambda_{\min}(\Omega)}{1 - \lambda_{\min}(\Omega)}I$$

We can see from the graph in Figure 13.18 that the higher the value of α, the tighter is the range of the eigenvalues. So instead of reducing only the percentage of explained variance of the "market factor" as in the spectral method, we reduce all the eigenvalues above unity and increase all those below unity.

Using the Rayleigh–Ritz method we obtain the changes in the correlation structure shown in Figure 13.19.

13.3.3 Comparison

In order to assess the impact of both transformations on the original correlation matrix Ω (not Ω_0), we use the Frobenius norm as in Kim *et al.* (1999), which will help us assess how close the new matrix is to the old and inconsistent one. This will help us assess which one of the methods is the most efficient.

Let us recall the Frobenius norm of a matrix Ω:

$$\|\Omega\| = \left(\sum_{i=1}^{n}\sum_{j=1}^{n}|\Omega_{ij}|^2\right)^{\frac{1}{2}}$$

To determine the distortion (in percentage terms) generated by an algorithm, we need to calculate the following ratio: $\Delta = \|\Omega^* - \Omega\|/\|\Omega\|$. When we measure the distortion generated by the spectral method on the previous example (JPM hedged in USD), the distortion Δ is equal to 2.45%; when we use the Rayleigh–Ritz method, the distortion is much higher at 8.56%. The changes implied by the Rayleigh–Ritz algorithm are more important (as shown in Figure 13.19), because the "shrinking" is operated across the whole correlation structure, whereas the spectral decomposition is more efficient because it is correcting only the required elements.

The implications in terms of portfolio management are important.

- The Rayleigh–Ritz method will tend to decrease the general level of correlation towards zero when we stress the level of correlation upwards, and vice versa. So the portfolio VaR will tend to be lower than expected by the changes applied to the correlation structure in the first place. On the other hand, if one manages portfolios against a benchmark, this will increase the tracking error of the portfolio.
- The spectral method is very efficient in correcting the inconsistencies of the correlation structure, so the portfolio VaR will tend to be closer to the "ideal" stress scenario envisaged in the first place. On the other hand, for relative risk purposes it will understate the risk compared to the Rayleigh–Ritz method.

The following table summarises our findings:

Stressing correlations	Implications in terms of VaR	Implications in terms of tracking error
Upwards	Spectral VaR > R–R VaR	Rayleigh–Ritz TE > spectral TE
Downwards	Spectral VaR > R–R VaR	Rayleigh–Ritz TE > Spectral TE

13.4   CONCLUSION

We have seen that the methodology used to calculate correlation could have a dramatic impact on the accuracy of the Value at Risk and/or the tracking error of a portfolio. But it is not the only key to a successful risk management system. When the variance/covariance approach is used in that context, it is useful to stress the correlation structure in order to provide insight regarding the portfolio risk exposures. We define a crisis indicator based on the ratio of the current risk divided by the maximum risk attainable with the current portfolio weights and volatilities. In order to stress the portfolio VaR or tracking error we provide two main solutions: stress either the general level of correlation within the portfolio or individual correlations. The first method requires the risk manager to stress only the general average "implied" correlation within the portfolio. We also provide the boundaries for this number and show how it is related to the crisis indicator. The second method is to stress individual correlations within the correlation matrix. We provide two ways to do it: the spectral and the shrinkage method and recommend which one to use in which context.

REFERENCES

Alexander, C. (1998). *Risk Management and Analysis Vol. 1, Measuring and Modelling Financial Risk*. New York: Wiley; p. 128.
Baba, Y., R.F. Engle, D. Kraft and K. Kroner (1989). "Multivariate Simultaneous Generalized ARCH", UCSD discussion paper.
Best, P. (1998). *Implementing Value at Risk*, New York: Wiley.
Bollerslev, T. (1986). "Generalized Autoregressive Conditional Heteroscedasticity", *Journal of Econometrics* **31**, 307–327.
Bollerslev, T., R.Y. Chou and K. Kroner (1992). "ARCH Modelling in Finance: A Review of the Theory and Empirical Evidence", *Journal of Econometrics* **52**, 5–59.
Bourgoin, F. (1999). "Large Scale Conditional Correlation Estimation". In C. Dunis (ed.), *Advances in Quantitative Asset Management*. Boston: Kluwer Academic; 139–178.
Dunbar, N. (1998). "Meriwether's Meltdown", *Risk Magazine* **October**, 32–36.
Engle, R.F. (1982). "Autoregressive Conditional Heteroscedasticity with Estimates of the Variance of UK Inflation", *Econometrica* **50**, 987–1008.
Engle, R.F. and K. Kroner (1995). "Multivariate Simultaneous GARCH", *Econometric Theory* **11**, 122–150.
Engle, R.F. and J. Mezrich (1995). "Grappling with GARCH", *Risk Magazine* **8**(9), 112–17.
Engle, R.F. and J. Mezrich (1996). "GARCH for Groups', *Risk Magazine* **9**(8), 36–40.
Finger, C.C. (1997). "A Methodology To Stress Correlations", *RiskMetrics Monitors 4th Quarter*, 3–11.
Finger, C.C. (2000). "Why is RMCI so low?", working paper no. 99-11, RiskMetrics Group.
Harville, D.A. (1997). *Matrix Algebra From a Statistician's Perspective*. New York: Springer.
Horn, R.A. and C.R. Johnson (1999a). *Matrix Analysis*. Cambridge: Cambridge University Press.
Horn, R.A. and C.R. Johnson (1999b). *Topics in Matrix Analysis*. Cambridge: Cambridge University Press.
Jorion, P. (1999). "Risk Management Lessons From Long-Term Capital Management", working paper, UC at Irvine.

JP Morgan (1995). *RiskMetrics Technical Document*, 4th edition www.riskmetrics.com.

Kim, J., A. Malz and J. Mina (1999). *Long Run Technical Document*. RiskMetrics © Group: 151–152.

Laloux, L., P. Cizeau, J.P. Bouchaud and M. Potters (1998). "Noise Dressing of Financial Correlation Matrices", Science & Finance working paper.

Ledoit, O. (1996). "A Well-conditioned Estimator For Large Dimensional Covariance Matrix", working paper, UCLA.

Ledoit, O. (1998). "Factor Selection for Beta Pricing Models", working paper, UCLA.

Ledoit, O. (1999). "Improved Estimation of the Covariance Matrix of Stock Returns with an Application to Portfolio Selection", working paper, UCLA.

Rebonato, R. and P. Jackel (2000). "The Most General Methodology for Creating a Valid Correlation Matrix for Risk Management and Option Pricing Purposes", *The Journal of Risk* **2**(2), 17–27.

INDEX

Oblique Classifier (OC1)   130, 131, 132, 137
one-tail Z test   129
output layer   123
percentage of variance explained (PVE) 127–9
Principal Components (PCs)   122
Probabilistic Neural Network (PNN)   130, 131, 132, 135
results   127–33
RIPPER Rule Induction (RRI) algorithm 130, 139
sigmoidal activation functions   123
variation   117, 118
Neural networks,
classification algorithms   86
forecasting models   29
PNN see Probabilistic Neural Network
predictability   82
Newton methods   123
Nikkei 225   xx, 22, 160, 179, 188, 189
Noise,
population-based algorithm   15, 17
pruning rule sets   94, 95
sampling error   7
Nonincreasing Absolute Risk Aversion (NIARA),
assumption   247
cubic utility function   246
utility class   243, 244
Nonspherical distributions   244
Nonstationarities,
data generation   7
exchange rate forecasts   47, 48, 50, 57
forecasting models   27
rolling samples   57
Normal distributions,
Capital Asset Pricing Model (CAPM) 239–40
Mean Lower Partial Moment (MLPM) 216, 217
mixture see Mixture of normal distributions
residual   xx
Normalisation,
discrimination   96
neural network linear (NN-PCA)   126
neural network nonlinear (NN-NLPCA) 126

Oblique Classifier (OC1),
annual returns   131, 132, 139
classification performance   130, 131, 137
composite classifiers   99
decision trees   91–4, 125
excess returns   132, 133, 141
high/low performing shares   82, 91–4, 125, 131, 132

hyperplanes   93–4
misclassification   126
neural network linear (NN-PCA)   130, 131, 132, 137
neural network nonlinear (NN-NLPCA) 130, 131, 132, 137
overfitting   97, 126
Principal Components Analysis (PCA) 130, 131, 132, 137
results   100–7, 110–20, 131, 132
OMX   22
Optimal trading performance, volatility of forecasts   9
Optimisation,
criterion risk   xviii, 3–26
dynamic investment model   215
Incremental Reduced Error Pruning   95
indirect see Indirect optimisation
joint see Joint optimisation
L-BFGS   126
Lower Partial Moment (LPM)   216, 217
portfolios see Portfolio optimisation
single see Single optimisation
SOFI see System Optimisation by Fusion of Information
Option pricing models, exchange rate forecasts   45, 46
Out-of-sample sets,
classification methods   97, 98, 100–7, 110–20
exchange rate forecasts   46, 47, 53, 54, 57–69, 78
forecasts fusion   63–9
population-based algorithm   17, 18
statistical arbitrage models   40, 41, 42
Outliers, long memory   xx, 160, 171
Overfitting, classification methods   97, 125, 126

Parameter estimation,
abstract   xx, 179
application   188–93
conclusions   193–4
Error Correction Model (ECM)   189
grid-search procedure   192
introduction   179–82
long memory   179–94
Pseudo-maximum Likelihood (PML) estimation   190, 193
semiparametric estimation (SP)   182–6
two-step method   192
Pareto-optimal equilibrium model   255, 257, 258, 270–1
Path dependence,
GARCH model   150
Markov switching (MS)   151

Printed and bound by CPI Group (UK) Ltd, Croydon, CR0 4YY

23/04/2025

14660967-0004